Scriptures, Scholarship,
and the People of God

Scriptures, Scholarship, *and the* People of God

Essays in Honour of Sven K. Soderlund

Edited by Stuart T. Rochester
and Joseph H. S. Lee

REGENT COLLEGE PUBLISHING
Vancouver, British Columbia

Scriptures, Scholarship, and the People of God
Copyright © 2021 Stuart T. Rochester and Joseph H. S. Lee

Regent College Publishing
5800 University Boulevard
Vancouver, BC V6T 2E4 Canada

All rights reserved. No part of this publication may be reproduced, stored in a retrieval system, or transmitted, in any form or by any means, electronic, mechanical, photocopying, recording or otherwise, without the prior written permission of the author, except in the case of brief quotations embodied in critical articles and reviews.

Regent College Publishing is an imprint of the Regent Bookstore (RegentBookstore.com). Views expressed in works published by Regent College Publishing are those of the author and do not necessarily represent the official position of Regent College (Regent-College.edu).

ISBN: 978-1-57383-595-4

Cover painting: Laura Sportack, "Arbutus Tree," South Pender Island, British Columbia

Contents

Introduction   1

Part 1: Scriptures

1. Uneasy Lies the Head: The Enthronement of the King James Version and the Right of Succession *Robert P. Gordon*   7
2. Who Is the *Gēr* ("Sojourner")? *Bruce K. Waltke*   38
3. It's All Going to Burn: Holy Scripture, Our "Environment," and Climate Change *Iain W. Provan*   61
4. The Colossian Hymn: Christ and the Church in Creation *Mariam Kamell Kovalishyn*   83

Part 2: Scholarship

5. What If Jesus Is Not in This Parable?: How Historical Context Provides an Interpretive Key to the Parable of the Minas in Luke 19:11-27 *Marcus K. M. Tso*   105
6. Faith in Greek Isaiah *Ken M. Penner*   136
7. Alliance Groups within the Textual Tradition of Paul's Letter to the Philippians *James M. Leonard*   149
8. The Nameless Scripture and the Name Above All Names: The Early Jewish and Christian Scribal Praxis and Paul's *ONOMA*-Christology in His Letters *Joseph H. S. Lee*   174

Part 3: The People of God

9. A Passion for the Word: Scriptural Piety and Meaningful Mission *Jay T. Smith*   203
10. From Library to Pulpit: The Role of Research in Expositional Preaching *David Montgomery*   228
11. Disability and Dependency: Toward a Theology of Weakness *Toni Kim*   257
12. Accounting for the "Good" in "Toronto the Good" *Bill Reimer*   280

Select Bibliography   307
Appendix to Chapter 7   309
Editors and Contributors   319

SVEN SODERLUND (BA, Toronto; MA Central Bible College; MCS, Regent College; PhD, Glasgow), Professor Emeritus of Biblical Studies at Regent College, first started teaching at Regent College in 1978 and became Associate Professor of Biblical Studies in 1986. During his time at Regent, he taught courses in both Greek and Hebrew, Old Testament Prophets, Luke-Acts, Pauline Letters, and Hebrews. In addition to serving on the faculty, he was also Dean of Students from 1989 to 2005. Since his retirement in 2006, Dr. Soderlund has continued teaching at Regent, offering courses in Exegesis and Interpretation, Acts, and Pauline Letters. His academic studies have been enriched by several overseas ministry experiences in Europe and Latin America, as well as by visits to biblical sites associated with the travels of Paul in Asia Minor (modern Turkey) and Greece. He has a heart for the integration of biblical scholarship and biblical spirituality in both the church and the academy. His current research interests lie in exploring the church-planting and church-nurturing mission of the apostle Paul, together with implications for ministry and church life in our neo-pagan, post-Christian twenty-first century.

Introduction

Scriptures, Scholarship and the People of God summarizes Sven K. Soderlund's life-long endeavours in biblical studies. Trained as a textual critic of the Septuagint (LXX), Sven could have pursued a critical and scientific approach in biblical scholarship (not suggesting anything wrong with such a process). Instead, he focused on biblical exegesis, language and theology to educate pastors, leaders, and laity to edify and build up the church.

It is challenging to narrow down Sven's biblical and theological work to one or two representative themes, considering his teaching and scholarship in both the Hebrew Bible and the New Testament, not forgetting to mention that he has also taught courses in Second Temple Jewish history and literature. But one study that truly captures Sven's scholarship was Paul as Pastor, which he introduced a few years ago in one of the spring schools at Regent College. Although Apostle Paul never referred to himself as a pastor in his letters, the study's premise is that Paul was thoroughly pastoral at heart, as reflected in his letters. Such a pastoral heart and theology were also at the core of Sven's teaching, scholarship and spirituality. To this day, the drumbeat of his pastoral heart is still loud and clear as Sven continues to teach Scriptures for the church, even after his retirement in 2006, at various places in North and South America, Asia, Europe and now online via Zoom (on account of the pandemic).

To best represent Sven's life-long commitment to biblical scholarship for the church, we have set the present articles in the three sections that correspond to the volume's title: Scriptures, Scholarship and the People of God. In *Scriptures*, we have essays from Sven's former colleagues who offered papers engaging with scriptural issues. **Robert P. Gordon** contributes a historical article, originally delivered as a lecture on the King James Version of the English Bible and how it became one of the most significant works in English literary history. **Bruce K. Waltke** offers an important and timely word study on the term *gēr* (sojourner) and its literary contexts in the Hebrew Bible. **Iain W. Provan** provides a critical discussion on how the study of the Scriptures should shape our engagement with God's good creation, frequently referred to as our environment. As if not all three senior scholars of the Hebrew Bible and their contributions are sufficient, **Mariam Kamell Kovalishyn**, representing the guild of NT scholarship, writes on one of the books dear to Sven, as he has often taught Paul's letter to the Colossians. In the paper, she discusses the Christ hymn of Colossians 1:15-20 for its Christological message and implications for the church.

In the *Scholarship* section there are four essays written by his former students. **Marcus K. M. Tso** offers exegetical research on the Parable of the Minas from the Gospel of Luke (19:11-28). **Ken M. Penner** discusses the word 'faith' in the Septuagint version of Isaiah. With Penner's recent commentary on Isaiah from the Codex Sinaiticus, this paper provides a glimpse of his extensive study on the LXX. **James M. Leonard** provides text-critical research on Paul's letter to the Philippians and its manuscripts' genealogical relationships. Leonard's work truly displays to what extent Sven's interest in text-critical study has inspired and influenced his students to advance beyond their studies at Regent. **Joseph H. S. Lee** has revised and expanded a paper that was originally presented to the NT seminar group at the University of Aberdeen in 2015, on the significance of the divine name evidenced in biblical literature. The text-critical part of this study had its origins and inspiration from the guided research that Lee had done with Sven on NT textual criticism at Regent College.

In *the People of God*, there are diverse topics on pastoral theology, ministry and church history, written by Sven's former students. **Jay T. Smith** offers a critical article that explores the role of the Scriptures in formulating the church's theology of mission. **David Montgomery** contributes a piece on the relationship between biblical scholarship and expository preaching, answering an important question, "What is the role of biblical research for developing and delivering a homily based on a biblical text?" **Toni Kim** has provided an invaluable discussion on disability in the light of a biblical theology of weakness. Such a synthesis of biblical studies and spirituality is a good representation of the expansion of Sven's legacy in the work and reflection of his students. **Bill Reimer** covertly interviewed Sven about his upbringing and childhood in Estonia and Canada. He offers a biographical sketch of Sven's early life as the opening part of his more extensive historical research into the late nineteenth-century Christian movements and their legacy in Toronto.

Introduction

In this volume, the trajectory and order of the essays try to sum up Sven Soderlund's scholarship and journey – from biblical studies to textual-linguistic research, then to the synthesis of biblical exegesis, spirituality and pastoral theology for the church. Many people came to Regent College, met Sven and gravitated toward him because of his kind-hearted spirit. More than this, his passion for the Scriptures and the church inspired all of us. It is an honour to celebrate Sven's eightieth birthday with this collection of essays written by his colleagues and former students, who have been privileged to call Sven their dear friend or mentor.

Part 1

Scriptures

Uneasy Lies the Head

The Enthronement of the King James Version and the Right of Succession

Robert P. Gordon

It is a great pleasure to join colleagues and students of Sven Soderlund in honouring his contribution to Christian scholarship and to the mission of Regent College over many years. My wife Ruth and I became friends of Sven and Rose in days long ago when Sven was writing his doctoral dissertation on the Septuagint of Jeremiah at Glasgow University under the supervision of Professor Robert Davidson. Neither the miles nor the years have weakened the friendship, or our immense admiration for what Sven and Rose have achieved in the greatest of causes. Since Sven lists among his "areas of expertise" the "history of Bible translations" my enthusiasm in offering the following essay is tempered just a little, but I am sure that it will be received with the trademark graciousness that we have all recognised and so much admired.

The King James translation of the Bible (KJV) represents a monument, a colossus, in the history of religion, literature and culture, and not just in the United Kingdom, or even the English-speaking world. Perhaps this is deservedly so, though of course much of its fame properly belongs to the underlying biblical text itself, and some of it to those who had already been labouring in the field of Bible translation—William Tyndale in particular. The usefulness and effectiveness of the KJV continue right up to the present, even if this is now largely because many in the Christian fold will not allow their Lord and Master to use any other English version.

A hundred and sixty years before the KJV, the invention of the printing press, as Elizabeth Eisenstein reminds us, had far-reaching effects socially and intellectually right across the world.[1] As she also observes, the move from script to type, as earlier from scroll to codex (or book), had big implications for the study and dissemination of the Judeo-Christian scriptures. Now people could begin to think of a mass-produced, fixed text in a way that was not possible before. We have only to think of the looseness with which names, and spellings generally, were treated for centuries, to be reminded that "fixed text" was a long time in coming. In Old English (to AD 1150) spellings are so variable that, to lessen the difficulties for modern readers, Old English texts are generally "normalised"—printed in accordance with what scholars think is a good representative form for each word.[2] That kind of variation continued through the medieval period and beyond. From the fifteenth century and the appearance of printed texts, standardisation in spelling became a theoretical possibility, but it did not happen all at once. In the biblical field, not only orthographical variation but, more importantly, growing awareness of the existence of multiple New Testament texts, no two of which agreed precisely, made the creation of a standardised, finalised text seem more remote, unless one took refuge in the so-called "Textus Receptus," or "Received Text."[3]

---

1. Elizabeth L. Eisenstein, *The Printing Press as an Agent of Change*, 2 vols. (Cambridge: Cambridge University Press, 1979), 1, 303-450 ("The Scriptural Tradition Recast: Resetting the Stage for the Reformation").

2. See Suzanne Kemmer, "The History of English: Spelling and Standardization in English: Historical Overview," Linguistics/English 395, Rice University, Spring 2009 (http://www.ruf.rice.edu/~kemmer/Histengl/spelling.html).

3. For example, in his *Novum Testamentum Graecum, cum lectionibus variantibus Mss. exemplarium, versionum, editionum, SS. patrum et scriptorum ecclesiasticorum; et in easdem notis* (Oxford: E Theatro Sheldoniano, 1707; 2nd edn; Leipzig, 1723), which presented unchanged Robert Stephanus's 1550 text, John Mill (1645–1707) noted approximately 30,000 textual variants among his manuscripts and printed editions. See Bruce M. Metzger, *The Text of the New Testament: Its Transmission, Corruption, and Restoration* (2nd edn; Oxford: Clarendon, 1968), 107-8; Peter J. Gurry, "The Number of Variants in the Greek New Testament: A Proposed Estimate," *New Testament Studies* 62/1 (2016): 97-121 (https://doi.

Not even the publication of the King James translation altered this situation. As David Norton has noted of popular attitudes in the seventeenth century, "most people were not concerned with the precise verbal form of their Bible: one translation was as good as another."[4] This is reflected in the way in which people quoted from the Bible at the time. Apart from the correction of printer's errors in the original KJV of 1611, some standardising of spelling continued through several decades of printing, and even yet there are archaic forms that have never been modernised (publick, musick, Syriack, and Leviathan's "neesings" in Job 41:18).

Early Reception of the KJV

The KJV took a while to establish its nonpareil status within the English-speaking world, and not for reasons of orthography. It was greeted by Hugh Broughton ("the choleric and controversial Hugh Broughton"[5]) with the following message intended for King James and often quoted since then:

> The late Bible, Right Worshipful, was sent me to cēsure [assess]: which bred in me a sadnes that will greeve me while I breath. It is so ill done. Tell his Maiest. that I had rather be rent in pieces with wilde horses, then any such translation by my consent should bee vrged vpon poore Churches.[6]

In fairness, Broughton had forewarned the king, writing in 1610 to James in protest against the ongoing King James Bible project, and offering to make

---

org/10.1017/S0028688515000314). Cf. Adam Fox, *John Mill and Richard Bentley: A Study of the Textual Criticism of the New Testament, 1675–1729* (Oxford: Basil Blackwell, 1954).

4. *A History of the English Bible as Literature* (Cambridge: Cambridge University Press, 2000), 74.

5. Rocío G. Sumillera, "Hugh Broughton's *Censure* to the King James Bible," in Mauricio D. Aguilera Linde, María José de la Torre Moreno and Laura Torres Zúñiga (eds.), *Into Another's Skin: Selected Essays in Honour of María Luisa Dañobeitia* (Granada: Universidad de Granada, 2012), 47–57 (47).

6. Hugh Broughton, *A Censure of the late translation for our Churches: sent vnto a Right Worshipfull knight, Attendant vpon the King* (Middelburg: R. Schilders, ca. 1611). Cf. F. F. Bruce, *History of the Bible in English: From the Earliest Versions*, 3rd edn (Guildford: Lutterworth, 1979), 106-7.

a last-minute rescue effort.[7] Broughton made many striking comments, but one stands out: his complaint that even the considerable number of translators involved would not be capable of properly rendering the "Hebraeo-graecos Apostolos" ("Hebraeo-Hellenic Apostles"), since there were in fact "vix duo ... in toto orbe" ("scarcely two men ... in the whole world") who could manage such a task. In his review of the KJV, Broughton highlighted representative errors, or "howlers" as he, seldom knowingly understated, would have called them nowadays. They and many more like them, he believed, were urgently in need of correction. Some of his complaints had to do with chronology and the meaning of individual words such as *qesitah* in Genesis 33:19, where, he lamented, the right word ("lambs") was in the margin and the wrong one ("pieces of money") in the main text. He had considerable support in the ancient translations of Genesis 33:19, but modern lexicographers would disagree with him.[8]

It was no help that it took a while for the KJV text to settle down. As well as those printings that were simply error-ridden, a few achieved infamy. Of course, there's the "Wicked Bible" of 1631, with its "Thou shalt commit adultery," and a deliberate-looking piece of irreverence at Deuteronomy 5:24.[9] Already, in 1645, in a sermon preached before the House of Commons, the Hebraist John Lightfoot called for a revision of the KJV.[10] As well as other improvements, he wanted the Apocrypha omitted. In 1657 Parliament appointed a committee to facilitate revision, but the impetus was lost and the revision came to nothing. Then in 1659 Robert Gell de-

---

7. See Kirsten Macfarlane, "Translating the 'Hebraeo-Hellenic Apostles': Hugh Broughton and the Scholarly Context of the English New Testament," *The Review of English Studies* 68 (issue 286, September, 2017), 689-707.

8. See Broughton, *A Censure*, par. V:3.

9. Cf. Gordon Campbell, *Bible: The Story of the King James Version 1611-2011* (Oxford: Oxford University Press, 2010), 109-11. There are photographic reproductions of the offending version of Deut. 5:24, from surviving copies, on p. 110. Several other printing mishaps produced, for example, "The Unrighteous Bible" (1653), "The Vinegar Bible" (1717), and "The Murderer's Bible" (1795). See Paul D. Wegner, *The Journey from Texts to Translations: The Origin and Development of the Bible* (Grand Rapids: Baker Academic, 1999 [corrected printing 2000]), 312.

10. See Samuel Newth, *Lectures on Bible Revision* (London: Hodder and Stoughton, 1881), 92; A. E. Hill, "The King James Bible Apocrypha: When and Why Lost?", in D. G. Burke, J. F. Kutsko and P. H. Towner, eds., *The King James Version at 400: Assessing Its Genius as Bible Translation and Its Literary Influence* (Atlanta, GA: SBL, 2013), 345-57 (350).

clared his support for a revision of the KJV. He exculpated the translators themselves since they had to work within unacceptable limits, but he gives the KJV faint enough praise: "though I think our last Translation *good*, [...] yet I doubt not but *Ours* may be made *much better* then it is."[11]

The flagging of the deficiencies of the KJV did not dissipate in the next hundred years after Gell. In the later eighteenth century, Robert Lowth, one-time Professor of Poetry at Oxford and Bishop of London, highlighted the need for a revision of KJV on various occasions. In a sermon preached in Durham in 1758 he observed how well the KJV would be served in the eyes of its readers if seen "in a more advantageous and just light," meaning that it was in serious need of revision.[12] Lowth had just traced a history of Christian opposition to religious falsehood across the centuries, and went on to show how, for example, better knowledge of Hebrew and increased "knowledge of antiquity" since 1611 made it possible to improve on the work of King James's men (p. 86). In his commentary on Isaiah published in 1778 Lowth looks forward to the "necessary work" of making a completely new translation, or at the least of revising the KJV "for the use of our Church." A little later he settles for revision, "the expediency of which grows every day more and more evident."[13] Lowth, as is well known, led the way in demonstrating the essentially poetic nature of much of Hebrew prophecy—something that was not represented in KJV, nor even, for reasons the Revisers give in their Preface, in the Revised Version of the Old Testament published in 1885.

In the same general period, John Wesley was issuing his edition of the New Testament, published as *Explanatory Notes Upon the New Testament* (1755) and consisting of commentary and translation. The translation was published separately in 1790. In his Preface, dated 4th January, 1754, Wesley says that he will take the liberty "as occasion may require, to make here and there a small alteration." He followed J. A. Bengel's critical edition of the

---

11. Robert Gell, *An Essay toward the Amendment of the Last English-Translation of the Bible* (London: Andrew Crook, 1659), 29-30.

12. *Sermons, and Other Remains of Robert Lowth D.D.* (London: J. G. and F. Rivington, 1834 [repr. London: Routledge/Thoemmes Press, 1995], 85-87 [85]).

13. Robert Lowth, *Isaiah: A New Translation. With a Preliminary Dissertation, and Notes Critical, Philological, and Explanatory* (London: J. Dodsley and T. Cadell, 1778), lxix, lxxii-lxxiii.

New Testament (1734) fairly closely, and in fact introduced about 12,000 changes in all, according to one calculation.[14] Various other attempts to revise the KJV were undertaken in the eighteenth and nineteenth centuries, in advance of the official revision of 1881 (NT) and 1885 (OT).

These included the translation endeavours of John Nelson Darby. He is associated with translations of the Bible into German and French, which were done in collaboration with native speakers from fellowships that he had established in Switzerland, France and Germany from the 1830s onward. The German Elberfelder Bibel New Testament was first published in 1855 and the Old Testament in 1871.[15] Darby did not produce a translation of the Bible into English, but published in 1865-67 fascicles of what became (abbreviatedly) *A New Translation* of the New Testament (1867; 2nd edn 1872; 3rd 1884).[16] The English translation of the Old Testament that goes by his name was actually created by adherents of Darby on the basis of the German and French editions, and was joined with the New Testament text to form *The Holy Scriptures: A New Translation from the Original Languages* (1890).[17] In the preface to his New Testament Darby shows how he applies principles of textual criticism that move beyond the KJV and the Textus Receptus, drawing on the work of major textual critics such as Griesbach, Lachmann and Tischendorf. No manuscripts are regarded as so old as to be free of "ecclesiastical" interference: to accept the readings of the oldest manuscripts without weighing and comparing would be poor policy. Darby, in fact, always gives the Textus Receptus in the margin where he departs from it (except for Revelation).

Extreme caution is also the burden of the "Introductory Notice" to the 1884 edition of the New Testament, published two years after Darby's death. It is noted, and variously illustrated, that the conscientious adherence of modern editors to their "systems of comparative criticism" can "lead to singular mistakes"; and yet it is concluded, albeit with great caveats

---

14. See Frank Baker, "John Wesley, Biblical Commentator," *BJRL* 71 (1989): 109-120 (110-11).

15. *Die Heilige Schrift aus dem Urtext übersetzt: Elberfelder Bibel* (Elberfeld: Brockhaus).

16. See Edwin N. Cross, "Appendix 5: Darby's Bible Translation work," in W. G. Turner, *Unknown and Well Known: A Biography of John Nelson Darby*, rev. edn (London: Chapter Two, 2006), 143-53 (143). The Revised Preface to the second edition is dated 1871.

17. See Cross, in Turner, *Unknown and Well Known*, 144.

and cautions, that "many facts tend to shew (sic) that, as a general rule, the so-called Alexandrian readings come nearest to the primitive text." Again, "[e]very passage has to be examined apart on its own merits…." So there is no apotheosis of the Textus Receptus, but a commending of a policy of respectful eclecticism in the face of so many textual witnesses.

It would be easy to demonstrate that some of the "errors" attributed to modern versions already had the patronage of Darby, and this because modern textual criticism is generally not governed by doctrinal bias or prejudice but by honest-to-goodness evaluation of readings with a view to recovering the form of the original insofar as this may be imaginable and attainable. As F. F. Bruce notes, Darby's New Testament translation was consulted by the Revisers responsible for the 1881 edition of the New Testament, quite possibly on account of the unusual amount of text-critical and philological notes with which it was supplied.[18]

Given Darby's influence on contemporary Christian fundamentalist interpretation of the Bible, and not only in relation to dispensationalism and the neoconservative project, it will be instructive to look briefly at his comments on three textual and theological *causes célèbres*. In the "Revised Preface to the Second Edition of the New Testament (1871)," Darby introduces them as the "three greatest questions" posed by the manuscript evidence. 1 Timothy 3:16 is a key text for many evangelical Christians because the textual variation at this point appears to involve the doctrine of the deity of Christ. The KJV translates the crucial phrase with "God was manifest in the flesh," whereas many more recent translations have the equivalent of "He was manifest in the flesh." Darby appears ambivalent as to which is the correct reading. In his translation he has "God has been manifested in flesh," but says in a footnote, "I do not enter on the criticism of this text. It very likely should read 'He who has,' &c." So, basically, he thinks that the correct reading is probably "He," but in his translation he keeps the peace with the adherents of KJV. It is worth noting, then, that the issue is not the deity of Christ, or attempts to deny it.

As was pointed out when the verse came up for discussion by the Revisers, the non-KJV reading was accepted by Griesbach, Lachmann,

---

18. Bruce, *History of the Bible in English*, 132.

Tischendorf, Tregelles and Alford on the basis of the manuscript evidence.[19] The structure of the verse suggests that an excerpt from a hymn or credal composition is possibly being quoted, in which Christ is the subject of each verb. And if the verse was extracted from within a longer composition, it is likely that "He" builds on a previous verse in which God or Christ, or Christ as God, is specifically mentioned. A ready analogy in that case would be Charles Wesley's hymn "O for a thousand tongues to sing," with the verse beginning "He breaks the power of cancelled sin/He sets the prisoner free" building on the mention of "Jesus" in the previous verse. In his *Synopsis of the Books of the Bible* (1857-67) Darby emphasises, when commenting on 1 Timothy 3:16, that it is God who is "manifest in flesh." This essentially remains the case whether the reading is "God" or "He," though Darby probably gives his readers the impression that he is supporting the KJV reading.

The two other of "the greatest questions" can be introduced more summarily. First, Darby accepts the *pericope de adultera* as it is, where it is, in John 7:53–8:11, with the comment "I do not doubt its genuineness." He cites Augustine's testimony that the pericope was omitted in some "untrustworthy" manuscripts "because it was thought injurious to morality," and he supports this with the observation that he had personally inspected one of the best manuscripts of the Old Latin, two pages of which had been removed at the crucial place, with further loss of text on either side of the pericope. To say the least, it is an interesting alliance of Augustine, Darby and an Old Latin manuscript. When Darby deals with Mark 16:9-20 he summarises the resurrection appearances in Matthew and Luke, noting what would be called their Galilean and Jerusalem perspectives, and he finds them appropriate to their respective Gospels. He observes that Mark 16:1-8 aligns with Matthew. Then, in words better transcribed than paraphrased on account of their opaqueness, he notes: "from verse nine a summary of the Bethany and ascension scene, and facts related in Luke and John." Here his eye catches sight of a fence on which to sit: "It is a distinct part, a kind of appendix, so to speak." In his *Synopsis* he says, simply, "This

---

19. See Alan H. Cadwallader, *The Politics of the Revised Version: A Tale of Two New Testament Revision Companies* (Scriptural Traces: Critical Perspectives on the Reception and Influence of the Bible, 14 [=LHBOTS 637]; London: T&T Clark, 2019), 102.

is another testimony." As with the *pericope de adultera*, there is no indication in Darby's translation of the disputed status of Mark 16:9-20, much less of the existence of more than one "ending" to the Gospel.

It is hard not to see the weight of tradition pressing heavily on Darby at these junctures, causing him to sidestep the kinds of issues that in other circumstances he would have addressed with relish and fervour. The need to reassure nervous audiences that all is well of course only increases the more the audience is protected from the "real Bible," and this is especially regrettable when, as often, a more frank statement of facts would increase awareness of the workings of Scripture, and not only of textual criticism, without undermining basic doctrines whose support does not depend on single texts or disputed interpretations of them.

History Repeats

This is a good point at which to pause and reflect on the way in which the reception history of Bible translations keeps repeating itself. The earliest of them all, the so-called Septuagint translation of the Old Testament into Greek, produced in the third to first centuries BC, really was the translation that "was good enough for Paul," for he and his colleagues used it repeatedly. Legends grew up around the Septuagint, starting with the charter myth in the "Letter of Aristeas," which tells how seventy-two scholars summoned to translate the Pentateuch worked expeditiously in pairs for seventy-two days, and when they had finished, their work was deemed to be of such excellence that a curse was imposed on anyone who should dare to alter the sacred text.

The eulogising continued, and by the fourth century the Septuagint was held to be as inspired as the original, only more so. According to Augustine, even the deviations from the Hebrew original were sound and, because of the prophetic status of the translators, possessed an authority equal to that of the original text ("just as if the prophet himself had said both").[20] So, in the Latin-speaking world, by AD 400 the "Old Latin" renderings based on the Septuagint had become so firmly established as Latin Christendom's "Authorised Version" that Jerome's much improved "Revised Version," known to succeeding centuries as the "Vulgate," ran into a wall of

---

20. Augustine, *City of God*, 18:43.

opposition.[21] Augustine, like many others, objected to Jerome's abandoning of the Old Latin Bible and his reinstatement of the Hebrew-Aramaic text of the Old Testament as the proper authority and basis for translation. In a letter written to Jerome in AD 394 or 395 Augustine expresses the hope that, if Jerome makes a Latin translation of the Hebrew Old Testament, he will show clearly where his version differs from the Septuagint. Like some modern devotees of the King James Version, he also suggests that it is by now unlikely that Jerome's efforts will be rewarded with much that has escaped the notice of previous translators of the Hebrew text.[22]

These were the circumstances in which Jerome wrote the preface to his translation of Samuel-Kings, his *Prologus Galeatus* ("Helmeted Prologue")—"helmeted" because he felt the need to protect himself against the "mad dogs who bark and rage" who, like the "two-legged asses" in his letter to Marcella (*Letters*, 27:3), railed against his translation. Augustine eventually conceded that Jerome's "Vulgate" project was useful, and explained that he was concerned lest any version of Scripture read in public should cause offence to the worshipping community.[23] Or, as the KJV translators themselves wrote, preemptively, in their address to King James:

> His Majesty ... knew full well ... that whosoever attempteth anything for the public (specially if it appertain to religion, and to the opening and clearing of the word of God), the same setteth himself upon a stage to be glouted upon by every evil eye; yea he casteth himself headlong upon pikes, to be gored by every sharp tongue.[24]

And so it was also with the Revised Version of 1881–85. The Revisers had been required to work to operational guidelines that proved a veritable hair shirt for some of them. The first two of the "General Principles" to be followed by the Old Testament and New Testament "Companies" were as

---

21. The comparison between the Vulgate and the Revised Version is suggested by Henry Chadwick, *The Early Church* (Penguin History of the Church, 1; revd edn; London: Penguin Books, 1993), 65.

22. Augustine, *Letters*, 28:2.

23. Augustine, *Letters*, 82:5.

24. *The Translators to the Reader: The Original Preface of the KING JAMES VERSION of 1611 Revisited*, ed. Erroll F. Rhodes and Liana Lupas (New York: American Bible Society, 1997), 29.

follows:

1. To introduce as few alterations as possible into the text of the Authorised Version consistently with faithfulness.

2. To limit, as far as possible, the expression of such alterations to the language of the Authorised and earlier English Versions.[25]

One of the Revisers was William Wright, a Semitist who began life in Scotland, spent several years in Dublin (1856-61), and then moved to Cambridge. Wright had a white parrot as a pet—a truly eccentric member of the Wright household that could be described as "having attitude." The Egyptologist Wallis Budge recalled a dinner party at which the parrot was very jolly, so that eventually a large handkerchief was put over his cage to silence him. However, during a pause in conversation the parrot was heard to call down damnation on the Minor Prophets, in a tone of voice awfully like that of his owner. Wright explained to his friends, when they had stopped laughing, that the parrot must have learned this from the young man who worked in the garden. It was ungallant of him. In fact, Wright was having a frustrating time working on the Minor Prophets for the Revised Version.[26]

When it was published, the revision won grudging praise in some quarters, with more of the praise falling on the Old Testament committee. There was, of course, Dean Burgon, the Hugh Broughton of the later nineteenth century, for whom the revision failed at all levels.

> My one object has been to defeat the mischievous attempt which was made in 1881 to thrust upon this Church and Realm a Revision of the Sacred Text, which—recommended though it be by eminent names—I am thoroughly convinced, and am able to prove, is untrustworthy from beginning to end. Their uncouth phraseology and their jerky sentences, their pedantic obscurity and their unidiomatic English, contrast painfully with "the happy turns of expression, the music of the cadences, the felicities of the rhythm" of our Authorised Version. The transition from one to the other, as the Bishop of Lincoln remarks, is like exchang-

---

25. Cadwallader, *The Politics of the Revised Version*, 216 ("Appendix B").

26. See Bernhard Maier, *Semitic Studies in Victorian Britain: A portrait of William Wright and his world through his Letters*, Arbeitsmaterialien zum Orient, 26 (Würzburg: Ergon Verlag, 2011), 36.

ing a well-built carriage for a vehicle without springs, in which you get jolted to death on a newly-mended and rarely-traversed road. But the "Revised Version" is inaccurate as well; exhibits defective scholarship, I mean, in countless places.[27]

A commemorative article in the London *Times*, on 14th May 1935, pronounced on the merits and demerits of the revision. In the Old Testament the Revisers "clarified the sense of the Authorised Version while respecting its consecrated rhythms." As a result of their work, "numerous passages in the poetical and prophetical books ... were found to have beauty of thought as well as beauty of sound." The New Testament received a meaner encomium. The Revisers "included no men of letters versed in the rhythm, cadence, and euphony of good English. The Revisers began by setting before themselves a pedantic code, and for the sake of conformity with that code they cheerfully ruined many of the loveliest passages in English literature."[28]

The impertinence of the production of the Revised Version, as some saw it, is caught by Frederick Brittain and Bernard Lord Manning in their marvellously titled *Babylon bruis'd and Mount Moriah mended; Being a compendiouse & authentick Narracioun of yͤ Proceedinges of yͤ Wᵐ Dowsing Societie in a Visitatione of all yͤ Parisshe Churches & college chapels of Cambridge during a longe Vacation (1940)*, in which they imagined a reenactment by William Dowsing and his Cromwellian band of their iconoclastic visitation of the churches and chapels of Cambridgeshire in 1643-44. It includes the following: "In yͤ chapel at Ridley Hall we turned yͤ lecterne straight. We tooke awaye therefrom .i. superstitiouse booke called yͤ Revised Version and did put yͤ Bible in place thereof."[29]

Canonical Status

The same unwelcoming attitude towards any translation other than the KJV continues through to our own day and, in some quarters, will confront any attempt to render the Scriptures more accurately or more intelligibly.

---

27. John W. Burgon, *The Revision Revised* (1883), quoted from Dover Publications (New York, 1971), 4-5 (original, pp. v-vi).
28. See Wegner, *The Journey from Texts to Translations*, 318.
29. Published by Heffer, Cambridge. A reprint was issued in 1968 ("to be hadde of divers booksellers"). See Bruce, *History of the Bible in English*, 152.

The anathematising of the Revised English Bible of 1989 as "The Antichrist Bible" is one of the more extreme examples of this.[30] By the nineteenth century, however, there was also developing the contrary tendency to exalt the KJV to a position of canonical invincibility. It had endured, it was familiar, and it was ingrained in the culture of the English-speaking world. This canonicity is illustrated no better than in the production of concordances, already starting with Alexander Cruden in 1737,[31] but reaching new levels with the publications of Robert Young in 1879 and James Strong in 1890.

Cruden published his concordance in late 1737, presenting a copy to Queen Caroline in November, just two weeks before her death. A grateful reviewer in the London *Times* pointed out that he had omitted the personal name of Buz, son of Nahor and Milcah and brother of Uz (KJV Huz) in Genesis 22:21, and had subsumed "sneeze" under "neeze."[32] In his concordance of 1879, Robert Young explicitly excuses himself from recording every word, and especially Hebrew particles, but he still presents an extremely useful text in which occurrences are subdivided according to the underlying Hebrew or Greek roots.[33]

However, it is Strong's concordance of 1890 that epitomises the canonical process.[34] Strong concordances the standard lexical stock, garnishing it with his well-known system of numerical notation, but, in a work of true Protestant supererogation, adds an appendix giving occurrences of forty-seven words, or "particles," cited by reference only. These include the

---

30. Ian R. K. Paisley, *The Revised English Bible: The Antichrist Bible: An Exposure* (Belfast: Martyrs Memorial Free Presbyterian Church, 1989). Occasional justified criticisms mingle here with startling expressions of ignorance. When this writer picked out at random three REB renderings criticised by Paisley and compared them with the ESV, the latter was found to agree with REB against KJV in each case. It is just a matter of interpreting the manuscript evidence, which is sometimes evenly balanced but often enough clearly disposed one way or another. The present writer, as a revision panel member for REB, savours this particular Paisley bouquet.

31. Alexander Cruden, *A Complete Concordance to the Holy Scriptures of the Old and New Testament* (London: for D. Midwinter et al., 1738 [sic]).

32. See J. A. Gere and John Sparrow (eds.), *Geoffrey Madan's Notebooks* (Oxford: Oxford University Press, 1981), 16.

33. Robert Young, *Analytical Concordance to the Holy Bible* (Edinburgh: George Adam Young, 1879).

34. James Strong, *The Exhaustive Concordance of the Bible* (Cincinnati: Jennings and Graham, 1890).

indefinite article ("a," "an"), the conjunction "and," pronouns, prepositions (including "in," "of"), the definite article, and lots more. On a very rough calculation, that amounts to about a quarter of a million references. The industry is remarkable, and the point of it would be questionable even in the era of computerisation. But the deeper significance, no doubt, lies in the status that is accorded the KJV text. Every word, right down to the indefinite article, is worthy of listing: the text has achieved a level of fixity appropriate to a canonical text.[35]

This marks a very special point in KJV reception history, emblematising the attitude of many users of the version up until that time, and the judgment of many since then. It crystallises a situation that had not obtained before in Christian history. In biblical times, books and collections of books achieved their final form in a process that meant that by the time, say, Chronicles in the Old Testament was more or less finalised in the fourth century, some prophetic texts, psalms and other material already had a long history of transmission, and there had been sufficient time for manuscripts with variant readings to make their appearance. Something similar holds for the New Testament, despite its much shorter historical span: by the time of the canonising of the collection, there were manuscripts with variants in circulation, and the awareness of this never fully escaped the notice or attention of those whose business it was to study, translate and conserve the transmitted text in the succeeding centuries.

There were, to be sure, earlier and parallel concordancing ventures on the Latin Vulgate, undertaken by scholars from the thirteenth century on, and on the Hebrew Bible, starting somewhat later. Similar ventures on the Greek New Testament and the Septuagint could also be noted. In English, Thomas Gybson's concordance of the New Testament was published in 1535, and John Marbeck's concordance of the whole Bible in 1550. Already the idea of a fixed text of the Old Testament had been embraced by the Masoretes, who had counted every word and letter in the standardised Hebrew text of each Pentateuchal book. What we have, then, by the time of Young and Strong are two countervailing developments within the English

---

35. The edition of the concordance published by Thomas Nelson as *The New Strong's Compact Bible Concordance* (Nashville, 2004) eliminates 168 words "that the reader is not likely to use in searching for particular passages in Scripture" and condenses entries for forty other words "by retaining the more important passages" (from the Preface).

Bible tradition: (1) the increasing availability of New Testament manuscripts and the perceived need for a more exact science of textual criticism and the deployment of knowledge that had become available since 1611, and (2) the enthronement of the KJV among a wide circle of Bible users for whom the version had become identical with the "Word of God."

Challenging the Charges

From the publication of the Revised Version onward—and not forgetting other attempts at revision and improvement before then—the story has been of the ageing monarch of the KJV fending off upstart aspirants to his throne. And whatever the merits of a new arrival, the same charges against it, and in favour of the KJV, tend to surface. It will be worth headlining some of them, since they are so persistent.

First, modern versions are said to use New Testament texts that are deficient, and we have already adverted to that. This is not the place to enter into detailed discussion of what has been comprehensively answered again and again by competent authority. Arguments for providential preservation of a favoured group of texts wear very thin in the face of the total evidence. "Textus Receptus," "Majority Text" and "Neutral Text" all have Achilles heels, and yet all together add up to a body of evidence that is massive, and more than sufficient for the accomplishment of the church's mission on earth. The commonsensical approach to the manuscript evidence is to proceed eclectically with them all in play, and without denying oneself solid testimony for the sake of a dogmatic *a priori*. We do have a "Textus Receptus" for the Old Testament—the Masoretic Text—and yet the Old Testament quotations in the New Testament quite often differ in some detail from this Hebrew "Textus Receptus," which raises a question or two about fideistic approaches to textual criticism of the Bible.

Second, the KJV is said to be more reverent. Perhaps it sounds so, but so much of this depends on the use of "thou," "thee" and "thine" and their associated verb forms. As has been endlessly pointed out, this usage makes the translation sound more holy than the original, since in the original languages there were no special pronouns for Deity, but only differentiations between singular and plural. This distinction between singular and plural, which has nothing to do with reverence or sanctity, is what accounts for the KJV's use of "thou," "thee" and "thine" in divine address. But not only that: those who know tell us that the language of the KJV was already archaic in some respects in 1611, and this may be relevant for "thou" and its congeners. In his study written to mark the KJV quadricentenary, Gordon Campbell comments on this archaic aspect of "thou," which by 1611 had become a marker of social relationship rather than number.[36] And it worked in a way opposite from what is often assumed. "You" was the deferential term, and those deferred to might reply with "thou." So in *Twelfth Night*, Sir Toby Belshaw advises Sir Andrew Aguecheek on how to be rude to Cesario/Viola: "if thou 'thou'st' him some thrice, it shall not be amiss." In other words, "if you use 'thou,' you'll take him down a peg." In the same way, Sir Walter Raleigh was addressed at his trial in 1603: "thou viper, for I 'thou' thee, thou traitor." That is not quite the whole story, but it is a spoke in the wheel of those who insist that only "Thou" is reverential before God. Archaism *can* be a way of expressing awe before the divine majesty. A few Hebrew scrolls among the Dead Sea cache turn back to the old ("Phoenician") script when they reproduce the Divine Name, the Tetragrammaton. And it can even happen in manuscripts of the *Greek* Old Testament, as in the Minor Prophets scroll from Nahal Hever.[37]

Thirdly, the KJV is presented as the repository and the touchstone of sound doctrine. Yet the instances where modern translators have let personal biases influence their handling of the text are very few. It was different with the ancient translators. They were not averse to letting their biases insert themselves into their renderings. A theologically unfraught or neutral example is provided by the Syriac translator of 1 Chronicles in the Peshitta version. He was working at some point in the early Christian centuries, and he betrays in several places a decided antipathy against the use of musical instruments in worship. Of course, this should not interfere with his translation of the biblical text, but it does. The books of Chronicles mention musical instruments in connection with the arrangements for the temple worship in Jerusalem, especially as these were put in place by King David, who has an enhanced role in Chronicles as the founder of Israel's temple praise. Sometimes in the Syriac the list of instruments is shortened

---

36. Campbell, *Bible*, 74-75.
37. There is also, of course, the tradition of the *nomina sacra* in, for example, Greek manuscripts of the New Testament, whereby "Lord," "God," "Jesus," and "Christ" are represented by abbreviations.

or simply passed over, but there is one text that merits description as outright "converse translation," which is the term used to describe translations that convert a text into saying the opposite of what is intended, for the sake of consistency with the context or related texts, or with theological or other norms. At 1 Chronicles 16:42, a statement about a certain Heman and Jeduthun being responsible for "the sounding of the trumpets and cymbals and for the playing of other instruments of sacred song" is stood on its head: "These righteous ones were giving praise: *not* with instruments of praise, nor with tambourines, nor with tabors, but with pleasing mouth and prayer that was pure."[38] This anticipates by centuries John Milton's sketch of *a cappella* worship by Adam and Eve in the Garden of Eden: "More tunable than needed lute or harp/To add more sweetness" (*Paradise Lost*, 5:151-52).

There are exceptions to the general translator fidelity in the modern period, but the charges of "infidelity" are out of all proportion to the actual number of questionable renderings that would remain after detailed examination of the evidence. At the same time, if, for example, we were to take a sampling of renderings relating to the deity of Christ, it would become apparent that modern translations are as orthodox as the versions of the 16th and 17th centuries. In his book *The King James Version Debate: A Plea for Realism* (1978) Don Carson has a table of eight debated texts, which scores translations in terms of orthodoxy of rendering. KJV, RSV and NEB all score 4 out of 8, and NIV 7 out of 8. Both Douay-Rheims and the Jerusalem Bible score 5 out of 8. But Carson is careful to point out that this exercise has to do with text-critical decisions rather than commitment to orthodoxy.[39]

Modern translators may even surprise us by occasionally gilding the orthodox lily. At Hebrews 1:9 the NEB translators create a new proof-text for the deity of Christ: where KJV has "therefore God, even thy God, hath anointed thee with the oil of gladness above thy fellows," NEB has "therefore, O God, thy God has set thee above thy fellows, by anointing with the

---

38. See Robert P. Gordon, George A. Kiraz and Joseph Bali, *The Syriac Peshitta Bible with English Translation: Chronicles* (Piscataway: Gorgias Press, 2019), XXV, 108-9.

39. Donald A. Carson, *The King James Version Debate: A Plea for Realism* (Grand Rapids: Baker, 1978), 64.

oil of exultation."⁴⁰ By using the vocative "O God," NEB strengthens the idea that the deity of Christ is anticipated in Psalm 45. It is not the most likely explanation of the quotation, and NEB does not handle the original text in Psalm 45:8(7) in this way, but the point is that at Hebrews 1:9 NEB is, if anything, ultra-orthodox. Another example of orthodoxy from, according to some, an unlikely source, concerns the extremely difficult text of John 1:18, although this rendering did not actually make it into the Revised Version. Westcott and Hort argued that the original reading in this verse was not "only-begotten Son" but "only-begotten God," which would be a fuller than usual ascription of deity to Christ (cf. ESV "the only God, who is at the Father's side, he has made him known"), but the traditional "only-begotten Son" won the vote and the strong preference of these two "modernisers" fell.⁴¹

Fourthly, the KJV is lauded for the stateliness of its language, with which subsequent versions are invariably compared to their disadvantage. There is something in this, but it is also fair to say that the KJV is sometimes stately-sounding when the original itself may be more pedestrian, and it is stately-sounding not least when it is unintelligible. Again, some of that exquisiteness of expression derives from the fact that the translators often followed the sentence structure of the biblical source language, and what is slightly unnatural as English can sound more stately or elevated. This was observed, famously, by Msgr Ronald Knox in his *The Trials of a Translator*. He held up for special disapprobation the following verse from Mark's Gospel in the KJV: "For the Pharisees, and all the Jews, except they wash their hands oft, eat not, holding the tradition of the elders" (7:3). Knox complains that this is typical KJV, because the translators worked only with the words and not the sentence: "it gives you an English sentence which would get any man the sack, and rightly, from Fleet Street."⁴² This is indeed "translationese," but perhaps not so strange for the seventeenth century. Here is an excerpt from the diary of Samuel Pepys for 1st January,

---

40. REB agrees with NEB on this point, though it introduces changes to the wording elsewhere in the verse.

41. See Cadwallader, *The Politics of the Revised Version*, 126. There is a separate issue as to whether *monogenēs* should be translated "only-begotten" (KJV) or "only" (NIV; ESV).

42. Ronald Knox, *The Trials of a Translator* (New York: Sheed and Ward, 1949), 5-6 (cf. 75-76).

1662: "Waking this morning out of my sleep on a sudden, I did with my elbow hit my wife a great blow over her face and nose, which waked her with pain, at which I was sorry, and to sleep again." This kind of "speak" was parodied by Dale Spender in the spoof diary she created for Pepys's young wife Elizabeth, as in the entry for 22nd December, 1655: "This day I did with Eliza meet, though not to market we did go, for still no monies do I have, and greatly does this vex me."[43]

Fifthly, there's memorability. People, it is asserted, can memorise the KJV better than its unmelodious competitors. This is a particularly weak point. In the first place, there are many texts in modern versions that sound almost identical to their Jacobean predecessor. The omission of a few -eths and -ests should make no difference in that respect. Texts such as Genesis 1:26, Matthew 11:28, John 1:29, John 14:6, and so on, sound perfectly familiar in RV, RSV, NRSV, ESV, and to an extent NIV, for the simple reason that they position themselves within the KJV tradition of translation, just as the KJV itself stands in the Tyndale tradition. If anyone wishes to see a translation clearly not from the KJV stable, they could consult NEB, REB, JB, NJB, or NABRE. But there are other aspects to memorability. Often the complainants about modern versions are past the peak of their memorising ability. The KJV would be at least as challenging, if the exercise of memorising were to begin now. Here we are dealing with the "roses-don't-smell-as-they-used-to" argument, which is true, and the reason usually given is cross-breeding. But there are other reasons. One's sense of smell may not be what it used to be. And there was a time in childhood when flowers smelt so lovely because one's nose was rather nearer the ground where the roses grow.

Three Modern Versions

There have been many attempts to bring the words of Scripture more accurately and intelligibly to readers in the 20th and 21st centuries. I shall comment briefly on three that are most likely to interest readers of this essay, viz. NIV, ESV and NKJV. Of these the big seller is undoubtedly NIV, first

---

43. Quoted in Irene and Alan Taylor, eds., *The Assassin's Cloak: An Anthology of the World's Greatest Diarists* (Edinburgh: Canongate, 2000), 621; taken from Dale Spender, *The Diary of Elizabeth Pepys* (London: Grafton, 1991).

marketed as a complete Bible in 1978. The translators "go beyond a formal word-for-word rendering" because they wish to "recreate as far as possible the experience of the original audience." In other words, they do not set out to produce a "literal"—if that word is sufficiently meaningful—translation but, rather, something describable as "dynamic equivalence." They also claim to "preserve a measure of continuity with the long tradition of translating the Scriptures into English," which I understand to mean that they regard themselves as belonging within the fellowship of independent KJV affiliates. The version has not only been an outstanding marketing success, but has helped many to appreciate and engage with the message of the biblical text. The "Committee on Bible Translation" is up front about its policy of regular revision and updating, in the light of new information and changes in English usage. Perhaps this is too much a feature of NIV printings, and at times the translation seems to bob about among the other little translational ships, with changes as likely to reflect uncertainty about the translation of difficult or ambiguous readings as to bring new information to the fore. It seems scarcely credible, at the same time, that in Philippians 2:8, after centuries of preacherly nuancing of KJV's "became obedient unto death, even the death of the cross" so that it was understood to mean "became obedient as far as death," NIV through all its gradations has maintained "humbled himself by becoming obedient *to* death—even death on a cross!"[44]

The Preface to the 2011 commemorative publication mentions revisions in 1984 and 2005, with the 2011 publication itself also representing a new edition, just six years after its predecessor. There was also one in 1996—the ill-fated "Inclusive Language NIV." It purported to "respond to the significant changes that are taking place within the English language in regard to gender issues." The idea was to "mute the patriarchalism of the culture of the biblical writers through gender-inclusive language when this could be done without compromising the message of the Spirit." This is the "fire-fighter," "shooter" approach, where "workman" becomes "worker," and so on. But not everyone was clear as to what was going on. The trans-

---

44. "Nor was it to death that Christ rendered obedience (as might be inferred from KJV); it was to the Father's will that he rendered obedience as far as death" (F. F. Bruce, *Philippians*, NIBCNT [Peabody, MA: Hendrickson, 1989], 79).

lation committee were depatriarchalising culturally-bound texts, whereas the blurb was also claiming that the inclusive language was bringing the reader nearer to what the biblical writers actually meant to communicate. Sometimes it has to be one or the other of these two. In fact, the revisers were editing the Bible in favour of a contemporary politically correct agenda.

It had at least one interesting result at the textual level. In Luke 2:25-38 we have the accounts of two elderly Jerusalemites, Simeon and Anna, encountering the baby Jesus. When Simeon meets the child, he utters his "Nunc Dimittis" and speaks a personal word to Mary. Then the text says, "And there was a prophetess, Anna, the daughter of Phanuel, of the tribe of Asher." That makes perfect sense. First Simeon, then Anna the prophetess. Simeon is not actually called a prophet, but so much that is said about him calls out "prophet!" (And "prophet" was a term very generously applied in New Testament times, so there would be no problem in recognising him as such.) The Holy Spirit is "upon him," a revelation has been made to him, moved by the Spirit he comes to the temple at the right time, he recognises in the baby "the light for revelation to the Gentiles," and he prophesies about Messiah's mission, and of the sword that would pierce Mary's heart. So when the text then says that there was a *prophetess* called Anna, this is to be read in the light of the Simeon account. Unfortunately, NIV's alteration of "prophetess" to "prophet" makes it sound as if prophecy is making its début in the chapter with the appearance of Anna: "There was also a prophet…" (so also NIV 2011). And with the retention of "also" from earlier editions NIV goes further out on the branch. This is clumsy. The "Inclusive Language Edition" was trialled in the United Kingdom and there was an outcry, with the result that it was never issued in North America.

This is not to say that inclusivisation should have no place in modern revisions. Bruce Metzger, chairman of the committee of translators of the NRSV, used to cite "there shall be two *men* in one bed" (KJV Luke 17:34) and "if any man hear my voice, and open the door, I will come in to him" (KJV Rev. 3:20) as examples of the unnecessary masculinisation of the text (whatever the KJV wording may have signified in 1611). There is, for example, a strong case for translating Greek *adelphoi*, traditionally rendered "brothers" (KJV "brethren"), by "brothers and sisters," as is the growing tendency in versions outside the KJV. There is the Old Testament precedent of Deuteronomy 15:12 where, in a quasi-legal setting, the case of the so-called "Hebrew servant" is introduced with "If your brother, a Hebrew man or a Hebrew woman." Here the word "brother" is clearly subdivided into male and female. However, at the root of this inclusivising tendency is the fact that in both Hebrew and Greek the words for "brother" and "sister" are basically the same and are differentiated only by gendered endings.

The ESV was first published in 2001. It was undertaken by a group of evangelical biblical scholars who took the 1971 text of the RSV as the starting point for their work. As far as language and style are concerned, they have positioned themselves within the Tyndale-King James tradition, which indeed applied broadly to the old RSV itself. They describe the ESV as "essentially literal," with word-for-word rendering wherever this appears adequate. It is also noted in the Preface that "every translation is at many points a trade-off between literal precision and readability, between 'formal equivalence' in expression and 'functional equivalence' in communication." One of the problems with the NIV, by contrast, has been that in its pursuit of dynamic equivalence it fails to pay attention to terms that are deliberately repeated, in the way of leitmotif, within a passage. Multiple, or at least plural, equivalence is important as a translation principle if texts are to be rendered intelligibly, nevertheless there are places where repetition is of the essence of a passage and ought to be represented in translation. The word "face" in the story of the reconciliation of Jacob and Esau in Genesis 32-33 is a case in point, and so also the threefold occurrence of *bēma* ("judgment seat") in the story of Paul before Gallio in Acts 18, in which story justice is denied and the reminders that this is supposed to be a *bēma* are more than incidental. ESV scores well in both passages, in the case of Genesis 32:20 with the help of a couple of explanatory footnotes.

For this and other reasons, the ESV is a better translation than the NIV for serious study purposes. Even so, it is interesting that, so soon after an official revision of the RSV had been carried out under the chairmanship of Bruce M. Metzger of Princeton—himself a credal Christian believer—resulting in the New Revised Standard Version (NRSV) of 1989, an evangelical revision based on the same RSV should be thought necessary.[45]

---

45. For reflections by Metzger of an autobiographical nature, including chapters on the RSV (pp. 76-88) and NRSV (pp. 89-102), see Bruce M. Metzger, *Reminiscences of an Octo-*

Leland Ryken, a member of the oversight committee responsible for the ESV, suggests that, since the NRSV is a dynamic equivalence translation, its place as the heir to the old RSV "in terms of translation philosophy and literary excellence" has been ceded to the ESV.[46] Since Ryken estimates that the changes made to the RSV text in the preparation of the ESV amounted to about six percent of the total (p. 55), most of the credit for literary excellence would seem to lie in the parent text.

It is not as if the NRSV and ESV are in fundamental disagreement theologically. They even agree at Romans 9:5 on who is "God blessed forever," while at Romans 3:25 the NRSV has "sacrifice of atonement by his blood" and ESV "propitiation by his blood," which are different, but not vastly so. But there remains, of course, the old bellwether of Isaiah 7:14, and here the two differ, NRSV having "the young woman is with child" (with footnote recording that the Septuagint has "the virgin") and ESV "the virgin shall conceive" (cf. Gen. 24:43: NIV, NRSV "young woman," KJV, ESV "virgin.") But the evidence supports NRSV. The word *'almah* is not so specific as "virgin," though it may have such a connotation. The masculine equivalent is used twice of David in 1 Samuel 17:58 and 20:22, and even Robert Young's *Literal Translation* has "young man" in both places.[47]

---

genarian (Peabody, MA: Hendrickson, 1997). On p. 78 is a reproduction of a photograph of an urn containing the ashes of a copy of the Revised Standard Version (1952) that had been burned by a pastor from North Carolina because it was "heretical" and "communist-inspired." Metzger, as was his wont, remarked that it was good to live in happier times when it was a copy of the translation and not the translator himself that was consigned to the flames (p. 79).

46. L. Ryken, *The Word of God in English: Criteria for Excellence in Bible Translation* (Wheaton, IL: Crossway Books, 2002), 53. Ryken makes a very strong case against rampant "dynamic equivalence." It would have been interesting to hear him further, in dialogue with, for example, Ronald A. Knox, on the subject of Bible translation.

47. For the sake of balance, I record the following observations by F. F. Bruce who, at the time he wrote the following, was minded to make a case for the KJV rendering. "It is true that *bethulah* rather than *'almah* is the word that actually asserts virginity, but *'almah* normally implies it. (In the new Dutch version mentioned above it is translated by *jonkvrouw*, which according to Professor Aalders can mean either a young girl who is still a virgin or a young woman already married.) But since the new revisers have enlisted the aid of the Ras Shamra documents elsewhere, they might have done so here. For Isaiah's announcement of the birth of the child Immanuel is couched in language reminiscent of the Ugaritic formula for announcing the birth of a hero. And in that formula the Ugaritic equivalents of Hebrew *'almah* and *bethulah* appear in synonymous parallelism! There are overtones in Isaiah 7:14

The reason is that Christian faith recognises only one virginal conception, and Isaiah 7 very specifically refers to circumstances in the eighth century BC; and Matthew, citing the Septuagint, finds a deeper significance in relation to the birth of Christ. Two further points may be made. First, if Matthew's citing of Isaiah 7:14 were more often discussed in the context of his several other Old Testament quotations in the infancy narratives, and with particular regard to the degree of "fit" in each of those cases, a better approach to the original sense of the Isaiah reference might be achievable. Secondly, given the possibility that the definite article in "the young woman" is generic (as even KJV's "a virgin" appears to recognise), and that, with two millennia of Christian history behind us, "the virgin" might easily be construed as a very specific reference to Mary the mother of Jesus, and as thereby excluding a referent in the eighth century as the context demands, the ESV rendering is potentially misleading and therefore regrettable. This is an important point with a more general implication, since front-ranking academic institutions tend to favour the NRSV over the NIV and ESV because they reckon that it is a "neutral text" that avoids *parti pris*.

There was a further twist in the ESV story when a Roman Catholic edition (ESV-CE), also to become known as The Augustine Bible, was published in 2018. The main difference from the original ESV is the inclusion of the deuterocanonical books, though an edition with the Apocrypha included had already been published in 2009 by Oxford University Press. More recently, the decision by the Catholic Bishops' Conferences in United Kingdom to use this version in the liturgy has been greeted with protests about the version's failure to embrace inclusive language. The complaint is that it excludes at least half of the membership of the Christian church with its retention of masculine language, presumably in such matters as the translation of *adelphoi* simply as "brothers." The old RSV is obviously on an interesting trajectory, first being adapted to suit conservative evangelical needs and then in its slightly altered ESV form being augmented in order to appeal to Roman Catholic readers. Issues of principle begin to arise, in the first place because a light revision of the RSV does not amount to a new

---

which are not satisfied by the RSV rendering. The prophet's words probably rang a bell in the minds of his hearers, just as did the reference of his contemporary Micah to 'the time when she who is in travail has brought forth' (Mic. 5:3, RSV)." See F. F. Bruce, "A British Scholar Looks at the RSV Old Testament," *Eternity* (May, 1954): 12-13, 42-47 (46-47).

translation or "version," and secondly because it is not a good policy to adjust Bible versions in this way. Perhaps it is particularly a North American problem. The writer recalls being invited by a North American publisher a good number of years ago to discuss the translation into English of a standard German work on the Old Testament, which would have involved omitting the more "critical" elements in the original. It was necessary to point out that this would be considered unacceptable in the academic community, and in the end a much better solution was found.[48]

The New King James Version (1979 and onward) observes the principle of "complete equivalence," according to which all elements in the text—the interjection "behold" is mentioned illustratively in the Preface—are represented. The archaic forms "thou," "thee," "thy" and "thine" (also "ye") are modernised, but respect for deity is preserved by capitalising the initial letter of "You," "Your," and "Yours." Obsolete verb endings are abandoned. The "Textus Receptus" that stands behind the KJV New Testament is maintained, with other readings, "Critical" and "Majority Text," noted in the centre column of each page. The grounds for this textual conservatism are introduced in a less than comprehensive fashion—the evidence of the papyri and of the ancient versions could have been given due weight—but it is fairly noted that there is overwhelming agreement among the differing text-types: "fully eighty-five percent of the New Testament text is the same in the Textus Receptus, the Alexandrian Text, and the Majority Text."

This nervousness over readings is a weakness in the NKJV, for when a better reading is relegated to the centre column something is lost. Revelation 1:5 illustrates this well. This verse in the KJV includes the words: "Unto him that loved us, and washed us from our sins in his own blood…"

---

48. Among the correspondence of C. S. Lewis there is discussion of a request by an American missionary publisher for permission to translate his best-selling *Miracles* into Japanese, with potentially upsetting elements omitted. Lewis resisted the thought of such "expurgations," not wanting to be "disguised as a fundamentalist and a non-smoker." The translator "may, if he pleases, add notes of his own, warning readers that the book is at these points, in his opinion, pernicious. But he must not remove them" (letter to Jocelyn Gibb [publisher], from Magdalene College, Cambridge, dated 9 May, 1960). See *C. S. Lewis: Collected Letters*, Volume III, *Narnia, Cambridge and Joy 1950-1963*, ed. Walter Hooper (London: HarperCollins, 2006), 1150. Lewis refers in a subsequent letter (*ibid.*, 1151) to "the Japanese Bowdler." For the record, I should mention that I acted as a "Translation Review Scholar" (to use the term in the Preface) for the book of Amos in the original ESV.

Modern translations differ from the KJV in two main respects. First, they have the present tense, "To him who loves us" and, secondly, they have "and *freed us* from our sins by[49] his blood" instead of "*washed us* from our sins in his own blood." While a statement about a past expression of Christ's love would command interest (cf. "who loved me and gave himself for me," Gal. 2:20), John is thinking of that love as a present and continuing reality. The difference between the verbs "freed" and "washed" is minimal graphically, and aurally they are indistinguishable (*luein* and *louein*), but both readings cannot be original. The better attested reading (with the support of Papyrus 18) is "freed," and this strengthens the comparison with the deliverance theme in Exodus that the passage already suggests. Following the unique blood ritual of the Passover night (Exod. 12:7, 13), the Israelites were delivered ("freed") from Egypt, now to fulfil God's purpose for them: they were to become a "kingdom of priests and a holy nation" (Exod. 19:6), which idea is picked up in Revelation 1:6. To Moses, who led the people out of Egypt, God had revealed himself as "LORD" (Exod. 3:13-15; 6:2-3), just as in Revelation 1:4 that divine Name is "unpacked" in "Grace and peace to you from him who is, and who was, and who is to come." Coincidentally, the other side of Papyrus 18, which is the oldest witness to Revelation 1:4-7, contains the last verses of the book of Exodus in Greek.[50]

Acceptance of "freed" instead of "washed" dissolves the statement about Christians being "washed in the blood" of Christ. This is language that, though popular in evangelical hymnology (both older and more recent), is not supported elsewhere in Scripture. The "great multitude" in Revelation 7:9-14 wash *their robes* in the blood of the Lamb (v. 14).[51] One of the most popular hymns about being "washed in the blood of the Lamb"—"Have you been to Jesus for the cleansing power?"—is generally understood as meaning just what it says. On a sympathetic reading, and

---

49. The preposition *en* can as easily mean "by" as "in" in Rev. 1:5.
50. See A. S. Hunt, *The Oxyrhynchus Papyri*, Part VIII (London: Egypt Exploration Fund, 1911), 13–14; Brent Nongbri, "Losing a Curious Christian Scroll but Gaining a Curious Christian Codex: An Oxyrhynchus Papyrus of Exodus and Revelation," *NovT* 55 (2013): 77–88; Philip W. Comfort and David P. Barrett, eds., *The Text of the Earliest New Testament Greek Manuscripts: New and Complete Transcriptions and Photographs* (Wheaton, IL: Tyndale House, 2001), 103–105.
51. According to Heb. 10:22, Christians should have their bodies "washed with pure water."

taking into account its references to "garments," one might just conclude that the washing of the garments equates to being "washed in the blood of the Lamb," but it is more likely that the writer of the hymn has simply conflated the two ideas from Revelation 1:5 (according to KJV) and 7:14. Most curiously, in the closing verse the addressee is bidden to "lay aside the garments that are stained with sin, and be washed in the blood of the Lamb," which rather turns Revelation 7:14 on its head, for there it is the garments (cf. vv. 9, 13) that have been washed.

Simple modernising of the English of the KJV, as in the NKJV, does not address these sorts of issues in the way they deserve, even when alternative readings are noted in the centre column.[52] At the same time, the criterion for deciding readings is not whether the language offends reader sensitivity, but whether the reading on which the translation is based has the requisite claim to authenticity. In John 6:53 Christ talks of "eating the flesh" and "drinking the blood" of the Son of Man, and textual criticism will not alter that figure, though it did alienate many followers of Christ at the time.

Many Witnesses

As we survey the translation industry of the past century and more, the differences in rendering of texts, and the stylistic variations between one version and another, it would be easy to lose a sense of proportion and even of faith in translations. But it is the very enduring power of the Scriptures themselves that makes all these projects defensible, and the results beneficial. All seminal works attract translators. The translation of Scripture began early, with the Septuagint, which appears to have been the first translation of an oriental book into Greek. Already in the New Testament we can see evidence not only of the dominant Septuagint version in the quotations from the Old Testament, but also traces of several other versions within the broader Greek tradition, as well as very occasional trace elements from the Aramaic Targum tradition.[53] By such means faith was

---

52. The editors note that at Rev. 1:5 the NU text (Nestle-Aland and United Bible Societies) has "loves us and freed" and that the Majority Text has "loves us and washed."

53. Cf. the following observation on quotations from the Greek Old Testament in the New Testament, published under the aegis of the Wuppertal Septuagint project: "It was observed that the *quotations in the New Testament* bear similarities to different branches of the Septuagint tradition. There are important reflections of the Old Greek (most of the

nurtured, and the gospel disseminated to the wider world.

The history of Bible translation bears out the maxim that there is safety in numbers, and it is, with rare exception, one of noble endeavour. The first translation had a large translation committee that was—if we were to believe the ancient spin rather than the sight of our eyes—unbelievably successful. Since then there have been innumerable translation enterprises, by individuals and by teams, with the common purpose of bringing out the sense of the original as best that may be done for people whose language, cultural background and historical experience would otherwise cut them off from the generations that produced the original texts.

The KJV had, of course, its panels of translators, and even the greatest of them had to argue his case on individual words and phrases. The name of the polymathic Lancelot Andrewes, originally of Pembroke College, Cambridge, and said to be proficient in most of the languages of Europe, stood at the head of the list of translators. But on such a text as Genesis 4:13 ("My punishment is greater than I can bear"), Andrewes lost out. He is on record as preferring the reading that ended up in the margin: "Mine iniquity is greater than that it may be forgiven."[54]

Appendix: A Note on KJV Hosea 6:5

David Norton, a leading authority on the history of the English Bible, has made an interesting discovery about the KJV text, and what lies behind the text, at Hosea 6:5. In current printings God says, "Therefore have I hewed *them* by the prophets; I have slain them by the words of my mouth," which represents accurately the sense of the underlying Hebrew and its striking language about the potentially destructive effects of prophetic speech. Some translators and commentators pursue an alternative route and make the prophets themselves the object of the divine action, but this

---

quotations belong to that category) as well as some relevant evidence for the Antiochene text (Rom 11:4 / 3 Kgdms [1 Kgs] 19:18 etc.; cf. above). Sometimes a 'kaige'-text (see καί γε in Acts 2:18 and Joel 3:2) or preparations for the so-called newer translations can be identified (e.g. Symmachus Deut 32:35 with Rom 12:19; Heb 10:30)" (J. de Vries and M. Karrer, eds., *Textual History and the Reception of Scripture in Early Christianity / Textgeschichte und Schriftrezeption im Frühen Christentum*, SCS 60 [Atlanta, GA: SBL, 2013], 11).

54. See S. L. Bray and J. F. Hobbins, *Genesis 1-11: A New Old Translation for Readers, Scholars, and Translators* (Wilmore, KY: GlossaHouse, 2017), 136n. 288.

gives an improbable sense and would unnecessarily complicate the present discussion.

The earliest printing of the KJV had, on the other hand, "shewed" for "hewed." This was immediately amended in subsequent printings, and it has commonly been assumed that "shewed" was a simple misprint for "hewed." Norton, however, found that a copy of the 1602 edition of the Bishops' Bible, which was used by the KJV translators and is preserved in the Bodleian Library, Oxford (Bod 1602), has the words "cut down" struck out and replaced by "shewed."[55] It seems, therefore, that "shewed" was the intention of the translator(s), which would leave the subsequent printing of "hewed" as a hypercorrection that turned out to be strictly correct.

The language of Hosea 6:5 is by all accounts stark and violent, and it was already giving the ancient translators pause. Whether it threw the Septuagint translator off course when he misrendered, "Therefore I cut off your prophets," is not clear since the language remains stark also in this version. Symmachus, one of the translators of the so-called "minor" Greek versions, has "I did not spare," in what is clearly an attempt at tonal moderation. Norton, aware that the KJV translators consulted quite widely among the ancient commentaries and versions, concluded that their likeliest source of authority was the Aramaic Targum to Hosea 6:5, which paraphrases with "Because I warned them through the mission of my prophets and they did not repent..." Apart from its reconfiguration of the syntax, the Targum has clearly moderated "hewed" to "warned," interpreting the figure of sharp, warning words. Amelioration or attenuation where the divine speech is strong and colourful is characteristic and commonplace in the Targums. And if support for the original KJV is to be found in the ancient versions, Norton's nomination of the Targum has something in its favour, even if the rider "*faute de mieux*" has to be added.

Two or three additional considerations deserve airing. First, there is possibly further evidence of toning down within the Targumic tradition, in the Targum text of the famous Codex Reuchlinianus (copied AD 1105), which has "Because I held them back..." However, there is enough graphic similarity between the majority reading *d'zhrt[y]nwn* and the unique

---

55. David Norton, *A Textual History of the King James Bible* (Cambridge: Cambridge University Press, 2005), 38-40.

variant *d'whrtynwn* (where "h" is the letter *heth*) to make mechanical error a possibility, with Reuchlinianus still providing a generally appropriate sense. The editor of the Targum text of Reuchlinianus, Paul de Lagarde, noted the majority reading and said that he nevertheless was unwilling to alter his text (*nolui mutare*).[56]

Secondly, the possibility of this confusion of "shewed" and "hewed" was uncannily present from the start because "hewed" would not only be a good equivalent for the Hebrew verb in question, it is the KJV equivalent for fourteen of its twenty-four occurrences elsewhere in the Old Testament (including Isa. 5:2 where it is a marginal alternative). Moreover, other early English versions tended not to be too troubled by the idea of God "hewing" (cf. Wycliffe, Douay-Rheims "hewed" and Geneva, Bishops' "cut down").

Thirdly, although the idea of God "hewing" by means of his prophets creates an unusual image in the Old Testament, there is a semantic parallel to "hewed" in this rare sense in 1 Samuel 24:8(7): "So David cleft his men with words." Even though this is not divine speech, translators in all periods have had difficulty with what should have been relatively straightforward, since the idea of cutting and cleaving with words is not unique to Hebrew and can be paralleled in various languages. The Targum in this case moderates to "persuaded," and so also did the Septuagint before it (cf. also Douay-Rheims;[57] ESV). The Hebrew lexicon of Brown-Driver-Briggs thinks that the Hebrew expression "gives too violent a meaning,"[58] so that it is small wonder that English versions also depress the tone, as already in KJV "So David stayed his men with these words," where the addition of "these" shows that the translators failed to recognise that "cleft ... with words" is figurative, with the clue in the addition of "with words."[59]

Norton (p. 38) explains "shewed" in the original KJV of Hosea 6:5 as originating partly in response to the first note to the verse in the Geneva Bible, which talks of God still labouring by means of his prophets to

---

56. Paul de Lagarde, *Prophetae Chaldaice* (Leipzig: B. G. Teubner, 1872), XL.
57. Checked in 1635 reprint.
58. F. Brown, S. R. Driver and C. A. Briggs, *A Hebrew and English Lexicon of the Old Testament* (Oxford: Clarendon, 1907), 1042.
59. See R. P. Gordon, "Word-Play and Verse-Order in 1 Samuel xxiv 5-8," *VT* 40 (1990): 139-44 (= idem, *Hebrew Bible and Ancient Versions*, SOTSMS [Aldershot: Ashgate, 2006], 33-37).

bring the people to amendment of their ways, so that "laboured by my prophets" in the Geneva note was, in effect, replaced with "shewed *them* by the prophets" in the original KJV. The discovery of the annotation in Bod 1602 certainly changes the terms of the discussion as regards KJV Hosea 6:5, though in the light of 1 Samuel 24:8(7) and KJV's opting for "stayed," when other versions either aligned with the Septuagint or made a contextual guess (cf. Wycliffe "brake," Geneva "overcame," Bishops' "kept of," Douay-Rheims "perswaded"), we may wonder whether Targum's "warned" really was the source of the original KJV "shewed."

2

Who Is the *Gēr* ("Sojourner")?

Bruce K. Waltke

I am honored to contribute this essay for the FS of my esteemed colleague at Regent College, Sven Soderlund. Sven and I, having offices next to one another, spent many pleasant and profitable hours discussing exegesis, theology and spiritual life. Sven is the tree planted by the waters of God's Word and Spirit; never withering, he bears the nine fruits of the Spirit.

The essay aims to coin the best English gloss for the Hebrew term gēr, prompted by my dissatisfaction with its glosses in all translations. The study serendipitously yielded unexpected exegetical insights in several texts, called into question the putative dates of Wellhausen's documentary hypothesis, and contributed to new insights into theology and the religion of Israel.

The essay first explores glosses offered in the ancient versions, lexicons, and theological word books. Then it culls from the about 90 uses of the term six defining characteristics of the gēr. In that light, and after critically appraising glosses in popular English translations and theological word books, a new gloss is coined. Finally, the essay suggests how the study contributes to a better understanding of selected texts, of source criticism, theology, and the religion of Israel.

Ancient Versions, Lexicons, and Theological Word Books

The LXX twice transliterates *gēr* by γειώρας (Exod. 12:19; Isa. 14:1); several times glosses it by πάροικος ("neighbor," "foreigner" [Exod. 2:22]); and

Who Is the Gēr ("Sojourner")?

about sixty times by προσήλυτος ("proselyte," e.g., Exod. 12:48). The Vulgate commonly glosses *gēr* by *advena* ("stranger," "foreigner" [Exod. 2:22; 6:4; 12:19; 18:2; Josh. 8:33; 2 Sam. 1:13]) and *peregrinos* ("to stay or travel in a foreign country" [Deut. 1:16; 5:14; 10:19; 14:21;1 Chr. 29:15]), and rarely by *colonus* (a "colonist" [Exod. 12:48f.]) and *proselytus* (1 Chr. 22:2). Aramaic versions offer its Aramaic equivalent, *giyyôrā'*, glossed "proselyte" by Bauer[1] and mostly "sojourner" by Jay Palmer.[2]

Of the lexicons, BDB[3] defines the term as "1. *sojourner, temporary dweller, new-comer (no inherited rights)....* 2. *usually of gērim in Israel...; dwellers in Israel with certain conceded, not inherited rights....*"; *HALOT*[4] glosses "*protected citizen, stranger*"; and *CDCH*[5] gives "*sojourner, resident alien.*"

Of the theological word books, H.G. Stiger[6] proposes "*alien*," "*sojourner*," "*stranger*"; A. H. Konkel[7] "*sojourner*" or "*alien*"; and D. Kellerman[8] "*protected citizen*" in legal literature. A. Martin-Achard[9] transliterates the Hebrew word.

In sum, common glosses in these sources are "sojourner," "stranger," "foreigner," "alien," "proselyte." All but "proselyte" occur as glosses in the English versions.

---

1. Cited in *Hebrew and Aramaic Lexicon of OT* [*HALOT*], edited by Koehler & Baumgartner (Leiden: Brill, 1994 [*HALOT*], 201, s.v. גֵּר.
2. Targum Onkelos on the Pentateuch: An English translation complied and adapted by Jay Palmer, cited in Bible Works 10.
3. Brown, Driver & Briggs, *A Hebrew and English Lexicon of the Old Testament* (Oxford: Clarendon House, 1907) 158, s.v. גֵּר.
4. *HALOT*, 201, s.v. גֵּר.
5. *Concise Dictionary of Classical Hebrew*, edited by D. J. A. Clines (Sheffield: Sheffield Phoenix Press, 2009), 70, s.v. גֵּר.
6. H. G. Stiger, *Theological Word Book of the Old Testament*, edited by R. L. Harris et al. (Chicago: Moody Press,1980), I:155f., s.v. גֵּר.
7. A. H. Konkel, *New International Dictionary of Old Testament Theology and Exegesis* [*NIDOTTE*], edited by Van Gemeren et al. (Grand Rapids: Zondervan, 1997), I:837, s.v. גור.
8. D. Kellerman, *Theological Dictionary of the Old Testament* [*TDOT*], edited by G. J. Botterweck and H. Ringgren (Grand Rapids: Eerdmans, 1974), 2:439–449, esp. 443f., s.v. גור.
9. A. Martin-Achard, *Theological Lexicon of the OT* [*TLOT*], edited by Ernst Jenni, Claus Westermann (Peabody, MA: Hendrickson, 1997), 2:307–310, esp. 309, s.v. גור.

Defining Characteristics of the *Gēr*

The noun *gēr* occurs over 90 times: Genesis 2x; Exodus 12x (mostly in the putative P document[10] or covenant code [Exod. 20 – 23:19]); Leviticus 20x (mostly putative P or Holiness Code [chs. 17–26]); Numbers 11x (mostly putative P); Deuteronomy 22x (putative frame, chs. 1–11, 27–34 and law code chs. 12–16); Joshua 3x; 2 Samuel 1x; Chronicles 3x; Job 2x; Psalms 4x; Isaiah 14:1; Jeremiah 3x; Ezekiel 4x; Zechariah 7:10; Malachi 1x. In sum, the majority of its use occurs in Exodus to Deuteronomy.

As is well known, traditionally church and synagogue agreed that the Books of Moses came from the hand of that great founder and lawgiver of Israel. In the nineteenth century, however, critics denied the Mosaic authorship and the literary integrity of the Pentateuch, and on the basis of isolating literary sources (see n. 10) they set about to reconstruct the history of Israel's religion that differed considerably from the traditional understanding. This literary approach was reoriented in the twentieth century by form and tradition criticisms, which dealt with the putative oral and written traditions behind the earlier reconstructed literary sources. At some indeterminate point, however, before any extant evidence, the Pentateuch was regarded as a unified document. Today there is a movement, known as "the canonical approach," to read the text not according to its putative reconstructed sources but holistically as a witness to its own understanding.

The source critical way versus the canonical way of reading the text leads to different understandings of the *gēr* in the history of the orthodox Israelite religion.[11] Mark Glanville notes "the near consensus in the [critical] scholarship that the framework [of Deuteronomy] (chs. 1–11, 27–34) initiates a new religious inclusivism [of the *gēr*] that is not to be found in the (earlier) law corpus (chs. 12–16)."[12] Read canonically, however, the con-

---

10. Academics analyze the Pentateuch as composed of at least four putative literary sources: J[ahwistic] document (ca. 950 BC), E[lohistic] document (ca. 850 BC), Deuteronomistic Code (ca. 625 BCE) [early post-exilic], and P[riestly] document (early post-exilic).

11. By "orthodox" is meant the religion of Moses in the extant Pentateuch and in the canonical prophets. Many other religions had political sanction during the history of ancient Israel. See Richard S. Hess, *Israelite Religions* (Grand Rapids, 2007).

12. Mark Glanville ("The *Gēr* [Stranger] in Deuteronomy," *JBL* 137, no. 3 (2018): 599–623, here 617) cogently argues that this consensus "underestimates the religious significance of the *gēr* appearing in Dtn feasting texts 'before YHWH your God' (לִפְנֵי יְהוָה

trast between the framework and code could signify that the *gēr* belongs to a religious category of legally recognized foreign subjects other than native-born Israelites. Indeed, reading the Pentateuch holistically, as a unified document, this essay proposes that the orthodox Israelite religion had a caste[13] system that was similar to the caste system of the Hindu religion in political India.

What then are the defining characteristics of the *gēr* as extrapolated from reflecting on all uses of the noun *gēr*?[14]

Foreigner

The native Israelites, who were unified by their common blood, common land, common memory, and common government, regarded the *gēr* as an outsider accepted into their kinship group. No reason is given in the text to explain the reception of the *gēr* into this kinship group. In narrative texts the *gēr* is reckoned a foreigner: Israel in Egypt (Gen. 15:3; cf. Deut. 23:7 [Heb. 8]); Abraham at Hebron (Gen 23:4); Jacob in Aram (32:4); the patriarchs in Canaan (Exod. 6:4) and Moses in Midian (Exod. 2:22). The youth who reported Saul's death to David, and so probably a soldier in the Israelite army, describes himself as an Amalekite- *gēr*:

וַיֹּאמֶר דָּוִד אֶל־הַנַּעַר הַמַּגִּיד לוֹ אֵי מִזֶּה אָתָּה וַיֹּאמֶר בֶּן־אִישׁ גֵּר עֲמָלֵקִי אָנֹכִי:

"And David said unto the young man that told him: 'Whence art thou?' And he answered: 'I am the son of an Amalekite *gēr*.'" (2 Sam. 1:13 JPS)

Most legal texts referring to the *gēr* distinguish the *gēr* from the native-born Israelites (e.g., Josh 8:35). Several explicitly distinguish them:

וְכִי־יָגוּר אִתְּכֶם גֵּר וְעָשָׂה פֶסַח לַיהוָה כְּחֻקַּת הַפֶּסַח וּכְמִשְׁפָּטוֹ כֵּן יַעֲשֶׂה חֻקָּה אַחַת יִהְיֶה לָכֶם וְלַגֵּר וּלְאֶזְרַח הָאָרֶץ:

"A *gēr* residing among you is also to celebrate the LORD's Passover in accordance with its rules and regulations. You must have the same regula-

---

16:11, אֱלֹהֶיךָ etc.)."

13. "Caste" means "a system of rigid social stratification characterized by hereditary status, endogamy, and social barriers sanctioned by custom, law, or religion." https://www.merriam-webster.com/dictionary/caste

14. Translations are from the NIV, unless otherwise indicated, but *gēr* and *tôšāb* are transliterated or glossed differently from the version.

tions for both the *gēr* and the native-born)." (Num. 9:14[15])

The *gērîm* [plural of *gēr*] felt keenly their alienation as foreigners among the natives:

וְגֵר לֹא תִלְחָץ וְאַתֶּם יְדַעְתֶּם אֶת־נֶפֶשׁ הַגֵּר כִּי־גֵרִים הֱיִיתֶם בְּאֶרֶץ מִצְרָיִם׃

"Do not oppress a *gēr*; you yourselves know how it feels to be a *gēr*, because you were *gērîm* in Egypt." (Exod. 23:9[16])

Mark Glanville, however, albeit admitting that most scholars conceptualize the *gēr* from without Israel, defines the *gēr* in Deuteronomy more broadly as "a dependent 'outsider' in relation to the kinship grouping within which that person resides."[17] In his view the diverse kinship groupings could also be within all Israel. His preferred translation of *gēr* is "stranger," for this translation allows him to identify the *gēr* as potentially within the clans of Israel. Since he restricts his study of *gēr* to Deuteronomy, he does not interact with the *gēr—native born* contrast in several texts (Num 9:14 and note 15). In his own study of "kinship and covenant" (Deut. 10:12–11:1. esp. 10:17–19), he distinguishes "native Israelites" from "the stranger," diagramming their relationship as a triangle:

YHWH the divine kinsperson
Covenant
Kinship
Emotions
Native Israelites   Stranger[18]

Finally, let it be noted that many texts distinguish between the native Israelite and the *gēr*, and that none equates them.

Immigrant

The legal literature envisions the *gēr* as a person who has left behind his

---

15. See also Exod. 12:49; Lev. 25:35; Num. 9:14; 15:29, 30; Deut. 12:19; 14:21; 24:14; Josh. 8:33; Ezek. 47:22.

16. See also Exod. 2:21 [Heb. 2:20]; cf. Exod 6:4.

17. Mark Glanville, "The *Ger* (Stranger) in Deuteronomy: Family for the Displaced," *JLB* 137, no. 3 (2018): 599–623.

18. Ibid., 618.

Who Is the Gēr ("Sojourner")?

homeland and kinship group to live permanently, not temporarily, among the Israelites. Frank Anthony Spina suggested the gloss" immigrant" for the *gēr*.[19] *HALOT* (see n. 4) and Kellerman (see n. 8) gloss the term by "protected citizen." The legal texts grafted the *gēr* into Israel's economic, political, religious and social structure. Glanville argues persuasively that "Deuteronomy's response to displacement was to foster the incorporation of the *gēr* within kinship groupings, namely, within a household, a clan, and the nation."[20]

As for the *gēr*'s inclusion within a household, the term commonly occurs with the pronoun "your" (i.e., Israel) *gēr*," implying the *gēr* was reckoned as part of a household, similar to "your son," and "your slave." Consider the well-known Sabbath law:

וְיוֹם הַשְּׁבִיעִי שַׁבָּת ׀ לַיהוָה אֱלֹהֶיךָ לֹא תַעֲשֶׂה כָל־מְלָאכָה אַתָּה וּבִנְךָ־וּבִתֶּךָ וְעַבְדְּךָ־וַאֲמָתֶךָ וְשׁוֹרְךָ וַחֲמֹרְךָ וְכָל־בְּהֶמְתֶּךָ וְגֵרְךָ אֲשֶׁר בִּשְׁעָרֶיךָ לְמַעַן יָנוּחַ עַבְדְּךָ וַאֲמָתְךָ כָּמוֹךָ:

"But the seventh day *is* the Sabbath of the LORD your God. *In it* you shall do no work: you, nor your son, nor your daughter, nor your male servant, nor your female servant, nor your ox, nor your donkey, nor any of your cattle, nor *your* [mine] *gēr* who *is* within your gates, that your male servant and your female servant may rest as well as you." (Deut. 5:14 NKJ[21]; cf. Exod. 20:10; 23:12)

Glanville comments: "The list of participants is structured, as it were, in concentric circles of natural affiliation within the household, progressing from the paterfamilias at the center, outwards to בן ("son") and בת ("daughter"), then to household slaves …, and outward again to vulnerable people who also participated in the life of the household."[22]

As for the clan, the many references to the *gēr* in the integration formula ("living within your gates") suggests that the *gēr* was principally understood as grafted into a clan. In this formula "gates" is a synecdoche for the whole town or city, and "your," according to E. Otto, "shows clearly that this lexeme [*ša'ar*, "gate"] … has not only a local connotation but also

---

19. Ibid., 613.
20. Glanville, "The *Gēr* (Stranger) in Deuteronomy," 601.
21. Many English versions arbitrarily omit the pronominal suffix "your."
22. Glanville, "The *Gēr* (Stranger) in Deuteronomy," 613.

a genealogical connotation, in the sense of 'clan' or 'extended family' (cf. Ruth 3:11; 4:10)."[23]

As for the inclusion of the *gērîm* into all Israel, they participated in the covenant renewal ceremony that bound YHWH with his adopted "son," Israel:

טַפְּכֶם נְשֵׁיכֶם וְגֵרְךָ אֲשֶׁר בְּקֶרֶב מַחֲנֶיךָ מֵחֹטֵב עֵצֶיךָ עַד שֹׁאֵב מֵימֶיךָ

לְעָבְרְךָ בִּבְרִית יְהוָה אֱלֹהֶיךָ וּבְאָלָתוֹ אֲשֶׁר יְהוָה אֱלֹהֶיךָ כֹּרֵת עִמְּךָ הַיּוֹם:

לְמַעַן הָקִים־אֹתְךָ הַיּוֹם לוֹ לְעָם וְהוּא יִהְיֶה־לְּךָ לֵאלֹהִים כַּאֲשֶׁר דִּבֶּר־לָךְ וְכַאֲשֶׁר נִשְׁבַּע לַאֲבֹתֶיךָ לְאַבְרָהָם לְיִצְחָק וּלְיַעֲקֹב:

"Ye are standing this day all of you before the LORD your God: your heads, your tribes, your elders, and your officers, even all the men of Israel, your little ones, your wives, and thy[24] *gēr* that is in the midst of thy camp, from the hewer of thy wood unto the drawer of thy water; that thou shouldest enter into the covenant of the LORD thy God - and into His oath which the LORD thy God maketh with thee this day." (Deut. 29:10–12 [Heb. 9–11] JPS)

Furthermore, the *gēr* took on the obligation to participate in the seventh-year reading of Torah:

הַקְהֵל אֶת־הָעָם הָאֲנָשִׁים וְהַנָּשִׁים וְהַטַּף וְגֵרְךָ אֲשֶׁר בִּשְׁעָרֶיךָ לְמַעַן יִשְׁמְעוּ וּלְמַעַן יִלְמְדוּ וְיָרְאוּ אֶת־יְהוָה אֱלֹהֵיכֶם וְשָׁמְרוּ לַעֲשׂוֹת אֶת־כָּל־דִּבְרֵי הַתּוֹרָה הַזֹּאת: וּבְנֵיהֶם אֲשֶׁר לֹא־יָדְעוּ יִשְׁמְעוּ וְלָמְדוּ לְיִרְאָה אֶת־יְהוָה אֱלֹהֵיכֶם כָּל־הַיָּמִים אֲשֶׁר אַתֶּם חַיִּים עַל־הָאֲדָמָה אֲשֶׁר אַתֶּם עֹבְרִים אֶת־הַיַּרְדֵּן שָׁמָּה לְרִשְׁתָּהּ:

"Gather the people together, men, and women, and children, and thy *gēr* that is within thy gates, that they may hear, and that they may learn, and fear the LORD your God, and observe to do all the words of this law, and that their children, which have not known anything, may hear, and learn to fear the LORD your God, as long as ye live in the land whither ye go over Jordan to possess it." (Deut. 31:12f. KJV)

Significantly, the children of the *gērîm* are "to hear and learn to fear YHWH," implying the *gēr* was reckoned as a permanent citizen within Israel, not a temporary "sojourner." In sum, the *gēr* is a citizen (i.e., a legally

---

23. Eckart Otto, "שַׁעַר," *TDOT*, 15:359–405; here 380.
24. See n. 19.

recognized subject of the leaders of Israel), but is characterized as residing among the Israelites and so never equated as an Israelite.

A Religious Proselyte

In addition to Num. 9:14; Deut. 5:14; 29:11 and 31:12f., other texts also demonstrate that the *gēr* participated fully in Israel's religion. The same laws applied to the *gēr* as to the Israelite, as illustrated by regulations for the Passover:

הַקָּהָל חֻקָּה אַחַת לָכֶם וְלַגֵּר הַגָּר חֻקַּת עוֹלָם לְדֹרֹתֵיכֶם כָּכֶם כַּגֵּר יִהְיֶה לִפְנֵי יְהוָה

"The community is to have the same rules for you and for the *gēr* residing among you; this is a lasting ordinance for the generations to come. You and the *gēr* shall be the same before the LORD." (Num. 15:15; cf. 15:16; Exod. 12:48)[25]

If the community of Israel failed unintentionally to keep the law and were forgiven, so were the *gērîm* residing among the Israelites:

וְנִסְלַח לְכָל־עֲדַת בְּנֵי יִשְׂרָאֵל וְלַגֵּר הַגָּר בְּתוֹכָם כִּי לְכָל־הָעָם בִּשְׁגָגָה:

"The whole Israelite community and the *gēr* residing among them will be forgiven, because all the people were involved in the unintentional wrong." (Num. 15:26)

The *gēr* offered sacrifices:

דַּבֵּר אֶל־אַהֲרֹן וְאֶל־בָּנָיו וְאֶל כָּל־בְּנֵי יִשְׂרָאֵל וְאָמַרְתָּ אֲלֵהֶם אִישׁ אִישׁ מִבֵּית יִשְׂרָאֵל וּמִן־הַגֵּר בְּיִשְׂרָאֵל אֲשֶׁר יַקְרִיב קָרְבָּנוֹ לְכָל־נִדְרֵיהֶם וּלְכָל־נִדְבוֹתָם אֲשֶׁר־יַקְרִיבוּ לַיהוָה לְעֹלָה:

"Speak to Aaron and his sons and to all the Israelites and say to them: 'If any of you—whether an Israelite or a *gēr* residing in Israel—presents a gift for a burnt offering to the LORD, either to fulfill a vow or as a freewill offering...'" (Lev. 22:18)[26]

The circumcised *gēr* also participated in Israel's sacred season. As for the Passover, the law stipulates:

וְכִי־יָגוּר אִתְּךָ גֵּר וְעָשָׂה פֶסַח לַיהוָה הִמּוֹל לוֹ כָל־זָכָר וְאָז יִקְרַב לַעֲשֹׂתוֹ וְהָיָה כְּאֶזְרַח הָאָרֶץ וְכָל־עָרֵל לֹא־יֹאכַל בּוֹ:

---

25. See also Num. 19:10.
26. See also Lev. 17:8; Num. 15:14

תּוֹרָה אַחַת יִהְיֶה לָאֶזְרָח וְלַגֵּר הַגָּר בְּתוֹכְכֶם:

"A *gēr* residing among you who wants to celebrate the LORD's Passover must have all the males in his household circumcised; then he may take part like one born in the land. No uncircumcised male may eat it." (Exod. 12:48)

The *gēr* also participated in the festivals of Weeks (Deut. 16:10f.) and of Booths (Deut. 16:13)[27]:

וְשָׂמַחְתָּ בְּחַגֶּךָ אַתָּה וּבִנְךָ וּבִתֶּךָ וְעַבְדְּךָ וַאֲמָתֶךָ וְהַלֵּוִי וְהַגֵּר וְהַיָּתוֹם וְהָאַלְמָנָה אֲשֶׁר בִּשְׁעָרֶיךָ:

"Be joyful at your festival—you, your sons and daughters, your male and female servants, and the Levites, the *gēr*, the fatherless and the widows who live in your towns." (Deut. 16:14)[28]

The *gēr* was cleansed of sin on the Day of Atonement:

וְהָיְתָה לָכֶם לְחֻקַּת עוֹלָם בַּחֹדֶשׁ הַשְּׁבִיעִי בֶּעָשׂוֹר לַחֹדֶשׁ תְּעַנּוּ אֶת־נַפְשֹׁתֵיכֶם וְכָל־מְלָאכָה לֹא תַעֲשׂוּ הָאֶזְרָח וְהַגֵּר הַגָּר בְּתוֹכְכֶם: כִּי־בַיּוֹם הַזֶּה יְכַפֵּר עֲלֵיכֶם לְטַהֵר אֶתְכֶם מִכֹּל חַטֹּאתֵיכֶם לִפְנֵי יְהוָה תִּטְהָרוּ:

"This is to be a lasting ordinance for you: On the tenth day of the seventh month you must deny yourselves and not do any work—whether native-born or the *gēr* residing among you—because on this day atonement will be made for you, to cleanse you. Then, before the LORD, you will be clean from all your sins." (Lev. 16:29f. cf. Deut. 16:14)

A *gēr* who blasphemes was put to death (Lev. 24:16, 22), and YHWH cuts off from the midst of Israel a *gēr* who worships idols or eats blood:

כִּי אִישׁ אִישׁ מִבֵּית יִשְׂרָאֵל וּמֵהַגֵּר אֲשֶׁר־יָגוּר בְּיִשְׂרָאֵל וְיִנָּזֵר מֵאַחֲרַי וְיַעַל גִּלּוּלָיו אֶל־לִבּוֹ וּמִכְשׁוֹל עֲוֺנוֹ יָשִׂים נֹכַח פָּנָיו וּבָא אֶל־הַנָּבִיא לִדְרָשׁ־לוֹ בִי אֲנִי יְהוָה נַעֲנֶה־לּוֹ בִּי:

וְנָתַתִּי פָנַי בָּאִישׁ הַהוּא וַהֲשִׁמֹּתִיהוּ לְאוֹת וְלִמְשָׁלִים וְהִכְרַתִּיו מִתּוֹךְ עַמִּי וִידַעְתֶּם כִּי־אֲנִי יְהוָה:

"'When any of the Israelites or any *gēr* residing in Israel separate themselves from me and set up idols in their hearts and put a wicked stumbling

---

27. Only native-born Israelites without the *gērîm*, however, lived in shelters for the historical experience was unique to them (Lev. 23:43).

28. See also 26:11.

Who Is the Gēr ("Sojourner")?

block before their faces and then go to a prophet to inquire of me, I the LORD will answer them myself." (Ezek. 14:7)[29]

וְאִישׁ אִישׁ מִבֵּית יִשְׂרָאֵל וּמִן־הַגֵּר הַגָּר בְּתוֹכָם אֲשֶׁר יֹאכַל כָּל־דָּם וְנָתַתִּי פָנַי בַּנֶּפֶשׁ הָאֹכֶלֶת אֶת־הַדָּם וְהִכְרַתִּי אֹתָהּ מִקֶּרֶב עַמָּהּ׃

"I will set my face against any Israelite or any *gēr* residing among them who eats blood, and I will cut them off from the people." (Lev. 17:10 [cf. 17:12f.]).

The *gēr* underwent the same special cleansing rites as the native (Lev. 17:15f, Num. 19:10), and the laws of sexual chastity (Lev. 18:1—25) applied to the *gēr* as well as to the native-born:

וּשְׁמַרְתֶּם אַתֶּם אֶת־חֻקֹּתַי וְאֶת־מִשְׁפָּטַי וְלֹא תַעֲשׂוּ מִכֹּל הַתּוֹעֵבֹת הָאֵלֶּה הָאֶזְרָח וְהַגֵּר הַגָּר בְּתוֹכְכֶם׃

"But you must keep my decrees and my laws. The native-born and the *gēr* residing among you must not do any of these detestable things." (Lev. 18:26)

Landless

The characterization of the *gēr* as landless is implicit, not explicit, yet certain. This is so because each native Israelite family enjoyed the patrimony of the Land, which was owned by YHWH. They inherited portions of it as a usufruct[30] when Joshua and the leaders distributed the Land (Josh. 14:1–5; 17:8–10).[31] Moreover, the Law forbade the Israelites from selling their inheritance permanently:

וְהָאָרֶץ לֹא תִמָּכֵר לִצְמִתֻת כִּי־לִי הָאָרֶץ כִּי־גֵרִים וְתוֹשָׁבִים אַתֶּם עִמָּדִי׃

"The land shall not be sold in permanently, because the land is mine and you reside in my land as *gērim* and *tôšābîm*." (Lev. 25:23)

If land was sold, in the Year of Jubilee it was returned to its original owners (Lev. 25:28). These laws excluded the *gēr* from any patrimony in the Land. Centuries later Naboth refused to dispose of his land to king

---

29. See also Lev. 17:12f.

30. "The legal right of using and enjoying the fruits or profits of something belonging to another" (Merriam-Webster's Collegiate Dictionary, 11th ed.)

31. See Bruce K. Waltke with Charles Yu, *An Old Testament Theology* (Grand Rapids: Zondervan, 2007), 528.

Ahab based on his conviction the Land was YHWH's, that the Land was distributed as a perpetual usufruct to each Israelite family, and the family had a sacred duty to preserve the family's permanent inheritance in the Land (1 Kgs. 21:3).

The *gēr*'s lack of land gave rise in part to *gērîm*'s characterization as dependents of and social inferiors to native Israelites.

Dependent for Provision and Protection

D. Kellermann comments: "[The *gēr*'s] status and privileges are dependent on the hospitality that has played an important role in the ancient Near East ever since ancient times." Job defends his honor, claiming:

בַּחוּץ לֹא־יָלִין גֵּר דְּלָתַי לָאֹרַח אֶפְתָּח׃

"The *gēr* has not lodged in the street; I have opened my doors to the traveler." (Job 31:32)

Separated from the native land and from kindred by birth, the *gēr* is vulnerable and in need of protection. As a proselyte, the *gēr* stands under divine protection:

יְהוָה שֹׁמֵר אֶת־גֵּרִים יָתוֹם וְאַלְמָנָה יְעוֹדֵד וְדֶרֶךְ רְשָׁעִים יְעַוֵּת

"The LORD watches over the *gēr* and sustains the fatherless and the widow, but he frustrates the ways of the wicked." (Ps. 146:9)[32]

The psalmist condemns the proud for slaying the *gēr* (Ps. 94:6). The *gēr* was to be judged fairly, even in disputes with a native-born Israelite:

וָאֲצַוֶּה אֶת־שֹׁפְטֵיכֶם בָּעֵת הַהִוא לֵאמֹר שָׁמֹעַ בֵּין־אֲחֵיכֶם וּשְׁפַטְתֶּם צֶדֶק בֵּין־אִישׁ וּבֵין־אָחִיו וּבֵין גֵּרוֹ׃

"And I [Moses] charged your judges at that time, 'hear the disputes between your people and judge fairly, whether the case is between two Israelites or between an Israelite and a *gēr*.'" (Deut. 1:16)

Anyone who withheld justice from the *gēr* was cursed:

אָרוּר מַטֶּה מִשְׁפַּט גֵּר־יָתוֹם וְאַלְמָנָה וְאָמַר כָּל־הָעָם אָמֵן

"'Cursed is anyone who withholds justice from the *gēr*, the fatherless or the widow.' Then all the people shall say, 'Amen!'" (Deut. 27:19)

---

32. See also Mal. 3:5.

Who Is the Gēr ("Sojourner")?

The *gēr* guilty of manslaughter could flee to a city of refuge:

אֵלֶּה הָיוּ עָרֵי הַמּוּעָדָה לְכֹל ׀ בְּנֵי יִשְׂרָאֵל וְלַגֵּר הַגָּר בְּתוֹכָם לָנוּס שָׁמָּה כָּל־מַכֵּה־נֶפֶשׁ בִּשְׁגָגָה וְלֹא יָמוּת בְּיַד גֹּאֵל הַדָּם עַד־עָמְדוֹ לִפְנֵי הָעֵדָה׃

(Josh. 20:9 WTT)

"Any of the Israelites or any *gēr* residing among them who killed someone accidentally could flee to these designated cities and not be killed by the avenger of blood prior to standing trial before the assembly." (Josh. 20:9; cf. Num. 35:15)

Kindness to the *gēr* came as an inseparable twin to the vulnerable *gēr* (cf. Lev. 19:10), and oppression was prohibited:

וְכִי־יָגוּר אִתְּךָ גֵּר בְּאַרְצְכֶם לֹא תוֹנוּ אֹתוֹ׃ כְּאֶזְרָח מִכֶּם יִהְיֶה לָכֶם הַגֵּר ׀ הַגָּר אִתְּכֶם וְאָהַבְתָּ לוֹ כָּמוֹךָ כִּי־גֵרִים הֱיִיתֶם בְּאֶרֶץ מִצְרָיִם אֲנִי יְהוָה אֱלֹהֵיכֶם׃

"When a *gēr* resides among you in your land, do not mistreat them. The *gēr* residing among you must be treated as your native-born. Love them as yourself, for you were a *gēr* in Egypt. I am the LORD your God." (Lev. 19:33f.)[33]

YHWH loves the *gēr* and so provisions them:

עֹשֶׂה מִשְׁפַּט יָתוֹם וְאַלְמָנָה וְאֹהֵב גֵּר לָתֶת לוֹ לֶחֶם וְשִׂמְלָה׃

"who executes justice for the orphan and the widow, and who loves the *gēr*, providing them food and clothing." (Deut. 10:18 NRS)[34]

Providence provides for the *gēr* to share in the fruit of the Land and its abundance by deeding to the *gēr*, the orphan and widow what is left behind after reaping the fields in the spring, and after beating of the olive trees and gathering of the grapes in the fall:

וְכַרְמְךָ לֹא תְעוֹלֵל וּפֶרֶט כַּרְמְךָ לֹא תְלַקֵּט לֶעָנִי וְלַגֵּר תַּעֲזֹב אֹתָם אֲנִי יְהוָה אֱלֹהֵיכֶם׃

לֹא תִּגְנֹבוּ וְלֹא־תְכַחֲשׁוּ וְלֹא־תְשַׁקְּרוּ אִישׁ בַּעֲמִיתוֹ׃

"When you reap the harvest of your land, you shall not reap to the very edges of your field, or gather the gleanings of your harvest. [10] You shall not strip your vineyard bare, or gather the fallen grapes of your vineyard; you shall leave them for the poor and the *gēr*: I am the LORD your God." (Lev.

---

33. See also Exod. 23:9; Deut. 10:19; Jer. 7:6.
34. See also Deut. 24:21.

19:9f., cf. 23:22)³⁵

Obviously, the effectiveness of YHWH's provision depends on Israel's obedience. The term also occurs in connection with the tithe for the Levites and the needy triad of the widow, the fatherless, and the *gēr*:

כִּי תְכַלֶּה לַעְשֵׂר אֶת־כָּל־מַעְשַׂר תְּבוּאָתְךָ בַּשָּׁנָה הַשְּׁלִישִׁת שְׁנַת הַמַּעֲשֵׂר וְנָתַתָּה לַלֵּוִי לַגֵּר לַיָּתוֹם וְלָאַלְמָנָה וְאָכְלוּ בִשְׁעָרֶיךָ וְשָׂבֵעוּ

"When you have finished setting aside a tenth of all your produce in the third year, the year of the tithe, you shall give it to the Levite, the *gēr*, the fatherless, and the widow, so that they may eat in your towns and be satisfied." (Deut. 26:12, cf. 14:29)

The landless *gēr* in an agricultural economy was financially poor and so in need of support, as can be inferred from the comparison with a poor relative:

וְכִי־יָמוּךְ אָחִיךָ וּמָטָה יָדוֹ עִמָּךְ וְהֶחֱזַקְתָּ בּוֹ גֵּר וְתוֹשָׁב וָחַי עִמָּךְ

"If any of your fellow Israelites become poor and are unable to support themselves among you, help them as you would a *gēr* and *tôšāb*, so they can continue to live among you." (Lev. 25:35)

Socially Inferior to the Israelites

Though the *gēr* was grafted into Israel with the ethic of a family member and included fully into Israel's religion, the *gēr* was socially inferior to the native-born. Job reckons the *gēr* on a par with a female slave:

גָּרֵי בֵיתִי וְאַמְהֹתַי לְזָר תַּחְשְׁבֻנִי נָכְרִי הָיִיתִי בְעֵינֵיהֶם׃

"My dependents and maidservants regard me as a stranger; I am an outsider to them." (Job 19:15)

In truth the *gēr* is often listed after, and presumably inferior to, the Israelite slave, probably because the Israelite slaves regained their land in the Year of Jubilee. The *gērîm*'s social inferiority can be inferred from their dependence on the Israelites (see above Lev. 19:9; Deut. 26:12).³⁶ The *gērîm* are depicted as those "who chop your wood and carry your water" (Deut. 29:11 [Heb. 10]) and as stonecutters (1 Chr. 22:2).

---

35. See also Deut. 24:19f.
36. See also Deut. 24:17; 26:13; Jer. 76; Mal. 3:5.

Who Is the Gēr ("Sojourner")?

Nevertheless, Samuel Eliot Morison, the official historian for the US Navy in World War II, likened life to a card game. The Sovereign deals all of us a hand, and then we must play that hand. He deals some a good hand and others a poor hand. If you are dealt a good hand and play it well, you will excel, but if you don't play it well, you will lose to a person who is dealt a poor hand but plays it well. The same reality plays itself out in the relationship the *gēr-'ezrah* relationship:

וְכִי תַשִּׂיג יַד גֵּר וְתוֹשָׁב עִמָּךְ וּמָךְ אָחִיךָ עִמּוֹ וְנִמְכַּר לְגֵר תּוֹשָׁב עִמָּךְ אוֹ לְעֵקֶר מִשְׁפַּחַת גֵּר

"If a *gēr* or *tôšāb* residing among you becomes rich and any of your fellow Israelites become poor and sell themselves to the *gēr* or *tôšāb*..." (Lev. 25:47)

The prediction that the *gēr* would rise higher than the native Israelite proves the characterization of *gēr* as the social inferior to the native Israelites[37] for that topsy-turvy situation occurs as part of the curse against faithless Israel:

הַגֵּר אֲשֶׁר בְּקִרְבְּךָ יַעֲלֶה עָלֶיךָ מַעְלָה מָּעְלָה וְאַתָּה תֵרֵד מַטָּה מָּטָּה

"The *gēr* who reside among you will rise above you higher and higher, but you will sink lower and lower." (Deut. 28:43)

Moreover, although the *gēr* was a religious proselyte who participated fully in the Israelite religion, the *gēr*, not the native-born Israelite, was permitted to eat the נְבֵלָה (*niblâ*, "corpse"):

לֹא תֹאכְלוּ כָל־נְבֵלָה לַגֵּר אֲשֶׁר־בִּשְׁעָרֶיךָ תִּתְּנֶנָּה וַאֲכָלָהּ אוֹ מָכֹר לְנָכְרִי כִּי עַם קָדוֹשׁ אַתָּה לַיהוָה אֱלֹהֶיךָ

"You [the holy people, cf. 14:2] must not eat anything that has died a natural death. You may give it to a *gēr* living in your town, or you may sell it to a stranger. But do not eat it yourselves, for you are set apart as holy to the LORD your God. You must not cook a young goat in its mother's milk." (Deut. 14:21 NLT)

This law distinguishes the *gēr* from the native Israelite,[38] not only in diet but also in status: the Israelite, not the *gēr*, is regarded as holy (cf. Exod.

---

37. *Pace* Kellerman ("gûr," 446).
38. *Pace*, Glanville, "The *Gēr* in Deuteronomy," 608.

19:5). Most scholars think "the Deuteronomic legislators did not regard the *gērim* as members of Israel."[39] Nevertheless, the *gērîm* lived among the kinship group of Israelites as citizens with the same rights and privileges of the native-born, and as proselytes to the orthodox religion of Israel. Their status is similar to a person in India: a citizen of India and also belonging to one of the categories of the Hindu religion: Brahmins, Kshatriyas, Vaishyas or Shudras.

English Glosses of *Gēr*

There is no precise English equivalent for *gēr*. This is so because in the English-speaking world, aside from royalty in the United Kingdom, there are no castes, no ranking by birth, among commoners. All are regarded as social equals. And languages do not have appellatives for a non-existing situation. And so the best that can be achieved is to coin a term of one or two English words that most closely approximates the *ger*'s six defining characteristics. This can be done by critically appraising glosses in the English versions, as sampled from Exodus 2:22 and Deuteronomy 5:4, and other hyponyms of the superordinate "an outsider" proposed by academics:

"Settler" (so NIDOTTE)

"Settler" signifies a relatively permanent outsider residing in a new cultural context. It fails to capture any of the six defining characters of the *gēr*.

"Sojourner" (so ASV,[40] ESV, NAS, RSV, YLT)

Many scholars mistakenly have opted for the gloss "sojourner" because they assume the meaning of the noun *gēr* is related to the verb *gûr* ("to stay temporarily"). Besides being archaic, "sojourner" (i.e., "temporary resident") does not satisfy the defining characteristics of "foreigner," "immigrant" and "proselyte." Although the patriarchs, as *gērîm*, happened to dwell temporarily in Canaan, and Israel, as a *gēr*, happened to dwell in Egypt over 400 years, a defining characteristic of the *gēr* in legal literature

---

39. Rainer Albertz, "From Aliens to Proselytes: Non-Priestly and Priestly Legislation concerning Strangers," in *The Foreigner and the Law: Perspectives from the Hebrew Bible and the Ancient Near East*, ed. Reinhard Achenbach, Rainer Albertz, and Jakob Wöhrle, BZABR 16 (Wiesbaden: Harrassowitz, 2011), 55.

40. Exod. 2:22.

Who Is the Gēr ("Sojourner")?

is not a "temporary resident." As argued above, in the Torah the *gērîm* is reckoned as an immigrant, a permanent member within the Israelite social structure. Israel's law even commanded the *gērîm* to teach their children the Torah (Deut. 31:12f., above)

In some poetic literature, as in narrative, the *gēr* could be understood as a "sojourner" (e.g. Ps. 119:19), but no text demands that sense, and others exclude it:

כִּי יְרַחֵם יְהוָה אֶת־יַעֲקֹב וּבָחַר עוֹד בְּיִשְׂרָאֵל וְהִנִּיחָם עַל־אַדְמָתָם וְנִלְוָה הַגֵּר עֲלֵיהֶם וְנִסְפְּחוּ עַל־בֵּית יַעֲקֹב:

"The LORD will have compassion on Jacob; once again he will choose Israel and will settle them in their own land. The *gēr* will join them and unite with the descendants of Jacob." (Isa. 14:1)

"Proselyte" (so LXX, Vulgate)

"Proselyte" signifies "a person who has converted from one opinion, religion, or party to another," and so the gloss "proselyte" satisfies this defining characteristic of the *gēr*. It fails, however, to satisfy the other five characteristics of the *gēr*: foreigner, immigrant, landless, dependent and socially inferior.

"Foreigner" (so CJB, CSB, NET, NIV, NJB, NLT)

"Foreigner" refers to a person residing in one nation while belonging to and owning allegiance to another.[41] This gloss, popular in recent translations, is stylistically felicitous but it fails in several ways. First, Hebrew has terms for "foreigner": נָכְרִי (*nokrî*) and בֶּן־נֵכָר (*ben-nēkār*). Second, if no distinction is made between נָכְרִי and גֵּר, the English-speaking audience is left with contradictions, anomalies and misunderstandings. Note the contradiction in Exodus 12:43 and 48 caused by glossing both *gēr* and *ben-nēkār* by "foreigner":

וַיֹּאמֶר יְהוָה אֶל־מֹשֶׁה וְאַהֲרֹן זֹאת חֻקַּת הַפָּסַח כָּל־בֶּן־נֵכָר לֹא־יֹאכַל בּוֹ

"These are the regulations for the Passover meal: "No *foreigner* (בֶּן־נֵכָר) may eat it" (Exod. 12:43)

---

41. www.merriam-webster.com/dictionary/foreigner.

וְכִי־יָגוּר אִתְּךָ גֵּר וְעָשָׂה פֶסַח לַיהוָה הִמּוֹל לוֹ כָל־זָכָר וְאָז יִקְרַב לַעֲשֹׂתוֹ וְהָיָה כְּאֶזְרַח הָאָרֶץ וְכָל־עָרֵל לֹא־יֹאכַל בּוֹ׃

"A *foreigner* (גֵּר) residing among you who wants to celebrate the LORD's Passover must have all the males in his household circumcised; then he may take part like one born in the land. No uncircumcised male may eat it." (Exod. 12:48)

One could lamely rationalize that the foreigner prohibited to eat the Passover was not circumcised but that harmonization would be wrong for reasons shown above. Moreover, without distinguishing between גֵּר and בְּנֵי נֵכָר (*ben-nēkār*), a proselyte could be understood as David's enemy who cower before him (2 Sam. 22:45); YHWH sets his face against apostate foreigners, an oxymoron (Ezek. 14:7); and Israel should have the same welfare program for foreigners as for the needy widow, fatherless, and *gēr*. Israelites *gave* the *niblâ* to the *gēr* but *sold* it to the *nokrî* ("foreigner") (Deut. 14:21). The *nokrî* must repay debts (Deut. 15:3) and may be charged interest (23:20 [Heb.21]).

In sum, "foreigner" would identify the *gēr* as a member of the abandoned country, not as a proselyte to the religion of Israel nor an immigrant entitled to the rights and privileges of the Israelites; nor as dependent upon them for protection provisions.

"Stranger" (so ASV,[42] JPS, [N]KJ, TNK)

"Stranger" denotes a person whom one does not know or with whom one is not familiar. This gloss fails to signify some essential defining characteristics of the *gēr*: foreigner, proselyte. and a vulnerable immigrant entitled to the rights and privileges of the native-born Israelite. "Stranger" may in fact connote a person "to be protected from," not a person in need of protection.

"Resident alien" (so NAB, NRS)

A "resident alien" is "a foreign national living on an official basis in a country of which they are not a citizen." This gloss does not fit well the defining characteristics of the *gēr*, who is no longer identified as a foreign national but as an immigrant, as a citizen of Israel. Moreover, "resident

---

42. Deut. 5:14.

alien" does not denote a proselyte nor connote a dependent. Finally, the gloss is more appropriate for the *tôšāb* (see below) than the *gēr*,

"Protected citizen" (so HALOT, Kellerman)

As noted, the *gēr* is vulnerable and dependent citizen in need of protection and provisions, but the gloss "protected citizen" fails to capture other defining characteristics of the *gēr*: foreigner, immigrant, landless, and a religious proselyte.

"Immigrant" (so E. Otto, see above)

An "immigrant" is "a person who comes to live permanently in a foreign country." On the one hand, "immigrant" satisfies the *gēr*'s essential characteristics as a foreigner whom the natives have allowed to participate in their economy, rules, and religion. On the other hand, it does not signify a landless, poor, dependent person similar to the widow and fatherless; a social inferior to the native kinship group. This lack can be mitigated by the collocation "landless-immigrant."

"Landless-immigrant"

In an agricultural culture "landless-immigrant" connotes dependence and social inferiority. None of the above glosses captures the notion of proselyte, other than the term itself. The gloss "landless-immigrant" sits comfortably in every context, including narrative.

Three Exegetical Insights

Genesis 23:4

גֵּר־וְתוֹשָׁב אָנֹכִי עִמָּכֶם תְּנוּ לִי אֲחֻזַּת־קֶבֶר עִמָּכֶם וְאֶקְבְּרָה מֵתִי מִלְּפָנָי׃

"I [Abraham] am a landless-immigrant—a landless alien[43] living among you. Sell me some property for a burial site here so I can bury my dead."

The gloss "landless-immigrant" signifies the Hittites showed Abraham's family hospitality and accepted them with all the rights and privi-

---

43. In a forthcoming essay it will be argued the *tôšāb* is best glossed by "landless alien."

leges of an immigrant. In that light, one better understands why Abraham asked the Hittites to cede land to him so he could bury Sarah; why Esau married Hittites (Gen. 26:34—35); and why Abraham qualified his status as a *ger* by adding a *tôšāb* ("landless alien," see n. 43 and below), to wit, to exclude himself from being a proselyte to the Hittite gods. Moreover, that the Hittites reckoned the landless-immigrant Abraham a נָשִׂיא (*něśî'*, "mighty prince," Gen. 23:6) demonstrates how exceptional was YHWH's blessing on him.

Exodus 2:22

וַתֵּלֶד בֵּן וַיִּקְרָא אֶת־שְׁמוֹ גֵּרְשֹׁם כִּי אָמַר גֵּר הָיִיתִי בְּאֶרֶץ נָכְרִיָּה׃

Zipporah gave birth to a son, and Moses named him *Ger*shom, saying, "I have become a landless-immigrant in a foreign land." (Exod. 18:3)

The Midianites allowed Moses to live among them—he even married one of them—but Moses was an unhappy camper. The birth of his son made him acutely aware of his inferior status, probably having no hope of owning land to give his son as a patrimony. He is the first "Jew" in search of a homeland and so is psychology prepared for YHWH's revelation at the burning bush that Moses would lead his fellow Hebrews to the promised land (Exodus 3–4).

Ezekiel 47:22f.

וְהָיָה תַּפִּלוּ אוֹתָהּ בְּנַחֲלָה לָכֶם וּלְהַגֵּרִים הַגָּרִים בְּתוֹכְכֶם אֲשֶׁר־הוֹלִדוּ בָנִים בְּתוֹכְכֶם וְהָיוּ לָכֶם כְּאֶזְרָח בִּבְנֵי יִשְׂרָאֵל אִתְּכֶם יִפְּלוּ בְנַחֲלָה בְּתוֹךְ שִׁבְטֵי יִשְׂרָאֵל׃ וְהָיָה בַשֵּׁבֶט אֲשֶׁר־גָּר הַגֵּר אִתּוֹ שָׁם תִּתְּנוּ נַחֲלָתוֹ נְאֻם אֲדֹנָי יְהוִה

"'You are to allot it [the land] as an inheritance for yourselves and for the landless-immigrant[44] residing among you and who have children. You are to consider them as native-born Israelites; along with you they are to be allotted an inheritance among the tribes of Israel. In whatever tribe a landless-immigrant[45] resides, there you are to give them their inheritance,' declares the Sovereign LORD." (Ezek. 47:22–23)

Unlike the old dispensation, in Ezekiel's vision of Israel's idealistic fu-

---

44. NIV "foreigner."
45. See n. 24.

ture the formerly landless-immigrant will own portions of YHWH's land along with the clans of the אֶזְרָח (*'ezrāh*, "native born"). This vision anticipates the Pauline mystery (i.e., heretofore not revealed truth) of Jew and Gentile as co-heirs in the promises God: "εἶναι τὰ ἔθνη συγκληρονόμα καὶ σύσσωμα καὶ συμμέτοχα τῆς ἐπαγγελίας ἐν Χριστῷ Ἰησοῦ διὰ τοῦ εὐαγγελίου" ("This mystery is that through the gospel the Gentiles are heirs together with Israel, members together of one body, and sharers together in the promise in Christ Jesus" [Eph. 3:6]).

Source Criticism

The numerous laws about the landless-immigrant imply that they comprised a significant percentage of the population, an implication confirmed by Solomon's census:

וַיִּסְפֹּר שְׁלֹמֹה כָּל־הָאֲנָשִׁים הַגֵּירִים אֲשֶׁר בְּאֶרֶץ יִשְׂרָאֵל אַחֲרֵי הַסְּפָר אֲשֶׁר סְפָרָם דָּוִיד אָבִיו וַיִּמָּצְאוּ מֵאָה וַחֲמִשִּׁים אֶלֶף וּשְׁלֹשֶׁת אֲלָפִים וְשֵׁשׁ מֵאוֹת׃

"Solomon took a census of all the landless immigrants residing in Israel, after the census his father David had taken; and they were found to be 153,600." (2 Chr. 2:17 [Heb. 16])

The number pertains only to workers (see v. 18). If we add to them women and children, as seems reasonable, the total number of landless-immigrants could easily be as high as 500,000. What are the origins of so many displaced persons?

Source critics commonly allege that the Deuteronomic code (chapters 12–26) originated in the northern kingdom and that "the fugitives from the northern kingdom after the fall of Samaria in 722 BC" brought the Deuteronomic code with them.[46] But migrants from the northern kingdom into Judah are never called *gērîm* (cf. 2 Chr. 11:16; 15:9). In fact, the *gērîm* from the northern kingdom who participated in Hezekiah's Passover festival are distinguished from the native-born Israelites (2 Chr. 30:25). Source critics also assign the presumably large number assembled to hear the Law in Deuteronomy 31:9-13 to the postexilic period.[47] Glanville, however, rightly

---

46. Kellerman, "Gûr," 445.
47. Glanville ("The Ger (Stranger) in Deuteronomy," 621) cites Reinhard Achenbach, "Der Eintritt der Schutzbürger in den Bund (Dtn 29, 10–12): Distinktion und Integration von Fremden im Deuteronomium," in *Gerechtigkeit und Recht zu uben" (Gen 18,19): Stu-*

says that these scholars must explain why immigrants would have desired the 'harsh realities of life'[48] in Persian Yehud. The same critical question can be leveled against relating the implied many landless immigrants in the putative P document to the late exilic or early post-exilic periods. Glanville thinks his question debunks the notion that the landless-immigrants were exclusively foreigners. Rather, it debunks the notion of the late dating of P and of the frame of Deuteronomy.

Reading the canon holistically, the large number of landless immigrants is readily explained by the large mixed multitude that fled Egypt with Moses and Israel:

וְגַם־עֵרֶב רַב עָלָה אִתָּם

"An ethnically diverse crowd also went up with them." (Exod. 12:38 CSB)

Theology and the Religion of Israel

As for theology, the psalmists figuratively represent themselves as dependent, landless-immigrants before YHWH (Pss. 39:12 [Heb. 13]; 119:19)[49]; and Jeremiah complains that YHWH is like a landless-immigrant in the Land—that is to say, a vulnerable dependent, not a protector of Israel in her distress (Jer.14:8).

As for the religion of Israel, BDB says that *gērim* is a technical term in Gen. 23:4; Exod. 2:22; 18:3; Job 31:32;[50] A. H. Konkel says that the *gēr* "is recognized as having a special status,"[51] and A. Martin-Achard agrees;[52] D. Kellerman says: "The *gēr* occupies an intermediate position between

---

dien zur altorientalischen und biblischen Rechtsgeschichte, zur Religionsgeschichte Israels und zur Religionssoziologie: Festschrift fur Eckart Otto zum 65. Geburtstag, ed. Reinhard Achenbach and Martin Arneth, BZABR 13 (Wiesbaden: Harrassowitz, 2009), 240-55.

48. Glanville ("The *Ger* (Stranger) in Deuteronomy," 621) cites John Kessler, "Diaspora and Homeland in the Early Achaemenid Period: Community, Geography and Demography in Zechariah 1-8," in *Approaching Yehud: New Approaches to the Study of the Persian Period*, ed. Jon L. Berquist, Semeia Studies 50 (Atlanta: Society of Biblical Literature, 2007), 137-66, here 165.

49. See also Jer. 22:3.

50. BDB, 158, s.v. גֵּר.

51. A. H. Konkel, *NIDOTTE*, 1:837, s.v. גור.

52. A. Martin-Achard, *TLOT*, 1:308, גור.

Who Is the Gēr ("Sojourner")?

a native (*'ezrach*) ... and a foreigner (*nokhri*)."[53] The landless-immigrant should be understood more precisely than these vagaries, to wit, as a category within a caste system. The orthodox religion of Israel had four castes in a hierarchical arrangement according to proximity to YHWH.

The Levites (הַלְוִיִּם)

The highest caste was the Levites, who descended patrilineally from Levi, the third son of Jacob. Of them the high priest was the most holy of all. When Moses divided Transjordan and Joshua distributed Cis-Jordan, the Levites received cities but were not allowed to be landowners. This was so "because the Lord the God of Israel Himself is their inheritance" (Deut. 18:2). Many stipulations in Exodus 25-39 and Leviticus 1-16 pertain to YHWH's unique rules and regulations for the Levites. The Kohanim, a subset of the Levites, were the priests who served the temple. Those who were not Kohanim, were specifically assigned to singing and/or playing music in the Temple, serving as guards, or as carriers. In return for the services of the Levites, the landed tribes were expected to extend charity and give a tithe to support the Levites (Num. 18:21-25).

The Other Tribes of Israel (בְּנֵי יִשְׂרָאֵל)

The next caste were the other eleven tribes of Israel. They inherited as their patrimony of the land that YHWH uniquely owned, albeit he owned the universe. With respect to foreigners, the Israelites, above all the Levites, were YHWH's treasured possession, a kingdom of priests, and a holy nation (Exod. 19:6). The so-called Holiness Code (Lev. 17-26) and Deuteronomy pertain mostly to all Israel.

Landless-immigrant (גֵּרִים)

Third in the hierarchical caste system of Israel's religion were the proselytes, "the landless-immigrants." They could not own land but otherwise, apart from being given the *niblâ* as charity (Deut. 14:21), they participated fully in Israel's political, economic, judicial and religious life.[54] Deuterono-

---

53. D. Kellerman, *TDOT*, 2:443, s.v. *gur*
54. Nevertheless, after eating it the *gēr* must be ceremonially cleansed: וְכָל־נֶפֶשׁ אֲשֶׁר תֹּאכַל נְבֵלָה וּטְרֵפָה בָּאֶזְרָח וּבַגֵּר וְכִבֶּס בְּגָדָיו וְרָחַץ בַּמַּיִם וְטָמֵא עַד־הָעֶרֶב וְטָהֵר:
"Anyone, whether native-born or landless immigrant, who eats anything found dead or

my 14:21 makes it a point to contrast them with the holy people.

The Landless Alien (הַתּוֹשָׁבִים)

On the lowest rung of Israel's caste system was the *tôšāb*, who. we will argue in a forthcoming article, are best glossed by the term "landless alien." They, like the *gērim*, were also foreigners, landless and subjects of Israel's administrators (e.g., Lev. 25:47). Unlike the *gērim*, however, they were not religious proselytes: not circumcised, excluded from the Passover (Exod. 12:45) and from the Day of Atonement (cf. Lev. 16:29f). Also, unlike the landless immigrant (cf. Lev. 17:8), no provision was made for the תּוֹשָׁב (*tôšāb*) to bring a sacred offering. They could flee to a city of refuge (Num. 35:15) but listed with the שָׂכִיר ("hired worker" Lev. 22:10), not with the "widow, fatherless, and landless-immigrant" (cf. Deut. 10:13). Slaves could be bought from among the בְּנֵי הַתּוֹשָׁבִים along with slaves from nations around Israel, unlike fellow Israelites (Lev. 25:45).[55] In a separate article I will argue they were Canaanites who fled Egypt in the Exodus. Instead of being exterminated with the Canaanites in Joshua's conquest of the Land, they were protected but excluded from the orthodox religion of Israel. If so, the *ger*'s origins are probably not Canaanite, contrary to Kellerman's assertion that the *gērim* stone cutters in 1 Chr. 22:2 were "no doubt primarily the pre-Israelite Canaanite population."[56]

---

torn by wild animals must wash their clothes and bathe with water, and they will be ceremonially unclean till evening; then they will be clean." (Lev. 17:15)

55. An Israelite could sell himself as a slave but was not to be treated as such (Lev. 25:40).
56. Kellerman, "*gûr*," 444.

3

It's All Going to Burn

*Holy Scripture, Our "Environment,"
and Climate Change*

Iain Provan

In 1992 the United Nations sponsored what has informally become known as the first "Earth Summit."[1] It met in Rio de Janeiro in Brazil, and it produced *The Rio Declaration on Environment and Development*, which enunciated twenty-seven principles. The first claimed that "human beings are at the centre of concerns for sustainable development. They are entitled to a healthy and productive life in harmony with nature."[2] Principles two and three then asserted that political states possess "the sovereign right to exploit their own resources pursuant to their own environmental and developmental policies," but that "the right to development must be fulfilled so as to equitably meet developmental and environmental needs of present and future generations." Commitments were later entered to "co-operate in the essential task of eradicating poverty as an indispensable requirement for sustainable development" and to give careful consideration

---

1. This essay, which I am delighted to contribute to this Festschrift for my good friend and colleague Sven Soderlund, draws significantly on material that will be found in two chapters of a new book of mine to be published in late 2020: *Seeking What Is Right: The Old Testament and the Good Life* (Waco, TX: Baylor University Press).

2. The text may be found at https://www.cbd.int/doc/ref/rio-declaration.shtml, accessed February 18, 2020.

to "the least developed and ... most environmentally vulnerable" countries (principles five and six). Everything should be done "in a spirit of global partnership to conserve, protect and restore the health and integrity of the Earth's ecosystem" (principle seven). And so the *Declaration* continued.

The principles that lie at its heart are very familiar to many of us nowadays. They are indeed widely regarded as self-evidently sensible and virtuous, such that all right-thinking people will embrace and act upon them. It is worth pausing for a moment's critical reflection, then, to consider the significance of the fact that the great majority of human beings prior to the rise of modernity would certainly not have regarded these same principles as self-evidently sensible and virtuous—had they encountered them—nor would these principles have provided a basis for human action. The reason has to do with the way that pre-modern people commonly thought about the world around them and their relationship to it. To understand this important point we must delve into some historical background on the way to arriving at what this essay is fundamentally concerned to articulate—namely, what Holy Scripture has to say to Christians that is relevant to the matter of "environmental ethics" (or as we should call it, in our own language, "Creation care"), not least in a period of history marked by significant climate change.

A Convenient Myth

It is regularly claimed nowadays, among proponents of what contemporary author Bron Taylor has termed "dark green religion,"[3] that our contemporary ecological problems are the ultimate result of something that happened long ago: the advent of "civilization." Before the Neolithic agricultural revolution and the domestication of animals, it is claimed, human (Paleolithic) societies shared "intimacy with the world as the immanent basis of spirituality."[4] But then this "reverence for the earth-centered was

---

3. Bron Taylor, *Dark Green Religion: Nature Spirituality and the Planetary Future* (Berkeley: University of California, 2010).

4. John Zerzan, *Twilight of the Machines* (Port Townsend, WA: Feral House, 2008), 124. I discuss at more length this author and others who advocate for similar ideas in my *Convenient Myths: The Axial Age, Dark Green Religion, and the World That Never Was* (Waco, TX: Baylor University Press, 2013), chapter 4.

broken," and human beings began to dominate nature instead.[5] In order to save ourselves now, we must somehow retrieve a "religion that considers nature to be sacred ... and worthy of reverent care."[6] We must abandon modern world-religions that "promote and justify violence, bigotry, and anthropocentrism,"[7] and we must substitute for them a spirituality in which anthropocentrism is replaced with biocentrism. Contemporary indigenous peoples can help us greatly on this quest, since "scientists and indigenous peoples have similar insights regarding ecological interdependence, and . . . they often share common ethical and spiritual perceptions about the intrinsic value and sacredness of nature."[8] Indeed, these indigenous peoples represent the best remaining access that we possess to the crucially important spiritual and ecological knowledge that once enabled our ancient ancestors to live sustainably in harmony with their environment.

All of this is regularly claimed. There is, however, no good reason, empirically speaking, to believe it. We certainly lack direct evidence that, in reality, Paleolithic societies existed in such a state of bliss—in a kind of "dark green golden age." Further, the indirect evidence drawn from the observation and analysis of modern hunter-gatherer societies is not at all compelling.[9] I have offered an extensive summary of the modern research that bears on this question in another book, and there is no need to repeat much of that detail here.[10] However, it is worth reproducing a little of it in the present context, so that the reader can get a sense of where it leads us.

The Amazon

The native peoples of Amazonia have often been depicted in popular modern writing as possessing an innate "conservation ethic," preserved from ancient times, from which we might learn something important in our modern mission "to conserve, protect and restore the health and integrity

---

5. Zerzan, *Twilight*, 28.
6. Taylor, *Religion*, ix.
7. Taylor, *Religion*, 99-101.
8. Ibid., 147, referencing David Suzuki and Peter Knudtson, *Wisdom of the Elders: Honoring Sacred Native Visions of Nature* (Vancouver/Toronto: Greystone, 1992).
9. For a full discussion of the problems involved even in the *idea* that we might be able learn about the distant past by way of studying modern "primitive peoples," see Provan, *Convenient Myths*, chapter 5.
10. See Provan, *Convenient Myths*, chapter 6.

of the Earth's ecosystem" (*Rio Declaration*, principle seven). However, the evidence in fact suggests that what looks like "conservation" among these peoples arises in reality simply as an accidental by-product of the main business at hand: surviving as best one can in challenging circumstances. Their practices are driven by resource constraints, not by an environmental philosophy. As Michael Alvard has put it, "the appearance of balance between traditional native groups and their environment has more to do with low human population densities, lack of markets, and limited technology than it does with any natural harmonious relationship with nature."[11] As Allyn Stearman notes, this kind of claim is of course "certain to disturb those who romanticize indigenous peoples according to their own ethnocentric perceptions of how native societies relate to nature."[12] Since it is based on solid empirical evidence, however, it needs to be taken seriously.

North America

Other studies have tracked, in fact, just how destructive of their environments pre-modern people have often been, more generally, when resource constraints have not been in play—typically "using the richest resources with pitiless energetic efficiency" and thereby radically changing the world around them.[13] Contrary to the assumption of many modern people, for example, that "native North Americans had little impact on the flora and fauna of the continent," the truth is that these early native peoples "created the very ecosystem that we now consider 'natural'" in that part of the world.[14] Very likely they are to be implicated, first, in the eradication of some thirty-five genera of mostly large animals around 10,000 BC—the "Pleistocene

---

11. Michael S. Alvard, "Testing the 'Ecologically Noble Savage' Hypothesis: Interspecific Prey Choice by Piro Hunters in Amazonian Peru," *Human Ecology* 21 (1993): 355–87 (384).

12. Allyn MacLean Stearman, "Only Slaves Climb Trees: Revisiting the Myth of the Ecologically Noble Savage in Amazonia," *Human Nature* 5 (1994): 339–57 (351).

13. Atholl Anderson, "A Fragile Plenty: Pre-European Māori and the New Zealand Environment," in *Environmental Histories of New Zealand*, ed. Eric Pawson and Tom Brooking (Melbourne: Oxford University Press, 2002), 19–34 (32).

14. Michael S. Alvard, "Evolutionary Theory, Conservation and Human Environmental Impact," in *Wilderness and Political Ecology: Aboriginal Influences and the Original State of Nature*, ed. Charles E. Kay and Randy T. Simmons (Salt Lake City: University of Utah Press, 2002), 28–43 (29-30); Charles E. Kay, "Are Ecosystems Structured from the Top-Down or Bottom-Up?" in Kay and Simmons, *Wilderness and Political Ecology*, 215–37 (215).

extinctions." Even if they were not directly or entirely responsible for these extinctions, they certainly "drove populations of highly desirable 'target species' or 'preferred prey' to low levels, or even to local extinction,"[15] just as one would expect of a people pursuing "an optimal-foraging strategy with no effective conservation practices."[16] When Europeans first encountered North America, in fact, they generally found abundant wildlife only where the native inhabitants were absent or greatly diminished in number.[17] None of this speaks of "conservation practices" on the part of historical Native American peoples. It was, again, a matter of staying alive in the immediate circumstances. Ecological wisdom did not come into it.

Conservation Is Not a State of Being

These examples are aspects of a larger pattern, which has been described by Bobbi Low in her study of 186 traditional societies worldwide. People in such societies "do not, at least to their ethnographers, express a widely held conservation ethic," and "their low ecological impact ... results not from conscious conservation efforts, but from various combinations of low population density, inefficient extraction technology, and lack of profitable markets for extracted resources."[18] Consequently (as Thomas Neumann says), it is "important to surrender the image of the aboriginal peoples living in idyllic harmony with host ecological systems."[19] They have not done so recently, and there is no reason to think that they ever did so beforehand.

The most important point to grasp here is not only that pre-modern people have not typically practiced "conservation," but that the very concept has not arisen in their minds—and for good reason. Conservation (W. T. Vickers reminds us) "is not a state of being. It is a response to peo-

---

15. Paul S. Martin and Christine R. Szuter, "Revising the 'Wild West': Big Game Meets the Ultimate Keystone Species," in *Archaeology of Global Change: The Impact of Humans on their Environment*, ed. Charles L. Redman et. al. (Washington, DC: Smithsonian Books, 2004), 63–88 (64).
16. Kay, "Ecosystems," 225.
17. Provan, *Convenient Myths*, 74-9.
18. Bobbi S. Low, "Behavioral Ecology of Conservation in Traditional Societies," *Human Nature* 7 (1996): 353–79 (353, 368).
19. Thomas W. Neumann, "The Role of Prehistoric Peoples in Shaping Ecosystems in the Eastern United States: Implications for Restoration Ecology and Wilderness Management," in Kay and Simmons, *Wilderness and Political Ecology*, 141–78 (143).

ple's perceptions about the state of their environment and its resources, and a willingness to modify their behaviors to adjust to new realities."[20] In order for a "conservation ethic" to arise, then, two things are minimally necessary. First, there must be "stress on the resource base, made tangible through scarcity and/or increases in work effort, with significant repercussions for the user group."[21] Secondly, there must be a belief that human hunting or farming behavior (or whatever) is responsible in some way for the problem, and that changes to human habits will improve the situation. However, this is manifestly not how pre-modern people have typically looked at the world. On the one hand, they have often lived in the midst of plenty rather than scarcity (not least because of low population pressure on their environments). On the other hand, their belief systems have generally not led them to believe that there is any correlation between scarcity and their behavior (retrospectively or prospectively).

Ironically, it is precisely the pre-modern "nature-spirituality" so appreciated by the dark green religionists that has prevented the acquisition of "ecological wisdom" by the people who have practiced this spirituality! Consider the Plains Indians in North America, for example, who believed that buffalo were created in countless numbers underground, or in a certain lake, emerging each year onto the prairie to supply their needs. If the buffalo could not be seen, it was not because of population decline or some such modern concept. It was because they had not (yet) left their point of origin.[22] It is not easy to see how anything approaching a conservation ethic could ever have arisen out of such a belief system, and there is no evidence that it ever did, since "scarcity" here has no connection, conceptually, with human behavior. The following comments by the environmentalist David Suzuki, then, are partially but importantly misleading:

> It used to be understood that we have a sacred duty to pass on to future generations a world that is as rich as or richer than the one we came into ... For most of our existence, people knew that we were deeply

---

20. Cited in Flora Lu Holt, "The Catch-22 of Conservation: Indigenous Peoples, Biologists and Cultural Change," *Human Ecology* 33 (2005): 199–215 (209).
21. Holt, "Catch-22," 205–6.
22. Shepard Krech III, *The Ecological Indian: Myth and History* (New York: Norton, 1999), 121–49.

embedded in nature and that our very survival depended on nature's generosity. We understood that everything in the world was connected, that what we did had repercussions, and that therefore every act was laden with responsibility.[23]

It is true that many people in the past did understand that they were "deeply embedded in nature and that [their] very survival depended on nature's generosity"—that, indeed, "everything in the world was connected." This did not, however, lead them to believe that they had a role to play, much less a "sacred duty" to perform, in passing on "to future generations a world that is as rich as or richer than the one we came into." Their "responsibility" with respect to "repercussions" was simply not understood in such a manner.

The Rise of Modernity

To put this in a different way: in order even to conceive of the need for a document like the *Rio Declaration*, we already need to have registered that we have pressing environmental problems, that human beings have to some degree created them, and that we are also capable of doing something to solve them. We need to have already embraced a "modern" view of the world and our role in it, and to have abandoned pre-modern ones—at least the ones that I have just described.

I put the matter in precisely this way because of my convictions about where what we call "modernity" came from. Again, I have explained these convictions at great length in a different book, so here I shall simply outline them.[24] The core of the argument is this: that what we now call modernity arose out of a particular version of the Christian worldview that was deeply rooted in OT Scripture, which in the centuries BC had already set its face against the "nature spirituality" that was ubiquitous in the Ancient Near East. Modernity arose as this biblically-based worldview began fully to gain its own voice by freeing itself from the undue influence of certain streams of Greek philosophy (especially that of Aristotle) that had been dominant

---

23. David Suzuki, *The Legacy: An Elder's Vision for Our Sustainable Future* (Vancouver: Greystone Books, 2010), 55.

24. Iain Provan, *The Reformation and the Right Reading of Scripture* (Waco, TX: Baylor University Press, 2017), 383-413.

from the first to the fifteenth centuries. A biblical, Christian doctrine of Creation—so long prevented from radically changing the world by its unfortunate marriage to a Greek philosophy of nature, arranged by Christian theologians who were overly impressed with the latter—now began to reshape Western culture.[25] It did so in the first instance by way of modern science—a science now founded, not on Greek ideas about rationality and necessity, but on the conviction that both the heavens and the Earth are genuinely *created* entities that must be subject to empirical inquiry in order to discover their true nature. As Michael Foster puts it, "the modern investigators of nature were the first to take seriously *in their science* the Christian doctrine that nature is created."[26] The Reformation played a crucial role in this cultural shift, since it insisted on the authority of "the Bible alone," read according to its literal sense. Indeed, the new science was promoted most enthusiastically in those parts of Western Christendom where the older, medieval ideas had become the most marginalized—that is, in Protestant rather than in Roman Catholic areas of Europe.

For many of these early modern scientists, science was first and foremost about telling the truth about how the world works, first to the glory of the God who created it, and secondly so that we can live more holy lives within it. It did not take long, however, for modern science to begin to shake itself free of the constraints (as many saw it) of traditional Christian confession and to view "nature" (as it had once again come to be known) as a self-standing entity that could be studied using scientific method alone. Indeed, the potential of such study for producing fundamental *change* in the world was quickly appreciated. Already in the writings of the English philosopher Francis Bacon (1561–1626) in the early seventeenth century, we find that "reason exploring nature," unencumbered by any previous form of tradition, philosophy, or religion, is the path to true knowledge.[27]

---

25. "The medieval philosopher had of course believed the Christian doctrine that nature is created. But the belief had been efficacious only in his theology. In his science of nature ... he had continued to employ the methods of Aristotelian science, entirely oblivious of the fact that Aristotle's science was based upon the presupposition that nature is not created." Michael B. Foster, "The Christian Doctrine of Creation and the Rise of Modern Natural Science," *Mind* 43 (1934): 446–68 (453).

26. Foster, "Creation," 453.

27. John C. Briggs, "Bacon's Science and Religion," in *The Cambridge Companion to Bacon*, ed. Markku Peltonen (Cambridge: Cambridge University Press, 1996), 172–99.

This knowledge is to be acquired, moreover, in order to *master* nature—to bend everything in it to human ends. Here we already see foreshadowed the later development of modern science as a totalizing worldview in principle independent of the doctrinal and ethical constraints of Christian religion—or of any religion, for that matter. We are still dealing today with the consequences of the birth of this creature. It was indeed just at this point in history, and not before, that the seedbed was truly constructed out of which the flower of our current ecological crisis eventually emerged. A reductionistic science now set off on its quest for total knowledge of certain kinds concerning the totality of "nature," with a view to total mastery of it, convinced that such "progress" must always, in all respects, be a good thing. It did so without any apparent sense of obligation to account for itself in terms of larger, holistic ideas concerning what "the good" looked like, and with little reflection on whether some "goods" were in fact much more important than others. This journey was bound from the beginning to end badly. It simply took a few hundred years for us to realize just how bad the ending might be.

The Rise of Environmentalism

Strenuous objections to this new way of looking at the world already began to emerge in Europe and its colonies in the eighteenth and nineteenth centuries, associated with the movement typically referred to as "Romanticism"—a reaction against both the scientific rationalism of modernity and the massive changes happening in society as a result, as modern science harnessed natural forces and products to produce the Industrial Revolution and its attendant pollution, poverty, and ugliness. It was in fact just before and during this period that the above-discussed myth concerning the idyllic "state of nature" among pre-modern peoples first arose and was widely disseminated. It did so as influential people expressed their own dissatisfaction with how early modern civilization was turning out, and contrasted it with native society (especially in the Americas), celebrating over against the "civilized" the spontaneous, the visceral, and the natural. Romanticism not only contributed in general ways to what became environmentalism, but also in very specific ones, for out of this context emerged some important writings that have had a long-lasting influence on modern culture. Among these were Henry David Thoreau's *Walden* (1854) and the various writings of John Muir about the Sierra Nevada (1872–1913). The passionate interest in nature that is evident in such authors is also reflected in the creation of various early-modern organizations designed to protect aspects of it from the further encroachment of modern industrialist capitalism—for example, the Sierra Club, established by Muir and others to preserve Yosemite National Park.

What these and other initiatives have in common is a keen awareness that humanity in the modern period has been drastically changing the environment far more significantly than ever before, and must now—for the benefit of all creatures—constrain its activity and alter its habits. This awareness has greatly increased since the middle of the twentieth century. A significant moment in this process was the publication in 1962 of *Silent Spring* by Rachel Carson, which warned of the severe harm that pesticides, particularly DDT, were causing to birds and other creatures. Stunning visual evidence of the modern human capacity to do harm was provided a few years later, in 1969, when an oil rig in California blew out, and the subsequent oil slick killed ten thousand birds and sea-creatures. With "environmental issues" firmly on the table in the United States as a result, the first Earth Day in 1970 brought twenty million Americans out of their homes to demonstrate in favor of a healthy, sustainable environment. By the time we got to the Rio Declaration in 1992, the world had witnessed many other alarming events, including the opening of a hole in the ozone layer over Antarctica. It is not surprising, then, that one of the major international agreements concluded at Rio concerned global climate change.

It's All Going to Burn

It is clear that the "dark green religionists" referred to above do not believe that Christian faith has made any kind of positive contribution to sustaining care for the environment, but only a markedly negative one. This is a view that is in fact widely shared within the environmental "movement," with its overall "critique of Abrahamic anthropocentrism, which is believed to separate humans from nature."[28] It is famously represented in an influential 1967 essay written by Lynn White, in which he claimed that, in Christian faith, God is viewed as planning Creation "explicitly for man's

---

28. Taylor, *Religion*, 75.

benefit and rule: no item in the physical creation had any purpose save to serve man's purposes."[29] The judgment at which White arrived on the basis of his analysis, in fact, was that "especially in its Western form, Christianity is the most anthropocentric religion the world has seen."[30] This perspective on Christian faith has continually resurfaced in "green" publications ever since. An early example is James Lovelock, who is well known for his "Gaia theory" about the biosphere as a self-regulating organism (Gaia being the Greek goddess of the Earth). Lovelock's opinion was that "our religions have not yet given us the rules and guidance for our relationship with Gaia."[31] He believed that neither "the humanist concept of sustainable development" nor "the Christian concept of stewardship" were fit for purpose in this respect, because both "are flawed by unconscious hubris."[32] Human beings, in both worldviews, are conceptually simply too far up the chain of being, and that is a major problem for the planet. People who think that God has given us "dominion" over the earth are the last people who are going to take the radical steps necessary to save it.

This critique hits the mark to some degree. It is not at all difficult to find marked anthropocentrism in the Christian tradition attached to biblical ideas concerning human "dominion" over nature (Gen. 1:26-28). Consider the theology of Thomas Aquinas, for example, which one modern author characterizes as follows: "the entire changeable universe is finally for the sake of the human good and species."[33] John Calvin writes, similarly, that "it was chiefly for the sake of mankind that the world was made ... this [is] the end which God has in view in the government of it."[34] The "end for which all things were created ... [was] that none of the conveniences and neces-

---

29. Lynn White, "The Historical Roots of Our Ecologic Crisis," *Science* 155 (1967): 1203-7. This essay was reproduced in I. G. Barbour, ed., *Western Man and Environmental Ethics* (Reading: Addison-Wesley, 1973), 18-30, and the quote in that version is to be found on p. 25.

30. White, "Crisis," 25.

31. Cited in Taylor, *Religion*, 36.

32. Ibid.

33. Francisco Benzoni, "Thomas Aquinas and Environmental Ethics: A Reconsideration of Providence and Salvation," *Journal of Religion* 85 (2005): 76-446 (446) .

34. John Calvin, *Institutes of the Christian Religion*, ed. John T. McNeill, trans. Ford L. Battles (Louisville: Westminster John Knox, 2011), 1.16.6.

saries of life might be wanting to men."[35] This kind of view of Creation has then often been wedded to a view of redemption that focuses on human salvation and says little or nothing about the cosmos as a whole. In fact, wherever Greco-Roman Gnosticism has deeply penetrated into Christian theology (and it often has), we find little interest shown in *materiality* at all, since in Gnosticism salvation is all about human souls escaping their imprisonment in evil matter. The Christian gospel, influenced by this idea, comes to concern the redemption of human souls rather than their bodies. The material world as such, then, becomes of little importance. In the words of the old song, it is a place that "I'm just a-passing through" and in which it is quite wrong to "feel at home," since our "treasures are laid up somewhere beyond the blue."[36] In the words of a newer song, we are souls "stranded in some skin and bones" and waiting only for our rescue at "the dawn."[37]

The present world exists, on this view, to provide for us the "necessaries of life" while we wait for a future in which "the heavens will disappear with a roar, the elements will be destroyed by fire, and the earth and everything done in it will be laid bare … everything will be destroyed" (2 Pet. 3:10-11) and human souls will enter a much better, spiritual eternity. There is indeed *not* much in this way of looking at things that provides an incentive for looking after the environment. "It's all going to burn anyway," as people have quite often said in certain Christian circles—"so why worry too much about it?" Why monitor global warming except as another sign of the end-times (as a number of so-called "prophecy websites" are now actually doing)? Why bother legislating environmental protections? This kind of perspective is often found nowadays in Protestant dispensationalist circles, where the earth is regarded as "merely a temporary way station on the road to eternal life … unimportant except as a place of testing to get into heaven," created for the faithful to "use for profitable purposes on

---

35. John Calvin, *Commentaries on the First Book of Moses Called Genesis*, Calvin's Commentaries 1, ed. and trans. John King (London: Calvin Translation Society, 1847; repr., Grand Rapids: Baker, 1981), 64-65, 96.

36. The full text can be found at https://genius.com/Jim-reeves-this-world-is-not-my-home-annotated, accessed April 24, 2019.

37. The full text can be found at https://genius.com/U2-yahweh-lyrics, accessed April 24, 2019.

their way to the hereafter."[38] We do not need to plunge into the depths of Protestant dispensationalism, however, in order to come across marked Christian anthropocentrism. Consider *Caritas in veritate* (2009) for example—the last encyclical of Pope Benedict XVI. It is a wonderful, modern restatement of the long tradition of Christian humanism, laying out for us in a very helpful way our human duties and responsibilities toward other human beings. However, its love and justice are indeed predominantly, perhaps entirely, for men and women. Creation as a whole serves mainly only as the backdrop against which the human drama is played out.

The pragmatic, instrumentalist view of non-human Creation that tends to emerge from such theology is well illustrated by a large glass case containing a stuffed brown bear that I encountered a number of years ago in the airport waiting area in Anchorage, Alaska. Inscribed on the accompanying plaque was some helpful information telling the reader when this bear had been "harvested." When you can talk about "harvesting" a bear, it is no longer a living creature with its own dignified existence apart from your own, but simply an object serving your own ends.

The Hermeneutics of Creation Care

What are we to make if this kind of biblical hermeneutic, as developed by some Christians and critiqued by many environmentalists? Is this the right way in which to read the biblical story as it touches upon "nature"?

From the Ground

"In the beginning God created"—a God whom we soon discover has a tremendous interest in *what* he has created and what is for its good. It is true that human beings are designed to play an important role in this Creation. However, this does not mean that we are intrinsically more important than the other creatures. Genesis 1 and 2 do set humans apart from other creatures, but they also go out of their way to make it clear that we are, like them, are *part of* Creation—a Creation that in Genesis 1 is already "good" before we come along. We do not have a day of Creation to ourselves, for example, but we share the sixth day with the other land creatures—emphasizing the commonality that exists between humans and

---

38. Ron Wolf, "God, James Watt, and the Public Land," *Audubon* 83 (1981): 58-65 (65).

the rest of the animal Creation. Genesis 2 underlines this commonality by telling us that humans are "produced" from the earth in the same way as the other animals (Gen. 2:7, 19). Humans are humus, made out of soil ("from the dust of the ground") and animated by God, who breathes into us the breath of life that makes a person "a living being" (2:7). In these respects we are no different from the other animals, for Genesis 1:20 uses the same phrase ("living being") of the sea creatures, and Genesis 2:19 uses it of the land animals and birds. We are important creatures, then—but we *are* creatures, formed "according to their kinds" just like all the others.

The conclusion of the Creation week occurs, indeed, not on the sixth day with the creation of human beings, but on the seventh when God "rested." It is this Sabbath rest, not the creation of humanity, which completes Creation and brings its days to the perfect biblical number of seven. And this Sabbath rest was of course later observed weekly in Israel, on which day it was again the *commonality* of all creatures that was emphasized, not the usefulness of some in respect of others (Exod. 20:8-11). On the Sabbath "you shall not do any work, neither you, nor your son or daughter, nor your manservant or maidservant, nor your animals" (v. 10). Other creatures have their own importance; we are not the only show in town. Job 38 and 39 later make exactly this same point, at considerable length.

Just Dominion

It is important next to be precise in the matter of how and for what reason human beings are "set apart" from the rest of Creation in Genesis 1-2. Just as Creation as a whole is conceived of in the OT as God's temple, so human beings are considered to be the images of God that ancient people used to place in *their* temples. Ancient kings also used to set up images of themselves in territories that they claimed as their own. It is not as autonomous beings, then, that humans are "made in God's image and likeness" in Genesis 1. We are instead God's representatives; we govern on behalf of the God who is the only true King, remembering all the while that "the earth is the LORD's, and everything in it" (Ps. 24:1). It does not belong to us.

What does being a king involve? It involves what ancient kings were expected to do on behalf of the gods generally: ruling and subduing. This implies that there is work to be done in the world, right from the beginning—that human beings are designed to go on working with God in his creative acts, bringing order out of chaos. But the language of kingship also implies *care* for the rest of Creation. For the vocation of kings in the ancient world involved not only ruling and subduing, but also looking after the welfare of their subjects and ensuring justice for all. The mandate to rule and subdue in Genesis 1, then, is not a mandate to exploit and ravage the earth in one's own self-interest. Genesis does not have in view here absolute and unfettered power that can be used as human beings will, with no moral restraint. Human rule is always to be exercised *on behalf of* the God in whose world we live. It is to be a just, peaceable dominion of the kind described in Psalm 72, governed by people who are able to "judge [their] people in righteousness, [their] afflicted ones with justice" (72:2).

Serving and Keeping

Genesis 2 makes it especially clear, as it exegetes "dominion" in terms of earth-keeping, what this looks like in relation to non-human Creation. The world is portrayed in this chapter as a garden—an enclosed parkland, in which human beings live in harmony with their kin (the animals) and with God. Here the language of monarchy gives way to the language of priesthood, and we find human beings placed in God's parkland "to work it and take care of it"—to "serve it and keep/guard it" (Hebrew *'abad* and *shamar*). This is religious language, which underlines the importance and sacred nature of the task: it is worship and conservation. It is precisely the language used in Numbers 3:7-8, when the work of the priests in the Tabernacle is described.[39] The world is a sacred place, like a temple, and human beings are its priests.

The dominion given to human beings in Genesis 1, then, is evidently not a *lording it over* the rest of a Creation that is designed "explicitly for man's benefit" (White). This dominion is instead a sacrificial *looking after* Creation. Our creation in God's image has occurred with the purpose that we should imitate him in his creativity and in his providential care for creatures. In the Genesis story itself we get an early, extended picture of what

---

39. "They are to perform [*shamar*] duties for him and for the whole community at the Tent of Meeting by doing the work [*'abad*] of the tabernacle. They are to take care of [*shamar*] all the furnishings of the Tent of Meeting, fulfilling the obligations of the Israelites by doing the work [*'abad*] of the tabernacle."

this looks like in chapters six through nine, where Noah is "portrayed as uniquely righteous … [and] also the arch-conservationist who built an ark to preserve all kinds of life from being destroyed in the flood."[40]

All Creatures Great and Small

Much of the biblical narrative that follows Genesis 2 concerns not only how the human image-bearers treat each other, but also how they *should or should not* do so. "People-keeping" (in the language of Gen. 4:9) is therefore a major concern of OT Scripture. Yet "earth-keeping" is also, "from the beginning," very important. In the OT literature both inside and outside Genesis, in fact, people-keeping and earth-keeping go hand in hand. For Creation can only function properly to the extent that the image-bearers delegated to look after it are able to do their job. Conversely, human dysfunction—whether individual or communal—inevitably impacts the rest of Creation grievously. This is precisely *because* the whole of Creation is conceived of in biblical faith as a single "circle of being," in which what happens to one part inevitably affects the remainder. Hosea 4:1-3 starkly describes this reality in the context of the Israel of the eighth century BC:

> There is no faithfulness, no love, no acknowledgment of God in the land. There is only cursing, lying and murder, stealing and adultery; they break all bounds, and bloodshed follows bloodshed. Because of this the land mourns, and all who live in it waste away; the beasts of the field and the birds of the air and the fish of the sea are dying.

Here we see communal dysfunction—people-keepers failing to keep each other properly. They break many of the Ten Commandments, and this disables the earth-keepers from keeping the earth properly, which results in grief and death for all.

Sometimes there is damage because human violence *directly* impacts the Earth—a possibility envisaged in Deuteronomy 20:19, for example. Here the text recognizes that war (even in ancient times) could be disastrous for the rest of Creation, and it urges combatants, when they fight, to try to limit the damage: "When you lay siege to a city for a long time, fighting against it to capture it, do not destroy its trees by putting an ax to

---

40. Gordon J. Wenham, *Genesis 1–15*, WBC 1 (Waco, TX: Word Books, 1987), 33.

them, because you can eat their fruit. Do not cut them down. Are the trees people, that you should besiege them?" If there must be war, then at least leave the trees alone. This is partly for pragmatic reasons (they provide fruit), but partly simply because the trees do not deserve to be caught up in the conflict. Trees have rights.

Another reason that communal dysfunction can impact the rest of Creation is that it distorts the relationship between the earth-keepers and what they are called to keep. That is, it places the Earth disproportionately in the hands of those who do not care for God's laws, and who certainly do not accept that "the land is mine and you reside in my land as foreigners and strangers" (Lev. 25:23). The prophets also have a lot to say about this dimension of the problem. In Isaiah 5:8-10, for example, we find "woe" laid upon those "who add house to house and join field to field till no space is left and you live alone in the land."

Just as the whole of Creation thus suffers along with humanity in its fallen state, so the whole of Creation is envisaged in the OT as being redeemed along with its flawed "keepers." Among the OT passages that address this reality is Isaiah 11:6-9, with its vision of a future in which "the wolf will live with the lamb, the leopard will lie down with the goat ... They will neither harm nor destroy on all my holy mountain, for the earth will be full of the knowledge of the LORD as the waters cover the sea." Hosea 2:18 goes on to envisage a day when God "will make a covenant for them with the beasts of the field, the birds of the air, and the creatures that move along the ground. Bow and sword and battle I will abolish from the land, so that all may lie down in safety."

The Earth and Everything in It

As we come to the NT, we find (unsurprisingly) that the whole world remains God's world: "From him and through him and to him are all things," writes Paul, "the earth ... and everything in it" (Rom. 11:36; 1 Cor. 10:26; cf. Rev. 4:11). Into this world comes the one in whom human image-bearing reaches its high point—"the image of the invisible God," of whom Paul says that "all things were created by him and for him ... in him all things hold together" (Col. 1:15-20). He it is who "fulfills God's design for all creation and displays what had always been intended for all humankind."[41] The redemption that Christ initiates is naturally cosmic in its scope—as broad as the original Creation: "God was pleased ... through him to reconcile to himself *all things* [my emphasis], whether things on earth or things in heaven" (Col. 1:19).

For this cosmic redemption the entirety of non-human Creation waits, looking "in eager expectation for the children of God to be revealed"; it is currently "groaning as in the pains of childbirth," waiting for the new heavens and the new earth to be born as a result (Rom. 8:19, 22). Currently "subjected to frustration" (8:20)—it does not function properly, because of human dysfunction (sin)—it looks to be released from this frustrated condition. It *will* be released, once human beings themselves are fully redeemed: "Just as the resurrection hope is hope of a resurrection body, so resurrection life is to be part of a complete creation."[42]

Our thinking about Creation in relation to New Creation needs to stress continuity as well as discontinuity—an important balance that needs to be maintained in *all* our Bible reading. A text like 2 Peter 3:10 might well at first appear to tell us about a complete disjunction between present and future reality—"it's all going to burn." However, such an interpretation would place this text well outside the mainstream of biblical thinking concerning the future, in which what is new represents an "evolution," as it were, from what has come before, rather than a complete break from it. "The wolf will live with the lamb" (Isa. 11:6), "the meek ... will inherit the earth" (Matt. 5:5), the present will give birth to the future, and our resurrection bodies will be similar to as well as different from our present ones. The present reality may be passing away, and it may indeed be destined for "fire" (Heb. 1:10-12; 12:26-29), but it seems that it must pass through fire only to become a more purified version of itself. The new heaven and the new earth are, after all, just *that*, not something entirely different (2 Pet. 3:13). Moreover, our human destiny is to live with God in the New Jerusalem that in Revelation 21:1-3 comes down out of heaven to Earth. We do not fly away (without our bodies) to another destination.

There is nothing in any of this NT material that suggests that God has ceased to care for all of Creation, or that we human beings are no longer

---

41. William L. Lane, *Hebrews 1-8*, WBC 47A (Dallas: Word Books, 1991), 48.
42. James D. G. Dunn, *Romans 1-8*, WBC 38A (Dallas: Word Books, 1988), 471.

called to look after it on God's behalf. Earth-keeping remains one aspect of our human calling, just as destroying the Earth represents a grievous departure from it. And in the New Creation we shall in fact still be "kings and priests," just as we are now (Rev. 5:10).

Christians and "the Environment"

While it is true, then, that there are versions of Christian theology that are attacked by environmentalists as overly anthropocentric and insufficiently focused on Creation-in-general, these theologies are not well grounded in Christian Scripture. In fact, they owe much to Francis Bacon, "who hijacked the Genesis text to authorize the project of scientific knowledge and technological exploitation whose excesses have given us the ecological crisis."[43] There is much in the genuinely Christian tradition that is, to the contrary, well rooted in Scripture, whose teaching provides Christians with every reason to continue to be involved in the "environmental movement," as they *have been* in fact, in large numbers, for decades now. The good life in Scripture is a life marked by love, not only for our image-bearing neighbors, but also for the remainder of what we rightly think of as God's Creation (and not merely "the environment"). So it is that "the righteous care for the needs of their animals" (Prov. 12:10; cf. Deut. 22:1-6). The well-being of the remainder of Creation is in fact intrinsically bound up with our own and our neighbors' flourishing, as both Scripture and our own contemporary experience teach us: it is especially the poorest people in the world who suffer the most from negative ecological developments.[44]

We are likewise called, not only to care for the whole of Creation as we find it now, but also to seek to correct the mistakes that we have made in the past, in the belief that God has delegated to us enormous responsibility in "ruling" and "keeping" the planet, and that our decisions will necessarily be very important in determining how things play out. Whether this is a welcome truth or not, it is a matter of scriptural and empirical fact that

---

43. Richard Bauckham, *Bible and Ecology: Rediscovering the Community of Creation* (London: Darton, Longman and Todd, 2010), 6.
44. So, e.g., Pushpam Kumar and Makiko Yashiro, "The Marginal Poor and their Dependence on Ecosystem Services: Evidence from South Asia and Sub-Saharan Africa," in Joachim von Braun and Franz W. Gatzweiler, eds., *Marginality: Addressing the Nexus of Poverty, Exclusion and Ecology* (Dordrecht: Springer, 2014), 169-80.

human beings do possess "dominion" over Creation. This is why, at all the Earth Summits ever held, the delegates were drawn from only one species (as my friend Loren Wilkinson once said to me). It was not because their organizers were "overly anthropocentric," but because among all of God's creatures it is only human beings who possess the kind of agency that is capable of drastically changing the world for good or for ill, and it is only human beings who might even be concerned or worried about doing so.

Climate Change

This brings us in the end to the highly contemporary matter of global climate change. As we reflect on this particular matter from the standpoint of the biblical teaching outlined above, we immediately understand that the Christian should find nothing at all surprising in the idea that human behavior might have contributed to significant global warming. The associated idea of consequent, severe impact on the flourishing of both human beings and other creatures in different parts of God's world also makes biblical and theological sense. These are absolutely *not* ideas that only make sense in connection with (for example) "the rising political clout of modern feminism," as one conservative Christian writer has recently put it.[45]

Whether contemporary global warming is in fact an empirical reality has of course been much debated in recent decades, and significant numbers of people remain skeptical about it. Among conservative Republicans in the USA, for example, recent figures suggest that only forty-two percent agree that it is a reality, and indeed analysis of Gallup Poll data from 1990 through 2015 suggests that among US Christians, in particular, "the likelihood that a … respondent expressed a great deal of concern about climate change dropped by about a third between 1990 and 2015."[46] It is always important, of course, to interrogate properly the empirical evidence

---

45. James Wanliss, *Resisting the Green Dragon: Dominion not Death* (Burke, VA: Cornwall Alliance for the Stewardship of Creation, 2010), chapter 2, Kindle.

46. Ari Natter, "Republicans Who Couldn't Beat Climate Debate Now Seek to Join It," Bloomberg, March 5, 2019, accessed February 18, 2020, https://www.bloomberg.com/news/articles/2019-03-05/republicans-who-couldn-t-beat-climate-debate-now-seek-to-join-it. See further Jim Hanchett, "Polls Suggest Less Environmentalism among U.S. Christians," Futurity, February 1, 2018, accessed February 18, 2020, https://www.futurity.org/christians-environment-opinion-1670122./.

upon which scientific claims are based, in order to check that they are well founded. Yet the evidence in this case appears to be overwhelmingly supportive of the thesis, such that "most of the leading scientific organizations worldwide have issued public statements endorsing" the view "that climate-warming trends over the past century are extremely likely due to human activities."[47]

We may, of course, choose to adopt a skeptical posture in relation to the scientific community that "agrees" on this matter. However, we must recognize the risk in doing so without very good reason—that as people who identify as truth-seekers, we shall in fact end up by deliberately cutting ourselves off from important aspects of the truth. Christians have found themselves in this kind of position before. A great many believers in seventeenth- and eighteenth-century Europe, for example, simply refused to swap their medieval cosmology for the new Copernican one, even as the empirical evidence in support of the latter became overwhelming.[48] This kind of commitment to ignorance has only ever had devastating consequences for the credibility of the Christian faith in the public square. This is even more serious in the present case. How are we to fulfil our vocation to look after God's garden, if we simply refuse to look at the evidence pertaining to what might be ailing it?

Even if there *were* any doubt about the extent of global warming and its main causes, we should still be obliged by Scripture to respond as creatively and constructively as we could to its negative effects, so far as we could ascertain them—the erosion of human and animal habitats, for example, and consequent loss of species. As Christians in search of biblical righteousness we should not need to agree on every fine point of the debate about the significance and causes of climate change in order to agree on our duty of care for a planet that is currently clearly suffering from its effects. Global warming ought to matter to us, and we ought to be fully engaged with others in responding to its challenges as well as we can. Whether we ourselves initially warm to this idea or not, we must hear the divine imperative in Scripture to do what is right in this area of our lives, even if others choose

---

47. See "Climate Change: How Do We Know?" NASA, accessed February 18, 2020, https://climate.nasa.gov/evidence/, with references to the academic literature.
48. Provan, *Right Reading*, 368-69.

to ignore it—including our Christian neighbors, or our political allies. So it comes down to this: created as earth-keepers, we should be striving to live in ecologically-committed ways in our personal lives and in our Christian communities. In the realm of public discourse, we should be urging our politicians to consider in all of their decision-making the common good not only of all *people*, but of all *creatures*. People are important, and their interests should certainly not be ignored in pursuing the common good of all, but nor should human interests lead us to neglect the interests of our non-human neighbors.

Conclusion

The question, as I suggested above, is not whether humanity has dominion over Creation, but only how we shall use it. The biblical story tells us how we *should* use it, and indeed provides us with the hope that we need in order to persevere in the task even when it seems difficult and even impossible. For it calls us to live in anticipation of a time when not only human society will be ordered perfectly justly, but the entire cosmos will be redeemed—a new Creation. And we have every reason to believe that God himself will gather up everything that is good in this present Creation, including our smallest and seemingly futile actions, and will carry it forward into the new one, where the righteous who cared for the first version will also get to care for the second. It does not seem likely on the basis of biblical teaching that the unrepentant who failed to look after the first will also get a chance to mess up the latter—which is precisely why "all [will] lie down in safety" (Hos. 2:18). So contrary to the sentiments of authors like James Lovelock, people who truly believe that God has given humanity "dominion" over the earth are in fact likely to be the *first* people who will take the radical steps necessary to save it. It is simply that many people do not truly believe it, even if they generally claim to be Bible-believing Christians.

4

The Colossian Hymn

Christ and the Church in Creation

Mariam Kamell Kovalishyn

It is with a deep sense of gratitude that I dedicate an essay on Colossians to Sven Soderlund. When I first arrived at Regent, it was to see him teaching Advanced Exegesis in Colossians and Philemon, courses I now (as then!) wish I had taken. His breadth of knowledge in both the Hebrew and Greek texts and his attention to detail, his humility to take on whatever courses needed teaching (Advanced Hebrew exegesis? *Sure.* Advanced Greek? *No problem.* Basic Exegesis? *Of course!* A book study? OT or NT?), combined with a deep pastoral concern for the lives of his students and colleagues, provided the richest of blessings for this young upstart. Sven's faithful dedication to pointing students to the Jesus in the text, to clearly delighting in the Jesus revealed by the text, to living the character of the Jesus taught through the text of the whole of Scripture has always stood out as a model of how a teacher ought to be. I hope that this essay on the character of the Jesus he taught so well indicates, in at least a small way, my respect for him and my honor of having worked alongside him for several years.

In 1989, Depeche Mode had a hit called "Your Own Personal Jesus," who was summarized as "Someone to hear your prayers, Someone who cares." Its reception in the church at the time was, unsurprisingly, not particularly keen. Unfortunately, the band was ahead of their time. I accidentally eavesdropped in on a conversation between two Christians who were chatting about how other Christians were acting, decisions other Christians were making, choices other Christians were opting for, and they were unconvinced of the "Christian-ness" of those choices. The line that stayed with me, has haunted me, ever since then, was the comment, "My Jesus would never do that."

"My Jesus." As if we own him. As if he is ours to dictate to, to describe, to control. As if he acts in accordance with the ways we think he ought to act. That phrase has haunted me since I heard it, because it reflects our unconscious thoughts: "I have read the Bible and have filtered it according to my preferences. Now, all my theology, all my future Bible reading, all my future decisions will be based on my version of Jesus." But while this instinct to make Jesus our own may be unconscious, the Bible has a harsh term for those who attempt to control God in some way or another by creating for him the image we think he should have. When we talk about "my Jesus" or "my God" in such a way, the Bible says we are committing idolatry. Biblically, idolatry is when we decide God is too much, too demanding, too distant, too *something*, and so we create a "safer" God to worship, one that aligns with how we think the world should operate. Whenever we participate in taming God to our liking, then we incidentally create our own idol to worship instead of God.

Again, this is likely unintentional. It is not easy to keep all of God's "Godness" in our head at any one given time. However, we perhaps need to be aware of how our culture is affecting our theology. Our culture, right now, is focused on individualism, and, more concerningly, the practice of individual self-creation, self-identification. And talking about "my Jesus" fits right into that cultural moment. To some, "My Jesus" is more important than the Jesus of the Bible, because it is the one they feel attached to and the one they identify with. It emerged as part of their journey of self-discovery, and now it encourages them to continue on the way they were, because it is part of their authentic self-journey. And thus, we become the gods, and God becomes our creature. But he's not. As the oft-quoted Mr. Beaver said in *The Lion, the Witch, and the Wardrobe*, "Safe? ... don't you hear what Mrs. Beaver tells you? Who said anything about safe? 'Course he isn't safe. But he's good. He's the King, I tell you."[1]

---

1. C. S. Lewis, *The Chronicles of Narnia: The Lion, the Witch, and the Wardrobe* (Grand

C. S. Lewis might have been improvising on the theme from Colossians 1. The writings of the New Testament do not arise in a vacuum, but rather they were written in response to varying situations. In Colossians, the situation was one in which people were uncertain whether Jesus was *all* that was needed, so they added a little philosophy and some additional religious actions to update the Christianity they had received. Indeed, that situation is not that far from today: one person needs to be in some mountains to worship, another legislates being at church twice on Sunday and every Wednesday to maintain holy status, another has a little "buddy Jesus" on the dashboard, and we update Christianity to our modern sensibilities. But this leads many of us to fall into what Christian Smith called "Moral Therapeutic Deism," a functional religion that often is unconsciously substituted for Christianity.[2] In this belief system, people will believe that a God exists who created and ordered the world and watches over human life on earth—good creational theology. This God, then, wants people to be good, nice, and fair to each other, and go to heaven when they die—good Canadian values, and even, depending on how one defines the terms, possibly even Christian. But Moral Therapeutic Deism adds the modern ideas that the central goal of life is to be happy and to feel good about oneself, and that God does not need to be particularly involved in one's life except when he is needed to resolve a problem.

This, unfortunately, is a common theology of our age. To counter it, I suggest that we study Paul's grand hymn in Colossians 1, rightly considered to be one of the more famous theological statements of the New Testament.[3] It leaves no room for a "my Jesus" approach. While this hymn may already have been in circulation around the early church, and Paul simply quotes it here, it also reflects the impact of Paul's encounter with Christ on the Damascus road. After that incident, the scales fell from his eyes, and he could never worship Jesus as anything less than the fullness of God dwelling with us.

Rapids: HarperCollins, 1950, 2001), 146.

2. See Christian Smith and Melina Lundquist Denton, *Soul Searching: The Religious and Spiritual Lives of American Teenagers* (New York: Oxford University Press, 2005).

3. I refer to "Paul" as the author simply because that is the presented author in the text. None of the conclusions of this paper require Pauline authorship, and that debate is outside the scope of this paper.

> The Son is the image of the invisible God, the firstborn over all creation. For in him all things were created: things in heaven and on earth, visible and invisible, whether thrones or powers or rulers or authorities; all things have been created through him and for him. He is before all things, and in him all things hold together. And he is the head of the body, the church; he is the beginning and the firstborn from among the dead, so that in everything he might have the supremacy. For God was pleased to have all his fullness dwell in him, and through him to reconcile to himself all things, whether things on earth or things in heaven, by making peace through his blood, shed on the cross. (Col 1:15-20, NIV)

This paper will not be able to go into every detail of this hymn, not least because it was written in the days of COVID-19 combined with maternity leave, and my access to time and resources was limited. Moreover, there are obviously many scholarly writings on the hymn available. Rather, this paper is an attempt to do a close reading of the hymn and see how it helps to counter the impulse of our age for a self-made "Jesus." We will look at the text in three parts. Verses 15-17 show Christ's incredible identity and his rule. Verse 18 then shows Christ's relation to the Church. Finally, verses 19-20 show his reconciliation work. Through it all, we will see that the focus of this hymn is on the identity and work of the Son, calling the Church to remember and live according to both his cosmic and peacemaking personhood. As Margaret MacDonald summarizes, "The Christ-hymn ... draws believers back into the arena of worship where they discover and renew their experience of the lordship of Christ."[4]

Verses 15-17: Christ's Cosmic Nature

Verses 15-17 show that Christ is fully God. While we may acknowledge this when we say the Nicene Creed, "true God from true God, begotten, not made; of the same essence as the Father," what does it really *mean*? The hymn begins by announcing that Jesus is the "image (εἰκών) of the invisible God," revealing the infinite God to the world. This line is reminiscent of dialogue in the Gospel of John, where Jesus says that to have seen him is to

---

4. Margaret Y. MacDonald, *Sacra Pagina: Colossians and Ephesians* (Collegeville, MN: Liturgical Press, 2008), 68.

have seen the Father (Jn 14:9). When we look at Jesus, we are seeing God.[5] We are not seeing a "wise teacher" who simply teaches us to be good, moral people; we are looking at God, the God who created us.[6] Fee argues that Paul "is intending something very much like what he says in 2 Cor 4:4–6: that God is now to be known not through personified Wisdom but in his beloved Son (Col 1:13), who alone bears the true image of the Father to whom Paul has been giving thanks (v. 12)."[7] Or, as Jeal describes it, "the words ὅς ἐστιν εἰκὼν τοῦ θεοῦ τοῦ ἀοράτου indicate both a functional and an ontological presence. As the image of God, Christ manifests the actual presence of God from eternity."[8] The hymn thus begins with a dramatic claim about Jesus's divinity: Jesus is the very image of the eternal God, an irreducible part of the Godhead.[9] As Dunne notes, "In the opening of the Colossian 'hymn,' then, we likely have an assertion that Christ is restoring the rule that humanity was meant to have."[10] Whereas humans are made *in* the image of God, "Jesus simply 'is' the image," God made manifest.[11] In Christ, we see God.

But in an argument intriguingly related to my concern about idolatry, Matthew Bates reminds us to consider the "image" language from anoth-

---

5. John Anthony Dunne, "The Regal Status of Christ In the Colossian 'Christ-Hymn': A Re-evaluation of the Influence of Wisdom Traditions," *Trinity Journal* 32, (2011), 9, suggests that "it seems preferable to view the use of εἰκών as an allusion to Gen 1:26–28."

6. See Gordon Fee, "Wisdom Christology in Paul: A Dissenting View," in *The Way of Wisdom: Essays in Honor of Bruce K. Waltke*, ed. J. I. Packer and Sven K. Soderlund (Grand Rapids: Zondervan, 2000), pp. 257-60 in particular, for his argument against reading this text as promoting a "Wisdom Christology." Of this phrase he notes that "personified Wisdom [in Ps-Solomon] is not 'the εἰκών of *God*,' but is merely 'an image of his *goodness*.'"

7. Ibid., 259.

8. Roy R. Jeal, "Starting Before the Beginning: Precreation Discourse in Colossians," *Religion & Theology* 18, (2011), 292.

9. A similar claim can be seen in Philippians 2:6, although the vocabulary is different: "ἐν μορφῇ θεοῦ ὑπάρχων." The same language, along with the claim of the greatness of the good news that this is, appears in 2 Corinthians 4:4: "τὸν φωτισμὸν τοῦ εὐαγγελίου τῆς δόξης τοῦ Χριστοῦ, ὅς ἐστιν εἰκὼν τοῦ θεοῦ."

10. Dunne, "The Regal Status of Christ," 13.

11. Grant Macaskill, "Union(s) with Christ: Colossians 1:15-20," *Ex Auditu* 33, (2017), 94. Constantine R. Campbell, "Response to Macaskill," ibid., 109, rightly pushes Macaskill's comment further, noting that "the phrase 'image of the invisible God' (*eikōn tou theou tou aoratou*) plainly evokes the juxtaposition of 'image' with the invisibility of God. In this way, it seems that the plainest meaning of the phrase has to do with the *revelation* of God."

er perspective, that of idols. Indeed, "idols or images in the ancient Near Eastern world… were believed to make the heavenly deity local, concrete, truly present on earth."[12] However, this image is not blind and deaf wood or stone, but in continuity with the biblical creation narrative, a person. "Jesus in the flesh is the truly human one, the apex of God's design for humanity as made in God's image."[13] And this hymn focuses not merely on the moment of incarnation that makes Jesus the image, but rather, as Beale argues, "Christ's preexistence as God's divine 'image' is the focus.… This eternal status in God's image refers to eternity past (the focus here), the incarnation and exaltation and Christ's exalted status into eternity future."[14] The gnomic present of the ἐστίν here makes clear Christ's eternal status as the true image of God. Thus, it becomes imperative that we look closely at him and learn, because "our allegiance to him and his self-emptying ways will also involve a transformation into his image."[15] Christ, the true image of God, reveals to us the fullness of what humanity is to be.

The second line of the first stanza then observes that Jesus is the "firstborn over all creation" (πρωτότοκος πάσης κτίσεως). The observation that he is the "firstborn" isn't solely—or even predominantly—a statement of birth order, but a statement of status.[16] This line reveals that "Christ *as Son* holds the rights of primogeniture with regard to every created thing, since they were all created *through* him and *for* him."[17] The firstborn is the one who inherits. The firstborn is the one who holds the father's property together and who passes on the family identity.[18] It is not a statement present-

---

12. Matthew W. Bates, *Salvation by Allegiance Alone* (Grand Rapids: Baker, 2017), 157.
13. Ibid., 157.
14. G. K. Beale, *Colossians and Philemon*, BECNT (Grand Rapids: Baker, 2019), 81.
15. Bates, *Salvation*, 157.
16. Cf. Walter Bauer, *A Greek-English Lexicon of the New Testament and other Early Christian Literature*, ed. Frederic William Danker, third ed. (Chicago: University of Chicago Press, 2000), 894: "pert. to having special status associated with a firstborn, *firstborn*."
17. Fee, "Wisdom Christology in Paul," 259. Dunne, "The Regal Status of Christ," 5, observes that "One area of particular dissimilarity [between Christ and Wisdom] arises from one of the key terms of the hymn, πρωτότοκος… Although the term πρωτότοκος is not used for Wisdom, the sense of 'firstborn' that can be attributed to Wisdom is not a titular sense of primogeniture … but the sense of being the first created thing."
18. Beale, *Colossians*, 86, observes that "The OT repeatedly asserts that the 'firstborn' of every Israelite family gains authority by virtue of being given a double share of inheritance rights (e.g., Deut. 21:17)."

ing him as a created being, as the next lines make clear, for verses 16-17 "in effect distance him from creation."[19] Rather, this claim of firstborn status elucidates that there is nothing in all of the universe that holds more prestige, priority, or status than Jesus. Beale is convinced that the reference here to "firstborn" alludes back to "Ps. 89 (88 LXX), which refers to David and (typologically) to the coming eschatological messianic king as having God as his 'Father,' being 'firstborn' (πρωτότοκος, *prōtotokos*), and inheriting a position 'higher than the kings of the earth,' with a 'throne' that lasts forever (Ps. 89:27-29, 37 [99:28-30, 38]). The emphasis on ruling instead of on temporal priority in Psalm 89 is apparent from recalling that David was the youngest among his brothers (1 Sam. 16:11), yet in this psalm he is called 'firstborn.'"[20] Jesus may have been made apparent only at the incarnation, but his status is unquestionable.

But part of the reason for this status is that, to quote the Creed again, "Through him all things were made." Verses 16-17 begin a series of extravagant claims. In the next five verses, there are eight appearances of a word for "all" or "every". This passage is about as universal as it can get. But more pointedly, in these verses, all things were made *through* and *for* Jesus. This reality makes senseless the Colossians' act of trying to supplement their worship of Jesus with other practical combinations. If Jesus is the head of everything and the one holding everything together, this "makes redundant any extra ritual or practice."[21] Moreover, even the powers, the other entities that might need to be placated, are included into this "everything." Viljoen calls verses 16b-17 "the refrain," which "once again states the ultimate superiority of Christ compared to all powers. All of them have been created through and for Christ, and they can't continue to exist without him."[22] Without Jesus, the whole universe vanishes, the good and the opposition, and thus we need not fear any other powers. Our worship—and our lives—reflect that confidence.

---

19. Moises Silva, *New International Dictionary of New Testament Theology and Exegesis*, 2nd ed., 5 vols. (Grand Rapids: Zondervan, 2014), 4:178.

20. Beale, *Colossians*, 87.

21. Harry O. Maier, "A Sly Civility: Colossians and Empire," *JSNT* 27, no. 3 (2005): 327.

22. Francois P. Viljoen, "Perspectives from the Christ hymn in Colossians 1:13-20 on cosmic powers and spiritual forces within an African context," *In die Skriflig* 53, no. 4 (2019): 8.

Jesus is holding all things together, but we also catch a glimpse of the purpose of creation in this when Paul writes that "all things have been created through him *and for* him." Paul's "range of prepositions reflects a range of relationships, all of which reinforces the sense that however one looks at the world, whichever angle one takes, one sees things that are related to Jesus. They are in him, through him, and for him."[23] We can see that all of creation, humanity most particularly, is not praising God at all times. But everything is created *for Christ's sake*. Thus, it makes no sense when we say things like "my Jesus," because the hymn's equation is turned around; Jesus is *for our sake*, not us for *his* sake.

Finally, Christ is said to be "before all things, and in him all things hold together." For Baugh, this line is the "center of the chiasm, and thus should be seen as the focus of the poem."[24] In this, he finds support from Beasley-Murray, who notes that "both in the sphere of creation and in the sphere of redemption all things find their unity in Christ."[25] While this essay finds a slightly different emphasis at the center, as will be argued below,[26] there is no question that this line anchors the "all things" of this first section. All things center on Christ. And "just as Christ holds all things together in the universe, he ensures the cohesion of the community,"[27] and thus we find our place in him and in reality.

In fact, as Paul will argue later in the letter, our worship goes astray when we fail to worship Jesus as he truly is, for *who* he truly is. So often we live as if our lives are our own to claim, and that creation itself is our own to use as we want. But as Abraham Kuyper famously said, "There is not a square inch in the whole domain of our human existence over which Christ, who is Sovereign over all, does not cry: 'Mine!'"[28] It is worth con-

---

23. Macaskill, "Union(s) with Christ," 97.
24. Steven M. Baugh, "The Poetic Form of Col 1:15–20," *WTJ* 47, (1985): 237.
25. Paul Beasley-Murray, "Colossians 1:15-20: An Early Christian Hymn Celebrating the Lordship of Christ," in *Pauline Studies: Essays Presented to Professor F. F. Bruce on His 70th Birthday*, ed. Donald A. Hagner and Murray J. Harris (1980), 170. Beale, *Colossians*, 101, agrees that this line is the center of a chiastic reading of this hymn.
26. I find myself closer to the outline of John Behr, "Colossians 1:13–20: A Chiastic Reading," *St. Vladimir's Theological Quarterly* 40, no. 4 (1996): 248, although his verse range is wider than my chosen range.
27. MacDonald, *Colossians*, 68.
28. James D. Bratt, ed. *Abraham Kuyper: A Centennial Reader* (Grand Rapids: Eerdmans,

sidering who claims the lordship. "In the Roman peace, what makes all this possible is an emperor—in the Neronian imperial ideology (contemporary with Colossians), the vice-regent of the gods, if not incarnate deity—who holds all things together in the body of his Empire of which he is head, and which he maintains in health and security. In the Colossian vision, it is the incarnate Son, in whom the fullness of God dwells bodily, who exercises a universal reign."[29] Today it is easy to see people's hopes pinned on political leaders, or celebrities, or conspiracy theories. But Christians ought always to raise our eyes to see and find rest in the certainty of the Lordship of Christ, the one who is creator of all (τὰ πάντα) "thrones or powers or rulers or authorities," who is "before all things (πρὸ πάντων)," and in whom "all things hold together (τὰ πάντα ἐν αὐτῷ συνέστηκεν)."[30]

Verse 18: The Relation of Christ to the Church

And that takes us to the second point, the relation of Christ to the Church[31] as pictured in verse 18: "He is the head of the body, the church (αὐτός ἐστιν ἡ κεφαλὴ τοῦ σώματος τῆς ἐκκλησίας)." Paul uses the image of "head" two further times in Chapter 2 (vv. 10 and 19), where Christ's authority and sustaining power are again intertwined, again revealing how central this hymn is to the argument of Colossians more broadly. Schweizer notes that there is a historical jump here: "Between creation and reconciliation nothing is mentioned of the fall of man. The singing community does not need to tell Christ about this, or about its repentance and belief, he knows all that. They are singing face to face to him, the creator and the reconciler, praising him jubilantly for being this. There is no need to speak about how

---

1998), 488.

29. Maier, "Sly Civility," 328.

30. Viljoen, "Perspectives from the Christ hymn," 8, adds the encouragement, "Paul inserts this hymn into this letter to assure them that the Son has authority over whatever kind of power or authority there might be, whether visible or invisible, earthly or heavenly, personal or impersonal. God has created all these powers through and for his Son. The living Christ, who reigns over all creation, can dissolve the concerns of the false teachings. Believers are under the authority of the Son and need not fear any cosmological power, in whatever form."

31. I use the capitalized "Church," not in reference to any particular branch of the church as we see it, but to the cosmological reality of the Body of Christ as the "one holy catholic and apostolic church" of all who worship Christ.

his creatures on our earth today still oppose what he has already fulfilled."³² Schweizer's point helpfully reminds us that this hymn is intended as a statement of reality, for Jesus *is* the Lord of the Church and all of creation, and an affirmation of relationship, for he is the head of a newly constituted body of people who worship him.

The very act of worship subverts the expectations of the rulers of our age who believe they have the power, and allows God's people to remember their new identity as part of the Body of Christ. As Colossians 2:19 reminds us, the danger comes if we "have lost connection with the head, from whom the whole body, supported and held together by its ligaments and sinews, grows as God causes it to grow." Beale argues that the headship metaphor has multiple implications: "the head connected to a body suggests both authoritative direction and cause of growth, *as well as unity*."³³ The body is sustained only insofar as it remains connected to its head, as a united whole. Therefore, by celebrating Christ's headship, we also renew our commitment to remaining in him, and our commitment to each other. Moreover, "The 'head' and 'body' metaphor here indicates that Christ, the precreational image of God, is also the precreational source and sustainer of the church."³⁴ According to the hymn and to Paul, the Body of Christ originates from and exists only through the headship of Christ, the image of God and source of all of creation.

But he is also the head of the Body because he died for the Body. The text does not explicitly say that, but it is implicitly clear from the line "he is the beginning and the firstborn from among the dead (πρωτότοκος ἐκ τῶν νεκρῶν)." In God raising him from the dead, in God vindicating the work he did on the cross, in God bringing him forth as the firstborn from the dead—both in time and in preeminence—Jesus began a new body of people, a newly created people of whom he is the leader. Macaskill points to a profound parallelism between this line and verses 15–17: "These complex relations are all connected to the nature(s) or being of the Son-Icon: he is able to sustain the created realm because of his own creatureliness (he is the firstborn of every creature) and is able to bring life to the dead

---

32. Eduard Schweizer, "Colossians 1:15–20," *Review and Expositor* 87, (1990): 97.
33. Beale, *Colossians*, 102-3.
34. Jeal, "Starting Before the Beginning," 292.

because he shares in their mortality (he is the firstborn from the dead). The relations, in other words, rest upon shared natures."[35] Jesus shows us the certainty of the new creation ("he is the beginning," ἀρχή),[36] and the certainty of the resurrection ("firstborn from among the dead"). Only insofar as we are in Christ do we have hope of being among those who follow the firstborn from the dead.[37]

Additionally, by vindicating him, God declared his supremacy over not just creation, but also the new creation people, the Body. The outcome of the resurrection is "that in everything he might have the supremacy (γένηται ἐν πᾶσιν αὐτὸς πρωτεύων)." While "supremacy" works as a translation, BDAG translates this line as "that he might come to have first place in everything."[38] He is the first, both in time of resurrection as well as in honor accorded to him. He is the πρωτότοκος, again indicating his status of primogeniture, but as Dunne notes, it also indicates his status as king: "We not only see his position of authority over the dead by virtue of being the first to rise from the dead, but the imagery rings with Davidic overtones as Paul often associates the resurrection of Christ with the Davidic covenant."[39] He is not merely a wise leader who gives pointers on how to

---

35. Macaskill, "Union(s) with Christ," 99.

36. Dunne, "The Regal Status of Christ," 15-16, argues strongly that ἀρχή ought to be translated as "ruler" rather than "beginning," noting both the consistency of LXX usage when referring to people, as well as the close parallel in Rev. 1:5: "and from Jesus Christ, who is the faithful witness, the firstborn from the dead, and the ruler of the kings of the earth (πρωτότοκος τῶν νεκρῶν καὶ ὁ ἄρχων τῶν βασιλέων τῆς γῆς)."

37. Cf. Rom. 8:29: "For those God foreknew he also predestined to be conformed to the image of his Son, (συμμόρφους τῆς εἰκόνος τοῦ υἱοῦ αὐτοῦ), that he might be the firstborn among many brothers and sisters (εἰς τὸ εἶναι αὐτὸν πρωτότοκον ἐν πολλοῖς ἀδελφοῖς)." This verse intriguingly ties together our growth into a new identity as the "image of the Son" with Christ's identity as the firstborn of this new community.

38. Bauer, *Greek-English Lexicon*, 892. The basic definition given for πρωτεύω is "to hold the highest rank in a group, *be first, have first place.*" The significance of this here is the recognition that there is a specific group for which Christ is the highest. Beale, *Colossians*, 106, notes that this word is a NT *hapax*, but is used in "the LXX and Josephus as well as other early Jewish writings.... the idea of the word generally is that of being first in rank, along with authoritative overtones.... This is not a restatement that Christ would be the 'first' of the ensuing new creation in chronological order (though that is partly expressed by 'firstborn from the dead') but that he would hold the 'preeminent' position in the new creation, from its inception until its consummation."

39. Dunne, "The Regal Status of Christ," 13.

live a better life, he is King. Being a Christian is not about being moral, or "good" people, it is about submitting to the Lordship of Christ, submitting to his supremacy in the Church. This submission entails obedience to Jesus, which includes growth in "morality" and "goodness," of course, but it also entails realizing that what we are as the Body is the beginning of the re-creation of all things under Christ's Lordship.

Verses 19-20: The Lordship of Christ

These last two verses of the hymn map out what the Lordship of Christ entails: the restoration of all things through the reconciling work of Christ on the cross. These verses begin by reminding the hearer again of the image-language from the start of the hymn. Here, it is said that "God was pleased to have all his fullness dwell in him (ἐν αὐτῷ εὐδόκησεν πᾶν τὸ πλήρωμα κατοικῆσαι)." As before, this reminds the hearer that "all of God's divine essence and glory are found in Christ."[40] Bates draws out the significance of this line, that "although Jesus is not the only human to bear God's image, he is the only one who imaged God in a *complete* manner."[41]

The importance of this reality is such that Paul reiterates it in 2:9: "in Christ all the fullness of the Deity lives in bodily form (ἐν αὐτῷ κατοικεῖ πᾶν τὸ πλήρωμα τῆς θεότητος σωματικῶς)." The language of πλήρωμα in both references indicates superabundance and completion, reiterated here by Paul, "who encountered the *šĕkînâ* glory of the risen Lord."[42] Helyer is right to use the language of the *šĕkînâ* glory, for that is exactly what Colossians 1:19 indicates. The full glory of God, present in the Exodus, present in the Temple, is finally fully present with humanity in Jesus.[43]

---

40. Gary L. Shultz Jr, "The Reconciliation of All Things in Christ," *BSac* 167, (2010): 450.

41. Bates, *Salvation*, 157. He continues, "For all humans, apart from Jesus, the image and God's divine presence do not fully align, so that the divine presence is not perfectly mediated by the image—it is eclipsed or occluded. But with Jesus there is flawless alignment and pervasive presence." He then also notes the connection to 2:9.

42. Larry L. Helyer, "Cosmic Christology and Col 1:15–20," *JETS* 37, no. 2 (1994): 245.

43. Elsewhere, in Ephesians, Paul uses similar language to call the believers up to their intended re-creation. For instance, in Ephesians 3:19 Paul prays "that you may be filled to the measure of all the fullness of God" (ἵνα πληρωθῆτε εἰς πᾶν τὸ πλήρωμα τοῦ θεοῦ), a prayer that draws believers to mirror the fullness of God in Christ. More specifically, again in 4:19, Paul points toward the goal of the Church to be to work "until we all reach unity in the faith and in the knowledge of the Son of God and become mature, attaining to the whole

The purpose of having his šĕkînâ glory resting on Jesus is stated in verse 20: to "reconcile" (ἀποκαταλλάξαι) and to "make peace" (εἰρηνοποιήσας). Meier notes that "these terms were especially at home in ancient diplomatic and political contexts to describe the cessation of hostility and the reconciliation of hostile parties."[44] God-in-Christ came on a diplomatic mission, as it were, to restore what was broken in the fall, the relationship of God with humans (and all creation). The first term, ἀποκαταλλάξαι, occurs almost instantly again in 1:22, where Paul further elucidates the implications of the reconciliation: that through Christ's physical death we will be "holy in his sight, without blemish and free from accusation."[45] The work of God in Christ is for the restoration of our Edenic relationship with God. The latter term, εἰρηνοποιήσας, occurs only here in the New Testament, but is the verbal form for the noun that occurs only in Matthew 5:9: "Blessed are the peacemakers (εἰρηνοποιοί), for they will be called children of God." Just as the Firstborn is making peace, so all who would be children of God shall likewise make peace.

The cosmic scope of this reconciliation and peacemaking is again highlighted with the reiteration of all-encompassing language: ἀποκαταλλάξαι τὰ πάντα … εἴτε τὰ ἐπὶ τῆς γῆς εἴτε τὰ ἐν τοῖς οὐρανοῖς. The merism of "earth" and "heaven" encompasses the entirety of physical beings and spiritual powers, reiterating the creative power of God-in-Christ from verse 16, that "in him all things (τὰ πάντα) were created": things "ἐν τοῖς οὐρανοῖς καὶ ἐπὶ τῆς γῆς, τὰ ὁρατὰ καὶ τὰ ἀόρατα, εἴτε θρόνοι εἴτε κυριότητες εἴτε ἀρχαὶ εἴτε ἐξουσίαι." All things, which have rebelled, which oppose God, which the Colossians feared or tried to placate, all those things were not only created by God but also still come under his power as he is now reconciling all things. As Maier notes, the "overall effect of 1:15-23 is to offer a vision of a universal reconciliation in which earthly civic ὁμόνοια mirrors heavenly concord and peace assured and won by the creating and recon-

---

measure of the fullness of Christ (εἰς ἄνδρα τέλειον, εἰς μέτρον ἡλικίας τοῦ πληρώματος τοῦ Χριστοῦ)."

44. Maier, "Sly Civility," 329.

45. Shultz, "Reconciliation of all things," 452, is right to caution here that "There is clearly a difference between the reconciliation accomplished by Christ in verse 20 and the reconciliation of the Colossians in verses 21-23 and the redemption of the Colossians in verses 12-14. Universal salvation is never implied by Paul's idea of universal reconciliation."

ciling/pacifying work of the Son."[46] The reconciliation and peacemaking of God-in-Christ are not merely for our individual relationship with Christ, although that is included, but the scope reaches the sum total of everything. Too often, our vision of the impact of the gospel has been too influenced by Western individualism, and so we think of it solely in terms of our own personal relationship with Christ. Again, it is not less than that, but it is far more. "A day is coming when the entire universe, including those who are forever lost, will experience universal reconciliation."[47] This passage calls the reader to revel in the reality that God is indeed on the throne, and despite the uncertainty we face as we navigate the unreconciled world with its hostile powers, that is not the final piece of the story.

The central moment of power in all of history is "his blood, shed on the cross (διὰ τοῦ αἵματος τοῦ σταυροῦ αὐτοῦ)."[48] "Reconciliation comes through the death of the ruler, not the ruled,"[49] and by this, first those who believe in him and then ultimately *everything*, are being brought into a restored relationship with God. Christ is the reconciler; he was the plan of God to redeem his fallen creation, and through his crucifixion, resurrection, and Lordship, reconciliation *is occurring*. "With this highly poetical hymn, Paul stresses the fact that the salvific work of Christ is complete and sufficient. There is no power in the entire cosmos, whether human, demonic, personal or impersonal, that could ever be as great as that of Christ, because Christ created the cosmos and is renewing it."[50] Even more, through his work on the cross, Christ is bringing peace to a hostile, warring creation. "Here cosmology and soteriology meet with a Christological scope. God is fully at work in Christ for human salvation and for the transformation of the world. No human argumentation or rejection can alter that divine plan fulfilled in Christ."[51]

---

46. Maier, "Sly Civility," 333.
47. Shultz, "Reconciliation of all things," 458.
48. Behr, "Colossians 1:13–20," 263-64, calls this line "the key to the whole passage.... all the Christological assertions are based upon and through 'the blood of the Cross.'"
49. Maier, "Sly Civility," 348.
50. Viljoen, "Perspectives from the Christ hymn," 9.
51. Teresa Okure, "'In him all things hold together': a missiological reading of Colossians 1:15-20," *International Review of Mission* 91, no. 360 (2002): 68.

An Additional Note About Christ and the Church

There are many deeply helpful—and also quite varied—diagrams mapping out the flow of this passage, whether conceptually or grammatically. I will not try to duplicate any of them here, but for this paper there is one note I want to highlight about this passage, specifically about the Church's location within the cosmological scope of this hymn. The hymn, as I've followed it in this exploration, breaks into three parts that might be depicted as follows:[52]

Verses 15-17
-Image of the Invisible God
-Firstborn of creation
-Creator and Sustainer of all things (earthly, heavenly, etc.)

Verse 18
-Head and Ruler of the Church
-Firstborn from the dead
-Preeminent in all things

Verses 19-20
-Fullness of God Dwells
-Peacemaker through the Cross
-Reconciler of all things (earthly and heavenly)

When laid out like this, we can see again the emphasis on *all things* that come under Jesus' Lordship and work. But also amidst the glorious focus on *all things* comes an equally glorious centering of the Church amidst that focus. The Church is not an afterthought; rather, its identity comes directly from its identification with the One who is himself identified with God. The high point of the hymn, amidst all the cosmic work, is Christ's work in forming the Body. And it is in his work in creating the Church that his preeminence, his supremacy is made real. Behr argues that this line "explains the relationship between Jesus Christ and the whole of cre-

---

52. Beale, *Colossians*, 101-2, concedes that a thematic approach lays out as I have done so, where the "main point is in v. 18, with vv. 19-20 being the supporting basis ['because'] of that main point." He, however, supports a threefold chiastic pattern which centers on v. 17b.

ation more precisely.... the Church is, therefore, creation in so far as it has been (re)created and reconciled to God in Christ as its head."[53] Christ, the firstborn from the dead, has started the work not merely of creation but of re-creation, and the Church stands at the center of this work.

This new creation reality has implications for the work, worship, and lives of believers. Okure cautions the reader that "Paul therefore challenges the Colossians to become aware of their new dignity and status and not allow themselves to be held again in bondage by any other religious authority. In short, the Christological issue in the letter is treated from a primarily soteriological standpoint, in terms of what it signifies for the believer and for the entire creation."[54] The Church, his Body, becomes the locus from which the reconciliation and restoration of all things flow outward. As Maier describes it, "We have here the making of a Quiet Revolution."[55] If the Church, in its worship, takes the lordship of Christ over all things seriously, and if its members live into our own call from Jesus to be peacemakers (εἰρηνοποιοί, Matt. 5:9) in emulation of our Head (εἰρηνοποιήσας, Col. 1:20), then the reconciling work of Christ will continue to flow outward.

In the passage just prior to the hymn, Paul tells the Colossians his prayer for them: that they would "live a life worthy of the Lord and please him in every way: bearing fruit in every good work, growing in the knowledge of God, being strengthened with all power according to his glorious might so that you may have great endurance and patience, and giving joyful thanks to the Father" (vv. 10–12). And we give thanks because "he has rescued us from the dominion of darkness and brought us into the kingdom of the Son he loves, in whom we have redemption, the forgiveness of sins" (13–14).[56] The prayer and the theological exposition of the hymn flow together. Paul praises God for the redemption the Colossian believers have experienced, and then immediately praises God that through Christ he is in the work of reconciling *all* things—with the Church at the center of that. And he prays

---

53. Behr, "Colossians 1:13–20," 260.
54. Okure, "In Him all things hold together," 69.
55. Maier, "Sly Civility," 340.
56. Behr, "Colossians 1:13–20," 263, argues for the necessity of verses 13-14 for understanding the hymn according to his chiastic layout. Without necessitating the chiasm he maps out, it is reasonable to suspect that Paul included the hymn after the prayer in specific conversation with each other.

that they would be "strengthened with all power" and "knowledge of God," and immediately reveals to them what that power is and teaches them *who* Christ is so that their knowledge of God might indeed grow.

Moreover, in the passage just following the hymn, Paul ties the reconciling work of Christ much more overtly to the Church. In his initial exposition, "he specifically changes the object of ἀποκαταλλάξαι from the universe (τα πάντα) in 1:19 to 'you' (the Christian church, ὑμάς... ἀποκατήλλαξεν) in 1:21. The focus of reconciliation shifts from the crisis of cosmic disorder to that of personal hostility to God (1:21) and social disorder. The writer connects in a very explicit and intentional way the cosmic work of Christ with the historic, social and personal work of Christ and with the witness of the apostle."[57] The universal reconciling work of Christ gains its traction through the reconciliation and worship of the Church. In Christ is the image and fullness of God, so in coming to see Christ more clearly, we also come to see the Father. And when we begin to see Christ for who he truly is, then we can truly begin to bear fruit and please him in every way, thus fulfilling Paul's prayer for his readers.

Conclusion

This incredible hymn of Christ is Paul's answer to the Colossians' failure to take full account of who Christ is and their efforts to supplement him with other rituals. MacDonald argues that "the ethical implications for what is experienced in the midst of ritual are at the heart of the conflict in Colossae."[58] When the early Church sang this hymn, they reaffirmed reality and reoriented themselves to living as the Body. Paul's incorporation of this hymn in the introduction of his letter indicates the importance with which he views this Christology for the ongoing issues of life and worship in Colossae. Reading this passage should put us in mind of the moment when Jesus stilled the storm on the sea of Galilee. The disciples were suddenly faced with seeing that their friendly wisdom teacher somehow had power over the wind and waves. In that moment, when they *see* Jesus for who he is, they are terrified and ask each other, "Who is this?!" And they fall

---

57. Harold van Broekhoven, "The Social Profiles in the Colossian Debate," *JSNT* 66, (1997): 86.
58. MacDonald, *Colossians*, 68.

down and worship. When we truly see Christ, we cannot any longer speak of "my own personal Jesus." He is the fullness of God in human form, the one *through whom* all things were created, the one *for whom* all things were made, and the one *by whom* all things are being sustained and reconciled back to God.

But Macaskill adds an important pastoral consideration: nothing we can do can put us outside of the possibility of reconciliation: "God's dealings with the cosmos and its inhabitants have always been conditioned by the gospel of Jesus Christ; that is one crucial implication of Col 1:15–20. He related to the cosmos in Christ when he laid its foundations, he related to the cosmos in Christ when he first made humanity according to his image, he related to the cosmos in Christ when that paradigmatic first sin took place; all of his dealings are mediated and the same mediator is at the heart of all of them."[59] Redemption lies at the heart of the whole creation story because redemption is the work of the one who made everything. In an age of polarization, when disagreements lead to cutting off relationship, when it seems people gleefully rush to their keyboards to declare someone a sinner worthy of hell, it is worth remembering that the work that Christ completed on the cross was to open the possibility of the reconciliation of all things.

And this reconciliation is the work of which we, the Body, are called to participate in. Just as Jesus is *the* Peacemaker, so are we called to be peacemakers as restored children of God. The reconciling work of Christ "restores a right relationship, not only to God, but also to the whole creation. The purpose of God's salvation is not to escape the world, but to re-create it."[60] Our imaginations should be so consumed by the totality of Christ's lordship that we live, work, celebrate, and mourn, that we live all of our lives not as though God exists for us, but because we exist *for Christ*, to bring honor and glory to him in our dealings with humans and all of creation. The Body, as sustained and established in Christ, is to participate in his reconciling work of bringing all people and all things to God. So often we live with small and safe visions of Christianity, but Paul leaves no scope for small or safe. The universal lordship of Christ, the image and fullness

---

59. Macaskill, "Union(s) with Christ," 107.
60. Richard L. Christensen, "Colossians 1:15–28," *Interpretation* 61, (2007): 318.

of God incarnate, places the Church in the center of the reconciling and peacemaking work of our Head. The Colossian hymn calls the Church to mission under the universal lordship of Christ.

Part 2

Scholarship

5

What if Jesus Is Not in This Parable?

How Historical Context Provides an Interpretive Key to the Parable of the Minas in Luke 19:11-27[1]

Marcus Tso

1. The Curious Case of the Parable of the Minas

Among Jesus' numerous parables preserved in the synoptic Gospels, many make their points by using the trope of an authoritative figure's interactions with his subordinates.[2] One of these is the often-neglected parable of the minas in Luke 19:11-27.[3] Even when preached, it is often handled as a variant of a similar parable, the so-called parable of the talents in

---

1. It is my privilege to contribute an article to honour one of my beloved Regent professors, Dr. Sven Soderlund. Although I did not have the fortune of taking one of Sven's classes while I studied at Regent in the late 90s, the way he modeled how to be a scholar with a pastoral heart made a strong impression on me that has influenced me ever since. As he has once written, for travellers on the Emmaus road, all scriptures should be read canonically and christologically, see Sven Soderlund, "Burning Hearts and Open Minds: Exposition on the Emmaus Road," *Crux* 23 (1987):2-4. Notwithstanding the title of my present article, I heartily agree that even this Lukan parable is christological, just not necessarily in a straightforward way.

2. As is well known, most of Jesus' parables are found in Matthew and Luke, with Mark containing only a few. For the use of authoritative figures and subordinates as a typical structure in Jesus' parables, see Craig L. Blomberg, *Interpreting the Parables*, 2nd ed. (Downers Grove: IVP Academic, 2012).

3. For evidence of this neglect, at least in the 1980s, see note 1 in Luke Timothy Johnson, "The Lukan Kingship Parable (Lk. 19:11-27)," *NovT* 24 (1982):139-59.

Matthew 25:14-30.[4] Both parables share a similar plot: a master distributes money among his servants before going on a journey. Upon his return, he settles accounts with them, praising those that have been productive, and rebuking the one that did not produce as instructed. Indeed, the typical traditional interpretation and its variants read this parable in basically the same eschatological way that it reads Matthew's version, allegorizing the authoritative figure as Jesus, and the subordinates as his disciples. Section 2 below will examine these interpretations in greater detail.

However, in spite of the similarities between the two parables, Luke's parable has additional elements that are puzzling to uninitiated modern readers, raising various interpretive issues and demanding solutions that I will explore in Section 3 below. For example, what does it mean for a nobleman to go to a far country to receive a kingdom? Where is that kingdom and how does he get it? To whom are the citizens who reject the nobleman's rule making their appeals? The nobleman or someone else? Why does the nobleman not kill his detractors right away, but wait until his return? Why does Luke's version include these details and what do they add to the parable's meaning, if we assume it to be an expansion of the Matthean version, whether by Jesus himself on another occasion, or by Luke much later?[5] This paper will demonstrate that historical information about client kings of Rome in general, and Archelaus in particular, as presented in Section 3 below, is crucial for answering most of these questions, and opens the path for answering the last one.[6]

---

4. Cf. Mark 13:34 for a brief parabolic saying that contains some of the essential elements of these parables.

5. This essay will assume that the distinctive elements in Luke's version faithfully represent some tradition or traditions that reach back to Jesus' own telling of the parable. In other words, the extra details likely originated from Jesus' telling and were not invented or conflated by Luke. For an example of scholars who argue that Luke's Gospel tends to preserve Jesus' parables and sayings more faithfully than Matthew's Gospel, see John J. Pilch, "A Window into the Biblical World: The Parable of the Talents?" *Bible Today* 39 (2001):366-70. See also Garwood P. Anderson, "Seeking and Saving What Might Have Been Lost: Luke's Restoration of an Enigmatic Parable Tradition," *CBQ* 70 (2008):729-49. If this is incorrect, we can only explain their presence by Luke's communicative intent to his readers and not Jesus' to his hearers. Regardless, reading the parable canonically as contemporary readers, we must try to hear the rhetorical effects of the Lukan parable as closely as we can to how the original hearers of Jesus' parable or readers of Luke would have heard it.

6. Due to the nature of the sources, much of this historical information has been known

The traditional allegorical interpretations assume that both versions of the parable have the same allegorical referents, and that the master is a positive figure representing Jesus. In contrast, this essay challenges that assumption and asks, "What if Jesus is not in the version of the parable found in Luke?" Likewise, a growing body of more recent scholarship challenges the positive evaluation of the nobleman. Section 4 below, the main section of this paper, will showcase how that body of scholarship employs various methodological approaches to reach that alternative conclusion. Supported by such an emerging consensus, Section 4 will resume the argument, introduced in Section 3, that the parable's allusions to Archelaus are the strongest clues available to Jesus' original audience that would lead them to evaluate the nobleman negatively. Finally, Section 4 will conclude with an alternative interpretation, delineating how switching the evaluation of the nobleman would radically change the meaning of the parable, and what that meaning might be for ancient and modern readers alike.

2. The Traditional Allegorical Interpretations

While supporting an allegorical interpretation of this parable that I will challenge in this article, Craig Blomberg's model of the typical three-point parable is a helpful heuristic devise to analyze our parable, providing a simple means of contrasting various approaches of interpretation.[7] This model can be represented graphically as a triangle with one point on the top and two subordinating and contrasting points on the bottom.

Thus, what I am describing as traditional interpretations of this parable here can be modeled as having the nobleman in the authoritative-figure spot at the top point, representing Jesus. The two profitable servants, then, are in the positive-subordinate spot at one of the two bottom points, representing Jesus' faithful disciples. And lastly, the unprofitable servant is

---

for a long time, but often from a later Christian perspective that has not always fully explored the implications of this knowledge.

7. Blomberg, *Interpreting the Parables*, 29, 197, and esp. 269-80. Blomberg rightly distinguishes between allegory and allegorizing, acknowledging that while a parable may indeed contain allegorical elements (elements that point to non-literal referents), allegorizing is the improper imposition of figurative meanings on parts of a parable that are not originally intended. The way Blomberg interprets both parables is in spite of recognizing them not to be true parallels. See Craig L. Blomberg, "When Is a Parallel Really a Parallel? A Test Case: The Lucan Parables," *WTJ* 46 (1984):78-103.

in the negative-subordinate spot at the other bottom point, representing unfaithful disciples. (Fig. 1) This is more or less the same traditional interpretation as the parable of the talents in Matthew 25:14–30. In this view, both parables taught that Jesus was about to depart from this world for a while, but would eventually come back from heaven to rule. Meanwhile, his followers should remain faithful and do his work with what he had entrusted them. In both parables, the rhetorical point to all recipients has always been: "Don't be the servant who does nothing and is unprofitable!"[8]

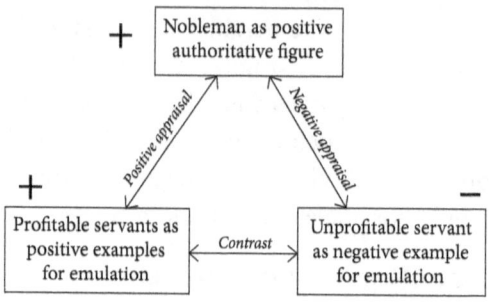

Fig. 1. Traditional allegorical interpretations represented by Blomberg's model.

This understanding of the parable has a long history, reaching back to the Church Fathers, with their propensity to allegorization and a straightforward Christological reading.[9] Notwithstanding the emergence of modern exegetical methods in the last few centuries, this traditional interpretation remains largely unquestioned.[10] As a result, it is still the majority

---

8. As the following will elaborate, this common interpretive strategy does not mean that its proponents do not see distinctive nuances in each parable. Indeed, many who make this basic role assignment in the model argue that the two parables are distinct and not two versions of the same parable.

9. E.g., Cyril of Alexandria, "Homily 128," *Commentary on the Gospel of Luke*. For a brief modern survey of such early allegorical interpretations, see esp. page 4 in Ernest Van Eck, "Do Not Question My Honour: A Social-Scientific Reading of the Parable of the Minas (Lk 19:12b-24, 27)," *HvTSt* 67 (2011):1–11. By "straightforward Christological reading," I mean reading one of the characters in the parable as a simple representation of Jesus Christ. This article argues for the possibility or even likelihood of an oblique Christological reading here, where the parable is Christological in that it shows who Christ is by using a foil.

10. For an example of an eighteenth-century interpretation of this parable, see Alfred

position among interpreters to date.[11]

According to many in this line of interpretation, the additional Lukan elements about the claimant king and his rebellious subjects are understood as an analogy about the unbelieving Jews who would perish for rejecting Jesus.[12] Furthermore, most in this majority position recognize other distinctive features of Luke's parable, but account for these differences as nuances in meaning rather than radical differences. Such nuances include an alleged Lukan concern to explain the delayed parousia, compared to the Matthean concern for how believers in Christ ought to live in the meantime.[13]

This traditional reading of the parable of the minas with a Matthean lens sometimes views Matthew's version as being normative and closer to the original, while the Lukan parable as a clumsy conflation of different parabolic fragments.[14] Such an assessment does not do justice to Luke's

---

Plummer, *A Critical and Exegetical Commentary on the Gospel according to St. Luke* (T&T Clark, 1896), 437-44. It is noteworthy that this relatively early work is already aware of the contextual information that will be cited below as evidence against the traditional reading.

11. Beside Blomberg cited above, other such interpreters include the following. James G. Simpson, "The Parable of the Pounds," *Expository Times* 37 (1926):299-303. Henry Clarence Thiessen, "The Parable of the Nobleman and the Earthly Kingdom: Luke 19:11-27," *Bibliotheca Sacra* 91 (1934):180-90. Johnson, "Lukan Kingship Parable." Laurie Guy, "The Interplay of the Present and Future in the Kingdom of God (Luke 19:11-44)," *Tyndale Bulletin* 48 (1997):119-37. Robert H. Stein, "Interpreting the Parables of Luke," *SwJT* 40 (1997):6-16. Arland J. Hultgren, *The Parables of Jesus: A Commentary* (Grand Rapids: Eerdmans, 2000). Klyne Snodgrass, *Stories with Intent: A Comprehensive Guide to the Parables of Jesus* (Grand Rapids: Eerdmans, 2008). Many of these scholars, like Plummer cited above, are aware of the contextual information, and attempt to account for it in various ways. Nevertheless, as I have alluded above, such information somehow did not cause them to reconsider their basic interpretive assumption that the nobleman represents Jesus.

12. For a non-eschatological reading that still argues for application to Jewish rejection of Jesus, see Adelbert Denaux, "The Parable of the King-Judge (Lk 19,12-28) and its Relation to the Entry Story (Lk 19,29-44)," *ZNW* 93 (2002):35-57.

13. See, e.g., Denaux, "Parable of the King-Judge," 41-42.

14. David Friedrich Strauss postulated early on that Luke's parable is an amalgam of Matthew's parable and a misplaced parable of the throne claimant and his rebellious subjects, cited in Plummer, *Luke*, 437. For an exegesis of that isolated fragment based on such a premise, see Francis D. Weinert, "Parable of the Throne Claimant (Luke 19:12, 14-15a, 27) Reconsidered," *CBQ* 39 (1977):505-14. For a recent source-critical argument supporting the view that Luke conflated elements from two parables, see Llewellyn Howes, "'Reaping Where You Did Not Sow': The Parable of the Entrusted Money (Q 19:12-13, 15-24, 26) and

demonstrated literary skills, and underestimates Luke's explicit claim for accuracy (Luke 1:1-4).[15]

3. The Problems with the Traditional Allegorical Interpretations

There are several noteworthy problems with the interpretations sketched out above. All of them read this parable in Luke more or less as a variant of the Matthean parable of the talent, only with shifts in emphasis and an additional point of warning to rebellious Jews.

First, this reading violates one of the cardinal rules of modern parable interpretation, that each parable should make one basic point and not multiple points.[16] In other words, Luke's parable in its original context, especially for Luke, was unlikely to be intended both to encourage faithful use of divine endowments and to warn against rejection of Jesus.

The second problem is closely related to the first. According to this traditional way of reading, not only was the parable intended to make two main points, these points were directed at two different groups: Jesus' followers and his opponents.[17] Granted, it is certainly possible for different groups to hear Jesus' original telling of the parables, or to read Luke's presentations of the same, and come away with different understandings of their points for them. Nevertheless, it is questionable whether Jesus or Luke intended different points for different groups in the same parable. For example, while the parable of the prodigal son (Luke 15:11–32) can be used to make a point to those who identify with the wayward son, that God's love and acceptance is unconditional (indeed it has more often been used this way), the literary context of that parable (Luke 15:1–3) clearly indicates that the intended target group of the whole series of parables in

---

the Redaction of Q," *Journal of Early Christian History* 6 (2016):18-54.

15. For an argument that Luke preserves the enigmatic nature of the parable traditions from Jesus, see Anderson, "Seeking and Saving What Might Have Been Lost."

16. For a summary of the historical development of this and other modern rules of parable interpretation, beginning with Adolf Jülicher in 1888, see Stein, "Interpreting the Parables of Luke," 7-10. See also the endorsement of such rules by yet another beloved Regent professor, Gordon Fee, in Gordon D. Fee and Douglas K. Stuart, *How to Read the Bible for All Its Worth*, 3rd ed. (Grand Rapids: Zondervan, 2003).

17. Although this problem is not exactly a violation of one of the rules adumbrated by Stein, it is related to his second and third rule about Jesus' and Luke's intended point to their original audience. See Stein, "Interpreting the Parables of Luke," 10-15.

this chapter was those who would identify with the older son. The details about the younger son help make the point about the older son. This is hardly true in the typical traditional reading of the parable of the minas. The additional details about the rebellious subjects in no way help make the supposed point about the unproductive servant. Instead, as shown below, these additional details help characterize the nobleman more than the servants.

Third, and most crucially, the additional details in Luke's parable closely match what ancient sources tell us about Jewish puppet rulers in the Greco-Roman period, particularly Herod Archelaus. While many proponents of the traditional reading are aware of these connections, none of these interpreters has offered an adequate account of how these correspondences might have functioned rhetorically. Let us examine and evaluate these correspondences that scholars have long observed.[18]

3.1. The nobleman who went to a distant country

First, Luke's parable begins by introducing the authoritative figure, not as a king, but as "a nobleman (Ἄνθρωπός τις εὐγενὴς) [who] went to a distant country to get royal power for himself and then return" (19:12).[19] As hinted above, such a description of the main character in the parable can cause much confusion for the modern reader who is unfamiliar with the political background of Jesus' times. One may misunderstand this figure to be an independent ruler who leaves his home base in a military or diplomatic campaign to gain control over some distant domain. However, interpreters familiar with the relevant historical context recognize that another picture is probably intended. The main source of that context is Josephus, who reports that after Herod the Great died and willed his kingdom to his son Herod Archelaus, the latter still had to leave Jerusalem and go to Rome to have Augustus Caesar confirm his appointment.

> [Ptolemy] opened and read [Herod's] testament, wherein Philip was to inherit Trachonitis, and the neighboring countries, and Antipas was to

---

18. For a succinct and impressive nine-point list of such correspondences, relying on *Antiquities of the Jews*, see Craig A. Evans, *Noncanonical Writings and New Testament Interpretation* (Peabody, MA: Hendrickson, 1992), 181.
19. Unless otherwise noted, English translations of biblical texts are from the NRSV.

be tetrarch, as we said before, and Archelaus was made king. [Ptolemy] had also been commanded to carry Herod's ring to Caesar, and the settlements he had made, sealed up, because Caesar ... was to confirm [Herod's] testament ... (Josephus, *War* 1.668-669 [1.33.8])[20]

The passage above illustrates well why Luke's authoritative figure is not described as a king outright. In the case of Archelaus, though he was one of King Herod's sons (a certain man of noble birth, Ἄνθρωπός τις εὐγενὴς), and the one whom Herod had named in his will as the heir to his throne, his succession was not automatic, but subject to imperial ratification. The following passage further sheds light on the necessity of the nobleman's long journey to secure his kingdom.

> Now the necessity which Archelaus was under of taking a journey to Rome was the occasion of new disturbances; for when he had mourned for his father seven days ... he put on a white garment, and went up to the temple, where the people accosted him with various acclamations. He also spoke kindly to the multitude, from an elevated seat and a throne of gold, and returned them thanks for the zeal they had shown about his father's funeral, and the submission they had made to him, as if he were already settled in the kingdom; but he told them withal, that he would not at present take upon him either the authority of a king, or the names thereto belonging, until Caesar, who is made lord of this whole affair by the testament, confirms the succession. (Josephus, *War* 2.1-2 [2.1.1])[21]

Evidently, if the nobleman is modeled after Archelaus, as I am arguing, the journey was not military, but a diplomatic mission to secure the political patronage of an overlord for a client king. In that case, the kingdom that the nobleman is to receive is not some distant domain, but the legitimacy to rule his own territory.

---

20. Unless otherwise noted, English translations of Josephus's works are from Flavius Josephus, *The Works of Josephus: Complete and Unabridged*, New updated ed., trans. William Whiston (Peabody, Mass.: Hendrickson, 1987). Cf. *Ant.* 17.188-89, 195 (17.8.1-2). For the partitioning of Herod's territories after his death, compare the historical note in Luke 3:1, referring to the situation during Tiberius's reign, years after Augustus deposed Archelaus and appointed Pontius Pilate to rule in his place.

21. Cf. *Ant.* 17.200-202 (17.8.4).

3.2. The nobleman opposed by rebellious subjects

Second, Luke's parable introduces the additional characters of the rebellious subject: "But the citizens of his country hated him and sent a delegation after him, saying, 'We do not want this man to rule over us'" (19:14). This is matched almost exactly by Josephus's account of Archelaus's rise to power. First, Josephus relates the opposition from within his own royal family:

> Archelaus went down now to the seaside with his mother and his friends, Poplas, and Ptolemy, and Nicolaus, and left behind him Philip, to be his steward in the palace, and to take care of his domestic affairs. Salome went also along with him with her sons, as did also the king's brethren and sons-in-law. These, in appearance, went to give him all the assistance they were able, in order to secure his succession, but in reality to accuse him for his breach of the laws by what he had done at the temple. (Josephus, *War* 2.14-15 [2.2.1])[22]

> The inclinations also of all Archelaus's kindred, who hated him, were removed to Antipas, when they came to Rome; although, in the first place, every one rather desired to live under their own laws [without a king], and to be under a Roman governor; but if they should fail in that point, these desired that Antipas might be their king. (Josephus, *War* 2.22 [2.2.3])

Archelaus's family hated him so much that they would rather be under direct Roman rule than to acquiesce to his reign. But this opposition was not limited to the inner circle of the royal court. It was widespread, as Josephus goes on to recount later:

> But now came another accusation from the Jews against Archelaus at Rome, which he was to answer to. It was made by those ambassadors who, before the revolt, had come, by Varus's permission, to plead for the liberty of their country; those that came were fifty in number, but there were more than eight thousand of the Jews at Rome who supported

---

22. Cf. *Ant.* 17.219-27 (17.9.3-4). Note also the correspondence between Archelaus entrusting his household affairs to someone prior to his trip and both versions of the parable in Matthew and Luke.

them. (Josephus, *War* 2.80 [2.6.1])[23]

So, beside members of his own family, a delegation of fifty Jews, joined by 8,000 in Rome, also opposed Archelaus. However, their motivation was very different from the royal family's. According to the context of this passage, this popular opposition was directed more at the entire Herodian dynasty than just Archelaus. The brutality of Herod the Great was cited as the main cause for their rejection of his heir.

These historical details about Archelaus once again provide a convincing clarification to another puzzle about this parable. The delegation opposing the rule of the nobleman in Luke is making an appeal not to him, but to an overlord, who has the authority to confirm or deny the nobleman's bid for kingship.

3.3. The nobleman's delayed retribution

Third and finally, Luke's parable states that the nobleman's response to his rebellious subjects is to massacre them upon his return: "But as for these enemies of mine who did not want me to be king over them—bring them here and slaughter them in my presence" (19:27). Although Josephus does not explicitly mention such a violent retaliation by Archelaus,[24] he does cite Archelaus's revenge against his old enemies when his rule was more or less secured:

> And now Archelaus took possession of his ethnarchy, and used not the Jews only, but the Samaritans also, barbarously; and this out of his resentment of their old quarrels with him. (Josephus, *War* 2.111 [2.7.3])

Furthermore, mass slaughter of opponents and trouble-makers is totally in character with the way Archelaus ruled, mimicking his father before him, as demonstrated by an account of how he suppressed a temple unrest before his journey to Rome:

> After which they [Jewish agitators in the Jerusalem Temple] betook

---

23. Cf. *Ant.* 17.299-300 (17.11.1).

24. Contra the claim made on pages 205 and 210 in Ernest Van Eck, "Social Memory and Identity: Luke 19:12b-24 and 27," *BTB* 41 (2011): 201-12.

themselves to their sacrifices, as if they had done no mischief; nor did it appear to Archelaus that the multitude could be restrained without bloodshed; so he sent his whole army upon them, the footmen in great multitudes, by the way of the city, and the horsemen by the way of the plain, who, falling upon them on the sudden, as they were offering their sacrifices, destroyed about three thousand of them; but the rest of the multitude were dispersed upon the adjoining mountains; these were followed by Archelaus's heralds, who commanded every one to retire to their own homes; whither they all went, and left the festival. (Josephus, *War* 2.12-13 [2.1.3])

Once again, the close correspondence between Josephus's account of Archelaus and the puzzling details of Luke's parable is illuminating^x'. The delayed retribution of the nobleman against his opponents matches the historical response of Archelaus, and reflects his ruthless brutality.

Granted that the historical details outlined above do not map on the parable precisely, the striking resemblance is too strong to dismiss.[25] Moreover, for the argument of this article to work, we do not need to prove that Jesus, Luke, or the first century recipients of this parable specifically associated the nobleman with Archelaus. The same rhetorical effect would be achieved if the recipients recognize in the nobleman someone like Archelaus, of whom there were many during the first century on either side of the turn of the era.[26]

In spite of how manifest the Archelaus connection is, many scholars ignore a key interpretive question: Why would Jesus use such an unpopular figure to represent himself?[27] Some attempted responses include using this figure as a rhetorical device, for shock value, to create incongruence, or simply circumstantial as Jesus happened to be around Jericho, the site

---

25. For an example of views critical or dismissive of the Archelaus connection, in spite of the evidence, see Jack T. Sanders, "The Parable of the Pounds and Lucan Anti-Semitism," *TS* 42 (1981): 660-68. See also more recently, Denaux, "Parable of the King-Judge," 53-54.

26. On this point I agree with Denaux, "Parable of the King-Judge," 53-54. See also page 76 in Richard Bolling Vinson, "The Minas Touch: Anti-Kingship Rhetoric in the Gospel of Luke," *PRSt* 35 (2008): 69-86.

27. This of course assumes the allusions were original with Jesus, the evidence for which is cited elsewhere in this paper. Even if they were Luke's contributions, the same question remains: Why would anyone use a negative figure to represent someone positively?

of Archelaus's palace.[28] But such explanations are not entirely satisfactory. These solutions do not take seriously enough how negative the allusion to an Archelaus-like figure must have been to Jesus' original listeners and even Luke's readers.[29] From the Jewish non-Herodian perspective, he was a ruthless tyrant who oppressed the Jewish people as an agent of the Empire. From the Roman perspective, he was merely an appointee without real power or merit. From a psychological perspective, it would be difficult to imagine the original recipients of this parable viewing the nobleman in a positive light and associating him with Jesus if they had picked up the clues that portray the nobleman negatively.[30] The negative association makes the traditional identification of the authority figure with Jesus untenable for Luke's parable, driving us to seek an alternative interpretation.

4. Toward an Alternative Interpretation

While all three lines of reasoning outlined in the previous section raise

---

28. For example, see Brian Schultz, "Jesus as Archelaus in the Parable of the Pounds (Lk 19:11-27)," *Novum testamentum* 49 (2007):105-27. Schultz correctly questions why such a negative character was used in the parable, and even deduces plausibly, in my view, that archaeological evidence suggests that the Archelaus elements were original with Jesus. However, failing to question the assumption that the nobleman refers to Jesus, Schultz unconvincingly explains the inclusion of the Archelaus elements as Jesus' rhetorical use, merely to add poignancy to the parable. A similar argument is made in David Seccombe, "Incongruity in the Gospel Parables," *Tyndale Bulletin* 62 (2011):161-72. Seccombe suggests persuasively that incongruity in the parables points to originality. That is, it reflects Jesus' rhetorical style. Nevertheless, he also asserts that such rhetorical techniques need not mean anything in the parable of the minas. Thus, those who argue similarly fail to show how such rhetorical use of incongruity can conceivably be effective in this case.

29. For an example of a contrived attempt to explain away the negative aspects, see J. Duncan M. Derrett, "A Horrid Passage in Luke Explained (Lk 19:27)," *ExpTim* 97 (1986):136-38.

30. While out of the scope of this article, my argument will likely be strengthened by research from a cognitive science perspective, such as measuring the unlikelihood of the human mind associating a positive figure with a negative one, and determining whether that tendency is widely appreciated, even intuitively, to influence one's rhetorical strategy. For a related discussion on metaphoric mapping with respect to biblical metaphors of God, see Eve Sweetser and Mary Therese DesCamp, "Motivating Biblical Metaphors for God: Refining the Cognitive Model," in *Cognitive Linguistic Explorations in Biblical Studies*, eds. Bonnie Howe and Joel B. Green (Berlin: de Gruyter, 2014), 7-23. For a succinct introduction to the emerging methodology of cognitive science of religion, see Risto Uro, "Cognitive Science in the Study of Early Christianity: Why It Is Helpful – and How?," *NTS* 63 (2017): 516-33.

questions about the validity of the traditional allegorical readings, the final one about the Archelaus connection casts serious doubt on whether the nobleman was originally intended to be understood as a positive authoritative figure representing Jesus. What if the nobleman was not a positive figure, as most have assumed using a Matthean lens? He would then become a parodic foil for the kind of king Jesus would be.[31]

In fact, there is a growing body of scholarship in recent years that argues in that direction, or at least considers it to be a viable alternative reading.[32] While this group of interpreters all share the same conclusion that the nobleman in Luke's parable is a negative character, they have different methodologies, most of which do not in fact depend on the Archelaus connection. I will survey three representative approaches below, namely, the liberationist, literary, and social-scientific approaches.

4.1. Liberationist approaches

Among interpreters who see the nobleman mentioned in the parable of the minas as a negative figure are those who can be described broadly as liberationist. Liberationist interpreters of the Bible, like their theologian colleagues, approach their task from the perspective of currently oppressed groups, such as the poor, racial minorities, women, and sexual minorities.[33] Coming to the biblical text with this lens, liberationist interpreters tend to align themselves with characters in the text who are powerless, over against those who have power, especially coercive power.

The feminist Bible scholar Elizabeth Dowling is a case in point. In

---

31. The parable of the unrighteous judge in Luke 18:1-8 is a clear example of how an authoritative figure in Luke's parable serves not as a representation of God or Christ, but as a foil.

32. See, e.g., Ji-woon Yoo, "The Parable of Minas in Luke 19:11-27: A Parodied Parable of the Roman Imperial Patronage System," *Korea Presbyterian Journal of Theology* 49 (2017):37-63. Pilch, "Parable of the Talents." Richard L. Rohrbaugh, "A Peasant Reading of the Parable of the Talents/Pounds: A Text of Terror?," *BTB* 23 (1993): 32-39. Elizabeth V. Dowling, "Hearing the Voice of Earth in the Lukan Parable of the Pounds," *Colloq* 48 (2016): 35-46.

33. For a succinct survey of the history of liberationist biblical interpretation, see Pablo R. Andiñach and Alejandro F. Botta, "Introduction: The Bible and the Hermeneutics of Liberation: Worldwide Trends and Prospects," in *The Bible and the Hermeneutics of Liberation*, eds. Alejandro F. Botta and Pablo R. Andiñach (Atlanta: Society of Biblical Literature, 2009), 1-10.

several of her publications dealing with this parable, Dowling argues for a subversive reading where the master is not good, but the third slave is.[34] Her conclusion is determined to a large extent by identifying whose side she will take when reading the text,

> Against the majority opinion, I will argue that the Lukan parable is a story about the use and abuse of power. The parable is also the story of those who suffer adverse consequences when they oppose unjust power structures.[35]

As typical of liberationists, Dowling's reading is sensitive to the power inequality and class difference within a particular political and economic structure. This sensitivity to power and class oppositions is shown by statements such as these:

> In this reading of the Parable of the Pounds, a class difference between the characters creates an inequity in power. A further inequity is established by the imperialist structure whereby a foreign country has control over another country. As a result, the nobleman has power over his slaves and the citizens of his country, and the resistance of the third slave and the citizens is the resistance of those who challenge the dominating power structure.[36]

Not only is Dowling sensitive to instances of power disparity between the classes, she registers her protest against the abuse of power in such instances when she describes at least some of the slave parables in Luke as "texts of terror."[37]

---

34. Most notably, see her monograph, Elizabeth V. Dowling, *Taking Away the Pound: Women, Theology and the Parable of the Pounds in the Gospel of Luke* (London: T&T Clark, 2007). In Chapter 2 of this book, Dowling presents her analysis of the parable and uses insights from it to examine the theology in Luke's Gospel. Chapter 1 helpfully surveys the history of scholarship on this parable, providing a fuller account of the traditional readings outlined in Section 2 above. While she identifies her hermeneutical framework explicitly as feminist in this book (3), she specifies her approach as eco-feminist in Dowling, "Hearing the Voice of Earth."

35. Dowling, *Taking Away the Pound*, 1.

36. Dowling, *Taking Away the Pound*, 1-2.

37. Dowling follows Richard Rohrbaugh, cited above, for applying the term "text of terror" to this parable. Rohrbaugh, in turn, borrows the term from Phyllis Trible, *Texts of*

Several of the parables in the Gospel of Luke feature slaves and their masters, and demonstrate both the vulnerability of the slaves' bodies to physical abuse and the slaves' status as non-persons. As such, some of these parables may be considered Gospel "texts of terror."[38]

Also typical of liberationist readings of the Bible, Dowling disapproves of traditional interpretations of texts which accept and perpetuate such exploitative abuse of power, as when she critiques that "translations and interpretations frequently diminish the impact of the violence suffered by the slaves, the significance of the slaves' bodies."[39] Moreover, her criticism goes much further and reaches to the texts themselves, as indicated by her assertion that "any text or interpretation which ignores the violence inflicted on slaves calls for critique."[40]

Using this lens that favours the weak against their oppressors, Dowling's interpretation focuses on seeing the third slave as the sympathetic character in the parable, rather than on the nobleman as a negative figure.[41] Thus, although I strongly agree with her assessment of both the third slave vis-à-vis the nobleman and the first two slaves, we come to those conclusions from very different directions.

As outlined and illustrated above, the liberationist approaches certainly have their merits, such as recognizing the importance of the interpreters' contemporary and particular contexts, and using novel lenses when reading this parable. For one, highlighting the importance of the readers' contexts certainly makes the texts more relevant to their particular situations. More important for the purpose of this paper, liberationist hermeneutics

---

Terror: Literary-Feminist Readings of Biblical Narratives (Philadelphia: Fortress, 1984).

38. Elizabeth V. Dowling, "Slave Parables in the Gospel of Luke: Gospel 'Texts of Terror'?," *ABR* 56 (2008): 61-68.

39. Ibid., 61.

40. Dowling, "Slave Parables in the Gospel of Luke," 61. For another example of her critique of the texts themselves, and not just interpretations of those texts, see Elizabeth V. Dowling, "Luke-Acts: Good News for Slaves?," *Pacifica* 24 (2011): 123-40.

41. Dowling, *Taking Away the Pound*, 52-59. Elsewhere, Dowling summarizes her approbation of the third slave by concluding, "By refusing to continue the oppression of his master, the third slave acts in accord with the pronouncement by Jesus of release from oppression (4:18). In this parable, therefore, it is the third slave rather than his master who acts as Jesus acts, disrupting the master-slave dynamic somewhat." See also Dowling, "Luke-Acts," 135.

radically challenges the unexamined assumption that the authoritative figure in this parable is a positive character representing Christ.

However, this line of approaches has some limitations that need to be addressed. First, by starting with the contemporary context of one or more oppressed groups as a matter of methodology, liberationist hermeneutics prioritizes the perspectives and concerns of some contemporary exploited parties over the originally intended messages to the first recipients.[42] For example, Mary Ann Beavis summarizes the interpretive agenda of fellow feminist interpreters of parables featuring women as,

> ... placing the women characters at the center of the parables, questioning both traditional interpretations and the parables themselves insofar as they reflect the social realities of first-century women's lives, and asking whether they slight, demean, or honor the women they portray – and the women to whom they are preached.[43]

In the hand of the liberationists, originally intended messages of the parables can be irrelevant at best, and harmful and to be denounced at worst. Of course, no naïve dichotomy between original meanings and contemporary receptions is tenable, yet some control is still necessary to prevent an overly subjective approach to scripture.

Another issue with these approaches is that with the same methodology liberationists interpret many, if not all, authority figures in the parables negatively, such as the parable of the talents in Matthew.[44] Of course, liberationists are not the only interpreters to make this move, which this paper will argue is unnecessary and unwarranted. Nevertheless, liberationists are perhaps more likely to make such a value judgment as a result of their methodology.

However, liberationist interpreters of this parable do utilize arguments from the other two approaches we will turn to next: the literary and the

---

42. For an example of one paper starting with the problems of both ecological exploitation and human trafficking, see Dowling, "Hearing the Voice of Earth."

43. Mary Ann Beavis, "'Like Yeast That a Woman Took': Feminist Interpretations of the Parables," *RevExp* 109 (2012): 219-31. Cf. also her citation, on page 227, of Barbara Reid's description of the deconstructive goal of feminist methods.

44. For an example of doing the same value switch in both parables, from the social-scientific approach, see Rohrbaugh, "Peasant Reading."

social-scientific approaches.⁴⁵

4.2. Literary approaches

Beside the liberationists, other recent interpreters of this parable also come to read the nobleman negatively, but mainly on the basis of their literary analyses. With these literary analyses, they identify features of parody or irony in the details of this parable, which in turn fits the immediate literary context and/or the overall theological thrust of the whole Gospel as Luke's literary composition.⁴⁶

Richard Bolling Vinson, for example, showcases both of these results of literary analyses. While thoroughly aware of older readings that identify the nobleman as Jesus the soon-to-be king, he parts company with them. Citing his mentor, Vinson summarizes his argument for an alternative parodic reading:

> R. Alan Culpepper proposed that we should read the Parable as a parody of Jesus' understanding of the kingdom of God. The kingdom over which the parable's nobleman rules is nothing like God's, and the new king's way of ruling contradicts Jesus' teachings in several important ways. In what follows, I will argue that reading the parable as parody not only makes better sense of the story in its immediate context, but also better describes Luke's broader use of "king."⁴⁷

Vinson's first step is to clarify the rhetorical nature of this parable.

---

45. For the argument and demonstration that social-historical research is indispensable, and can be done in a distinctively feminist way, see Luise Schottroff, *Lydia's Impatient Sisters: A Feminist Social History of Early Christianity* (Louisville: Westminster John Knox, 1995), esp. 52-53. See also her use of social-historical analysis to identify the nobleman as negative and his profitable slaves as "exploiting people and the land to increase the wealth of their master." See also Luise Schottroff, *The Parables of Jesus*, trans. Linda M. Maloney (Minneapolis: Fortress, 2006), 185.

46. For the subversive nature of Luke's parables in general, and his use of rhetorical devices, see Matthew S. Rindge, "Luke's Artistic Parables: Narratives of Subversion, Imagination, and Transformation," *Int* 68 (2014):403-15. "Luke's parables are narratives of disorientation that subvert conventional wisdom about many issues such as the use of wealth and possessions. The parables use specific rhetorical strategies … in order to transform the lives of Luke's readers/hearers."

47. Vinson, "Minas Touch," 70. R. Alan Culpepper, *The Gospel of Luke* (Nashville: Abingdon, 1994), 361-64.

Arguing against the older consensus that the point of Luke's parable vis-à-vis Matthew's version is to explain the delayed parousia, Vinson offers an equally plausible purpose for the parable. While he agrees that Luke presents the parable as Jesus' response to the situation as he was entering Jerusalem, noted in 19:11, that people expected the kingdom of God would appear immediately, Vinson avers credibly, "The parable, however, does not resolve the temporal paradox of the Kingdom in Luke, but instead directs the reader's attention to what sort of King will come with it."[48]

What justifies that shift in understanding for the rhetorical purpose of this parable? Beside the wider textual evidence in Luke-Acts that Luke is not interested in speculating on the eschatological chronology, Vinson most helpfully highlights the internal features of the parable that signal its parodic or ironic nature.[49]

Such signals mostly have to do with how the original reader would have perceived the characterizations of the nobleman. Vinson notes first that compared to the master in Matthew's parable, Luke's nobleman "seems less generous, less trusting, and more clearly interested in profit."[50] This observation need not assume that Luke or his first readers have Matthew's version before them for comparison, but only points out that Luke's version contains characterizations that tend towards the negative.

Second, Vinson suggests that Luke's audience would have evaluated the nobleman negatively on the basis of the description that he went "to a far country," "to receive his own kingdom," the first element an intertextual allusion to the earlier Lukan parable of the prodigal son, and the whole thing a "cultural type scene." In his words, "No matter where Luke's audience lived, when the nobleman goes away to 'receive his own kingdom,' Luke's audience would understand 'from Rome.'"[51]

Third, Vinson deploys the same social-scientific arguments about how Luke's audience would have perceived the economic aspects in the parable,

---

48. Vinson, "Minas Touch," 73.
49. Ibid., 73.
50. Ibid., 74.
51. Ibid. Of course, the recognition of the throne-claimant motif as a cultural type scene depends in part on information supplied by the ancient historical sources, such as accounts about the Herodians in general and Archelaus in particular, that they portrayed the exploitative imperial system they were familiar with. Thus, this is yet another example of one interpretive approach relying on insights from other approaches.

with. I will examine these arguments in the next sub-section, but here it is important to note that such insights about historical context illuminate how the parable might have worked rhetorically. Such characterizations would have been expected to turn the audience against the nobleman, and not to endear them to him.

Finally, Vinson proposes that Luke's readers would have connected the nobleman's brutality against his rebellious subjects with a figure like Archelaus.[52] Again, this proposal depends on historical sources external to the text. Nevertheless, given the historical information, the literary conclusion is made all the more plausible.

Having built a persuasive case that the parable would have been perceived as a parody by Luke's first audience because of the many incongruities between Luke's characterizations of the nobleman and Jesus, Vinson goes on to argue that the Lukan corpus is generally negative in its portrayal of human kings, and applied the title of "king" to Jesus ironically after this parable. In other words, Luke uses the occasion of Jesus' entry into Jerusalem and the start of his passion narrative to present this parable about a despicable king, and begins to challenge his readers to wrestle with the nature of Jesus' kingdom and kingship.

More recently, Ji-woon Yoo offers another example of an alternative interpretation based largely on literary analyses that uncover both parody and theological coherence in this parable.[53] Like Vinson, Yoo also challenges the traditional identification of the nobleman as a Jesus figure. Building on Vinson and other scholars in the bad nobleman camp, Yoo presents an even more elaborate case. He showcases more rhetorical devices employed in the parable that mark it off as a parody, and gives a more thoroughgoing account of how the parodied message in Luke's parable is "an integral part of his overall narrative strategy".

However, unlike Vinson, who attends first to the characterizations of

---

52. Vinson, "Minas Touch," 76.
53. Yoo, "Parable of Minas." I thank Dr. Dongshin Chang of Northwest Baptist Seminary at Trinity Western University for acquiring this article for me. Beside the literary approach, following Vinson and Joel Green, Yoo also relies on the results of social-scientific approaches, such as those of Bruce Malina. Nevertheless, in this paper other scholars will serve as examples of the social-scientific approaches instead, because Yoo's contribution is clearly in the literary domain.

the nobleman in the parable, and then checks his result against how the theme of kingship and kingdom has been handled throughout Luke, Yoo has a more complex sequence of analysis. He first examines the near narrative context of the parable to establish that this parable is about kingship and not stewardship, severing the Matthean interpretive route. Yoo then follows through by examining the rhetorical devices within the parable to reveal how it is meant to be a parody. Finally, he correlates the parodic purpose of the parable with Luke's vision of a non-reciprocal patronage system, particularly as shown in the early chapters of Luke and the passion and resurrection narratives at the end.

In terms of the parable's near literary context in the overall narrative strategy of Luke, Yoo astutely observes the following connections. First, the parable (19:11-27) is located immediately between the pericopes about Zacchaeus (19:1-10) and the so-called "triumphal entry" (19:28-40), between Jericho and Jerusalem. The connections are tightened by the circumstantial clauses in v. 11 and 28, each linking the passage it introduces to the speech in the previous passage. Yoo notes that these circumstantial clauses form an inclusio.[54] This invites the readers to consider the meaning of the parable in light of its neighbouring narratives. In the former story, Jesus announces that he has come to seek and save the lost, as exemplified by Zacchaeus, and in the latter story, Jesus enters Jerusalem as a humble king of peace adored by a humble crowd, who echo the praise of angels before the shepherds in 2:14 with "glory to God in the highest."[55] Such portrayals of Jesus form a stark contrast with the nobleman in the parable that

---

54. Yoo, "Parable of Minas," 39. For seeing the literary framing of verse 28 in particular as a key to the interpretation of this parable, see Adam F. Braun, "Reframing the Parable of the Pounds in Lukan Narrative and Economic Context: Luke 19:11-28," *CurTM* 39 (2012):442-48. Braun's paper succinctly demonstrates the influence of all three lines of approach adumbrated in this section, as represented, e.g., by Dowling (liberationist), Vinson (literary), and Rohrbaugh (social-scientific).

55. Much more can be said about the literary connections between the Zacchaeus story and the parable of the minas, as Zacchaeus the tax-collector can be understood precisely as someone who has profited in an exploitative patron-client economic system, just like the servants in the parable were expected to do. Yet he is portrayed as having repented and renounced his former abuses, vowing to make restitutions. Such rejection of the oppressive imperial system stands in sharp contrast with the insistent demand of the nobleman and the compliance of the profitable servants.

does not sit well with the traditional interpretations.[56]

Second, Yoo moves from the immediate literary context of the parable to the wider context of the travel narrative (9:51 – 19:27), where the mentions of Jerusalem as Jesus' destination form another inclusion. Yoo notes that the parable signals the end of the travel narrative, and culminates a series of parables that "implicitly reveal a reciprocity-based patronage system under the Roman Empire."[57] This claim about what these earlier parables reveal can be argued more convincingly. Nevertheless, with the common motif of hoarding versus giving, these parables do create a pattern that implicitly criticizes the nobleman's acquisitiveness.

Third, in terms of context, Yoo traces how the Gospel of Luke handles the motifs of kingship, especially with the contrasting senses of words such as "kingdom" and "authority" when applied to Jesus and to the worldly kings. With Luke's propensity to portray worldly kings negatively, which Vinson also notes, Yoo suggests quite cogently that Luke's attentive audience "would doubt the kingship appearing in the parable is that of Jesus because of its similarity to the worldly kingship."[58] Thus, Yoo argues that Luke's narrative purpose is to set up his audience to ask the question, not when Jesus' reign would begin, but what kind of king he would be, in contrast to the brutal and greed-driven system of the world.

Turning from context to the rhetorical devices employed in the parable itself, Yoo identifies several types, including repetition, parallelism, and chiasm. For an example of parallelism and chiasm, Yoo notes the subtle verbal parallels in the text, and finds two chiastic structures within the parable, with verses 14 and 25 as their respective centres. Interestingly, both verses are unique to Luke's version, and insinuate protest against the nobleman-turned-king.[59] For an example of repetition, Yoo points out that 19:26 is a slightly modified repetition of 8:18, and remarks that the very

---

56. Cf. the similar conclusion in David E. Garland, *Luke* (Grand Rapids: Zondervan, 2011), ch. 59. "This parable should be read as a subtle subversion of Roman imperial ideology that highlights how Jesus' sovereignty differs: he is humble, gives his life for others, and dies forgiving his enemies. This king comes to seek and save the lost."

57. Yoo, "Parable of Minas," 42. These parables include "the rich fool" (12:13-21), "the great banquet" (14:15-24), "the shrewd manager" (16:1-9), and "the rich man and Lazarus" (16:19-31).

58. Yoo, "Parable of Minas," 45.

59. Ibid., 46-49.

different literary context makes Jesus' words in 8:18 ironic when spoken by the nobleman.[60]

As illustrated above, by attending to the literary features of the parable itself and its context in the Gospel of Luke, interpreters using literary approaches are able to recognize an alternative subversive reading, with or without help from liberationist perspectives. Garland sums up this rejection of the traditional reading well when he avers,

> This parable is *not* a salvation-history allegory in which the nobleman going to a far land represents Jesus' ascension to heaven to receive his kingdom, and his return and slaughter of the enemies represents the Parousia and final judgment, no matter how often this interpretation is repeated.[61]

This attentiveness to internal rhetorical features of the parable and its intertextual connections to the rest of Luke, as a feature of the literary approaches, is certainly illuminating. It gives due weight to the Gospel writer as an intentional agent aiming not merely to inform, but to transform the audience. This prioritizing of authorial intent is a helpful counterbalance to the liberationists' emphasis on the contemporary readers' concerns.

However, the literary approaches to this parable tend to assume that literary indicators for an alternative meaning are all Lukan in origin, that they can largely be attributed to Lukan shaping of traditional materials. This assumption makes the findings of the literary approaches less relevant for resolving what Jesus' purpose might have been if he told this parable more or less as Luke presents it. For one, the arguments from literary contexts would largely be irrelevant. If we isolate the parable from its literary context in Luke and assume for the sake of argument that Jesus told a parable in very much the same way to common Jews in Roman Palestine on some unknown occasion, can we still perceive any intended irony?[62] While literary observations about rhetorical devices used within the parable are still very helpful for that purpose, the importance of social-scientific ap-

---

60. Ibid., 49.
61. Garland, *Luke*, ch. 59.
62. For the suggestion that the vast majority of Jesus' original hearers would have been farmers, see Rohrbaugh, "Peasant Reading," 33.

proaches becomes particularly evident, as we will see below.

4.3. Social-scientific approaches

The distinctive contribution of social scientific approaches to this parable is information about the contexts of the original audience of Jesus and the Evangelist, and insights into the strategies used to bring about an effect on the audience given those contexts.[63] One of the earlier proponents of such approaches, Richard Rohrbaugh, states that his treatment of the common elements of the Lukan and Matthean versions of this parable focuses "on the social relations implied both in its narrative world and among the several audiences in which it has been heard."[64] He reminds us that parable interpretation requires imagination, and we must be critical of the modern imaginations we might bring to the text, and try to imagine as the ancients did. Furthermore, drawing on anthropologists and pioneers in the field of social-scientific biblical criticism, Rohrbaugh makes a number of sociological observations supportive of an alternative reading, two of which would suffice to illustrate his results.

The first of these observations is that most people in the first-century Mediterranean world lived in an agrarian economy of limited good, as opposed to a capitalistic economy of growth on investment, which was the world of the elites. From the agrarian context, or the peasants' perspective, wealth is a limited resource that can only be transferred and not created. Thus, accumulation of wealth necessarily involves acquiring what belongs to others, often through unjust means. From this perspective, the whole premise of making money grow and amassing wealth in the parable would have been met with disapproval by most in the audience except the urban elites.[65]

Second, citing Moses Finley's interpretation of the ancient Roman sources closer to our period, Rohrbaugh pegs legal interest rate at 12%

---

63. For a definitive work on social-scientific criticism, see John H. Elliott, *What Is Social-Scientific Criticism?*, GBS/NTS (Minneapolis: Fortress, 1993). See also Ernest Van Eck, *The Parables of Jesus the Galilean: Stories of a Social Prophet* (Eugene, OR: Wipf & Stock, 2016), 171, n. 1272.

64. Rohrbaugh, "Peasant Reading," 32.

65. See the textual evidence for such disapproval, even among what could be considered elite class, in Rohrbaugh, "Peasant Reading," 34-35.

then, when even rates well less than 50% were considered excessive. Such indications of social realities in the world of the New Testament would make the 500-1000% gain over apparently a short time outrageously high in Luke, likely evoking "an astonished gasp" from the audience.[66] On the basis of this information, not only would the rhetorical effect of this stratospheric profit be surprise and shock, it would likely insinuate profiteering or even extortion.

More recently, John Pilch basically reiterates Rohrbaugh's social-scientific argument, but is more explicit in his view that both Matthew and Luke took the initially ambiguous parable to an allegorical direction, especially in the case of Luke.[67] However, we cannot assume that Jesus only spoke one form of the parable with one intended purpose, from which form the Evangelists then developed their own forms and appropriated for their own purposes. Granted that the Evangelists evidently adapted their traditional materials into their literary frameworks with their rhetorical purposes, it cannot be reliably determined that the elements that are different between the two versions are totally the Evangelists' artistic inventions, disconnected from Jesus' original telling of the parable(s). Furthermore, Pilch's view that Luke took the parable into an allegorical direction begs the question of how Luke's parable should be interpreted. As this paper has been showing, a non-allegorical reading of Luke's parable is at the very least plausible, and even probably intended.

In view of these points, there is no compelling reason not to apply the contextual insights from Rohrbaugh and Pilch to both Jesus and Luke. As for the Matthean version, its own literary context clearly takes it in the direction of an allegory about Jesus and his eschatological return, for as Vinson aptly points out, "In Matthew's sequence, one would be hard-pressed not to read the absent thief/master/bridegroom as the Son of Man, the Coming One."[68] Whether that is completely attributable to Matthew, or reflects another telling by Jesus for a different purpose, is moot.

More recently still, Ernest van Eck has published some noteworthy articles on social-scientific readings of this parable, and advanced in a num-

---

66. Rohrbaugh, "Peasant Reading," 35.
67. Pilch, "Parable of the Talents."
68. Vinson, "Minas Touch," 72.

ber of significant ways the argument for reading the nobleman negatively.[69] Prior to his social-scientific analysis proper, he argues for delimiting the parable to Luke 19:12b-24, 27 as an integral and authentic unit that stems from Q and reaches towards the earliest layer of the Jesus tradition.[70] By retaining most of the distinctively Lukan materials and all of the materials having plausible connections with Archelaus, in contrast with Rohrbaugh, van Eck is able to show how the parable is a realistic portrayal of the social realities of Jewish Palestine during Jesus' life, including the social situation of slaves, peasants and elites, the economic practices under the Roman client-patron and taxation systems, and particularly the details about Archelaus's life.[71]

With the stage set with more allusions to realistic social and historical conditions than Rohrbaugh chose to cite, more quantitatively and specifically, van Eck proceeds to analyze the parable social-scientifically. He notes the historical allusions, social structures, as well as rhetorical strategies that assume and utilize those aspects of the historical contexts.

In terms of historical allusions, he identifies details of the parable that greatly resemble Josephus's accounts of Archelaus's life. This is very similar to the evidence presented in Section 3 above, but van Eck mentions an additional allusion that further strengthens the impression that the parable, by alluding to Archelaus, is a parody and not an allegory.

Citing Stephen Llewelyn, van Eck relates that Roman imperial taxation was entrusted to the cities, while slaves were forbidden to be tax collectors in Judea. Yet according to Josephus, appointing his slaves tax collectors for his own enrichment was precisely among the charges Archelaus' unwilling subjects levelled against him.[72]

> And, besides the annual impositions which [Archelaus] laid upon ev-

---

69. Van Eck, "Do Not Question My Honour." Revised and updated in Ernest Van Eck, "The Minas (Luke 19:12b-24, 27): Protesting for the Sake of the Kingdom," in *The Parables of Jesus the Galilean: Stories of a Social Prophet* (Eugene, OR: Wipf & Stock, 2016), 160-72. Van Eck, "Social Memory and Identity."

70. Van Eck, "Minas," 162-64.

71. Ibid., 164-65.

72. Van Eck, "Minas," 164-65. Stephen R. Llewelyn, "Taxation," in *A Review of the Greek Inscription and Papyri: Published 1984–85*, ed. Stephen R. Llewelyn (Grand Rapids: Eerdmans, 1998), 47-105.

ery one of them, they were to make liberal presents to himself, to his domestics and friends, and to such of his slaves as were vouchsafed the favor of being his tax gatherers, because there was no way of obtaining a freedom from unjust violence, without giving either gold or silver for it. (Josephus, *Ant.* 17.308 [17.11.2])

As van Eck suggests, this and other allusions to Archelaus plausibly reflect the collective memory of Jesus' Palestinian audience.[73] When they heard of a nobleman entrusting money to his slaves to earn exorbitant profits, and rewarding their high performance by granting them authority over cities, Jesus' audience, especially the non-elites, would probably associate the story with the exploitative and predatory loan system and the city-based and state-sanctioned tax rackets they were living under.

Regarding social structures, van Eck agrees with Luise Schottroff that it is the structure revealed by the historical allusions that is key, not the specific person they point to.[74] He accepts her view that the Archelaus allusions would have reminded the audience of the unfair system they were all too familiar with, of wealthy and powerful elites exploiting the poor and powerless non-elites.[75] By making this move, van Eck is able to clarify that

---

73. For an analysis of this parable as containing Jesus' social or collective memory about Archelaus, just as Josephus's two versions contain his social memory, used decades later than Jesus for two different purposes, see Van Eck, "Social Memory and Identity." For the rhetorical strategy of this parable to work, Jesus' audience needed to share that collective memory, which certainly seems probable. That may not be true for the non-elite audience of Luke's Gospel. But they would likewise recognize the patron-client system elsewhere in the empire. The elites among Luke's intended audience, Theophilus for one, may possibly be aware of some of the political scandals from Palestine. It would be interesting to explore how they might have heard the parables and what the intended rhetorical effect might have been.

74. Van Eck, "Minas," 165-66. This is in spite of his agreement with Jeremias that Jesus probably had the Archelaus story in mind when telling the parable.

75. Ibid. On the social opposition between elites and non-elites, see also Jacobs Theuns, "Social Conflict in Early Roman Palestine: A Heuristic Model," *Neot* 52 (2018): 115-39. Theuns, applying a social-scientific model of the conflict between elites and non-elites as a heuristic instrument on Luke 19, cogently concludes that since the Zacchaeus narrative and the entry narrative both take the non-elite perspective, so does the parable, leading him to conclude on page 134, "Jesus is not the client Throne Claimant. Rather, he is the socio-political antithesis of the Throne Claimant. If Jesus is the antithesis of what can be expected from Roman client-kings, it invites the reader to ponder with Luke the ways in which he differs from the socio-political norms of the day."

the parable was and is able to challenge the wider social, economic, and political structure, and not just one particularly notorious individual in the past.

With respect to rhetorical strategies, van Eck singles out the description of the third slave as the key to this parable's interpretation. Contrasting the violent and lethal reprisal the rebellious subjects receive with the relatively mild rebuke and punishment the third slave gets, van Eck perceives the parable's intent to contrast two ways of protesting against the exploitative system, one of which would literally be a dead-end.[76] Citing James C. Scott, van Eck interprets the parable to say that the only non-suicidal way to protest the system is to use "hidden transcript" or "coded talk". In that sense, this parable is a form of coded talk by Jesus.[77]

Van Eck's contributions, as illustrated above, allow him to conclude as follows:

> When the parable is read in a 30 CE context as a parable of Jesus the Galilean, with the help of the insights of social-scientific criticism, and when the strategy of the parable is taken seriously, the parable of the Minas is not about a man who leaves and then returns to judge those who were entrusted with the "gifts" he bestowed on them before he left (alluding to the ascension of Jesus, his parousia, and his judgment). It is not a parable about two good slaves and one bad slave. The parable is about the exploitative normalcies that were part and parcel of first-century Palestine: it is about the elite constantly seeking more honor, power, and privilege; it is about members of the elite using their power to exploit; it is also an example of the way the exploited could resist.[78]

As is the case with the liberationist and literary approaches, the social-scientific approaches outlined above have their distinctive values and limitations. They offer the strongest attempt to read the texts in their original contexts, trying to clarify the worlds shared by the communicators and their first audiences. Even the analyses of rhetorical strategies focus on

---

76. Van Eck, "Minas," 166.
77. Ibid., 166-67.
78. Ibid., 165. In the earlier version of this essay, van Eck is more specific about the premise of this conclusion, that it lies in the inclusion of the Archelaus narrative. Van Eck, "Do Not Question My Honour," 6.

the original contexts. However, it too needs to be supported by other approaches and sources. The importance of ancient texts and archaeology, for example, along with anthropological research and social-scientific models, inform practitioners in their analysis of ancient social realities.[79]

While details of interpretation vary among and within the approaches surveyed in this section, together they amount to a substantial cumulative argument for reading the nobleman as a negative figure.

The liberationist approaches focus on the parable from the perspective of contemporary marginalized readers. The literary approaches focus on the parable's internal rhetorical devices and its literary connection with the whole Gospel, assuming a coherent theological outlook and intent from the author. The social-scientific approaches focus on the historical and social contexts of the original communicative act, and the rhetorical strategies that assume those contexts. As seen above, not all approaches rely on making the Archelaus connection, but none is incompatible with it. Moreover, without Luke's literary context or a modern ideological lens, allusions to Archelaus would be the clearest rhetorical signal to Jesus' original hearers that he was being ironic.

So, these historical details about Archelaus, supported by an emerging consensus rehearsed above, demand a reconsideration of the parable's meaning, which I will outline below by returning to Blomberg's model cited in the beginning of Section 2.

4.4. Revising the referents in Blomberg's model

Key to parable interpretation is the identification of referents in the parable. Although Blomberg himself follows a traditional allegorical reading, his typical three-point model is still helpful here for developing an alternative allegorical reading that turns the traditional reading on its head. First, instead of identifying the nobleman as Christ, what if he represents evil worldly tyrants instead?[80] A reversal of value at the top of Blomberg's

---

79. For an example of how archaeology may inform the interpretation of this parable, see Joseph Anthony Giambrone, "A Note on Luke's Parable of the Minas and the Ancient Practice of Burying Coin Hoards," *NTS* 65 (2019): 589–97.

80. For how reversing the evaluation of the authority figure should revise the assessment of other figures in the parable, even though some scholars who recognize the negative aspects of the nobleman still interpret the third servant negatively, see Dowling, *Taking Away*

three-point model would have a domino effect on the value of the other two points, flipping them from positive to negative and vice versa.

Consequently, the profitable slaves whom the nobleman praises would refer to the tyrants' collaborators, taking part in their exploitative political-economic systems. They take the spot of the negative subordinates in the model. Conversely, the unprofitable slave rebuked by the nobleman would be among the passive resisters who refused to participate in the tyrants' exploitation, and thus got sidelined (not otherwise punished in the parable!). There are good reasons to put him in the positive spot in this upside-down parable, since he is the focal subordinate figure, and his passive resistance was generally the path that Jesus and the early church chose.

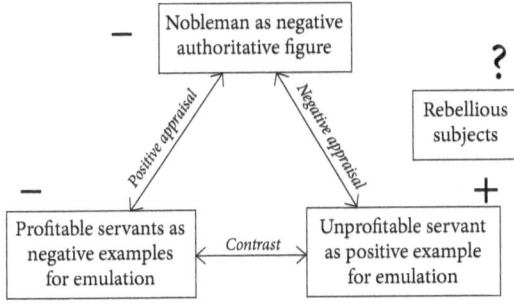

Fig. 2. Alternative interpretations represented by Blomberg's model.

The most difficult to place are the citizens who openly oppose the nobleman. In this reading, they would refer to those who actively opposed such puppets of the empire and were killed for their rebellions.[81] Do they belong to the positive or negative subordinates in the model for this parable?[82] One possibility is that they only serve as background details to

---

the Pound, 50.

81. The most extreme of these would include the zealots and others who eventually instigated the First Jewish War of the first century, with devastating results for the Jewish people and institutions. The militaristic ferment leading to that outbreak was certainly known to Jesus, and by the time Luke included this parable in his Gospel, the movement was even more notorious, if it had not already met its violent demise.

82. Liberationist readers of this parable would put both active and passive resisters into the positive subordinate category, and the collaborators in the negative. E.g., see Dowling, "Hearing the Voice of Earth," 44–45.

characterize the nobleman, and therefore, do not need to be placed in the Blomberg triangle. Otherwise, we have to group them with the others at one of the two subordinate spots, as the Blomberg model allows.

According to this model, characters in the positive spot are meant for emulation and those in the negative spot are counter examples. So, the question becomes, are the active resisters worthy of emulation because they also resist evil? Or is their approach another incorrect way to respond to the oppressive system, just as collaboration is incorrect?

Although the active resisters are not explicitly condemned in the parable, especially if the nobleman is read as a negative figure, their horrible fate does seem to be a caution against taking their course. Nevertheless, laying down one's life for the right kingdom is precisely what Jesus is about to do in Luke's narrative. The question might then be, for whose kingdom am I willing to die, and in what way?

There is a genuine ambiguity about whether the parable puts forward active resistance against evil political rule and oppressive power as a live option for the followers of Christ the King. What is clear in this reading of the parable is that complying with an evil system is identifying with evil, while direct confrontation with ungodly political power may cost one's life, as exemplified by Bonhoeffer and countless others.

5. Conclusion

Notwithstanding the strong case presented for an alternative reading of this parable based on a negative evaluation of the nobleman, the goal of this paper is not to invalidate all other options, especially the traditional readings. In the final analysis, which interpretation we take depends much on our perspectives and presuppositions, now as well as then, and at all times in between.[83] A healthy dose of self-awareness and humility is warranted in exegesis, especially when the conclusions are as divergent as shown.

Be that as it may, what can be said in conclusion? At the very least, as another beloved Regent professor, Eugene Peterson, helpfully points out, this parable challenges the expectations of what Jesus' kingdom is like.[84]

---

83. For using this parable to illustrate changes in interpretations through history, see Alan Cadwallader, "The Building of Awareness of Hermeneutics through the History of Interpretations of the Bible," *Colloq* 33 (2001):3-21.

84. Eugene H. Peterson, *Tell It Slant: A Conversation on the Language of Jesus in His*

What if Jesus Is Not in This Parable?

Going further, Amy-Jill Levine aptly avers,

> When we seek universal morals from a genre that is designed to surprise, challenge, shake up, or indict and look for a single meaning in a form that opens to multiple interpretations, we are necessarily limiting the parables and, so, ourselves.[85]

So, the value reversal this paper argues for is one among multiple interpretations. If this value reversal is accepted,[86] the parable provokes reflection on what sort of king Jesus is and what kind of kingdom he brings, as well as how his followers are to live in response. It uses a notorious example that the ancient recipients were familiar with, and yet might have hoped to achieve themselves—conquest by force and subjugation of the enemies. As modern readers, would we conform to the world of systemic oppressive power and exploitation, or would we resist it in spite of the threat of losing all, including our lives? If so, in what way?

Stories and Prayers (Grand Rapids: Eerdmans, 2008), 145 55. However, his reading of this parable is perhaps not slant enough in light of the discussion here.

85. Amy-Jill Levine, *Short Stories by Jesus: The Enigmatic Parables of a Controversial Rabbi* (New York: HarperOne, 2014), 4. True to her words here, she offers both a traditional and a non-traditional interpretation in her own commentary on this parable, Amy-Jill Levine and Ben Witherington, III, *The Gospel of Luke* (Cambridge: Cambridge University Press, 2018).

86. Even if the value reversal is not accepted, understanding how this parable alludes to aspects of a Jewish puppet ruler from Second Temple historical sources answers all our initial questions about this parable, and helps us focus on the question that provides the interpretive key: What did Luke or Jesus intend the nobleman to represent?

6

Faith in Greek Isaiah

Ken M. Penner

There is a tendency in some Christian circles to contrast two biblical means of salvation: the New Testament's "faith" with the Old Testament's "works". When Paul said, "It is by *faith* that you are saved, not by works, lest anyone should boast" in Greek, he used the word πίστις. This word and its cognates cover the semantic realm that includes faith, trust, belief, and confidence, and its corresponding verb πιστεύω appears in another of Jesus's most famous sayings: "For God so loved the world that he gave his only son, so that everyone who *believes* in him might not perish, but have eternal life." Yet the contrast of "faith" and "works" is far from clear in the biblical text. It has long been recognized that, as Bultmann said, "Trust in God is a basic feature in OT religion ... This is indicated by the prophetic message. Isaiah and Jeremiah in particular demand confidence in God and warn against false confidence in earthly powers."[1] In the book of Isaiah, Zion is judged for being a faithless city; king Ahaz is urged to trust God in the face of threats from Aram and Ephraim. Idols are not to be trusted, and neither is Egypt's military might. But despite the importance of faith in the message of Greek Isaiah, πίστις and πιστεύω together appear there only a dozen times. In other words, although the theme of trust is prevalent in Isaiah, it is not typically expressed using the common New Testament word πίστις.

---

1. Rudolf Bultmann, "Πείθω, Πεποίθησις, Πειθός, Πειθώ, Πεισμονή, Πειθαρχέω, Ἀπειθής, Ἀπειθέω, Ἀπείθεια," *TDNT* 6:5.

Because faith is central to Christian theology, the question of how the earliest Christian commentators interpreted faith when they read about it in Isaiah is of interest. Did they see continuity or discontinuity between the Old Testament and the New when it came to faith? Were the Church Fathers so saturated in the New Testament way of describing Christianity in terms of πίστις that they read this into Isaiah's prophecies even when that word wasn't there? When they did see the word πίστις in Isaiah, did they leap on the opportunity to elaborate on the significance of faith for a right relationship with God? These are questions I begin to address by examining how the earliest complete commentary on Isaiah interpreted faith.

Since 1932 we have had an almost complete early commentary on Isaiah in Greek. That year in Florence a manuscript of the Septuagint was discovered with marginal notes from a commentary on Isaiah written in the mid-fourth century by the famous bishop of Caesarea, Eusebius. Joseph Ziegler edited and published this work in 1975,[2] and it has recently been translated into English.[3]

One might expect a Christian such as Eusebius to interpret the trust he reads about in Isaiah in distinctively Christian ways by recasting the idea in terms of Christian πίστις. However, this expectation is generally not met when we read the commentary by Eusebius. In this essay, I will examine how Eusebius treats three kinds of passages in Isaiah: (1) where Isaiah uses the root πιστ-; (2) where Isaiah uses πεποιθ-; and (3) where Isaiah speaks of faith without using these two word groups. After this examination of Eusebius's treatment of faith when it *does* appear in Isaiah, I identify circumstances under which Eusebius introduces πιστ- words when they are *not* present in Isaiah.

Eusebius Interprets πίστις

First we will determine what Eusebius does when he encounters the root πιστ- in Isaiah.

---

2. Joseph Ziegler, ed., *Eusebius Werke, Band 9: Der Jesajakommentar*, GCS 56 (Berlin: Akademie Verlag, 1975).

3. Eusebius, *Commentary on Isaiah*, trans. Jonathan J Armstrong, ed. Joel C. Elowsky (Downers Grove, IL: InterVarsity Press, 2013).

Isaiah 1:21, 26

Already in the first chapter, it appears in its adjective form, πιστός. In 1:21 and 26, Zion is described as the faithful city. In this Isaianic context, faithfulness and justice are synonyms, and Eusebius simply retained this equivalence without expanding on what faithful might mean. It was a faithful city only because faithful people lived in it (Comm. Isa. 1.19). Eusebius claimed that now that God's people were governed by the Church of Christ, this "city" could once again be called "faithful."

Isaiah (source text)[4]	Comment by Eusebius
How did a faithful city, Zion, full of justice, in whom justice slept, become a harlot, but now murderers are in her? ... after these things it will be called City of Righteousness, Faithful Metropolis Zion. (1:21, 26)	The word teaches that faithful men of old built the city, and thus she was called a *faithful city* (one could also say it was a *city of the faithful*). At that time it was *full of justice* and *righteousness*, since it was then the dwelling-place of virtuous souls. (1.19)

Isaiah 7:9

In Isaiah 7:9, King Ahaz is exhorted to trust. Although Eusebius elaborated a bit, he did so without making any Christian connection to faith.

And the head of Ephraim is Samaria, and the head of Samaria is the son of Remaliah, and if you do not trust, neither will you understand. (7:9)	God appointed the prophet to speak these things to Ahaz himself and to the people under him, urging them on to turn to [God] and to have faith and not to disbelieve what had been said.... But being hard of heart and immersed in demonic deception, he refused and declined [to witness] a sign from God, and in this he proved himself to be *unfaithful* and unruly.... the house of David was exhorted to call on the name of Emmanuel instead of a charm [and to] be confident and *believe* that through him [they] will be saved from those 'two kings.' (1.48)

Isaiah 8:2

In chapter 8, Uriah and Zechariah are made witnesses because they are faithful. Eusebius missed the opportunity to make a point about faith here. In fact, when he quoted this section of Isaiah, he omitted the word

---

4. Translations of Greek Isaiah are taken from the first edition of the Lexham English Septuagint.

"faithful" and just called them witnesses.

... and make certain *faithful* people witnesses for me: Uriah and Zechariah son of Jeberechiah. (8:2)	For this very reason he says about these two men: Make for me witnesses; take a fresh roll of papyrus and get ready to write in it with a man's pen, and the witnesses who [shall] testify for me [shall] be present. (1.48)

Isaiah 17:10

According to Isaiah 17:10, those who abandon and forget God will plant an unfaithful seed. Eusebius put a Christian spin on this prophecy by describing the offending behavior in terms of faithfulness to Christ.

Because you abandoned God your savior, and you did not remember the Lord your helper; because of this, you will plant an *unfaithful* plant and an *unfaithful* seed. (17:10)	This is established in as far as they were not *faithful* to the Christ of God who shone forth from among them first. He says that if you plant this *unfaithful* seed and *unfaithful* plant in your soul, then you will be led astray. But if one should change and plant seed that will grow in the morning light of the gospel in the world, then one is sowing another seed in his understanding. (1.72)

Isaiah 22:23, 25

According to Isaiah 22:23, Eliakim would be set up in a secure place. Eusebius made nothing of the relevant word πιστός, "secure," even though he did interpret the prophecy in terms of Christ.

And I will set him up as leader in a *secure* place, and he will become a throne of the glory of his father's house ... on that day. This is what the Lord Sabaoth says: "The person who has been firmly set in a *secure* place will be removed and will be taken away and fall." (22:23, 25)	And Eliakim could be interpreted as a symbol of the resurrection of God to a new and fresh priesthood, which the resurrection of our Savior established in his church throughout the whole world. (1.82)

Isaiah 28:16

According to Isaiah 28, the one who trusts in the metaphorical "cornerstone" will not be disgraced. But Eusebius spent more time discussing a variant translation "will not be anxious" than he did discussing what it means to "believe". Then he discussed the phrase "they have entrusted themselves to death" without connecting this trust to Christian faith. Instead, in his view, the phrase simply meant "For you *pledged* yourselves to death."

Because of this, this is what the Lord God says: "Look, I am casting into the foundations of Zion a precious choice stone, a valuable cornerstone into its foundations, and the one who *trusts* will certainly not be disgraced. (28:16)	For, the one who *believes* will be patient and wait for the gospel of the word. This gospel is probably what the stone refers to and so would be the same rock concerning which the Savior said: "On the rock I will build my church" ... For you *pledged* yourselves to death and you surrendered yourselves to Hades. (1.93)

Isaiah 33:16

According to Isaiah 33:16, the water of one who lives in a rock cave will be "secure". In other words, he will be provided for. Eusebius overlooked any significance πιστός might have here and instead interpreted this prophecy to refer to ascetics.

This one will reside in a high cave of a strong rock; bread will be given to him, and his water will be *secure*. (33:16)	But, such a one as this who is disciplined in bread and water during the present life will have the glorious contemplation of the kingdom as a reward and fruit of his asceticism. (2.5)

Isaiah 43:10

In Isaiah 43:10, someone is called to be a witness in order to "know and believe and understand"; these are synonyms that have as their object the monotheistic claim "that I am." In Eusebius' view, faith in God was equivalent to *knowledge* of God and *understanding* of God, and nothing more.

"Be witnesses to me, and I am a witness," says the Lord God, "and the child, whom I have chosen, in order that you may know and *believe* and understand that I am; before me there is no other God, and there will be no one with me. (43:10)	For, the reason for the coming of Christ and for the witness of his apostles to every nation was nothing other than the preaching of the knowledge of God to everyone, and *faith* in him and understanding concerning him (τὴν τοῦ ἐπὶ πάντων θεοῦ γνῶσιν καὶ τὴν εἰς αὐτὸν πίστιν καὶ τὴν περὶ αὐτοῦ σύνεσιν) to those who were formerly void of understanding and to those who were *faithless* and disbelieving and to those who were ignorant concerning him, because the eyes of their minds were blinded and closed on account of the godless error of idolatry. (2.24)

Isaiah 49:7

In Isaiah 49:7, it is the Holy One of Israel who is faithful, and he promises to vindicate the lowly. Eusebius made no comment whatsoever involving this word; he only quoted the passage from Isaiah and commented on other aspects of the verse.

Rulers also will worship him for the sake of the Lord, because the Holy One of Israel is *faithful*, and I have chosen you." (49:7)	For, then all will do obeisance to him for the sake of the Lord, his Father, because the Holy One of Israel is *faithful*, the one who has chosen him. But, instead of "and I have chosen you" Symmachus says: "who chose you". (2.35)

Isaiah 53:1

According to Isaiah 53:1, the report (by which the arm of the Lord is revealed) is not believed. Eusebius explained this unbelief as the rejection of Jesus.

O Lord, who has *believed* our report? And to whom has the arm of the Lord been revealed? (53:1)	The prophets of God said these things, as they looked on in astonishment at the *unbelief* of the nation of the Jews and as they contemplated the conversion and obedience of the Gentiles. (2.42)

Isaiah 55:3

According to Isaiah 55:3, the holy things of David are *sure*. Eusebius merely paraphrased this prophecy, without adding any explanation.

I will establish an eternal covenant with you; the holy things of David are *sure*. (55:3)	And the sacred things of David which I promised to him, I will make sure, for I will substantiate my promise. (2.44)

Patterns in Eusebius's interpretation of πίστις

It is evident, therefore, that Eusebius missed more than half of the opportunities to elaborate on the significance of πίστις when he encountered this word in Isaiah. When he did comment on the meaning of πίστις, he did not have a tendency to import Christian theology into Isaiah's prophecies. In the few cases when Eusebius did import Christian theology into Isaiah's use of πίστις, the content of that faith tends to be restricted to something synonymous with knowledge of God and acknowledgement of Christ.

Eusebius Interprets πεποιθώς

The vocabulary of πίστις is only one aspect of faith in Eusebius's commentary on Isaiah. The concept of faith is also conveyed in Isaiah by means of vocabulary other than the characteristically Christian πίστις word family. Specifically, the words Greek Isaiah uses more commonly to express the message of trust are from the root πειθ-, always in the perfect tense, active voice (34 times), usually (29 times) as a participle (πεποιθώς). This kind of trust involves looking to someone or something for help. Yet Eusebius's commentary shows an aversion to the use of this vocabulary. Eusebius used πείθω only 25 percent more often than his source text (that is, only 45 times). By way of comparison, Eusebius used words from the verbal root πιστ- 204 times even though it appears in his source text only 17 times.

In the usage of Eusebius, the πεποιθώς word group generally carries a non-theological meaning, that is, of looking to someone for security (protection and provision). When Eusebius commented on the passages mentioning trust in God, he treated πεποιθώς and cognates as a synonym for such expressions as "fearing the God of the Jews," "receiving the gospel," "receiving Christ," "conversion to God," hanging their hopes on God, "waiting for grace," "being confident in the future life," and considering his promises "unerring". Among these usages, there are two clusters of meaning: (1) that "faith" is a matter of switching allegiances; and (2) that "faith" is an attitude to the future, i.e., a confident hope that God will make things good.

Without an object

That the security conveyed by πεποιθώς can be presented not as a real absence of danger but rather as a perception that there is no danger (what we might call "confidence") is demonstrated by Isaiah 36:4. "This is what the king says, the great king of the Assyrians: 'Why are you confident?'" Here it is a feeling; it is what the inhabitants of Jerusalem are looking for in the face of the Assyrians. Eusebius identified the object of this desire with help and protection.

The feeling of confidence also fits the context of 14:6, where God is confident; Eusebius renders it as "rested confidently".

| After striking a nation in wrath with an incurable blow, hitting a nation with a blow of wrath that he did not spare, he *rested, confident*. (14:6) | And again, instead of "it rested confidently, all the earth," Symmachus says: "it rested and enjoyed tranquility, all the earth." (1.30) |

Confidence is again what the women feel in 32:11 and 47:8, where the expression is in parallel with "hope," thinking no harm will happen to them. Eusebius calls them "boastful."

| Be astounded; grieve, you *confident* women… (32:11) | Therefore, what it is necessary for you to do in response to the things that have been predicted, he continues on and says: "Be amazed; be grieved, you *confident* women." (2.3) |
| But now hear these things, O delicate woman who sits, who *trusts*, who says in her heart, "I am, and there is no other woman. I will not sit as a widow or experience orphanhood." (47:8) | These verses are clearly about the arrogance of the kingdom of the Chaldeans. They describe the boastfulness of the men who ruled among them and record how they thought they would have a rule of immortal and unconquerable power. But, he says, at one and the same time, loss of husband and the death of children *shall come upon you*; the husband representing the one who rules among you and your children representing [20] your subjects. And these things *shall come upon you* all at once, and you shall be shown forth to be both a *widow* and *childless*. And these things shall happen to you not only on account of the prophecies but also *on account of the abundance of your witchcraft and your enchantments*. For, you placed your hope in them, and you were not only insolent but even said: *I am, and there is no other*. (2:32) |

Isaiah 32:17-19 says God's people will be secure. Eusebius interprets this to refer to "the conversion of the unbelieving nations to God." Although the prophecy in Isaiah might refer to a feeling, this time Eusebius interprets it as an objective reality.

| [17] And the deeds of righteousness will be peace, and righteousness will control rest, and they will be *secure* until eternity. [18] And his people will dwell in a city of peace, and they will dwell *confidently*, and they will rest with wealth. [19] And the hail, if it comes down, will not come upon you, and those who dwell in the forests will be *secure*, as in the plain. (32:17-19) | Therefore, he introduces similar things to those in this context when he says that in the place that was once a desert, "judgment and righteousness will rest," and there will be "works of righteousness" there. And he also says that in this very desert, "they will be *confident* forever; and his people will dwell in a city of peace." For, instead of that great and splendid city being demolished, God will establish another city, the church catholic, and he foretells the godly administration that will be in her. (2.32) |

With God as the object

When there is an *object* of the trust, that is, when Isaiah says someone trusts *in* something or someone, *God* is the object of the trust most of the time.

Isaiah 8:14, 17

Eusebius identified those who trust in 8:14 and 17 with "those who receive the gospel and who have been taught life according to the new covenant" and "the same ones who wait for grace through Jesus Christ" (1.52).

And if you *trust* him, he will become a sanctuary for you, and you will not encounter him as an obstacle of stone or like a fall from a rock. (8:14) ... "I will wait for God, who turned his face from the house Jacob, and I will *trust* him. (8:17)	"those who receive the gospel and who have been taught life according to the new covenant" and "the same ones who wait for grace through Jesus Christ." (1.52)

Isaiah 12:2

He made nothing of it in 10:20, but in 12:2, he commented, "now the Egyptians themselves have received the Christ of God" (1.64).

My God is my savior; I will *trust* him, and I will not be frightened (12:2)	... now the Egyptians themselves have received the Christ of God. (1.64)

Isaiah 17:7–8

In 17:7–8 he claimed that Isaiah "prophesies the conversion of the whole world to God" (1.72), and it is the prophet who trusts God in 33:2 (2.4).

On that day a person will *trust* the one who made him (17:7)	[Isaiah] prophesies the conversion of the whole world to God. (1.72)

Isaiah 50:10

Eusebius made nothing of trusting God in 36:7 and 37:10. To the mention of trust in 50:10 he added, "Only come and obey, and trust in the one who promises you salvation" (2.37).

| You who walk in darkness and have no light, *trust* in the name of the Lord and lean upon God! (50:10) | Those who walk in darkness and have no light, *trust* in the name of the Lord and lean on God. Only come and obey, and *trust* in the one who promises you salvation. (2.37) |

Isaiah 58:14

On the basis of 58:14, Eusebius explained that trusting in the Lord means "being confident in the future life and maintaining his promises to be unerring" (2.47). He did not describe trusting in God as an attitudinal change.

| ... and you will *trust* the Lord, and he will bring you up to the good places of the earth, and he will feed you with the inheritance of Jacob your father, for the mouth of the Lord has spoken these things. (58:14) | And so you shall *trust* in the Lord, being confident in the life to come and maintaining his promises to be unerring. (2.47) |

With something other than God as the object

Besides trusting in God, Isaiah described only one person as worthy of trust. Trust is properly placed in God's appointed leader Eliakim in 22:23-25 (mentioned earlier). "And I will set him up as leader in a *secure* place, and he will become a throne of the glory of his father's house ... on that day. This is what the Lord Sabaoth says: 'The person who has been firmly set in a *secure* place will be removed and will be taken away and fall'" (22:23, 25). Eusebius says that Eliakim represents resurrection of a new priesthood (1.82).

Other objects of trust are condemned. Trust is misplaced in idols (17:8), a lie (28:17; 30:12), things without avail (30:15; 59:4), and humans (20:5, 6; 30:3, 32; 32:3), especially their military might (31:1; 36:5-6, 9).

And they will certainly not *trust* the altars or in the works of their hands, which their fingers made, and they will not look to the trees or their abominations (17:8)	Trusting in idols is what Gentiles did "before they turned to fear the God of the Jews." (1.23)
And I will turn judgment into hope, and my mercy into balances, and those who *trust* a lie in vain; for a storm will not pass by you. (28:17)	They deceived themselves and expect another human Christ and tell mythic tales about him. (2.48)
And, being inferior, they will be ashamed because of the Ethiopians, whom the Egyptians *trusted*, who were an honor to them. (20:5)	They hung their hopes on men rather than the God of the whole world. (1.78)

Woe to you who go down to Egypt for aid, who *trust* horses and chariots (for they are many) and on horses (an exceeding multitude) but did not *trust* the Holy One of Israel and did not seek the Lord. (31:1)	And, through the whole history which has been discussed above, the word teaches that, in times of persecutions, when it may be that God judges his people or even delivers over his church to those who harass the service of God, it is necessary not to withdraw from the inspired *faith*, neither to abandon *trust* in God, nor to give up hope of reconciliation with God, nor even to desert the Egyptian way of life, but simply to desert the life of idolatry. For many in such times fall away from the word of true religion and attach their hopes on the aid of idolaters. (2.1)

Eusebius's comments explain that trusting in idols is what Gentiles did "before they turned to fear the God of the Jews" (1.23). Those who entrust themselves to death will receive God's wrath (1.93). He commented that Isaiah mentions trusting in vanities because "they deceived themselves and expect another human Christ and tell mythic tales about him" (2.48). Eusebius agreed with Isaiah in condemning misplaced trust in humans, but he rarely elaborated. The largest elaboration Eusebius provided is his comment on Isaiah 31:1, quoted above (2.1).

Patterns in Eusebius's interpretation of πεποιθώς

Because Eusebius did not often speak of faith with vocabulary other than these two word groups, πίστις and πεποιθώς, we can now summarize his treatment of "faith" when he encountered it in Greek Isaiah. Just as with πίστις, Eusebius did not tend to import Christian theology into Isaiah's prophecies. Rather, Eusebius generally used the word πεποιθώς with a non-theological meaning, that is, to convey looking to someone for security (protection and provision).

Eusebius Imports πίστις

Besides Eusebius' treatment of faith when he encounters it in Greek Isaiah, there is another piece of evidence for his understanding of faith: namely, what Eusebius intended when he introduced πίστις where that word did not appear in the text on which he was commenting.

In such places where Eusebius brings in πίστις without being prompted by that vocabulary in his source text, we can gain some idea of what Eusebius himself considered πίστις to be. This importation happens dozens of times, and the pattern can be summarized with some representative examples.

In Eusebius' usage, πίστις in Christ is comparable to a religion (1.73). Believing in him means switching allegiance and no longer blaspheming (1.73). There is a sharp line between the faithful and the unfaithful (1.75), and by the "faithful" Eusebius meant Christians (1.83). The church believes in the Lord (2.19). Faith is synonymous with reverence and acknowledging the Lord (1.76), with receiving him (1.26) and his word (1.63, 2.23) and the grace that comes through him (2.8). Faith especially distinguishes those Jews who became Jesus' followers (the apostles are specifically mentioned three times, in 1.32, 1.63, and 2.20) from those who did not. Faith means calling on Emmanuel (1.49). It is something one either attains, like excellence, or otherwise falls into unfaithfulness, like evil (1.81). It means receiving salvation (1.54). Faith is effected by fulfilment of prophecy (2.57); it involves believing the threats (1.36) and predictions (1.78) of the prophets (2.13), and the divine teachings (1.86), which appear to refer to the New Testament or perhaps Christian doctrine generally.

In Eusebius' view, the reward for faith in God is the kingdom of heaven (2.29). Nevertheless, he maintained that not everything is perfect for those who believe; they still need their earthly-mindedness done away with (1.62). However, the alternative to believing in God is to serve other kings (1.49) or even to perish (1.26). In other words, having faith in God could almost be synonymous with being a Christian, if it were not for one instance, in which πίστις is a synonym for hope (2.14).

I find that although Eusebius rarely introduced words from the πεποίθως group into his commentary, he often did mention πίστις where no πίστις was found in his source text. These instances reveal a pattern regarding what Eusebius himself thought πίστις was.

In Eusebius' usage, πίστις is not an attitude toward a person or things that corresponds to what we would call trust, the theme of the Jewish scriptures and Jesus. Nor is it a belief system like that referred to as "the faith" in the Pastoral Epistles of the New Testament, although this meaning is relatively common. Instead, Eusebius used πίστις primarily to refer to the acceptance or rejection of the divine Christ. In most cases, πίστις describes assent to Christ, particularly in recognizing pointers to Christ in the scriptural prophecies. Conversely, the unfaithful are those who do not acknowledge Jesus as the divine Christ, and are identified with the disobedient, rebels, and rejecters.

Conclusion

The patterns that emerge indicate that Eusebius did not have a tendency to import Christian theology into Isaiah's uses of πίστις, that Eusebius retained the generally non-theological use of the verbal root πειθ- in Isaiah, and that Eusebius did not often speak of faith with vocabulary other than these two words groups.

Eusebius tended not to connect passages in which the root πιστ- appears in Isaiah with the πίστις that Jesus and the apostles advocate for so prominently in the New Testament. In five passages, Eusebius did not add to what Isaiah says about πίστις (Isaiah 8:2; 22:23, 25; 49:7; 55:3). In two cases, Eusebius did add an interpretation about faith, but it was not distinctively Christian (Isaiah 1:21; 7:9). Only in five cases did he add some Christian interpretation (Isaiah 17:10; 28:16; 33:16; 43:10; 53:1).

What I draw from this pattern is that Eusebius was not concerned with many of the things modern theologians are interested in: the philosophy of faith, or sociological effects of faith, or the ethical implications of faith. He was not excited about the theme of trust in the Jewish scriptures to the point that he went looking for it in the prophet Isaiah. If anything, the thing he was seeking in the prophet Isaiah was an explanation for the Jewish rejection of the one he saw as their Messiah. He was concerned with the boundary between Christianity and other ways of viewing the world, in particular Gentile paganism and non-Christian Judaism. Ed Sanders famously said about the Apostle Paul's letters, "This is what Paul finds wrong in Judaism: it is not Christianity."[5]

Eusebius did the same with faith in Greek Isaiah. He did not *recast* the theme of trust in terms of Christian πίστις. Rather, he *ignored* the theme, and recast Christian πίστις in terms of assent to unspecified distinctively Christian doctrines.

---

5. E. P. Sanders, *Paul and Palestinian Judaism: A Comparison of Patterns of Religion* (Philadelphia, PA: Fortress, 1977), 522.

7

Paul's Letter to the Philippians

Alliance Groups within the Textual Tradition

James M. Leonard

One of my best academic experiences was serving as Sven's Teaching Assistant for his Biblical Exegesis course that he taught with Bruce Waltke, c. 1990. Along with a student-oriented passion, Sven brought a great love for Paul's letter to the Philippians, which was the focus of the NT section of this premier course. Even more evident than Sven's love for Philippians was that he took seriously Paul's words, "In your relationships with one another, have the same mindset as Christ Jesus" (Phil 2:5). Sven was all about establishing and building relationships, and still is. Perhaps, then, it is fitting that this Festschrift article is all about relationships, albeit relationships of *manuscripts* behind our critical texts of Philippians.

In those days at Regent College, there were three faculty members with text-critical specializations: Gordon Fee, Bruce Waltke (see his Harvard PhD dissertation, *Prolegomena to the Samaritan Pentateuch*), and our own dear Sven (see his Glasgow PhD monograph, *The Greek Text of Jeremiah: A Revised Hypothesis*). I am pleased to celebrate Sven as one of my mentors, with this text-critical perspective of a Pauline letter that he continues to model for us daily.

Goals

This is no attempt to create a genealogical history of the text. Mine is a simpler task—to show that a given manuscript has a strong or weak affinity with another, so that we might come to know a manuscript by its kinfolk or friends. In doing so, we might make more manageable the seemingly endless list of manuscript numbers that tend to convolute our critical apparatuses and discourage non-specialists. In the process, we will discover a plethora of unmined textual data helpful in characterizing a manuscript.

Materials

For any given variation unit in Philippians, one may count around 500 manuscripts that divide their support between two or more readings.[1] For a variation unit in Phil 1:3, for example, the massive work *Text und Textwert* (TuT) documents 583 Greek manuscripts in support of the reading adopted by our critical text (ευχαριστω τω θεω μου), and 16 other witnesses in support of six alternative readings.[2] To document the history of the text, the 28th edition of Nestle-Aland *Novum Testamentum Graece* (NA28)[3] has selected 28 of these hundreds of manuscripts to be "Consistently Cited Witnesses" for select variation units in Philippians.[4] These Consistently Cited Witnesses are the manuscripts represented by numbers and letters in the NA28 apparatus and on which our study in Philippians focuses:

> P16 P46 P61 01 02 03 04 06 010 012 016 018 020 025 044 075 0278 0282
> 33 81 104 365 630 1175 1505 1739 1881 2464[5]

---

1. Citations from versions and patristics would increase this number. The complexities of assessing versional and patristic readings—and especially early readings, rightly incites uncertainty in adducing their support for a variant. Although I have collected and noted versional and patristic data cited by NA28 in a larger project on Philippians, I deem them only secondarily interesting for the focus of this article.

2. *Text und Textwert der griechischen Handschriften des Neuen Testaments: II. Die paulinischen Briefe.* Kurt Aland, editor. Institute for New Testament Textual Research (INTF), Berlin: Walter de Gruyter, pp. 566-567.

3. Edited by Barbara and Kurt Aland, Johannes Karavidopoulos, Carlo M. Martini, and Bruce Metzger (Stuttgart: Deutsche Bibelgesellschaft, 2012).

4. NA28 actually lists 30 Consistently Cited Witnesses for Philippians. Minuscule 1506, however, is mistakenly listed (it preserves nothing of Philippians), and the palimpsest 048 is pervasively illegible.

5. With the discovery of more and more manuscripts, the older system of using alpha-

I examine these 28 Consistently Cited Witnesses in the context of 93 variation units in Philippians.[6] These variation units are listed and keyed for summary reference, with the respective passage address and the reading adopted by NA28, in table 7.1 (see Appendix for tables).

To facilitate the comparison of individual manuscripts to each other, I have adopted the categories used in the Text und Textwert (TuT) series to classify competing readings in a given variation unit. The categories are basic and essential, if not also intuitive. D. C. Parker notes, however, that while the descriptive categories provide "a unique tool for ascertaining information about the text of every manuscript," the system "has been so far largely ignored" (2008, 51):

TuT2: This category is for readings that have been adopted as the Text Reading (Txt Rdg), without the benefit of the majority of witnesses. For our purposes, it represents the text accepted by NA28, and is, putatively, the text from which all other variants of the variation unit derive.

TuT1/2: This category is the same as TuT2, except that these readings have the benefit of support from a majority of witnesses—the Text/Majority Reading (Txt/Maj Rdg).

TuT1: This category is for readings supported by the majority of witnesses (Maj Rdg), but have not been adopted by NA28.

TuT3: This category is for readings that are neither a text reading nor a majority reading. Such readings are designated as Special Readings. A variation unit may have more than one Special Reading, in which case, they are designated TuT4, TuT5, TuT6.... Special Readings as a class is referenced by the siglum TuT3⁺.

---

bet letters to represent specific manuscripts has become cumbersome. Following D. C. Parker's recommendations, I use the Gregory-Aland system (*An Introduction to the New Testament Manuscripts and Their Texts* [Cambridge: 2008, 37]). For basic information on manuscripts, see NA28, Appendix 1, pp. 792-819.

6. Hermeneia commentator Paul A. Holloway counts 102 variation units in Philippians, including four conjectures (*Philippians* [Minneapolis: Fortress, 2017], p. 55). I exclude NA28's first variation unit (συν επισκοποις/συνεπισκοποις), the four conjectures, a very few variation units of singular readings, and on rare occasion, I have combined two adjacent variation units into one, reducing the total number of variation units to 93. In contrast, TuT examines but 11 Test Passages for Philippians.

A variation unit has either a TuT2 reading (Txt Rdg), or a TuT1/2 reading (Txt/Maj Rdg), but not both. Likewise, a variation unit has either a TuT1/2 reading (Txt/Maj Rdg), or a TuT1 reading (Maj Rdg), but not both. TuT2 and TuT3 Rdgs are classed as non-Maj Rdgs. The siglum [pm] (Latin: permulti) indicates a variation unit in which the textual tradition is so evenly divided that there is no clear majority. In Philippians, this occurs but twice (Entries 42[pm] 79[pm]); the Txt Rdg is designated 1/2[pm] while the non-Txt Rdg is designated 1[pm]. The discussion herein builds upon these categories and assumes readers' acquaintance with them.

The system for tracking similarities and differences using the TuT categories is simple. There is no need for proprietary computer software; one might as easily track the data using graph paper.

Analyzing a Manuscript's Text

Authoritative classification of manuscripts by traditional categories of Primary or Secondary Alexandrian, Western, Byzantine or such, is often reported, but with little supporting data evidenced.[7] I have collected extensive data from NA28's 28 Consistently Cited Witnesses in 93 test passages representing the whole of NA28's critical apparatus for Philippians, and now focus on the 11th century minuscule 104 to illustrate the value of the data for assessing a manuscript's text. I have chosen 104 because it is not well known and lacks extraordinary features. The data allows statistical specificity that may supplant what otherwise may appear to be mere vague

---

7. For the Pauline epistles, see Bruce M. Metzger, *A Textual Commentary on the Greek New Testament* (Stuttgart: German Bible Society, 1994), pp. 15*-16*; James R. Royse, "The Early Text of Paul (and Hebrews)" in *The Early Text of the New Testament*, edited by Charles E. Hill and Michael J. Kruger (Oxford: University Press, 2012), pp. 178-180; and Michael Holmes, "Textual Criticism" in *Dictionary of Paul and His Letters*, edited by G. F. Hawthorne, R. P. Martin and Daniel G. Reid (Downers Grove: InterVarsity Press, 1993), pp. 927-932. The classification of manuscripts into *Categories I-IV* by Kurt and Barbara Aland is based on Text und Textwert test passages chosen to distinguish Byzantine manuscripts from non-Byzantine manuscripts (*The Text of the New Testament* [Grand Rapids: Eerdmans, 1987], 106-135). With the exception of the Byzantine text-type, the categorization of manuscripts by traditional text-types has become problematic, so much so that many have abandoned the term. Holmes' pre-publication article "The Text of the Pauline Corpus" in *The Oxford Handbook of Pauline Studies*, edited by Matthew V. Novenson and R. Barry Matlock is accessible online (10.1093/oxfordhb/9780199600489.013.16) and reflects the considerable changes in the discipline over the last two decades generally, and in the reference to text-types in particular.

impressions.

104 preserves readings for all 93 Entries, 63 of which agree with NA28 (68%; in bold):[8]

1 2 3 4 5 6 7 8 9 10 11 **12 13 14 15 16 17 18 19 20** 21 22 **23** 24 **25 26 27 28 29 30 31 32 33 34 35** 36 **37 38** 39 **40** 41 42 **43 44** 45 **46** 47 48 49 **50 51** 52 53 54 55 56 **57** 58 **59 60 61 62 63** 64 **65 66 67 68 69** 70 **71** 72 **73 74 75** 76 **77** 78 79 **80 81 82 83 84 85 86** 87 **88** 89 **90 91 92** 93

104's 68% agreement rate with NA28, highlighted in gray in table 7.2, can be immediately compared to the other 27 witnesses, as the table indicates.

Of the 28 Consistently Cited Witnesses, 104 is ranked last in the upper half in agreement rates with NA28, with 13 other witnesses having higher rates. By NA28 standards, 104's text is not as good or reliable as 1881 or 33, for example, but is still higher than P46's agreement rate.

Of course, each critical edition has its biases. In Philippians, NA28, SBL[9], and THGNT[10] agree in 88 of the 93 test passages, with the five differences delineated as follows, with Robinson-Pierpont's alliances indicated parenthetically:[11]

Entry 22 (Phil 1:24b): NA28 + SBL against THGNT (+ RP)
Entry 24 (Phil 1:27): NA28 + SBL against THGNT (+ RP)
Entry 65 (Phil 3:10): SBL + THGNT (+ RP) against NA28
Entry 69 (Phil 3:12c): [NA28] + THGNT (+ RP) against SBL
Entry 93 (Phil 4:23b): NA28 + SBL against THGNT (+ RP)

---

8. Some of the 28 Consistently Cited Witnesses are not fully extant for all 93 test passages, and a witness's support for a reading is sometimes indeterminable. In such cases, I so indicate by putting the Entry number (i.e., test passage) in gray; see for example Entry 80 in 1881, below.

9. *The Greek New Testament: SBL Edition*, edited by Michael Holmes (Atlanta: SBL, 2010).

10. *The Greek New Testament Published at Tyndale House* (Wheaton, IL: Crossway, 2017).

11. *The New Testament in the Original Greek: Byzantine Textform*, edited by Maurice A. Robinson and William G. Pierpont (Southborough, MA: Chilton Book Publishing, 2005).

104 fares nearly the same when compared to THGNT's text.[12] Moreover, the data may also be applied to detail 104's agreement rate with the Robinson-Pierpont Byzantine Textform. Indeed, 104's 68 agreements with Robinson-Pierpont yield an agreement rate of 73%, five points higher than its agreement rate with NA28 (table 7.3).[13]

The TuT categories reveal more about 104 than just agreement rates with our critical editions. 104's readings may be sorted according to TuT categories that may disclose other textual traits:

- **TuT2**: 11 readings (12%; Entries 8 13 14 20 23 26 32 36 38 66 92)
- **TuT1/2**: 53 readings (57%; Entries 1 2 5 7 9 11 12 15 16 17 18 19 22 27 28 29 30 31 33 34 35 37 40 43 44 46 48 50 51 57 59 60 61 62 63 65 67 68 69 71 73 74 75 77 80 81 82 83 84 85 86 88 90)
- **TuT1**: 16 readings (17%; Entries 3 24 39 41 42^{pm} 45 47 49 55 58 64 72 78 79^{pm} 87 93)
- **TuT3$^+$**: 13 readings (14%; Entries 4 6 10 21 25 52 53 54 56 70 76 89 91)

The combination of TuT2 Rdgs and TuT1/2 Rdgs yields a precise agreement rate with our critical editions. TuT data for 104 also reveals the extent to which its middling text depends on majority readings. Indeed, 104's agreements with NA28 are dominated by majority readings, and not by non-Maj Rdgs (TuT2), revealing a precise measure of Byzantine influence. A comparison of 104 with other witnesses, as in table 7.4, is telling (see appendix).

The chart demonstrates how the tracing of a manuscript's percentage of Txt/Maj Rdgs (TuT1/2) and non-Maj Txt Rdgs (TuT2) helps identify its place in the textual stream from the early text to the fully developed Byzantine text of the High and Late Middle Ages.

---

12. Most agreement rates remain marginally close whether compared against NA28 or THGNT. Some differences are noteworthy: 03's agreements with the Txt Rdg fares 3% better with NA28 than with THGNT; alternatively, 02 fares 4% better with THGNT; the largest percentage difference is 04 which is penalized by 6% if set against NA28, rather than THGNT.

13. For 104's disagreements with RP see Entries 4 6 8 10 13 14 20 21 23 25 26 32 36 38 42 52 53 54 56 66 70 76 89 91 92.

Tracking TuT3 Special Readings can likewise be revealing. Special Readings may be the poorly supported product of scribal idiosyncrasy (e.g., see 104's Special Readings in Entries 2 and 14), or have widespread support that just lacks sufficient justification for its adoption by a critical edition (e.g., Entries 4 and 10). In some instances, 104's Special Readings that are otherwise poorly supported may imply textual consanguinity with supporting witnesses (e.g., Entry 21 where 104 is joined by 03 0278 365 1175 1241 1505 2464). A disproportionate number of Special Readings may imply that the manuscript was produced in a relatively unstable textual tradition, while the lack thereof may reveal the opposite. Most of the 28 Consistently Cited Witnesses have Special Readings of percentages ranging between 15-20%, with some witnesses outside of the range, as table 7.5 indicates.[14]

As control over the manuscript tradition increased, the percentage of Special Readings tend to wane, although even early manuscripts can have a relatively low rate.

The overall data for 104 allows some characterization. Metzger characterized 104 as a Secondary Alexandrian witness, and Holmes agrees. Aland and Aland, based on highly selective test passages, place 104 in their Category III.[15] For Philippians, the TuT data from the indiscriminate 93 test passages indicate 104 is considerably more Byzantine than those manuscripts that have been traditionally deemed Alexandrian—or even Secondarily Alexandrian, calling into question its designation as a Secondary Alexandrian witness.[16] Indeed, there are but eight of the 28 Consistently Cited Witnesses that more consistently reflect the Byzantine text of the High and Late Middle Ages than 104 (630 020 018 1505 075 044 365 1175).

Alliance Groups in Philippians

TuT categories may facilitate the documentation of agreements and dis-

---

14. 0282 preserves only four readings in Philippians, but three happen to be Special Readings.

15. Category III: "Manuscripts of a distinctive character with an independent text... particularly important for the history of the text" Barbara and Kurt Aland, *The Text of the New Testament* (Grand Rapids: Eerdmans 1989), 106.

16. Metzger's list of Secondary Alexandrian for the Paulines include 02 (04) 016 044 33 81 104 326 1739.

agreements between manuscripts,[17] revealing high agreement rates not only between individual manuscripts, but also within groups of manuscripts; thus, TuT data might imply relative textual consanguinity between manuscripts and allied groups, and possibly imply an earlier archetype. One outstanding example is the well-known tenth century manuscript 1739 and its fourteenth century ally 1881.[18] Their readings for the 93 test passages are compared to each other in table 7.6.

1739 and 1881 have 84 agreements in their 92 commonly preserved entries, yielding a strikingly high agreement rate of 91%. This rate is only eclipsed by that of the well-known kindred manuscripts 010 and 012 which enjoy a 99% agreement rate. Not even the three most Byzantine of the 28 Consistently Cited Witnesses have an agreement rate higher than that of 1739 and 1881 in Philippians. What makes their agreement rate even more striking is the four centuries that separate the two.

High agreement rates between witnesses may not be a true indicator of textual consanguinity. The kinds of agreement are important. Note that the chart of combined agreements (table 7.6) differentiates majority agreements (TuT1 and TuT1/2) from non-majority agreements (TuT2 + TuT3⁺) by the representation of non-majority agreements in **bold**. High percentages of TuT2 and TuT3⁺ agreements more strongly indicate textual consanguinity than do high percentages of TuT1/2 and TuT1 agreements, since non-majority readings involve fewer supporting witnesses.

Another indicator of textual consanguinity is the frequency of recur-

---

17. The results of the Text und Textwert method have been documented summary in the TuT series for the Paulines, based on 251 highly selective test passages. The test passages were "chosen primarily to identify non-Byzantine members of the textual tradition and uncover instances of block mixture" (Michael Holmes, "The Text of the Pauline Corpus" in *The Oxford Handbook of Pauline Studies*, edited by Matthew V. Novenson and R. Barry Matlock (10.1093/oxfordhb/9780199600489.013.16; accessed July 13, 2020), p. 6. This extreme bias yields significantly different results and unlikely alliances than the indiscriminate use of all the variation units detailed in NA28's apparatus. Writing in 1995, T. C. Geer laments, "To that end, the [TuT] method still utilizes test passages rather than full collations" ("Analyzing and Categorizing New Testament Greek Manuscripts: Colwell Revisited" in *The Text of the New Testament in Contemporary Research: Essays on the Status Quaestionis*, edited by Bart D. Ehrman and Michael W. Holmes [Grand Rapids: Eerdmans, 1995], 259).

18. See J. N. Birdsall, *A Study of Ms. 1739 and its Relationship to Mss. 6, 424, 1908, and M* (unpublished PhD Dissertation, Nottingham University, 1959); T. C. Geer, Jr., *Family 1739 in Acts* (SBL: 1994).

rence of one manuscript in support of another's Special Readings—those readings that are neither Txt Rdgs (TuT2) nor Maj Rdgs (TuT1/2). In Philippians, 1739 has only eight Special Readings—a low percentage of TuT3⁺ Rdgs relative to the other 28 Consistently Cited Witnesses. Nonetheless, 1881 recurs in seven of 1739's nine Special Readings, three occurrences more than any other recurring witness. Reciprocally, 1881 has but nine Special Readings, with 1739 recurring eight times, two occurrences more than any other recurring witness.

1739 has the more primitive text than 1881. The two disagree in eight Entries (3 6 8 14 22 41 76 87). In six of these, 1739 supports the NA28 reading, against 1881; only in Entries 3 and 22 does 1881 support NA28 against 1739.[19] With the exception of Entry 22, there is no early artefactual support for any of 1881's readings against 1739. Indeed, 1881's other seven disagreements have little to be commended. The archetypal text implied by the affinity between 1739 and 1881 seems to be better preserved by 1739, with 1881 adding a mixture of readings unrelated to the archetype. Thus, when we suspect that 1739 might preserve a secondary reading, we can little expect that 1881 preserves the putative archetypal reading.[20]

Establishing three or more manuscripts as an alliance group requires further consideration. I commend the following standards as reasonable, based on introspection of the data:[21]

---

19. In Phil 1:5, 1739 joins the majority in the omission of the article in the text reading απο **της** πρωτης ημερας αχρι του νυν *from the first day until now* (Phil 1:5). The agreement between 1739 and the majority may be accidental and not genetically significant, so that in this one instance, 1881 may in fact preserve 1739's archetypal text. In Entry 22, 1739 supports the reading adopted by THGNT, while 1881 supports [NA28].

20. This may especially inform the assessment of external attestation for Entry 22 where 1881 supports NA28 against 1739's support for the THGNT text reading.

21. T. C. Geer writes, "Colwell's oft-repeated dictum that MSS of a text-type must agree with each over 70% and be separated from others by at least 10% (Colwell, *Studies*, 59) continues to be a helpful guideline…" and "…Richards is certainly correct in suggesting that one should not anticipate any particular level of agreement among MSS; rather the MSS themselves must set the different levels (Richards, *Classification*, 33-41" ("Analyzing and Categorizing New Testament Greek Manuscripts: Colwell Revisited" in *The Text of the New Testament in Contemporary Research: Essays on the Status Quaestionis*, edited by Bart D. Ehrman and Michael W. Holmes [Grand Rapids: Eerdmans, 1995], 261).

1. A proposed alliance group will consist of manuscripts that have agreement rates with each other of about 75% or more.
2. The agreement rate of the leading manuscript of the proposed group should not be separated by more than 5% difference between its closest ally and the weakest of its leading allies.
3. There should be a three-point separation or more between the agreement rate of the weakest of the leading allies from other witnesses.
4. Three-member alliance groups should have a combined agreement rate near 75%; a four-member alliance group should have a combined agreement rate of about 70%.
5. Textual consanguinity should be evident in average to high rates of non-majority agreements for proposed alliance groups.[22] High rates of non-majority agreements may compensate for marginal agreement rates, as exemplified for Alliance Group 01-02-33-04.
6. Textual consanguinity should be reflected in alliance members' mutual support for each member's Special Readings. Member recurrences in support for Special Readings may imply textual consanguinity more than agreement rates since Special Readings are relatively few in most manuscripts, and recurring support for Special Readings is rarer than support for Txt Rdgs and Maj Rdgs.

These six criteria must be conceived as ideal qualifications, and not as rigid standards.

Alliance Group 01-02-33-04 (B-Prime)

Our first alliance group is led by 01 with its individual leading allies 02 33 and 04. The four allies may combine variously to produce two three-member Alliance Groups (01-02-04 and 01-02-33), and a four-member Alliance Group (01-02-04-33). Regardless the specific formulation, agreement rates and other indicators of textual consanguinity are comparable. We will fo-

---

22. The Alands explanation for not reporting TuT1/2 readings in manuscript profiles, although offered in the context of distinguishing the Byzantine tradition, is instructive: "The reason is pragmatic: readings 1/2 are majority readings. Agreements in these passages [i.e., passages where a manuscript supports TuT1/2 readings] ultimately contribute nothing toward defining manuscript relationships" (*Text und Textwert* IV.1. Das Markusevangelium, p. 23*).

cus on the three-member alliance group 01-02-33, but will also include data for the four-member Alliance Group 01-02-04-33 in those readings that 04 preserves (only 39 of 93 total entries). See table 7.7.

The strength of these Alliance Groups and their textual consanguinity is suggested by

- the four members' high agreement with each other individually:
  - 01 and 02 = 83%; 01 and 04 = 82%; 01 and 33: 82%;
  - 02 and 04 = 84%; 02 and 33 = 79%;
  - 04 and 33 = 84%
- the cohesiveness of the alliance group
  - 01's agreement rate with alliance members is very tight, ranging between 83%-82%;
  - 01's next closest ally not in the group is 1739 which is separated from 01's weakest leading ally 04's 82% agreement rate by 10 percentage points;
- the homogeneity of the alliance group: alliance members have but two leading allies outside of the alliance group[23]
  - 02's fourth leading ally is 81, with which it agrees in 72 of 92 commonly preserved readings (78%);
  - 04's third leading ally is 1739, with which it agrees in 31 of 39 commonly preserved readings (80%).
- the astonishingly high percentage of non-Maj (TuT2 + TuT3⁺) agreements that undergird the alliance
  - 52% of the four-member alliance group's total combined agreements are TuT2 + TuT3⁺ Rdgs
  - 39% of the three-member alliance group's total combined agreements are TuT2 + TuT3⁺ Rdgs

---

23. I count as a manuscript's leading allies those witnesses with highest agreement rates, with a cutoff point wherever three to five percentage points separate the manuscript's leading allies from the next closest witness. 04's leading allies, for example are 33 (84%), 02 (80%), and 1739 (80%). Thereafter, there is a six-point spread from 04's weakest leading ally 1739 (80%) to 04's next closest ally 81 (74%).

- alliance members' prevalent recurrences in support of each members' Special Readings[24]
  - 01 (13 Special Readings): 02: 7x; 33: 6x; 04: 3x
  - 02 (14 Special Readings): 01: 7x; 33: 7x; 04: 3x
  - 04 (6 Special Readings): 01: 4x; 02: 5x; 33: 3x; 33:4x
  - 33 (14 Special Readings): 01: 7x; 02: 6x; 04: 2x

As a practical matter (i.e., for the sake of a shorter siglum), and because these manuscripts are key members of the B-Textual Cluster and identified traditionally with the Alexandrian text-type, I have denominated this alliance group as B-Prime. The siglum B' represents the alliance group when it unanimously supports a reading, while b' indicates only majority support.

Noteworthy is the absence of 03 = B from the alliance group, which is otherwise often regarded as the leading witness in the gospels. The data supporting the B' Alliance Group reinforces that, although 01 and 03 are strong allies in the gospels, they are not as closely aligned in the Paulines, having an agreement rate of only 68%.

Perhaps the most striking aspect of the B' Alliance Group is that it bears unanimous witness to 66 of their 92 (72%) commonly preserved readings. This unanimity may imply an earlier archetype worthy of further investigation. The readings of the alliance group may be sorted according to TuT categories:[25]

- Unanimously supported readings: 67 Entries
  - Non-Maj (TuT2) Rdgs: Entries 3 8 11 13 14 23 25 26 32 36 38 39 41 45 47 49 66 72 76 87 92 (21 Entries)
  - Txt/Maj (TuT1/2) Rdgs: Entries 1 2 7 9 12 15 16 17 18 19 21 28 30 33 34 37 40 43 48 53 56 57 59 61 63 67 71 73 75 77 79 83 84 85 86 88 90 (37 Entries)

---

24. In some cases, an alliance member may have more frequent support from a non-alliance member:

02's top recurring supporting witness is 81 (9x)

04's recurring supporting witnesses includes 06 (4x) which recurs once more than 01 and 33; 010 and 012 recur as often as 01 and 33

33's top recurring supporting witness is 81 (8x)

25. Note that 04's readings are unpreserved for Entries 1-17, 53, and 58-93; and that 33's support is not discernible in Entry 50. Inclusion of 04's readings produces incongruous number counts where 04 differs from the unanimous testimony of 01 + 02 + 33.

- Special (TuT3⁺) Rdgs: Entries 4 10 22 31 52 54 60 70 93 (9 Entries)
  - Note: 04 does not support the unanimous readings of 01 + 02 + 33 in Entries 26 (TuT2) and 48 (TuT1/2)
- Majority witness in support of the non-Maj Txt (TuT2) Rdg:
  - 01 + 02 + 04 against 33: Entries 44 51
  - 02 + 04 + 33 against 01: Entry 20
  - 01 + 02 +33 against 04: Entries 26 48
  - 01 + 04 + 33 against 02: Entry 27
  - 01 + 02 against 33: Entries 55 58 78 91
  - 01 + 33 against 02: 3 Entries 5 6 64 89
  - 02 + 33 against 01: 1 Entry = 20
- Majority witness in support of the Maj/Txt (TuT1/2) Rdg:
  - 01 + 02 + 04 against 33: Entry 29
  - 01 + 04 + 33 against 02: Entry 46
  - 01 + 02 against 33: Entries 69 80
  - 01 + 33 against 02: Entries 27 46 62 82
  - 02 + 03 against 01: Entries 68 74 81
- Majority witness in support of Special (TuT3⁺) Rdgs: (none)
- Majority witness in support of Maj (TuT1) Rdgs:
  - 02 + 04 + 33 against 01: Entries 24 42
- 3 different readings: Entry 65
- Evenly divided:
  - 01 + 04 in support of TuT1/2 against 02 + 33 in support of TuT3: Entry 35
  - 01 + 02 in support of TuT2 against 04 + 33 in support of TuT1: Entry 55

From the TuT data, one may entertain relationship dynamics that might otherwise go unnoticed. For example, although 01 has an agreement rate with NA28 that is only 5% higher than 02 (83% and 78% respectively), 01 joins b' in support of the Txt Rdg more than does 02 at a ratio of 4:3.[26]

An alliance group's unanimous readings proportionately increase the

---

26. 01 with b': 12 entries (5 6 26 27 44 48 51 55 58 64 8978 91); 02 with b': 9 entries (44 51 20 26 48 55 58 78 91).

perceptible weight for external attestation since they more assuredly hold promise of the preservation of an earlier archetype. Thus, B-Prime's unanimous support for the Special Reading Ιησου χριστου against the Txt Rdg χριστου Ιησου in Phil 1:6 (Entry 4) implies that an early archetype—earlier than 01's fourth century date, supports NA28's competing reading. Support for the Special Reading by B', then, is probably more than a matter of some individual manuscripts that might have transposed the words independently.[27]

When an alliance group is divided, its majority can still have prodigious weight for external attestation. The significance of 01 is well known and evokes confidence from users of the NA28 apparatus whenever it supports a given reading. Yet, its weight for external attestation is countered when the other B-Prime members support a competing reading. This is seen in Entry 20 where b' undercuts 01's support for the Maj Rdg (TuT1), and in Entry 24 where b-prime's support of the Special Reading counters 01*'s support of the Txt Rdg (TuT2).[28] While 01 may possibly preserve the archetypal reading, the other three alliance members suggest otherwise.

The considerable significance of Alliance Group B' for establishing the early text is reflected in

- its pronounced tendency to support readings adopted by NA28: The three-member group unanimously supports readings for 67 of their 92 commonly preserved readings (73%), with all but nine of those readings in support of NA28;
- its readings not adopted by NA28 nonetheless have considerable support from other significant early witnesses (Entries 4 10 31 52 54 60 70 93, the weakest of which is Entry 31 [2:2] where B' is amply supported by 016 81 1241 2464).

It goes without saying that all of B-Prime's readings are demonstrably early—preserved in artefactual evidence from the fourth and fifth

---

27. Stephen Carlson argues that in the genitive, "Paul has a strong preference for the order Ιησου Χριστου" (*The Text of Galatians and Its History* [Tübingen: Mohr Siebeck, 2015], 135).

28. Our critical editions are split in this variation unit: NA28 and SBL against THGNT.

centuries.[29]

The archetype that engendered the distinctive text preserved in B' is not only early but tends to comport with characteristics of a "scribally un-improved" text. Examples abound:

- Entry 11 (1:16-17—transposition of the two verses)—B' retains the Pauline chiastic order, prompting Silva to write, "…the variant [TuT1] is a convincing example of the tendency (common in the Byzantine or Majority text) to smooth what may have appeared stylistically awkward to some scribes."[30]
- Entry 14 (1:18a)—B' retains Paul's awkward construction πλην οτι that has been "improved" either by the omission of οτι (Maj) or of πλην (03).
- Entry 25 (1:28a)—B' retains Paul's Koine style that lacks the conjunction μεν that has otherwise been inserted by Maj in conformity with a more classical idiom.[31]

The textual reliability of B' is suggested by its agreement rate with NA28, as in table 7.8.

The ratio of B-Prime's support for the Txt Rdg is nearly 6:1 to that of its support for the reading not adopted by NA28.

The importance of B-Prime's textual reliability might well be emphasized because of its counterweight to the individual manuscripts P46 or 03, or to both of them together—two witnesses whose texts in Philippians may have an unduly high reputation (see B' readings in Entries 4 31 54 60 70).[32] Moreover, and finally, note that B' does not support a single non-Txt Maj Rdg (TuT1).

---

29. Similarly, noting that B' does not support any readings deemed patently secondary is hardly circular reasoning, for the weight of this group's external attestation for any given reading entails nearly automatic significance.

30. Moisés Silva, *Philippians*, BECNT, 2nd ed. (Grand Rapids: Baker, 2005), 66.

31. G. D. Fee, *Philippians*, NICNT (Grand Rapids: Eerdmans, 1995), 159, n. 15.

32. In Philippians, 01 has an agreement rate with NA28 3% higher than 03; 02 33 and 04 trail 03 by 2-6 percentage points, with P46 significantly lower than 01 by 18 percentage points.

Alliance Group 104-365-1175-81 (X-XII Prime)

In Philippians, the tenth, eleventh, and twelfth century manuscripts 104 365 1175 and 81 form a viable Alliance Group. See table 7.9.

This Alliance Group shares at least a moderate textual consanguinity, as suggested by

- the four members' high agreement rates with each other individually:
  - 104 and 365 (87%); 104 and 1175 (82%); 104 and 81 (80%);
  - 365 and 1175 (84%); 365 and 81 (76%);[33]
  - 1175 and 81 (85%).
- the homogeneity of the alliance group; only 1175 has a leading ally outside of the alliance group;[34]
- alliance group members' unanimity in 70% of their commonly preserved entries;
- its preservation of a moderate (or better) percentage of non-Maj (TuT2 + TuT3$^+$) Rdgs (27%);
- the strikingly high recurrences of alliance group members in support of each other's Special Readings:[35]
  - 104 (13 Special Readings): 365: 9x; 1175: 9x; 81: 9x;
  - 365 (13 Special Readings): 104: 11x; 1175: 10x; 81: 9x;
  - 1175 (15 Special Readings): 81: 9x; 365: 9x; 104: 8x;
  - 81 (16 Special Readings) 1175: 8x; 104: 7x; 365: 7x.

As a practical matter, and in reference to the centuries of their origin (tenth, eleventh, and twelfth), I have denominated this alliance group as X-XII', conveying that its moderating text is significant for its preservation of a considerable percentage (27%) of non-Maj (TuT2 + TuT3$^+$) Rdgs at a time when the Byzantine text was ascendant. When the alliance group

---

33. 365 and 81 have the lowest agreement rate (76%) in the alliance group, but even 76% is at least a moderate rate, or better.

34. With its ally 0278, 1175 shares 47 agreements in 57 commonly preserved entries (83%).

35. The only non-Alliance member that is a highly recurring witness in support of alliance members' Special Readings is 075 which occurs eight times in support of 365's 13 Special Readings.

is not unanimous, I denote a majority of the four members in lower case: x-xii'.

Alliance Group X-XII' has a text in Philippians that is relatively good considering its origins in the transition from the Early Middle Ages to the High Middle Ages. Its quality of text is evidenced by

- its pronounced tendency (a 10:3 ratio) to support readings adopted by NA28 rather than those readings unadopted:
  - 52 of the alliance group's 64 (58%) unanimous readings support the reading adopted by NA28 (see below under TuT categories)
  - In striking contrast, only 14 (16%) of its unanimous readings support readings not adopted by NA28;
- its tendency to support demonstrably early readings:[36] The alliance group unanimously supports readings in 64 Entries, all of which are demonstrably early except for those in six entries (47 **58 65 76 87 91**);
- its unanimous rejection of readings deemed patently secondary;[37]
- its consistent support for readings not adopted by NA28 yet have considerable support from other significant early witnesses (Entries 4 10 22 24 42 52 54 70 93).

X-XII Prime's unanimous readings may be sorted by TuT categories:

- Non-Maj (TuT2) Rdgs: 8 Entries = 10% (Entries 14 20 26 32 36 38 66 92)
- Txt/Maj (TuT1/2) Rdgs: 42 Entries = 47% (Entries 1 2 5 9 12 16

---

36. I consider demonstrably early readings those readings with artefactual evidence from the fifth century and earlier. In Philippians, I count 65 demonstrably early readings preserved in the textual tradition and noted in the apparatus of NA28. In some cases, a variation unit may have two or even three demonstrably early readings (e.g., Entry 52 has a reading supported by 03 [IV], another reading supported by 01* 02 04 [IV, V], and a third reading supported by P46 [III]).

37. A case can be made that, in Philippians, one or more readings in the following 48 entries (66 readings in total) are patently secondary: Entries 1 2 3 5 6 8 9 10 11 13 16 17 19 20 23 24 25 26 27 29 30 32 36 37 38 39 40 43 49 50 52 56 59 61 65 66 74 75 76 79 80 82 83 85 86 89 90 92. I do not deny the considerable subjectivity involved in this selection.

17 18 19 22 27 29 34 37 40 43 44 46 50 51 59 61 62 63 65 67 68 69 71 73 74 75 77 80 81 82 83 84 85 86 88 90)
- Non-Txt Maj (TuT1) Rdgs: 6 Entries = 7% (Entries 24 42 47 58 64 87)
- Special (TuT3+) Rdgs: 8 Entries = 9% (Entries 4 10 52 53 70 76 91 93)

Sorting by TuT categories can facilitate searches for vulnerable readings accepted by NA28, and test the strength of X-XII' readings.

Alliance Group 018-020-630 (RP-Prime)

In Philippians, the leading Byzantine witnesses of the 28 Consistently Cited Witnesses are the ninth century majuscules 018 and 020, and the twelfth or thirteenth century minuscule 630. As leading Byzantine witnesses, there is little surprise that they have high agreement rates with each other, but much depends on what Byzantine witnesses might be included in NA28's Consistently Cited Witnesses. The inclusion of 018 and 020 makes sense, for they are the earliest artefactual witnesses to the Byzantine Textform in the Pauline Epistles. The reason(s) for including 630, however, is not self-evident, and given the availability of the large number of Byzantine witnesses from the High and Late Middle Ages, one can imagine that 018 and 020 might have even closer allies than 630.[38] The most that can be said, then, is that of the 28 Consistently Cited Witnesses, 018 and 020 have their highest agreement rates with 630. See table 7.10.

There is evidence to justify the alliance group 018-020-630. Together, the alliance group has a strikingly high total combined agreement rate of 84%. As an alliance group, 018-020-630 unanimously supports Robinson-Pierpont in 77 of 89 commonly preserved entries (87%); accordingly, I have denominated the alliance group 018-020-630 as the RP-Prime Alliance Group (RP').

RP' alliance members have a high homogeneity; that is, alliance mem-

---

38. *Text und Textwert* lists "33 manuscripts whose profiles of variant readings come closest" to 018 (IV. Die synoptischen Evangelien: 1. Das Markusevangelium [Band 1.1], p. 25*), only three of which are included in NA28's Consistently Cited Witnesses: P16 016 and 020; 630 is not listed. TuT's limited and narrow selection of variation units has dramatically skewed the overall profile of P16 and 016, which are otherwise far removed from 018's alliances.

bers' closest allies are other alliance members:

- 018: 020 (88%); 630 (88%)
- 020: 630 (93%); 018 (88%)
- 630: 020 (92%); 018 (88%)

The highly controlled textual environment of Byzantium assures a notably low number of Special Readings for these three witnesses, so that the tracking of frequently recurring witnesses in support of their Special Readings produces no evidence of textual consanguinity. The controlled textual environment also tends to reduce the quantity of non-Maj Rdgs so that all RP' readings are Maj Rdgs (TuT1/2 + TuT1).

The value of conceiving 018-020-630 as an alliance group is two-fold. In practice, the reduction of three not well-known witnesses to the siglum RP' (or rp' to represent a majority of RP') is mentally and representatively convenient. Secondly, in the rare occasions when RP' or rp' supports a reading against Robinson-Pierpont, the disagreement may suggest an older reading that the Byzantine Textform ultimately rejected. There is, in fact, one reading where RP' unanimously supports a non-Robinson-Pierpont text reading (Entry 42[pm]) and five readings where a majority of the RP' Alliance Group supports a reading against the Robinson-Pierpont text. Tracking these readings is manageable with the use of TuT Categories:

- Unanimously supported readings: 75 of 89 commonly preserved Entries (84%)
  - Non-Maj (TuT2) Rdgs: (none)
  - Txt/Maj (TuT1/2) Rdgs: 51 Entries (1 2 3 5 7 9 15 16 17 18 19 21 22 24 27 28 31 34 35 40 44 46 50 51 52 53 56 57 59 60 61 62 63 65 67 68 69 70 71 72 73 75 80 81 82 83 84 85 86 88 90 91)
  - Non-Txt Maj (TuT1) Rdgs: 24 Entries (6 14 20 23 25 26 32 38 39 41 42[pm] 47 54 55 58 64 66 76 77 78 87 92 93)
  - Special (TuT3[+]) Rdgs: (none)
- Majority witness in support of the non-Maj Txt (TuT2) Rdgs: 1 Entry
  - 018 + 020 against: 630 (Entry 8)
- Majority witness in support of the Maj/Txt (TuT1/2) Rdgs: 6

Entries
- 020 + 630 against 018: (Entries 4 33 37 43)
- 018 + 630 against 020: (Entries 10 29 74)
- 018 + 020 against 630: (Entries 48 79[pm])
- Majority witness in support of Maj (TuT1) Rdgs: 3 Entries
  - 020 + 630 against 018: Entry = % (Entry 36 45 49)
- Majority witness in support of Special (TuT3+) Rdgs: (none)

RP' alliance group majority readings that do not support the Robinson-Pierpont text may be sorted according to TuT categories:

- An alliance majority in support of the non-Maj/Txt (TuT2) Rdg
  - 018 + 020 against 630: Entries 8 79
- An alliance majority in support of Special Reading (TuT3)
  - 018 + 630 against 020: Entry 30
  - 020 + 630 against 018: Entry 89

When the alliance is divided, 020 and 630 more often join together against 018, as reflected in 020's higher agreement rate with 630 by 5% higher than with 018.

While RP' is valuable for the history of the NT textual tradition, there is little to commend it for establishing the early text. Rarely is its weight for external attestation perceptible.[39] It attests but relatively few demonstrably early readings relative to other witnesses (56 of 75 = 75%). This contrasts with its relatively high percentage (15%) of readings deemed patently secondary (see Entries 3 23 25 26 32 38 39 49 66 76 92).[40] Moreover, RP' has a pronounced tendency to preserve scribally improved readings; three examples follow:

- In Entry 25 (Phil 1:28a), Paul contrasts a sign's interpretation: to unbelievers, the sign portends destruction, but for believers, it

---

39. One exception is Entry 42[pm] where RP' supports TuT1[pm], joining an impressive array of witnesses already arguably superior to the support for the Txt Rdg.

40. Compare with Alliance Group X-XII-Prime's support for 58 demonstrably early readings out of 64 unanimous readings (91%), and its total rejection of readings deemed patently secondary.

entails salvation. The Txt Rdg does so with only δε in the second element, while RP' supplies μεν in the first element. BDAG notes that μεν "is one of the commonest particles in Homer, Herodotus, et al., but its usage declines sharply in later times, found only 180 times in the NT" (629). Fee thus asserts that the later manuscript tradition "conforms Paul's Greek to a more classical idiom" and that the change "helps to make sense of a difficult clause, but it is scarcely original."[41]

- In Entry 32 (Phil 2:3), Paul urges the Philippians to do nothing out of selfish ambition or vain conceit. The Txt Rdg coordinates both motives with μηδε: μηδεν κατ εριθειαν μηδε κατα κενοδοξιαν, while the RP' reading reduces the conjunction to η. Silva denotes the variant readings[42] as "stylistic improvements" to a construction "though clear, is awkwardly expressed."[43]

- In Entry 72 (Phil 3:14), Paul reports that he presses on *toward* the prize. In the Txt Rdg, the preposition εις is used, while RP' attests επι. Lightfoot asserts that the Maj Rdg "is an obvious substitution for a more difficult reading." Kennedy agrees, and adds that the "explanatory gloss," perhaps was attracted by the directional preposition ανω in ανω κλησεως in the next clause.[44]

Alliance Groups in Practice

In assessing the value of alliance groups, consider Entry 52 (Phil 2:26), which tells of Epaphroditus' longing. Although NA28 cites five competing variants, we focus only on the Txt/Maj Rdg (TuT1/2) adopted by NA28 (and the other 13 editions I have checked) and a Special Reading (unsupported by any of the 14 editions). The NA28 apparatus might be represented as follows (see next page), with the Txt/Maj Rdg depicted above the competing Special Reading (less familiar witnesses are reduced in font size).

---

41. Fee, *Philippians*, 54 n. b; J. B. Lightfoot, *Saint Paul's Epistle to the Philippians*, (London: MacMIllan, 1898), 106.
42. NA28 lists two additional coordinating readings as variants: μηδε and η κατα.
43. Silva, *Philippians*, 109; Fee, *Philippians*, 174 n. 3.
44. Lightfoot, 153; H. A. A. Kennedy, *The Epistle to the Philippians*, Expositor's Greek Testament (Grand Rapids: Eerdmans, rprt 1980), 458.

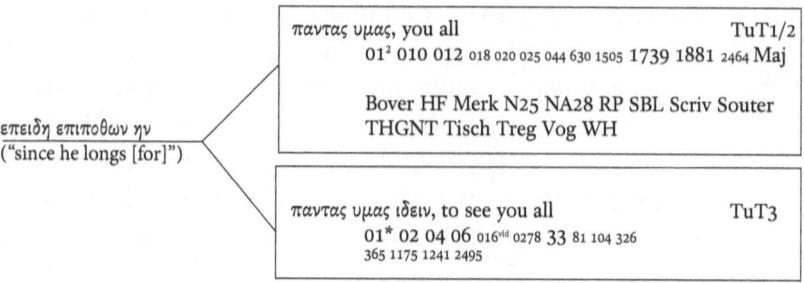

A well-practiced user of the NA28 might first note that the D-Text is split, with 010 and 012 supporting the Txt/Maj Rdg, and 06 supporting the Special Reading. The same user might then quickly discern that Maj (the Byzantine Textform) supports the Txt/Maj Rdg (TuT1/2). Thereafter, users may know that 01* 02 04 and 33, and ℓ739 are significant manuscripts, but often are clueless about the other 17 witnesses (printed in small type for illustrative purposes). Now, consider what an informed user of the NA28 might perceive if they were aware of key alliance groups and how alliance groups might work, if the attestation data from NA28 were depicted differently:

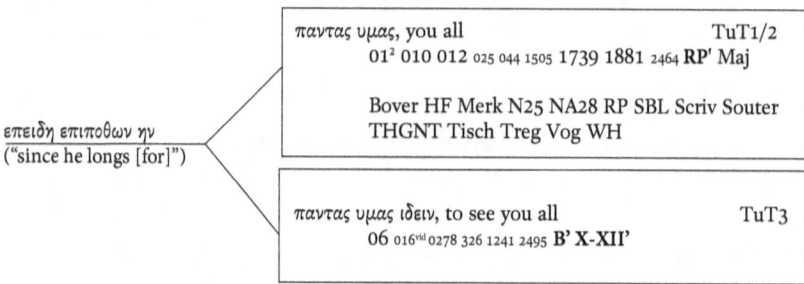

In this second representation of the variation unit, witnesses belonging to alliance groups are represented by their respective sigla (in **bold**). Accordingly, the number of less familiar witnesses has been narrowed from 17 to 9 (in reduced font). Thus, representation of a reading's support with reference to alliance groups does more than facilitate the weighing of external attestation; the use of alliance group sigla may also ameliorate the difficulty of introducing the uninitiated into the complex and specialized field of textual criticism.

Support Networks

Finally, we may increase our knowledge of a given manuscript by tracking data that can lead to identifying its Support Network. Two tables map out P46's Support Network for Philippians; table 7.11 indicates those witnesses in support of P46's readings adopted by NA28, and 7.12 of its readings rejected by NA28.

Much can be garnered from close scrutiny of the two charts. Even without quantifying specifics, one might sense from the first chart what level of support from other witnesses that the editors of NA28 deem generally necessary to adopt P46's readings and contrast it with those readings rejected by NA28. One might also note, for example, that 03 supports P46 44 times in its Txt Rdgs, and B' (unanimously) supports P46 35 times, and b' another 11 times, or that RP' and rp' support P46 29 times, just six more Entries than D-Txt and d-txt. The two charts represent a varying way to depict manuscript relationships to one another—an important goal for our complex discipline.

Summary and Prospective

In a scorching denunciation of our practice of textual criticism, 25 years ago (1995) Thomas C. Geer, Jr. wrote,

> A knowledge of the MSS is equally important for ... writing the history of the NT text. Nonetheless, even though Westcott-Hort clearly and emphatically stated that 'knowledge of documents should proceed final judgment upon readings,' still, more than a century later, few MSS are known with any sophisticated level of precision. Indeed, while it is at present an axiom within the text-critical discipline that MSS are to be weighed rather than counted, the general lack of acquaintance with the MSS themselves invites the simple procedure of counting.... Few are able to evaluate carefully the external evidence for variant readings in the NA or UBS because there is insufficient information given for the MSS presented. As a result, MS citations end up being *little more than a group of letters or numbers at the bottom of the page*. (emphasis added).[45]

---

45. "Analyzing and Categorizing New Testament Manuscripts," p. 253.

If what Geer wrote 25 years ago were true back then, it is ironically truer now since our easy access to manuscript images could hardly have been fathomed a generation ago. Yes, we now have significant monographs on the early majuscules and samplings of data from specific minuscules, and yes, we have identified many traits and tendencies of the scribes of important witnesses. I would suggest, however, that one of the better ways to get to know a manuscript's text is to know its allies.

In the Pauline letters, there is a dearth of research of manuscripts' relationships to one another. Too much hangs on Zuntz's groundbreaking 75-year-old work, and its narrow sampling of 2 Corinthians and Hebrews.[46] For example, Zuntz grouped P46 03 and 1739 together, denominated the group "proto-Alexandrian," writing that they 1) "are elements of one broad and ancient stream of the tradition, which we call 'Alexandrian'" and that 2) the ancestor of 1739 "contained an early form of it as do P46 and 03...," and that 3) their "most outstanding common feature is the presence of 'Western' ... traits...."[47] Such conclusions can hardly be sustained from the 93 text-critical samplings I have checked, based on the testimony of NA28's 28 Consistently Cited Witnesses in Philippians. P46 has a low agreement rate with 1739 (44 of 81 commonly preserved entries = 54%). P46's text is so idiosyncratic that none of the Consistently Cited Witnesses emerge as a viable P46 ally—the agreement rates with other manuscripts are all impressively low;[48] 1739 is but P46's fifth closest ally, and 06 follows as sixth. A testament to its idiosyncratic text is P46's exceptionally large number of Special Readings—26 in all, and while 06 does recur in support of P46's Special Readings, it does so only five times—a far lower percentage than the recurrences of X-XII' members in support of their own alliance members' Special Readings.[49]

---

46. Cf. Geer: "For too long in our discipline, too much has been based on too little" ("Analyzing and Categorizing New Testament Manuscripts", 265).

47. Zuntz concedes that this "proto-Alexandrian" group is not interdependent genealogically. One wonders if he is entertaining the notion that a text-type, or his proto-Alexandrian grouping is defined more in terms of the quality or characteristics of its text; that is, in terms of its tendency toward a scribally unimproved text. (*The Text of the Epistles: A Disquisition upon the Corpus Paulinum* [Eugene, Oregon: Wipf & Stock, 1953], 155-156).

48. 03 = 61%; 01 = 58%; 1175 = 57%; 02 = 56%; 1739 = 54%; 06 and 33 = 51%; etc., down to 630 = 3%.

49. More cogent is that P46, in Philippians, is not a leading recurring witness to 06's

Reconstruction of the textual history of the New Testament remains so complex, so interwoven and convoluted, and competing methodologies so uncertain that the simpler goal of identifying manuscript alliances on a smaller scale seems commendable as an intermediary goal. The collection and sorting of the data for Philippians' 93 test passages in 28 Consistently Cited Witnesses was not insurmountable, and doing so for the other Paulines can be achieved in short time so that a rather thorough representative analysis of the entire corpus is within reach.

Textual criticism has endured considerable, even radical changes over the last two or three decades. Eldon Epp famously wrote in 2005, "This, as the saying goes, is not your father's textual criticism, but an entrance into a brave new world...."[50] In this context, it is not the text that is preserved in the manuscript tradition that is decisive for faith, but that its content is indelibly written in the lives of people such as Sven Soderlund who undramatically live the cruciform life outlined in Paul's letter to the Philippians.

---

many Special Readings. Out of 06's 29 (!) Special Readings, 06 occurs but five times, with 010 and 012 occurring double as much, and 365 and 1175 still recurring more than P46. Where P46's text shows modest affinity with 06 is in four of 14 otherwise poorly supported readings: Entry 17 (P46 06*); Entry 46 (P46 02 06* 010 012); Entry 67 (P46 06 [010] [012]); Entry 88 (P46 06* 1505).

50. "The Oxyrhynchus New Testament Papyri: 'Not without Honor Except in their Hometown'? in *Perspectives in New Testament Textual Criticism: Collected Essays, 1962-2004* (Leiden: Brill, 2005), 748.

8

The Nameless Scriptures and the Name Above All Names

The Early Jewish and Christian Scribal Praxis and Paul's ONOMA-*Christology in His Letters*

Joseph H. S. Lee

I began studying the topic of this essay with Dr Sven Soderlund while working towards a ThM at Regent College. It is my great honour and pleasure to include this essay in the volume in honour of Sven's life, ministry and scholarship. The essay synthesizes studies in textual criticism, biblical allusion, and exegetical approaches.[1]

The divine name in the Hebrew Bible has been an important topic of inquiry throughout the eras of ancient Israel and early Judaism.[2] An important question is whether we are able to probe into the Hebrew and other Semitic language to draw out the true meaning and pronunciation of the

---

1. The essay is a revised form of a paper presented at the NT seminar at the University of Aberdeen.

2. Julian Obermann, "The Divine Name YHWH in the Light of Recent Discoveries," *JBL* 68 (1949): 301.

sacred name.³ In addition, since ancient Jews began using אדני ⁴ or אלהים ⁵ in Hebrew, שְׁמָא ⁶ or מָרֵא שְׁמַיָּא ⁷ in Aramaic, and Ἰαβέ, Ἰαουέ⁸ and κύριος in Greek⁹ for יהוה,¹⁰ it is difficult to elucidate the meaning and origin of the *tetragrammaton*.¹¹ However, it is extremely important to determine its significance in the religion of ancient Israel as represented in the Hebrew Bible in order to understand the history of religions. The *tetragrammaton* appears in every book of the Hebrew Bible (except the books of Esther, Ecclesiastes, and Song of Songs)¹² a total number of more than 6,800 times.¹³ However, the earliest extant evidence of the *tetragrammaton* was found in a non-biblical source in the paleo-Hebrew inscription of the Moabite Mesha

---

3. E. C. B. MacLaurin, "YHWH: The Origin of the Tetragrammaton," *VT* 12 (1962): 440-42.

4. Koog P. Hong, "The Euphemism for the Ineffable Name of God and Its Early Evidence in Chronicles," *JSOT* 37 (2013): 473-74; Hellmut Rosin, *The Lord Is God: The Translation of the Divine Names and the Missionary Calling of the Church* (Amsterdam: Nederlandsch Bijbelgenootschap, 1956), 112-121.

5. The *qere*-tradition of the Masoretic manuscripts reads אֱלֹהִים instead אֲדֹנָי of when the *tetragrammaton* stands together with אֲדֹנָי (i.e., אֲדֹנָי יְהוִה) in Gen 15:2 and Deut 3:24, for example (cf. The *qere* of Judg 16:28 consists of the full vocalization of אֱלֹהִים on the *tetragrammaton* on its own, even without אֲדֹנָי). See Martin Rösel, "The Reading and Translation of the Divine Name in the Masoretic Tradition and the Greek Pentateuch," *JSOT* 31 (2007): 412. The Samaritan Pentateuch also reads אֱלֹהִים for יְהוָה of the Masoretic Text (MT) in Exod 3:4, so while the Samaritan has אלהים twice, the Septuagint reads κύριος twice. See Robert J. Wilkinson, *Tetragrammaton: Western Christians and the Hebrew Name of God: From the Beginnings to the Seventeenth Century*, SHCT 179 (Leiden: Brill, 2015), 1; also Henry O. Thompson, "Yahweh," *ABD* 6:1011.

6. Rösel, "The Reading," 412-13.

7. Dan 5:23; See Joseph A. Fitzmyer, *A Wandering Aramean: Collected Aramaic Essays*, SBLM 25 (Chico: Scholars Press, 1979), 116-17.

8. Raymond Abba, "The Divine Name Yahweh," *JBL* 80 (1961): 320.

9. Rösel, "The Reading," 414-15; Fitzmyer, *A Wandering*, 121.

10. H. Rosin, in *The Lord Is God*, 21-23, illustrates his case study of how the name of God was proclaimed frequently in a missionary context in translations from the book of Jonah.

11. D. N. Freedman, "Yahweh," *TDOT*, 5:500.

12. Terence Fretheim, "Yahweh," *NIDOTTE* 4:1295.

13. If the *tetragrammaton* is considered separately, it would be 5,321 times while אלהים appears 2,555 times in the Hebrew OT; however, the number of 6800+ includes "the compounded and contracted usages of the name." See Stephen G. Brown, "The Tetragrammaton and Modern Scholarship" (ThM thesis, Western Conservative Baptist Seminary, 1970), 1; Abba, "Divine Name," 320.

stele from the 9th century B.C.E.[14]

If we also consider the textual evidence of the *tetragrammaton* in antiquity, we discover that the significance and veneration of the *nomina divina* (divine names) prevailed over an extensive period of the history of ancient Israel and Judaism. Neither the fall of Jerusalem in 587/6 B.C.E. along with the exile of the Judahites nor the Hellenization of Alexander the Great and his successors diminished the significance and veneration of the divine names in the history and religion of ancient Israel. Both from the Qumran and Masada manuscripts as well as the Old Greek Septuagint manuscripts, which all date later than the time of Alexander the Great, we find the ancient paleo-Hebrew scripts being used for the divine names, not exclusively for the *tetragrammaton* but also for other references to God.[15] Such phenomena of using paleo-Hebrew scripts for the divine name appear in some of the early manuscripts of the LXX as well. W. G. Waddell and C. H. Dodd also pointed out that the namelessness of God in the LXX is one of its unique features and contributes to 'the definition of monotheism'.[16] So, in spite of the Hellenization of the Palestinian Jews and Judaism and a need for the translation of the sacred writings from Hebrew to Greek during the Second Temple era, the Jewish veneration for the divine name seems to have contributed primarily to the rise of writing the *tetragrammaton* in the paleo-Hebrew scripts, as well as to the scribal phenomenon of *tentrapuncta*, i.e., four dots in place of the letters, in the scrolls from the Qumran caves and the early manuscripts of the Septuagint.[17]

---

14. Freedman and O'Connor, *TDOT*, 5:502. The Mesha inscription reads, "And I took from there the vessels of Yahweh and dragged them before Chemosh" in D. Winton Thomas, ed., *Documents from Old Testament Times* (London: Thomas Nelson and Son, 1958), 197. See also William W. Hallo, ed. *The Context of Scripture: Canonical Compositions, Monumental Inscriptions, and Archival Documents from the Biblical World*, 3 vols. (Leiden: Brill, 1997-2002), 2:138.

15. 1QH (Hôdāyôt) from the mid-2nd century B.C.E., for example, includes אל and אלי in the paleo-Hebrew scripts while substituting אדוני for יהוה in Exod 15:11. See Patrick W. Skehan, "The Divine Name At Qumran, in the Masada Scroll, and in the Septuagint," *BIOSCS* 13 (1980):17.

16. W. G. Waddell, "The Tetragrammaton in the LXX," *JTS* 45 (1944):158; C. H. Dodd, *The Bible and the Greeks* (London: Hodder and Stoughton, 1935), 4.

17. Daniel A. Machiela, "Lord or God? Tobit and the Tetragrammaton," *CBQ* 75 (2013):464; also see comprehensive lists and discussion for the *tetrapuncta* in Emanuel Tov, *Scribal Practices and Approaches Reflected in the Texts Found in the Judean Desert* (Leiden:

The Nameless Scriptures and the Name Above All Names

Now, considering the ways in which Paul rendered the *tetragrammaton* of the Hebrew Bible where he cites the Old Testament passages in the letters, it is clear that he used the word κύριος for the divine name of Israel's God (e.g., Rom 9:29; 10:13; 11:34). A number of studies have focused on Paul's use of the κύριος title in reference to Jesus, as well as to God, in the letters.[18] Nonetheless, there has not been, as far as I know, a study conducted considering Paul's use of κύριος for the divine name of the OT in light of the material evidences from the Jewish scribal praxis of the divine name from the Second Temple era.

Moreover, it is significant that when Paul refers to the name of Jesus, he writes the name either as κύριος or κύριος Ἰησοῦς, following after ὄνομα, thus τὸ ὄνομα τοῦ κυρίου [ἡμῶν] Ἰησοῦ Χριστοῦ, unless accompanied by the pronoun αὐτοῦ (e.g., Rom 1:5). One exception to such a Pauline ὄνομα construction is in Philippians 2:10, where it reads ἐν τῷ ὀνόματι Ἰησοῦ. Given that there is a concentration of the word ὄνομα in Philippians 2:9-11, we shall examine this passage more in depth later in this paper.

Thus, consideration of the name of the Lord construction in Paul, the use of שֵׁם יהוה in the Hebrew Bible, τὸ ὄνομα κυρίου in LXX, and the name (שֵׁם/ὄνομα) theology of the Old Testament are all important to this study. It should be noted also that the frequency of the phrase שֵׁם יהוה and τὸ ὄνομα κυρίου over שֵׁם אלהים and τὸ ὄνομα θεοῦ/τοῦ θεοῦ[19] is far greater in reference to the God of Israel in Israel's scriptures (both HB and LXX).[20] Such name-phrases and the theological significance of the OT may

---

Brill, 2004), 206.

18. Werner Kramer, *Christ, Lord, Son of God*, trans. B. Hardy, SBT 50 (London: SCM Press, 1966), 151-82; David B. Capes, *Old Testament Yahweh Texts in Paul's Christology*, WUNT II 47 (Tübingen: J.C.B. Mohr [Paul Siebeck], 1992); Carl Judson Davis, *The Name and Way of the Lord: Old Testament Themes, New Testament Christology*, JSNTSup 129 (Sheffield: Sheffield Academic Press, 1996); Gordon Fee, *Pauline Christology: An Exegetical-Theological Study* (Peabod, MA: Hendrickson, 2007).

19. τὸ ὄνομα θεοῦ is, at least for the half of the times it occurs in the HB, used in references to the gods other than the God of Israel (e.g., Exod 23:13; Duet 18:20; 1 Kgs 18:24 [LXX]). For the reference to the God of Israel, ἐν ὀνόματι θεοῦ αὐτοῦ is used in 2 Kings 5:11, with Ισραηλ in Ezra 5:1, and with the personal pronoun ἡμῶν in Psalm 19:6. On the other hand, the articular phrase τὸ ὄνομα τοῦ θεοῦ is strictly used in a reference to the God of Israel in Lev 19:12; 21:6; Josh 23:7; Ps 19:2; 43:21; 68:31; Prov 30:9; Amos 2:7; PSol 6:4; 8:22 (LXX).

20. The phrase שֵׁם אלהים appears 14 times and 87 שֵׁם יהוה times. As for LXX, the

be relevant when we study the Pauline phrase of "the name of our Lord Jesus Christ" (τὸ ὄνομα τοῦ κυρίου [ἡμῶν] Ἰησοῦ Χριστοῦ) since there are consistent patterns both for the name of the Lord God in the OT as well as for the name of the Lord Jesus in the Pauline corpus. Just as a substantial number of Paul's OT citations in reference to Jesus demonstrates a high, divine Christology, the apostle's ὄνομα construction, as I call it, also shows his high regard for Jesus. Thus, there is, in the Pauline corpus, a cogent ὄνομα-Christology, which demonstrates that Paul revered the name and person of Jesus Christ, and which, together with his use of the word κύριος, expresses a high reverence of the kind that ancient Israelites, early Christians, and early Jewish scribes would ascribe to the covenant name of the Lord God of Israel.

Aim and Methods

The purpose of the current discussion is, first, to give an analysis of the divine names in the biblical and *pesharim* scrolls from the Qumran caves, where the four paleo-Hebrew characters are used for the *tetragrammaton* in texts written in the Aramaic-square Hebrew script, I will also examine how the *tetragrammaton* is rendered in the early Old Greek Septuagint manuscripts and the later Jewish and Christian recensions of the LXX. Second, I will examine the divine names and titles in the early NT literature and textual tradition, reflected also in the *nomina sacra* from the earliest NT manuscripts. Thirdly, I will analyze the ὄνομα phrases pertaining to Jesus as Lord in the Pauline corpus, in comparison to the שֵׁם יהוה/τὸ ὄνομα κυρίου phrases from the HB and the LXX.

Through these textual, historical, and exegetical analyses, I will first point out that, although there may have been an evolution in how the divine names were rendered in various textual traditions, reverence for the God of Israel was the basis for most of these scribal practices surrounding the *nomina divina*. Second, Paul's ὄνομα κυρίου formulae (e.g., ἐν τῷ ὀνόματι κυρίου Ἰησοῦ Χριστοῦ)[21] follow closely to the structure of

---

phrase τὸ ὄνομα κυρίου/τοῦ κυρίου is used approximately 106 times and τὸ ὄνομα θεου/τοῦ θεοῦ 9 times.

21. Such as τὸ ὄνομα κυρίου/αὐτοῦ in Rom 1:5, 10:13, Col 3:17 and 2 Tim 2:19, as well as τὸ ὄνομα τοῦ κυρίου [ἡμῶν] Ἰησοῦ Χριστοῦ in 1 Cor 1:2, 10, 5:4, 6:11, 2 Thess 1:12, and 3:6. See also Phil 2:9 and Col 3:17 for τὸ ὄνομα Ἰησοῦ and ὄνομα κυρίου Ἰησοῦ respectively.

the *nomina divina* as reflected in the LXX (τὸ ὀνόματι κυρίου θεοῦ[22] or κυρίου τοῦ θεοῦ[23] or κυρίου θεοῦ Ισραηλ),[24] as well as שם יהוה אלהים [25] or שם יהוה אלהי ישראל.[26] Then, I shall posit that Paul's use of the ὄνομα κυρίου in reference to the name and divinity of Jesus was largely influenced by the ὄνομα κυρίου structure of the Old Testament as reflected in the early Christological hymn in Philippians 2:9-11.

In this study, however, I will not discuss in any depth the actual origin and the theological meaning of the *tetragrammaton* because of the complexities of these questions as mentioned earlier, because they are out of the scope of this study.

The Divine Names in the Hebrew Scrolls from the Qumran Caves

From the coins and fragments discovered in Qumran we are able to trace some of the scribal practices of using the paleo-Hebrew script well into the early Christian era although the Aramaic script had been the predominant scribal script since the Persian period.[27] In both biblical and non-biblical texts, some of the Qumran Scrolls feature the *tetrapuncta*,[28] as well as the paleo-Hebrew *tetragrammaton* for the divine name while the rest of the text is in Aramaic-square script.[29] We reserve discussion of the Greek text of the Qumran scrolls related to the Old Greek LXX for the next section.

---

22. τὸ ὀνόματι κυρίου θεοῦ (LXX) in Gen 21:33; 1 Kgs 5:17, 19; 8:17, 20; 1 Chr 22:7; 2 Chr 2:3; 6:7, 10; 33:18; 1 Esdr 6:1; Psa 19:8; Mic 4:5; Isa 48:1.

23. τὸ ὀνόματι κυρίου τοῦ θεοῦ (LXX) in Gen 4:26; Exod 20:7; Deut 5:11; 17:12; 18:7; Josh 9:9; 1 Kgs 18:24; Tob 13:13; Sir 47:18; Mic 5:3; Joel 2:26; Jer 33:16.

24. τὸ ὀνόματι κυρίου θεοῦ Ισραηλ (LXX) in 1 Kgs 8:17, 20; 2 Chr 6:7, 10; 33:18; 1 Esdra 6:1; Isa 48:1.

25. שם יהוה אלהים (HB) in Gen 21:33(אל rather than אלהים); Exod 20:7; Deut 5:11; 18:7; Josh 9:9; 1 Kgs 5:17, 19; 8:17, 20; 2 Kgs 5:11; Isa 24:15; 60:9; Jer 26:16; Joel 2:26; Mic 4:5; 5:3; Psa 20:8; 1 Chr 22:7; 2 Chr 2:3; 6:7, 10; 33:18.

26. שם יהוה אלהי ישראל (HB) in 1 Kgs 8:17, 20; Isa 24:16; 2 Chr 6:7, 10; 2 Chr 33:18.

27. Richard S. Hanson, "Paleo-Hebrew Scripts in the Hasmonean Age," *BASOR* 175 (1964): 42.

28. For example, 1QS VIII:14; 1QIsa[a] XXXIII:7 (Isa 40:7); 4QSamc I:3 (1 Sam 25:31); 4QTest (4Q175) lines 1, 19. See Tov, *Scribal Practices*, 206-207.

29. Bruce M. Metzger, *Manuscripts of the Greek Bible: An Introduction to Greek Paleography* (Oxford: Oxford University Press, 1981), 33.

1QpHab 1QPesher to Habakkuk

The text of 1QpHab or *Pesher Habakkuk* has survived in an extant manuscript from the first century B.C.E. It includes a commentary on Habakkuk chapters 1 and 2.³⁰ The significance of 1QpHab for biblical studies is that it provides us insightful examples of the Jewish sectarian exegesis.³¹ Moreover, 1QpHab contains not only the commentary on Habakkuk but also a number of figures and events that provide some clues about the sectarian community that was centered around the Teacher of Righteousness.³²

One of the significant textual features of 1QpHab for this study is that, even being a non-biblical scroll (non-biblical in the sense that it is a commentary rather than a copy of the biblical texts),³³ it contains the paleo-Hebrew *tetragrammaton* for the Habakkuk texts while using אל for the designation of God in the commentary section.³⁴ In 1QpHab col. VI, lines 12-16, for example, Habakkuk 2:1-2 is quoted almost verbatim³⁵ after the commentary on 1:17 in the lines 10-12a.³⁶ In line 14 for Habakkuk 2:2a, the Qumran text employs the four paleo-Hebrew characters for the *tetragrammaton*. Habakkuk 2:13 where it contains יהוה צבאות is also cited in 1QpHab col. X line 7 with the paleo-Hebrew letters.³⁷ Thus, within this *pesher* text the divine names from the scriptural citations are rendered consistently with the paleo-Hebrew letters.³⁸

---

30. Devorah Dimant, "Qumran Sectarian Literature," in *Jewish Writings of the Second Temple Period: Apocrypha, Pseudepigrapha, Qumran Sectarian Writings, Philo, Josephus*, CRINT 2, LJSPTT, vol. 2, ed. M. E. Stone (Assen: Van Gorcum, 1984), 508.

31. Craig A. Evans, *Noncanonical Writings and New Testament Interpretation* (Peabody: Hendrickson, 1992), 55.

32. Dimant, "Qumran," 508-509.

33. Tov, *Scribal Practices*, 229, writes, "Of the twenty-eight manuscirpts using paleo-Hebrew characters for the divine names, nineteen or twenty texts (if 1QPsᵇ is included) are nonbiblical; six or seven (if 1QPsᵇ is included) are biblical manuscripts."

34. Jonathan P. Siegel, "The Employment of Palaeo-Hebrew Characters for the Divine Names at Qumran in the Light of Tannaitic Sources," *HUCA* 42 (1971): 160-61.

35. From what is extant for 1QpHab, the text of col. VI, line 12 presents a *holem waw* in אעמודה whereas the MT text of Hab 2:1 reads אעמדה with a simple *holem*; also, the text of 1QpHab VI,14 reads וועני while the MT reads ויעני in Hab 2:2a.

36. Martin Abegg, ed., "1QpHab," in *The Dead Sea Scroll Reader, Part 2: Exegetical Texts* (eds. D. W. Parry and E. Tov; Leiden: Brill, 2004), 84-85.

37. Cf., 1QpHab X,14 (Hab 2:14); XI,10 (Hab 2:16).

38. Instances of the paleo-Hebrew *tetragrammaton* in a scriptural citation may also be

11QPsalms^a

11QPsalms^a

The biblical Psalter appears to have been significant to the life of the sectarian community since numerous copies of the Psalter were discovered in the Qumran caves, Masada and Nahal Hever.[39] Nearly 126 out of 150 canonical Psalms are attested in the forty extant scrolls from three locations,[40] composed between the second century B.C.E. and the first century C.E.[41] Among the extant Psalms scrolls, 11Q5 (11QPs^a) preserves the largest number of Psalms in its collection of forty-nine compositions.[42]

Significantly, there are about 145 occurrences of the paleo-Hebrew *tetragrammaton* in the extant texts of 11QPs^a including its small fragments and their attestations.[43] Moreover, the first scribe of the scroll seems to have left blank spaces where the text of Psalter attests to the *tetragrammaton*; the paleo-Hebrew characters were most likely added by the later hands.[44] Al Wolters has observed:

> [T]he spaces occupied by the tetragrammaton in 11QPsa show differences in size which are over three times as great as the normal handwriting of its scribe would lead us to expect. This would seem to indicate that those differences are not the result of the scribe's normal variation in leaving spaces between letters and words, but rather of his leaving

---

found in the following Qumran *pesher* texts for the prophetic literature – 4Q161 (4QpIsa^a) Frgs. 8-10, line 13 (Isa 11:3); 1Q15 (1QpZeph) line 4 (Zeph 2:2); 1Q14(1QpMic) Frgs. 1-5 (Mic 1:2).

39. Peter W. Flint, "The Book of Psalms in the Light of the Dead Sea Scrolls," *VT* 48 (1998):453.

40. There are 37 scrolls from the Qumran caves with 1Q10–12 (1QPs^{a-c}), 2Q14 (2QPs), 3Q2 (3QPs), 4Q83–98e (4QPs^{a-v}), 4Q236 (4QPs^w), 4Q522 (4QProphecy on Joshua), 5Q5 (5QPs), pap6Q5 (pap6QPs), 8Q2 (8QPs), 11Q5–9 (11QPs^{a-e}), and 11Q11 (11QPsAp^a), and 3 scrolls from Masada and Nahal Hever with MasPs^a (M1039-160), MasPs^b (M1103-1742), and 5/6Hev-SePs. See Flint, "The Book of Psalms," 454.

41. Ibid., 455.

42. In the order of Pss 101–103; 109; 118; 104; 147; 105; 146; 148 (+ 120); 121–132; 119; 135; 136 (with Catena); 145 (with postscript); 154; Plea for Deliverance; Ps 139; 137; 138; Sirach 51; Apostrophe to Zion; Ps 93; 141; 133; 144; 155; 142; 143; 149; 150; Hymn to the Creator; David's Last Words; David's Compositions; Pss 140; 134; 151A; 151B; blank column. See Flint, "The Book of Psalms," 458.

43. Al Wolters, "The Tetragrammaton in the Psalms Scroll," *Text* 18 (1995): 87; Siegel, "The Employment," 161-62.

44. Wolters, "The Tetragrammaton," 87-88.

word-length blanks.⁴⁵

The fragment Ci of 11QPsᵃ, for example, contains the fragmentary text of Psalms 101:5–102:2. For the line מעיר יהוה כל פעלי און in Psalm 101:8b, the fragment has survived with the words [פעלי און]הוה כול [מעיר י] and the size of its paleo-Hebrew letters and the spaces before and after these letters are slightly but distinctively larger than the Aramaic square-script texts. Thus, such discrepancy in the size of letters and spaces seems to be due to inserting the four paleo-Hebrew characters into the already deliberately left blank spaces.⁴⁶ Since 11QpIsaᵉ (4Q165) in 6,4 where Isaiah 32:6 is quoted, is left blank for the *tetragrammaton*, the hypothesis of the divine blank spaces has some warrant.⁴⁷ Even for the divine name following a preposition (e.g., ביהוה), the four letters are exclusively written in the paleo-Hebrew scripts (e.g., 11QPsᵃ XXVIII,5).⁴⁸

*4QIsaiah*ᶜ

From the biblical scrolls of the Qumran caves we have so far twenty-one copies for the book of Isaiah although a substantial number of manuscripts are fragmentary.⁴⁹ While the Great Isaiah Scroll (1QIsaᵃ) and other

---

45. Ibid., 90.
46. Al Wolters, against S. Talmon's single scribe hypothesis for 11QPsᵃ, additionally points out that "the basic shape of the letters is very consistent throughout the scroll" in "The Tetragrammaton," 96-97; however, there are also two occurrences in 11QPsᵃ where the paleo-Hebrew *tetragrammaton* was written unnecessarily. For these two superfluous instances, the scribe left the texts and added dots above and below the characters rather than erasing them. These dots, J. P. Siegel believes, were added as a device to prevent them from reading the divine names where they were superfluously added as well as from erasing the *tetragrammaton*. See Siegel, "The Employment," 162; and also Tov, *Scribal Practices*, 181-85. Moreover, Dennis Green argues against J. Siegel and points out that the dot or accentuations are not conclusive for non-erasure since there is diversity in how the *tetragrammaton* was represented in the Qumran practices in "Divine Titles: Rabbinic and Qumran Scribal Techniques," in *The Dead Sea Scrolls: Fifty Years After Their Discovery 1947 – 1997*, eds. L. H. Schiffman, E. Tov, and J. C. VanderKam (Jerusalem: Israel Exploration Society, 2000), 510-11.
47. Tov, *Scribal Practices*, 226-28.
48. Siegel, "Employment," 161-62.
49. 1QIsaᵃ, 1QIsaᵇ, 4QIsaᵃ⁻ᵒ, 4QpapIsaᵖ¹⁰, 4QIsaᵠ, 4QIsaʳ, and 5QIsa. See Emanuel Tov, "The Text of Isaiah at Qumran," in *Hebrew Bible, Greek Bible, and Qumran*, TSAJ 121 (Tübingen: Mohr Siebeck, 2008), 42; Francis James Morrow, Jr., "The Text of Isaiah at Qum-

Isaiah scrolls have the square-script *tetragrammata* for the divine name, 4Q57 (4QIs^c) uses the paleo-Hebrew letters.⁵⁰ Unlike the paleo-Hebrew characters in 11QPs^a, 4Q57 shows the prefixes and suffixes attached to the divine name including צבאות all written in the paleo-Hebrew script along with the divine name.⁵¹ The partial text of Isaiah 26:4a, for example, has survived in a fragment of 4QIs^c, and from the text of עדי ביהוה בטחו in Isaiah 26:4, the whole phrase ביהוה is in the paleo-Hebrew script. This distinctive characteristic of 4QIs^c among the Isaiah scrolls from the Qumran caves has suggested to some scholars the possibility of the fragments of 4QIs^c being part of a non-biblical scroll; however, as J. P. Siegel and Patrick W. Skehan have pointed out, the fragments of 4QIs^c "are extant from all parts of the book [of Isaiah]."⁵² Provided that the paleo-Hebrew *tetragrammata* are attested in other biblical scrolls such as 11QPs^a, such phenomena in 4QIs^c are not necessarily totally idiosyncratic in comparison with other biblical scrolls from the Qumran caves.

The Sectarian Community and Rabbinical Schools

The ways in which the divine names are represented in the Dead Sea Scrolls in Hebrew are not homogeneous but variegated. When it comes to the *tetragrammaton*, there are instances where the four letters were written in the square scripts just as in the rest of the scroll as well as in the paleo-Hebrew scripts either exclusively to the four letters or together with a preposition or modifier. Whether for the *tetrapuncta* or paleo-Hebrew *tetragrammata*, the intention of such scribal practices seems to be based on a scribe's veneration for the divine name and a desire to prohibit any indecent handling of it.⁵³ We have evidence that the community of the Qumran

---

ran" (PhD diss., The Catholic University of America, 1973), 6-9.

50. Morrow, "The Text of Isaiah," 37; Tov, *Scribal Practices*, 227; Patrick W. Skehan, "The Text of Isaias at Qumran," *CBQ* 17 (1955):162.

51. Siegel, "Employment," 163.

52. J. Siegel refers to Dr. N. M. Sarna's suggestion of the non-biblical status for the fragments of 4QIs^c, but Siegel also quotes Fr. Skehan's statement from "The Text of Isaias," 162 in n. 20 of Siegel, "Employment," 163.

53. Siegel, "Employment," 162; Green, "Divine Titles," 499. See also Lev 24:16; "One who blasphemes the name of the Lord shall be put to death; the whole congregation shall stone the blasphemer. Aliens as well as citizens, when they blaspheme the Name, shall be put to death." (NRSV; cf. Exod 20:7; Deut 5:11). Dennis Green pointed out that the seman-

scrolls practiced excommunication when the divine names were read frivolously.⁵⁴ Dennis Green also pointed out the later rabbinical prohibition for the pronouncement of the divine names, which reads, "All Israel have a portion in the world to come...But the following have no portion therein: ...Abba Saul says: Also one who pronounces the Divine Name as it is spelt" (*m. Sanh.* 11:1 [*b. Sanh.* 90a]).⁵⁵

The divine names were not represented distinctively in the paleo-Hebrew characters throughout the biblical and non-biblical scrolls; however, that does not imply that the square-script *tetragrammata* were necessarily less sacred than the ones written in paleo-Hebrew nor allowable for pronunciation, as observed rightly by J. P. Siegel:

> YHWH in square letters is no doubt as sacred as YHWH in palaeo-Hebrew characters. We need a m[o]re specific rationale for the occasional Qumran practice of writing the Tetragrammaton in palaeo-Hebrew characters. Such a rationale, I believe, is to be found in tannaitic literature.⁵⁶

Thus, Siegel concluded, rightly in my opinion, that the "occasional use of palaeo-Hebrew script for the Tetragrammaton" in the Dead Sea Scrolls is "to insure that such Tetragrammata are not erased."⁵⁷

---

tic range of the verb נקב may cover the sense of piercing, cursing, as well as blaspheming. Nevertheless, in Num 1:17 the verb נקב was used to mean "to name" or "to designate" by names. See Green, "Divine Titles," 498-99; "נקב," *HALAT*, 678-79.

54. Green, "Divine Titles," 503. See Martínez and Tigchelaar, *Dead Sea Scrolls*, 85-87; "[... Who]ever enunciates the Name (which is) honoured above all ... [...]... [W]hether blaspheming, or suddenly overtaken by misfortune or for any other reason, {...} or reading a book, or blessing, will be excluded and shall not go back ever to the Community council" (1QS VI,27b–VII,2a).

55. Green, "Divine Titles," 499.

56. Siegel, "Employment," 165, observed a tannaitic text from Yerushalmi *Megillah* 1:9, where there are specific rabbinical instructions on how to handle the divine names. The third one (ג) especially lists the divine names, including the *tetragrammaton* and other forms and titles, which may not be erased, as well as a few instances where partial texts might have been erased (e.g., אד from אדני). "The general principle is: If the [noun] resulting [from such word-division] is one which is sacred in another place [in the Hebrew Bible], then such a noun may not be erased" (*Meg.* 1:9c) in "Employment," 166-67.

57. Siegel, "Employment," 171.

The Divine Names in the Septuagint and the New Testament

One of the common features of the renderings of the *tetragrammaton* in the LXX and the citations of the Jewish scriptures in the NT is the use of the Greek word κύριος for the divine name. However, such a rendering of κύριος may not be true for some of the earliest extant manuscript evidence we have for the LXX. The earliest extant manuscripts of the Jewish Greek scriptures are found in the fragments of the Qumran scrolls dating back to the second century B.C.E., including the fragments from 7Q1 (Exodus), 4Q119 (Leviticus), 4Q122 (Deuteronomy) and 7Q2 (Letter of Jeremiah).[58] Considering that the *Letter of Aristeas* points us to the scene of Alexandria in the third century B.C.E. as the beginning of the Old Greek LXX at least for the Pentateuch,[59] the dating of the aforementioned fragments is significantly early. The manuscript evidence, nevertheless, with which we are concerned in this study come from the first century B.C.E. about a century after the aforementioned manuscript evidence, beginning with Papyrus Fouad 266 discovered in 1944 a few years prior to the discovery of the Qumran scrolls.[60] Hence, in this section we will examine and discuss the occurrences of the *nomina divina* and *sacra* in a diverse body of manuscripts from the first century B.C.E. in the Jewish Greek scriptures and their recensions, as well as in the NT manuscripts.

The Divine Names in the Early LXX Manuscripts

Although its provenance is unknown, P. Fouad 266 (Rahlfs 458) is a collection of the fragments of a papyrus scroll that consists of the Greek text of Deuteronomy from the middle of the first century B.C.E.[61] P. Fouad 266, however, does not render the divine name with the word κύριος but

---

58. Wilkinson, *Tetragrammaton*, 48-49.
59. Sven K. Soderlund, "Septuagint," *ISBE* 4:401-402; idem., "Text and MSS of the OT," *ISBE* 4:800.
60. Wilkinson, *Tetragrammaton*, 54.
61. The extant fragments of the scroll consist of the top margin of 25 mm long and 15 mm wide space between the columns, however, neither the ends of the lines nor the letter-size at the line-end are consistent. See E. G. Turner, *Greek Manuscripts of the Ancient World*, Bulletin Supplement 46, 2d ed., ed. P. J. Parsons (London: Institute of Classical Studies, 1987), 96-97; Metzger, *Manuscripts*, 60-61.

with the Aramaic square characters of יהוה.⁶² If one looks closely at the representation of the *tetragrammaton* in P. Fouad 266, the four letters are scribed within a large blank space. Not only that, the four letters were added either between or next to the two dots in the space. Scholars postulate that the two dots demonstrate the double yod (י י) indicating the divine name,⁶³ which is similar to the double yod abbreviation of the *tetragrammaton*, represented by two Greek letter Zs with a horizontal line through the middle (ƶƶ) in Papyrus Oxyrynchus (P.Oxy.) vii. 1007, a papyrus fragment of Genesis from the third century C.E.⁶⁴ Thus, when the Greek text of the Pentateuch was copied on a scroll, the scribes left a blank space in the place where the *tetragrammaton* occurs and then the four letters of the square Aramaic script seem to have been added later by a different hand.⁶⁵

We also have the manuscript evidence in Papyrus Rylands Greek 458, as well as 4QLXXNum (4Q121 Rahlfs 803), which contains blank spaces in place of the divine name.⁶⁶ It is unlikely but possible that when the Pentateuch was translated, the Greek word κύριος was not employed for the divine names in the first place as reflected in Martin Rösel's observation of W. G. Waddell's suggestion among others:⁶⁷

> Waddell concluded that in the Greek Bible the divine name was never translated by κύριος but was only represented by Hebrew consonants… Waddell's theory subsequently found support in the discoveries made in and around Qumran. In particular, the Greek Dodekapropheton Scroll from Nahal Hever (8Hever XII gr), a text dating from between 50 BCE and 50 CE.

The 8Hever XII gr of the Minor Prophets, "found in a cave (Nahal Hever) near Engedi in the Judean Desert," is considered as a manuscript from

---

62. Skehan, "The Divine Name," 31-32; Metzger, *Manuscripts*, 33-34; Wilkinson, *Tetragrammaton*, 54-55; Rösel, "The Reading," 415; Tov, *Scribal Practices*, 206.
63. Wilkinson, *Tetragrammaton*, 55.
64. Waddell, "The Tetragrammaton," 158; Arthur S. Hunt, ed., *The Oxyrhynchus Papyri, Part VII* (London: Egypt Exploration Fund, 1910), 1-3; Metzger, *Manuscripts*, 34; Wilkinson, *Tetragrammaton*, 84.
65. Wilkinson, *Tetragrammaton*, 55.
66. Rösel, "The Reading," 415; Wilkinson, *Tetragrammaton*, 58.
67. Rösel, "The Reading," 415.

the same period as P. Fouad 266 or slightly later.[68] The manuscript evidence of the Nahal Hever scroll (8Hever XII gr), as well as P. Oxy 3522 of Job 42:11-12 perhaps from the first century C.E., indicates the paleo-Hebrew *tetragrammaton* just as in some of the Qumran scrolls discussed above.[69] Thus, such scribal practice suggests that the reverence of the divine name continued outside of the sectarian circles to the wider Jewish communities in diaspora.

Ιαω, πιπι and κύριος in the LXX

Besides the phenomenon of the Hebrew *tetragrammaton* in the manuscript evidence of the LXX, the divine name is represented with the Greek word Ιαω in 4QpapLXXLev^b (4Q120; Rahlfs 802)[70] with a blank space before and after the word while the rest of the manuscript is in *scriptio continua*.[71] 4QpapLXXLev^b consists of the Greek text of Leviticus 2–5 and is considered to have originated from the first century B.C.E.[72] The Greek rendering of ΙΑΩ for the divine name can be traced from the writings of non-biblical authors such as Varro (116-27 B.C.E), Diodorus of Sicily (first century C.E.), Dioscorides Pedanius (40-90 C.E.) and Aelius Herodianus (180-250 C.E.).[73] For example, "Diodorus of Sicily (I, 94, 2) tells us that Moses referred his laws to τον Ιαω επικαλουμενον θεον,"[74] perhaps from the Greek phonetic rendering of יהו found in the Elephantine papyri.[75] Later Jerome (346-420 C.E.) also mentions that the *tetragrammaton* may be read as Ιαω.[76]

By contrast, Origen's massive *Hexapla* and the three Jewish revisions

---

68. Metzger, *Manuscripts*, 34.
69. Skehan, "The Divine Name," 32-33; Wilkinson, *Tetragrammaton*, 55-56.
70. Patrick W. Skehan, Eugene Ulrich and Judith E. Sanderson, eds., *Qumran Cave 4 IV: Paleo-Hebrew and Greek Biblica Manuscripts*, DJD 9 (Oxford: Clarendon Press, 1992), 168.
71. Tov, *Scribal Practices*, 208; Wilkinson, *Tetragrammaton*, 58; Rösel, "The Reading," 416.
72. Tov, *Scribal Practices*, 172, 208.
73. Wilkinson, *Tetragrammaton*, 65.
74. Skehan, "The Divine Name," 29.
75. Wilkinson, *Tetragrammaton*, 65; Rösel, "The Reading," 418-19.
76. Wilkinson, *Tetragrammaton*, 66. For a fuller discussion on the use of Ιαω in the LXX, see Frank Shaw, *The Earliest Non-Mystical Jewish Use of* Ιαω, CBET 70 (Leuven: Peeters, 2014).

of the LXX, namely Aquila, Symmachus, and Theodotion, show some distinctive features in how they represent the divine name, reflecting their Hebraizing tendency. Origen's *Hexapla* from the third century C.E. points us to the use of ΠΙΠΙ to represent the *tetragrammaton* in its meagre manuscript evidence (e.g., Q, 86, 8, 234ᵐᵍ, 264).[77] Aquila's version of 3 and 4 Reigns (or 1 and 2 Kings) has survived to us in an extant palimpsest from the sixth century C.E. Aquila's version contains *yhyh* in the paleo-Hebrew characters since it was difficult to differentiate between the paleo-*yod* and *waw*.[78] Similarly, a fragment thought to be part of the Symmachus version contains the paleo-Hebrew *tetragrammaton*.[79]

Because of all these diversified representations of the divine name in the manuscripts of the LXX (e.g., ΙΑΩ, ΠΙΠΙ and the paleo-Hebrew letters), and because of the lack of pre-Christian Jewish manuscript evidence for the use of κύριος in the LXX,[80] Emanuel Tov, in basic agreement with as W. G. Waddell,[81] has suggested that the use of κύριος in place of the *tetragrammaton* should be considered as a later Christian invention.[82] However, there is non-biblical textual evidence that attests to the use of κύριος for the *tetragrammaton* from the Jewish writings. For instance, Philo (20 B.C.E. – 50 C.E.) used the word κύριος to explain the divine name in *De Abrahamo* 121 and *De Plantatione* 85–90.[83] Also, the use of κύριος for the *tetragrammaton* is attested in the work of Aristobulus in his citation of Exodus 9:3, as well as in the citation of Deuteronomy 7:18-19 in the *Letter of Aristeas* 155.[84] Moreover, the Hebrew word אדני had been in use for the divine name as demonstrated in the Masada scroll of *Ben Sira*, as well as in 1QIsaᵃ.[85]

---

77. Metzger, *Manuscripts*, 35, 94; Wilkinson, *Tetragrammaton*, 72-73. P. W. Skehan ("The Divine Name," 32) has mentioned the consistent use of *pypy* in Syriac script from the attestation of the Syrohexaplar version.

78. Wilkinson, *Tetragrammaton*, 69; Metzger, *Manuscripts*, 35.

79. Wilkinson, *Tetragrammaton*, 72.

80. Ibid., 87.

81. Waddell, "The Tetragrammaton," 159.

82. Wilkinson, *Tetragrammaton*, 61-62. See E. Tov, "Greek Biblical Texts from the Judaean Desert," in *The Bible as Book: The Transmission of the Greek Text*, eds. Scott McKendrick and Orlaith A. O'Sullivan (London: The British Library, 2003), 112-113. Also, see Skehan, "The Divine Name," 34; Rösel, "The Reading," 416-17.

83. Wilkinson, *Tetragrammaton*, 85.

84. Rösel, "Divine Name," 424-25.

85. Skehan, "The Divine Name," 35.

Similarly, Thanksgiving Hymns (1QHodayot) from the mid-second century B.C.E. contains אדני for the divine name about twenty times, and the quotation of Exodus 15:11 in 1QH VII.28 from the mid-first century C.E. has אדני in place of the *tetragrammaton*.[86] Thus, contra Tov, it is more likely that the employment of the Greek word κύριος for the *tetragrammaton* was "pre-Christian in origin"[87] and also might have been in use because of the reverence for the divine name.

The Nomina Sacra in the NT

One of the key features of the NT use of Israel's scriptures is, without any doubt, the use of the word κύριος for the divine name (e.g., Isa 1:9 in Rom 9:29; Joel 3:5[2:32] in Rom 10:13; Isa 40:13 in Rom 11:34).[88] When the divine names and titles of God and Jesus, such as θεός, κύριος, Ἰησοῦς and χριστός, appeared in the early NT manuscripts, they were written in a short form, abbreviated to usually two or three letters with a straight line above. This phenomenon was mentioned first by Ludwig Traube in 1907,[89] and he coined the term now known to scholars as *"nomina sacra."*[90]

The above-mentioned four divine and sacred names and titles are the earliest *nomina sacra* (or the earliest five, since 𝔓46 from about 200 C.E.[91] also attests to the occurrence of ΠΝΣ for the word πνεύματος in Rom 15:30).[92] We are also able to trace other words treated as *nomina sacra*, apart from the earliest divine names and titles, including σταυρός, σταυρόω, πατήρ, ἄνθρωπος, Ἱερουσαλήμ, υἱός, Ἰσραήλ, πνευματικός, οὐρανός, μήτηρ, Δαυίδ and σωτήρ.[93] It is also significant that the earliest four (θεός, κύριος, Ἰησοῦς

---

86. Wilkinson, *Tetragrammaton*, 80.
87. Rösel, "Divine Name," 425.
88. Capes, *Old Testament Yahweh Texts*, 96-102; Wilkinson, *Tetragrammaton*, 89.
89. Ludwig Traube, *Nomina Sacra: Versuch einer Geschichte der christlichen Kürzung* (Munich: Beck, 1907) referenced in no. 4 in Larry W. Hurtado, "The Original of the *Nomina Sacra*: A Proposal," *JBL* 117 (1998): 655.
90. Hurtado, "The Original," 655-56; idem., *The Earliest Christian Artifacts: Manuscript and Christian Origins* (Grand Rapids: Eerdmans, 2006), 95-96.
91. Metzger, *Manuscript*, 64.
92. Tomas Bokedal, *The Formation and Significance of the Christian Biblical Canon: A Study in Text, Ritual and Interpretation* (London: Bloomsbury, 2014), 84-85.
93. Bokedal, *The Formation*, 89-90; Hurtado, "The Origin," 657; Wilkinson, *Tetragrammaton*, 89-90.

and χριστός) were abbreviated as *nomina sacra* for 99 percent of all their occurrences in the 74 earliest manuscripts from the second to the fourth century. The occurrence of abbreviations for other names and titles, apart from the earliest four, vary anywhere between 3 to 95 percent.[94] Thus, these visual data convey that there was such a high regard even among the early Christians for the divine names and titles of both God and Jesus, similar to that which caused the scribes of some manuscripts of the DSS and LXX to render the *tetragrammaton* distinctively from the rest of the text.[95]

However, Larry Hurtado has suggested that the Christian practice of the *nomina sacra* less likely has a Jewish derivation but is innovatively of an Christian origin, even though he acknowledges the phenomenological similarities between the Jewish and Christian scribal praxis of the *nomina divina*,.[96] As C. F. D. Moule pointed out in his work on the origin of early Christology, it was F. C. Burkitt who observed the abbreviation of ΚΥ for κυρίου at the end of the line in the manuscript of Aquila's version for the text of 2 Kings 23:24. This phenomenon, however, most likely does not mean that the Jewish scribes had a stylistic abbreviation of the *nomina divina* in the same way as in the earliest NT papyri.[97] But it probably suggests, as Burkitt pointed out, that in the Greek synagogues during the time of Aquila, the Jews used and read κύριος for the *tetragrammaton* in their scriptures.[98]

While the scribal practice of the *nomina sacra* might have been a distinctive Christian scribal feature, the motivation behind it was probably similar to that which led to the early Jewish scribal practices with the di-

---

94. Bokedal, *The Formation*, 89-90.
95. Hurtado, "The Origin," 663.
96. Hurtado, *The Earliest*, 106-111. Although Hurtado sees a similar 'religious motive' (p. 105) between the Jewish and Christian scribal praxis of the *nomina divina* and *sacra* in that both phenomena issue from their scribes' reverence towards the names and titles of God, as well as of Jesus in the case of the Christian scribes, Hurtado remains convinced, along with Tov and Tuckett, that the Christian scribal practice of the *nomina sacra* is an early Christian innovation and convention since the scribal mechanics and consistency differ significantly; see esp. 108-109.
97. C. F. D. Moule, *The Origin of Christology* (Cambridge: Cambridge University Press, 1977), 40; F. C. Burkitt, *Fragments of the Books of Kings According to the Translation of Aquila* (Cambridge: Cambridge University Press, 1897), 16.
98. Moule, *The Origin of Christology*, 40.

vine name as evidenced in some of the DSS and LXX manuscripts (e.g., P. Fouad 266).[99] That is, the Jewish and Christian scribal practices for the *nomina divina* and the *nomina sacra* respectively should be considered as the demonstration of their devotion to the God of Israel (cf., Gal 6:16), reflecting Exodus 20:7 and Deuteronomy 5:11. It is remarkable that the early Christian scribal practice presents the *nomina sacra* for the name of Jesus (Ἰησοῦς) and the title of messiah (χριστός) at the same level as θεός and κύριος.

The Divine Name in Israel's Scriptures and Paul's Letters

It is significant, as noted earlier,[100] that the name of the God of Israel, namely the *tetragrammaton*, occurs approximately more than 6,800 times in the Hebrew Bible. Within these occurrences of the *tetragrammaton* in the HB there are more than 800 occurrences where the *nomina divina* are followed by the word אלהים, usually translated in English as "the Lord God." Also, within these 800 examples of יהוה אלהים, there are 119 occurrences where the *tetragrammaton* is followed by a modifying phrase, the 'God of Israel', so 'the Lord God of Israel' as in יהוה אלהי ישראל. Moreover, there are 87 Hebrew construct phrases of the *tetragrammaton* with a noun word שֵׁם as its construct to mean "the name of the Lord," while among them there are 46 prepositional phrases with a preposition בְּ in the Hebrew Bible.[101]

For the construct phrase שם אלהים there are only 14 occurrences, distributed evenly between the reference to other deities and reference to the God of Israel.[102] For our interest, it is significant that when the authors

---

99. Hurtado, *The Earliest*, 105-106; idem., "The Origin," 663, 671-672.
100. See n. 12.
101. Gen 4:26; 12:8; 13:4; 16:13; 21:33; 26:25; Exod 20:7; 33:19; 34:5; Lev 24:16; Deut 5:11; 18:5, 7, 22; 21:5; 28:10; 32:3; Josh 9:9; 1 Sam 17:45; 20:42; 2 Sam 6:2, 18; 1 Kgs 3:2; 5:17, 19; 8:17, 20; 10:1; 18:24, 32; 22:16; 2 Kgs 2:24; 5:11; Isa 18:7; 24:15; 48:1; 50:10; 56:6; 59:19; 60:9; Jer 11:21; 26:9, 16, 20; 44:16; Joel 2:26; 3:5; Amos 6:10; Mic 4:5; 5:3; Zeph 3:9, 12; Zech 13:3; Pia 7:18; 20:8; 102:16, 22; 113:1; 116:4, 13, 17:118:10, 26; 122:4; 124:8; 129:8; 135:1; 148:5, 13; Job 1:21; Prov 18:10; 1 Chron 16:2; 21:9; 22:7, 19; 2 Chron 1:18; 2:3; 6:7, 10; 18:15; 33:18.
102. For שם אלהים in a reference to other deities, Exod 23:13; Deut 18:20; Josh 23:7; 1 Kgs 18:24, 25; Mic 4:5, and to the God of Israel, see Lev 18:21; 19:12; 21:6; Psa 20:2, 6; 44:21; 69:31; Prov 30:9. It is, however, significant that both in 1 Kgs 18:24 and Mic 4:5 שם יהוה in reference to the God of Israel is in an immediate opposition and contrast to שם אלהים in connection to other deities.

of the Hebrew Bible refer to the name of the God with the word שֵׁם, the construct form of the *tetragrammaton* was predominantly used either as שם יהוה or שם יהוה אלהים. Similarly, in the LXX there are a number of occurrences with the name of God either as τὸ ὄνομα κυρίου or τὸ ὄνομα κυρίου θεοῦ, which is more frequent than the phrase of τὸ ὄνομα θεοῦ. With these predominant phrases and construction for the divine name in mind, we are now concerned with the construct form of the divine name with other words in the Hebrew Bible, as well as with Paul's use of the name and titles of Jesus and the citation of Israel's scriptures in the letters.

The Covenant Formula and the Divine Name

The ways in which the divine name is represented in the word order of 'the Lord, God, Israel', thus שם יהוה אלהי ישראל and ὄνομα κυρίου θεοῦ Ισραηλ, are relevant and significant to this study, but also important is the aspect of the covenant, or the covenant formula (*die Bundesformel*),[103] for the divine name. For the scope of the current study, the texts of Genesis 17, for its foundational characteristic of the word בְּרִית for Israel, and Exodus 6, where God revealed the divine plan of redemption for Israel to Moses, are of interest.

As Rolf Rendtorff observed, in agreement with Rudolf Smend,[104] the covenant formula is show in the texts of Genesis 17:7-8, where it reads, להיות לך לאלהים...להם לאלהים (to be God to you... and [I will be] God to them), and Exodus 6:7, which reads, ולקחתי אתכם לי לעם והייתי לכם לאלהים (and I will take you to me as a people [i.e., my people] and will be to you as God [i.e., your God]).[105] This statement, 'I will be your God, and you shall be my people,' as expressed more fully in Exodus 6:7, is the covenant formula in a complete sense, since the Hebrew Bible often contains either one of the two sides, 'I will be God for you' or 'you shall be a people for me' in a number of places.[106]

---

103. Rolf Rendtorff, *The Covenant Formula: An Exegetical and Theological Investigation*, trans. Margaret Kohl (Edinburgh: T&T Clark, 1998).

104. Rudolf Smend, 'Die Bundesformel', ThSt(B) 68 (1963); reprinted in *Die Mitte des Alten Testaments: Gesammelte Studien 1*, BEvTh 99 (Munich, 1986; Tübingen: Mohr Siebeck, 2002), 11-39.

105. Rendtorff, *The Covenant*, 11-17.

106. Ibid., 13.

The Nameless Scriptures and the Name Above All Names

In Exodus 6:6-8 this covenant formula significantly takes a central place in the passage where God reveals the divine plan of redemption for Israel in relation to his divine name:[107]

> I am the LORD (אֲנִי יְהוָה)
>> I will free you from the burdens of the Egyptians
>> I will deliver you from slavery to them
>> I will redeem you with an outstretched arm...
>> **I will take you as my people, and**
>> **I will be your God. You shall know that**
>>> **I am the LORD your God** (אֲנִי יְהוָה אֱלֹהֵיכֶם)
>> who has freed you from the burden of the Egyptians
>> I will bring you into the land that I swore to give to...
>> I will give it to you for a possession
> I am the LORD (אֲנִי יְהוָה)

The covenant formula that depicts the relation between God and Israel is the crucial element for the revelation of the divine name, as well as the plan of redemption in Exodus 6:2-8 (cf. Exod 3:7-22). Such covenantal relationship between God and Israel explains the dominant number of occurrences of יהוה אלהים and שם יהוה אלהים in the Hebrew Bible since the divine name, as the covenant name, was revealed in the context of the establishment of Israel as a whole to be redeemed as the covenant people of God. Hence, considering the concepts of the covenant and redemption, the phrase of יהוה אלהי ישראל, which occurs 119 times in the Hebrew Bible, inherently depicts the covenant relation between God and Israel. The *tetragrammaton* represents the covenant name of God while אלהים signifies divinity and ישראל the one with whom this divine יהוה has established the covenant.

In sum, as we have observed from the text of Exodus 6:6-8, there is a covenant-name theology in the Hebrew Bible, depicting God, in connection to the divine name, as the one who establishes a covenant with and redeems his people. This dual aspect of covenant and redemption seems

---

107. For the structure analysis of Exodus 6:2-8 and the significance of the repeated phrase הוהי ינא within this passage, see Austin D. Surls, "Making Sense of the Divine Name in the Book of Exodus: From Etymology to Literary Onomastics" (PhD diss., Wheaton College, 2015), 136.

to be important for the revelation of the divine name as reflected with the phrase שם יהוה אלהי ישראל or τὸ ὄνομα κυρίου θεοῦ Ισραλη in Israel's scriptures. As we are moving on to the ὄνομα-κύριος theology in the Pauline corpus, this dual aspect of covenant and redemption in the name of the Lord seems to be crucial for our understanding of Pauline Christology.

Κύριος Ἰησοῦς and the Scriptural Citation in Romans 10:9-13

When Paul uses the word ὄνομα in relation to Jesus in his letters, he always uses the phrase τὸ ὄνομα τοῦ κρίου except the times when he uses the pronoun αὐτοῦ in reference to Jesus (τοῦ ὀνόματος αὐτοῦ, Rom 1:5) and when in Philippians 2:10 he writes ἐν τῷ ὀνόματι Ἰησοῦ πᾶν γόνυ κάμψῃ. Beside these two phrases with ὄνομα in reference to Jesus, the phrase τὸ ὄνομα κυρίου is used nine times for Jesus in the Pauline corpus.[108] If we consider the phrases κύριος Ἰησοῦς and κύριος Ἰησοῦς Χριστός, the frequency of Paul's use of the word κύριος in relation to Jesus becomes more significant with 36 and 21 times, respectively.[109] Considering the occurrences of 199 and 358 times for Ἰησοῦς and κύριος in the Pauline corpus, the aforementioned numbers are not trivial. Also, in view of Paul's citations from the LXX, which include κύριος as the divine name, his appropriation of this Hellenic Jewish representation of the divine name to the person of Jesus the Nazarene is significant for our understanding of Pauline Christology.[110]

For instance, in the text of Romans 10:9-13 Paul declares that when a person confesses with his or her mouth κύριον Ἰησοῦν and trusts in his or her heart that God raised him (Jesus) from death, that person shall be saved (v. 9) on the basis of the Israel's scriptures, namely from Isaiah 28:16 (for the aspect of faith in Romans 10:11) and from Joel 3:5[2:32] (for sal-

---

108. Rom 10:13; 1 Cor 1:2, 10; 5:4; 6:11; Eph 5:20; Col 3:17; 2 Thess 1:12; 3:6.

109. 36 times for κύριος Ιησους in Rom 1:7; 10:9; 13:14; 14:14; 1 Cor 1:3; 6:11; 8:6; 11:23; 12:3; 16:23; 2 Cor 1:2; 4:14; 11:31; 13:13; Gal 1:3; Eph 1:2, 15; Phil 1:2; 2:11, 19; 3:20; 4:23; Col 3:17; 1 Thess 1:1; 4:1(x2); 2 Thess 1:1 (x2), 7, 12; 2:8; 3:12; Philm 3, 5, 25; and among these 21 times for κύριος Ιησους Χριστός in Rom 1:7; 13:14; 1 Cor 1:3; 6:11; 8:6; 2 Cor 1:2; 13:13; Gal 1:3; Eph 1:2; 6:23; Phil 1:2; 2:11; 3:20; 4:23; 1 Thess 1:1; 2 Thess 1:1 (x2); 1:12; 3:12; Philm 3, 25.

110. Capes, *Old Testament Yahweh Texts*, 115-149; e.g., Joel 3:5 [2:32] in Rom 10:12-13; Jer 9:24 in 1 Cor 1:31; Isa 40:13 in 1 Cor 2:16; Num 16:5 in 2 Tim 2:19. See also Davis, *The Name and Way*, 129-140.

vation for those who confess κύριος Ἰησοῦς).[111] Both of these texts come from an eschatological context of יום יהוה (Isa 28:5; Joel 3:4[2:31]) and are centered around Zion. "Calling upon the name of the LORD" as well as "the LORD's calling" at the eschaton are the crucial aspects of this redemption as seen in Joel 3:5[2:32].[112] In Romans 10:13 Paul appropriates this calling on the name of YHWH (קרא בשם יהוה) from Joel 3:5[2:32] to ὁμολογέω κύριον Ἰησοῦν. Such a theological appropriation suggests that there is an 'ὄνομα-Christology' in Paul's thought, attributing the יהוה texts and divine κύριος name to Jesus[113] in the eschatological context of faith and salvation in Romans 10:9-13 (cf. Acts 9:14; 1 Cor 1:2; 12:3; 2 Tim 2:22).

The Christ-Hymn and an ONOMA-Christology in Paul

Paul's ὄνομα-Chirstology is apparent in his scripture citations in Romans 10, but it can also be perceived in the Christological hymn of Philippians 2:6-11. As debated by a number of scholars, this Christ-hymn of Philippians 2:6-11 was either of pre-Pauline origin or authored by Paul.[114] If the hymn originated from a pre-Pauline source, it may be that this hymn could have been one of the sources from which Paul had drawn and which had contributed to his ὄνομα-Christology, appropriating the divine

---

111. Paul the apostle follows almost, in part, verbatim to the LXX version of Isaiah 28:16 and Joel 3:5[2:32] in Romans 10:11 and 13 respectively, only adding the words πᾶς, prior to the Isaianic citation, and γάρ, into the text from Joel. Thus for Romans 10:11 πᾶς ὁ πιστεύων ἐπ'αὐτῷ οὐ καταισχυνθήσεται (Isa 28:16 except πᾶς; and also in the HB המאמין לא יחיש without the word כל); as for v. 13 πᾶς γὰρ ὃς ἂν ἐπικαλέσηται τὸ ὄνομα κυρίου σωθήσεται (Joel 3:5[2:32] except γάρ; also in HB כל אשר קרא בשם יהוה ימלט).

112. Davis, *The Name and Way*, 130-131.

113. C. E. B. Cranfield, *A Critical and Exegetical Commentary on the Epistle to the Romans* (2 vols.; ICC11; Edinburgh: T&T Clark, 1979), 2: 529; Robert Jewett, *Romans: A Commentary*, Hermeneia (Minneapolis, MN: Fortress Press, 2007), 633. See also C. Kavin Rowe, "Romans 10:13: What Is the Name of the Lord?," *HBT* 22 (2000): 135-173.

114. Ralph Martin, *Carmen Christi: Philippians ii.5–11 in Recent Interpretation and in the Setting of Early Christian Worship* (Cambridge: Cambridge University Press, 1967), 42-62, 287; Robert B. Strimple, "Philippians 2:5-11 in Recent Studies: Some Exegetical Conclusions," *WTJ* 41 (1979): 248-251; Takeshi Nagata, "Philippians 2:5-11: A Case Study in the Contextual Shaping of Early Christology" (PhD diss., Princeton Theological Seminary, 1981), 88-95; Gordon Fee, "Philippians 2:5-11: Hymn or Exalted Pauline Prose?," *BBR* 2 (1992): 34-37; Cătălin Varga, "The Pauline Background of the Christological Hymn in the Epistle to Philippians 2:6-11," *SUTO* 60 (2015): 65-66.

name and cultic devotion to the person and name of Jesus Christ.[115] If the hymn was composed originally by Paul in the letter, his allusion to Isaiah 45:23-24a[116] and its interpretation in Philippians 2:9-11 suggests Paul's ὄνομα-Christology.

There are three things to note concerning the literary context of Isaiah 45:23-24. First, the God of Israel is declared to be the sole exclusive creator of all things and redeemer for the people. Both monotheistic uniqueness and saving activity are the features that are part of Isaiah 45:23-24.[117] Significantly, Isaiah 45–46 conveys God's unique and exclusive character as creator (45:5-11; 46:1-11) and redeemer (45:13-17; 46:12-13) with such phrases as (אני יהוה ואין עוד) 45:5, 6, 18) and 46:8; 45:22) אני אל ואין עוד).

Second, the unique and exclusive divine prerogative in relation to the people is crucial for understanding Isaiah 45:23-24. The text of Isaiah 45:22-25 begins with "Turn to me and be saved" (v. 22), "By myself I have sworn" (v. 23), "only in YHWH" (v. 24) and again "in YHWH" (v. 25). The irrevocable word and promise of this unique and exclusive God of Israel in v. 23 is "To me every knee shall bow, every tongue shall swear." The author of the Christ-hymn, whether Paul or not, made a significantly modified citation of this connection to Jesus Christ in Philippians 2:9-11.

Third, and briefly, the LXX version of Isaiah 45:24 is correctly translates the Hebrew text and interprets it as the content of the confession of all tongues, but translates the *tetragrammaton* with the word θεός. We will return to this last point shortly as we consider the 'modified citation' of Isaiah 45:23-24 in Philippians 2:10-11.

Philippians 2:9-11, the Isaianic modified citation, follows closely to the LXX version of Isaiah 45:23-24, with a few phrasal differences as it is possible that the Hebrew text might also be in view as well here. Considering Paul's other verbatim citation of Isaiah 45:23 in verbatim in Romans 14:11,[118]

---

115. Ralph Martin, "Carmen Christi Revisited," in *Where Christology Began: Essays on Philippians 2*, eds. R. P. Martin and B. J. Dodd (Louisville: Westminster John Knox, 1998), 3.

116. Peter O'Brien, *The Epistle to the Philippians: A Commentary on the Greek Text* (Grand Rapids: Eerdmans, 1991), 241-242; Gordon D. Fee, *Paul's Letter to the Philippians*, NICNT (Grand Rapids: Eerdmans, 1995), 224.

117. Moisés Silva, *Philippians*, BECNT, 2nd ed. (Grand Rapids: Baker Academic, 2005), 112.

118. Markus Bockmuehl, *A Commentary on the Epistle to the Philippians*, BNC (London: A&C Black, 1997), 146.

such modification of the Isaianic text in Philippians 2:10-11, if intended by the apostle, is significantly important:

Isaiah 45:23b-24a (HB/MT):
כִּי־לִי תִּכְרַע כָּל־בֶּרֶךְ תִּשָּׁבַע כָּל־לָשׁוֹן אַךְ בַּיהוָה לִי אָמַר צְדָקוֹת וָעֹז עָדָיו

Isaiah 45:23b-24a (LXX):
ὅτι ἐμοὶ κάμψει πᾶν γόνυ καὶ ἐξομολογήσεται πᾶσα γλῶσσα τῷ θεῷ λέγων δικαιοσύνη καὶ **δόξα πρὸς αὐτὸν** ἥξουσιν...

Philippians 2:10-11 (NA28): ἵνα **ἐν τῷ ὀνόματι Ἰησοῦ** πᾶν γόνυ κάμψῃ ἐπουρανίων καὶ ἐπιγείων καὶ καταχθονίων **καὶ πᾶσα γλῶσσα ἐξομολογήσηται** ὅτι **κύριος Ἰησοῦς Χριστὸς εἰς δόξαν θεοῦ πατρός**.

Philippians 2:10 begins ἵνα ἐν τῷ ὀνόματι Ἰησοῦ in place of ὅτι ἐμοί from Isaiah 45:23 and adds the phrase ἐπουρανίων καὶ ἐπιγείων καὶ καταχθονίων before ἐξομολογήσεται πᾶσα γλῶσσα.[119] While Isaiah 45:23-24 reads, at its beginning, "to me" (לִי / ἐμοί) in reference to the God of Israel, the author of the Christ-hymn inserts the phrase ἐν τῷ ὀνόματι Ἰησοῦ, as in Philippians 2:10. Furthermore, where the Hebrew text of Isaiah 45:24 reads אַךְ בַּיהוָה לִי אָמַר, literally "only in the Lord, saying to me," which is translated as τῷ θεῷ λέγων in the LXX, the author of the hymn seems to apply κύριος Ἰησοῦς Χριστός as the full expression of the *nomen divinum*, 'the name above all names' (Phil 2:9) to the person and name of Jesus Christ. All this suggests that there is a lucid ὄνομα-Christology in this Christ-hymn of Philippians 2:9-11, whether Paul had composed it or incorporated it, seemingly, with the contextual and theological connection to Isaiah 45:23-24.

יהוה אלהי ישראל *in Israel's Scriptures and Κύριος Ἰησοῦς Χριστός in Paul*

We have seen that in Romans 10:9-13 and Philippians 2:9-11 the apostle appropriates the so-called YHWH texts and the divine name from Israel's scriptures to the person and name of Jesus Christ. As well, he connects the prophetic promise of Israel's restoration and redemption to the Christ event. We have also observed, in this paper, Paul's use of the phrase κύριος

---

119. Or πᾶσα γλῶσσα ἐξομολογήσεται as in Phil 2:11.

Ἰησους or κύριος Ἰησους Χριστός. When it comes to denoting the name of Jesus, the apostle almost always uses the τό ὄνομα κυρίου construction except in two instances, ὑπὲρ τοῦ ὀνόματος αὐτοῦ in Romans 1:5 and ἐν τῷ ὀνόματι Ἰησοῦ in Philippians 2:9. The reference of κυρίος Ἰησους Χριστός in immediate proximity to the two passages (Rom 1:4; Phil 2:10) indicates that τὸ ὄνομα τοῦ κυρίου is predominantly used in reference to the name of Jesus in the Pauline corpus.

Furthermore, the sheer number of occurrences of the phrases κύριος Ἰησους and κύριος Ἰησους Χριστός in the Pauline epistles is significant. If the *tetragrammaton* was the name of God in the context of the covenant and redemption in Israel's scriptures (Exod 6), Paul's use of the prophetic YHWH texts and the divine name for the person and name of Jesus and the Christ-event suggests Paul's particular Christological understanding of the identity and status of Jesus in the context of the covenant and redemption as well. Thus, if the phrase יהוה אלהי ישראל, the YHWH God of Israel, represents the covenant relationship between God and Israel in Israel's scriptures, κύριος Ἰησους Χριστός, Lord Jesus Christ, also describes the covenant relationship between the Lord Jesus Christ and his holy people,[120] to use a Pauline terminology, with the covenantal *nomen divinum*, κύριος.

Paul's use of new/renewed covenant language (καινὴ διαθήκη), of which the apostle uses only twice (1 Cor 11:25; 2 Cor 3:6), especially in the context of the Lord's Supper, supports that Paul's use of κύριος for Jesus has a covenantal significance. Paul mentions that he "received from the Lord," and again in the same sentence he emphasizes that it was ὁ κύριος Ἰησοῦς who broke the bread and took the cup of the new covenant (1 Cor 11:23-26). Who establishes a covenant with the people and asks them to remember him, if not the God of Israel?

Thus, in the Pauline corpus we may see the apostle's ὄνομα-Christology. This study suggests to us that such ὄνομα-Christology in Paul should be understood within the context of covenant and redemption and gives us somewhat of a window into how and why the apostles and the earliest Christians gave cultic devotion, exclusively appropriate to the God of Israel, to the person of Jesus the Nazarene. In addition, it suggests how and

---

120. For relationship to Christ as a significant element of Paul's Christology, see Chris Tilling, *Paul's Divine Christology* (Grand Rapids: Eerdmans, 2015).

why the early Christian scribes had regarded the name of Ἰησοῦς and the title of Χριστός as part of the *nomina sacra* with the same consistency as the words of κύριος and θεός in the scribal praxis of the early Christianity.

Conclusion

In this study we have examined the presentation of the divine names in the biblical and non-biblical texts of the Qumran scrolls, in the early LXX manuscripts and the Jewish recension of the LXX, as well as in the NT. Some of the Qumran scrolls contain the *tetragrammaton* in the paleo-Hebrew letters (e.g., 1QpHab), as well as the *tetrapuncta*, reflecting the community's veneration for the divine names, even preventing the pronunciation as well as the erasure of the *nomina divina*.

In the early manuscripts of the LXX there are a few fragments that include the Hebrew *tetragrammaton* in both paleo-Hebrew and Aramaic-square script (e.g., P. Fouad 266, 8⊠ever XII gr). Other manuscripts of the LXX contain ΙΑΩ in place of the *tetragrammaton* (4QpapLXXLev[b]) while in Jewish recensions of the LXX we find yhyh in the paleo-Hebrew script (Aquila) as well as the paleo-Hebrew *tetragrammaton* (Symmachus). Moreover, the word ΠΙΠΙ is found in some of the manuscript evidence for Origen's *Hexaplaric* text. Thus, it is significant that none of the pre-Christian LXX manuscripts contain the noun κύριος for the *tetragrammaton* while the OT citations in the text of the NT attest to κύριος in place of the *tetragrammaton*. There is, however, enough support that the word κύριος must have been used for the *tetragrammaton* even before the time of the NT (e.g., Philo's *De Abrahamo* 121, Exodus 15:11 in 1QH VII.28).

Subsequently, moving on to the NT we have seen the *nomina sacra* where the divine names and titles are abbreviated with a line above the two or three letters in the early NT manuscripts (e.g., θεός, κύριος, Ἰησοῦς and χριστός). Remarkably, these four *nomina sacra* occur in 99 percent of all the instances in the 74 manuscripts within the first four centuries C.E.

We have also considered how Paul the apostle appropriated the YHWH texts and *nomina divina* in connection to the person and name of Jesus Christ in the context of covenant and redemption, just as the divine plan of salvation for Israel in Exodus was centered around the divine name and covenant. Thus we may perceive, in the Pauline corpus, the apostle's ὄνομα-Christology. Since Paul the apostle was a devout Jew, his appropriation of the *nomina divina* to a human being was unthinkable for the first-century Jews.

Thus, all of these textual, intertextual and exegetical phenomena surrounding the *nomina divina* demonstrate that both the Jewish and Christian scribes, as well as Paul the apostle, handled the divine names with reverence when they were copying (or not copying, i.e., *tetrapuncta* with four dots and blank spaces) or incorporating them into their writings. The ways in which the Jewish and Christians scribes rendered the divine names demonstrate their devotion towards the One to whom the *nomina divina* refer. Hence, it is remarkable that Paul the apostle would apply the *nomina divina* within the OT texts to Jesus. This evidences the presence of an early ὄνομα-Christology within the wider scope of Paul's divine Christology. Such an understanding certainly must have been passed down to the earliest Christian scribes, who, in their devotion, copied Ἰησοῦς and χριστός as the *nomina sacra* with the same degree of consistency as κύριος and θεός throughout the first four centuries of early Christianity.

Part 3

The People of God

A Passion for the Word

Scriptural Piety and Meaningful Mission

Jay T. Smith

In the autumn of 1999, I registered for my first course in the Master of Theology program at Regent College. Like all new ThM students, I had enrolled in INDS 726, *Readings In Modern Protestant Thought*. This was akin to theological "boot camp" for scholarship-focused Masters of Theology students. The curriculum consisted in the reading of one major book on modern Protestant thought per week. Immanuel Kant, Friedrich Schleiermacher, Feuerbach and Strauss, among others, became our "tutors" for the semester. However, Ivan Gaetz, our instructor, gave us a break one particular day, and had a variety of Regent faculty members come to class. One of those faculty members was Sven Soderlund. In that modest encounter, I was immediately struck by his subdued yet positive demeanor, his love of the students, and his passion for Scripture. Although I never had the opportunity to enroll in one of Sven's courses, his kind and scholarly demeanor stayed with me, and continues to encourage my own scholarship to this day.

This essay touches on those topics that have been meaningful to Professor Soderlund: the priority of Scripture and mission in the life of the church. Scripture has been at the heart of the Protestant and evangelical movements for the last five hundred years, and has become the object of much debate in the last one hundred and fifty years. Hand-in-hand with the issue of Scripture has been the changing nature of the church's mission.

The lack of detail regarding the methodology of the church's mission in Scripture has led to a variety of interpretations, and a decline in traditional missional participation. This essay posits an approach to both Scripture and mission that recaptures a dynamic priority for each in the life of the church.

Christian Scripture: The Question of Authority

In the nineteenth century, the advent of modern scientific method began to influence biblical studies in a profound fashion.[1] For North American biblical studies scholars, the Scottish Commonsense Realism[2] of Thomas Reid became the predominant epistemological approach to the text. In an attempt to "prove" the soundness and "truthfulness" of the Bible in this modern age—an age marked by Darwinism, industrialism, and the rise of capitalism—the academy, led by the early Princeton theologians, began to construct an irrefutable foundation to ground the authority of the Bible.[3] This foundationalist approach to biblical authority did not garner universal approval from the church; indeed, it only exacerbated preexisting divisions. Early in the twentieth century, the divide became obvious in the "Fundamentalist-Modernist" controversy, where philosophical foundationalism and the uncritical appropriation of scientific theory met head to head.[4] In the years since, the divide has only widened as moderate-liberal and conservative-fundamentalist factions within the church have wrecked denominations, crippled individual congregations, and alienated at least

---

1. Stanley J. Grenz, *Renewing the Center: Evangelical Theology in a Post-Theological Era* (Grand Rapids: Baker Academic, 2000), 69f.
2. Mark A. Noll, *Princeton and the Republic 1786-1822* (Princeton, NJ: Princeton University Press, 1989), 36-37, 284-85.
3. Ernest R. Sandeen, *The Roots of Fundamentalism: British and American Millenarianism 1800-1930* (Chicago: University of Chicago Press, 1970), 114-131. Note: Sandeen's thesis is not without its critics. Scholars such as John Woodbridge, D. A. Carson, and Paul Helseth defend the Princeton understanding as the only legitimate *evangelical* position on Scripture. See John Woodbridge, *Biblical Authority: A Critique of the Roger-McKim Proposal* (Grand Rapids: Zondervan, 1982), and Paul K. Helseth and Millard Erickson, eds. *Reclaiming the Center: Confronting Evangelical Accommodation in Postmodern Times* (Wheaton, IL: Crossway, 2004).
4. Sandeen, 258-254. Also, Harry Emerson Fosdick, *The Modern Use of the Bible* (New York: Macmillan, 1927), and Fosdick, *A Guide to Understanding the Bible* (New York: Harper & Brothers, 1938).

three generations of young adults. The issue became so pronounced that at the end of the twentieth century, and the beginning of the twenty-first, scholars produced volume after volume on the authenticity, authority, and truthfulness of the Bible.[5]

There are several questions that needed to find answers. First, "How should the Christian understand the *authority* of the Bible?" Following this primary question, there are several derivative questions, all of which are debated at the Society of Biblical Literature meetings. For example, "How *is* the Bible the 'Word of God'?", "What makes the Bible the 'Word of God'?", "How does the Bible's standing as the 'Word of God' make it authoritative?", and "Does this standing make it authoritative for non-Christians?". Second, "How should Christians *interpret* the Bible?" Again, there are several derivative questions, all dependent upon how the first question is answered. For example, "Should there be a 'universal' approach or method to biblical interpretation?" "Can the content of the Bible be 'truth' if is not taken literally?" Currently, the majority of evangelically-oriented churches in North America affirm the Chicago Statement on Biblical Inerrancy (1978),[6] usually with some level of nuance. The Chicago Statement was produced in order to provide a definitive platform from which evangelicals could assert the authority of the Bible, and which would stand as an irrefutable foundation for theological and doctrinal construction in a modern, scientifically oriented era. However, the Chicago Statement moves beyond simply being a statement on the authority of Scripture, for it seeks to make statements about the quality of Scripture that shackles the text to a literal interpretative process—in a sense, limiting the Spirit's work in and through the text. The remaining Protestant churches affirm the Bible as central to

---

5. E.g. Meredith Kline, *The Structure of Biblical Authority* 2d ed. (Eugene, OR: Wipf & Stock, 1989); Kevin Vanhoozer, *Biblical Authority After Babel* (Grand Rapids: Brazos Press, 2016); *The Enduring Authority of the Christian Scriptures*, ed. D. A. Carson (Grand Rapids: Eerdmans, 2016); William Brown, *Engaging Biblical Authority: Perspectives on the Bible as Scripture* (Louisville: Westminster John Knox, 2007); Louis Countryman, *Biblical Authority or Biblical Tyranny: Scripture and the Christian Pilgrimage?* (Philadelphia: Fortress Press, 1982); Robert Price, *Inerrant the Wind: The Evangelical Crisis in Biblical Authority* (Amherst, NY: Prometheus, 2009);

6. The Short Statement of the 1978 Chicago Statement on Biblical Inerrancy is the simplest way of digesting this stance. Accessed at https://www.moodybible.org/beliefs/the-chicago-statement-on-biblical-inerrancy/ May 16, 2020.

their worship and discipleship, but do not necessarily affirm a specific position on authority or interpretation.

Grenz, the Spirit and the Scriptures

As Christians living in a postmodern context, we have inherited various approaches to the authority of Scripture that are grounded in modern philosophical presuppositions; yet these presuppositions are now being questioned. Understanding that problem, former Regent College professor Stanley Grenz suggested an alternative understanding of scriptural authority—the Bible as *the Spirit's book*. Grounding the authority of Scripture in the doctrine of the Trinity, Grenz outlined a theory of authority that was theologically coherent, philosophically meaningful, and *spiritually* dynamic. Through this theory, Grenz sought to avoid the long-standing evangelical reliance upon a foundationalist epistemology and a default hermeneutic linked to scientific method.[7] Grenz did not eschew contemporary biblical studies; on the contrary, he embraced them as a means of comprehending the nuances of the cultural context and scriptural message.[8]

However, by locating the authority of Scripture in the Holy Spirit, Grenz re-ordered the priorities of exegesis. To be able to interpret Scripture effectively, the interpreter first and foremost acknowledges the *theological and thus spiritual* nature of the text: God is speaking through the text; thus, God's speaking becomes God's dynamic Word. The divine speech, finding its origin in the Father, given shape and meaning by the Son, and communicated dynamically by the Holy Spirit, is inscribed in human hearts, and written as Scripture. God's speech in the text can be characterized as both polyphonic, and symphonic; it is many-voiced, with many thematic strands, and yet the speech itself forms a unity of beauty, truth, and goodness.[9] When God speaks, it is not simply "heard" but experienced; it resonates in the heart, the intellect, and penetrates to the furthest recesses of the soul. The quality of God's Word—God's Speaking—defies catego-

---

7. Grenz, *Renewing the Center*, 69-70.

8. For an example, see Grenz, *The Social God and the Relational Self: A Trinitarian Theology of the Imago Dei* (Louisville: Westminster John Knox, 2001).

9. See Hans Urs von Balthasar, *Truth is Symphonic: Aspects of Christian Pluralism* (San Francisco, CA: Ignatius, 1987) or Vern Poythress, *Symphonic Theology: The Validity of Multiple Perspectives in Theology* (Phillipsburg, NJ: P & R Publishing, 2001)

rization, and yet its truth cannot be reduced or dismissed. Indeed, there are passages of the biblical text that present as unreasonable, illogical, or even impossible according to contemporary scientific standards. Yet God's Word is not faithfully or accurately interpreted by these standards. The contemporary interpreter cannot be dismissive of the passages of text that seem irrational, nonsensical, or erroneous; rather, they require the interpreter, after performing a rigorous exegesis, to give interpretive priority to the spiritual nature and theological intent of the text.[10] *The Bible is the Spirit's book* through and through, from dynamic and continual inspiration to dynamic and particular illumination.[11] This would seem to be the position of the earliest church fathers and mothers as they understood the role of the Holy Spirit within the Trinity.[12] According to the apostle Paul, the Scriptures are sacred, and thus "profitable"[13] for teaching, reproof, correction and for training:

> But as for you, continue in what you have learned and firmly believed, knowing from whom you have learned it, and how from childhood you have known the sacred writings that are able to instruct you for salvation through faith in Christ Jesus. All Scripture is *inspired by God* and is *useful* for teaching, for reproof, for correction, and for training in righteousness; so that everyone who belongs to God may be proficient, equipped for every good work. (2 Timothy 3:14-18 NRSV)

If we seek to apply Paul's understanding of the function of Scripture, it means that the modern-day interpreter explores the geo-social context, character actions, and consequential results within the biblical text in order to construe theological content for coherent and meaningful contemporary application. The most prominent place where the spiritual

---

10. For the modern interpreter, immersed in a scientific worldview, texts such as 2 Kings 6:5-7 are beyond the scientific ability to affirm; therefore, the credibility and truth-bearing nature of the text is often dismissed or allegorized. The question that faces the interpreter should not be, how did the axe-head float? But rather, what purpose does the floating of the axe-head serve?

11. Stanley J. Grenz, *Theology for the Community of God* (Nashville, TN: Broadman Press, 1994), 379ff.

12. E.g. *The Epistle of Ignatius to the Philadelphians*, Chapter V.—Pray for me;

13. ὠφέλιμος – Strong's G5624 – *helpful, serviceable or advantageous: profitable.*

authority of the text is on display is in the sermon. It is here, in sermon preparation and delivery, that the pastor-exegete must practice exegetical expertise and spiritual wisdom. This exegetical process becomes even more important when studying passages of text that espouse an *ethos* that is at odds with contemporary moral standards and practice. The role of the interpreter is then expanded to rhetorician, with a concern for pastoral care and sensitive leadership in confronting the conflict in the sermon. With this exegetical and rhetorical responsibility there is a temptation to take "liberties" with the text in order to ground a particular theological point. This misuse, or abuse, of Scripture, actually weakens its spiritual authority and undermines the truth-carrying capacity of the text. Commonly called "Scripture twisting" or "proof-texting," this practice conflates the truth of the text with the theological proposition advocated by the exegete. A humility of spirit exercised through the character and ethos of the exegete is critical to the appropriate proclamation of the text.

The Bible in the Modern World

Many Protestants in Western culture have lost sight of what it means for the Scriptures to be "inspired"[14] and "authoritative" in our postmodern era. The root cause of this loss of vision is the manner in which the church has realized the function of Scripture in relation to our science-driven culture. There are generally two positions on this issue, conveniently generalized as "liberal" and "conservative." These positions have been "weaponized" in the war-like struggle between scriptural authority and cultural questions. The liberal-moderate side of this vision problem accepts the canons of science as definitive for the interpretation of Scripture, as well as its application to cultural issues. In this perspective, Scripture becomes a "moral reference"—a part of the liturgy, but not a universally applicable measure of divine truth. Thus, on cultural, cosmological, anthropological and physical issues, Scripture must yield to science in questions of the literal "truthfulness" of the narrative.[15] If contemporary "science"[16] judges that

---

14. θεόπνευστος – Strong's G2315 – divinely breathed in; Grenz, "God-spirited" – See Grenz, Theology for the Community of God, 380f.

15. Harry Emerson Fosdick, William Newton Clarke, Robert M. Price, Bart Ehrman, et al., in Sandeen.

16. By this we mean scientific fields of study – e.g., physics, mathematics, biology, med-

a narrative is unlikely, impossible, improbable, or hurtful, then the truth quality of the narrative is categorized as "moral mythology."

The conservative-fundamentalist side of the vision problem does not accept the canons of science as definitive for the interpretation of Scripture. However, the conservative vision of Scripture utilizes an aspect of early modern philosophy to ground its authority and truthfulness. Following Descartes' *Meditations on the First Philosophy,* the conservative side naively co-opted the concept of "foundations" in order to describe the authority of Scripture in relation to the Christian ethos and theology.[17] As its "foundation," Scripture embodies the essence of God's Word, and thus becomes the revelatory experience of the "Word of God." Although the Bible does not claim this status for itself, the "Word of God" concept was co-opted in order to anchor the truth claims of the Old and New Testaments in a world enamored of scientific method and philosophical foundationalism. The conservative side did not end its affection for modern philosophy with the concept of foundationalism. In the early nineteenth century, Princeton University, and consequently Princeton Seminary, made use of Scottish philosopher Thomas Reid's "commonsense realism," as a means of grounding the "universal truth" of Scripture. From this perspective, commonsense principles possess "the consent of ages and nations, of the learned and unlearned, [which] ought to have great authority with regard to first principles, where every man is a competent judge."[18] In the mid- to late nineteenth century, the commonsense realism of Reid, added to the Cartesian theory of foundationalism, became the preeminent philosophy used to ground the authority and truthfulness of Scripture.

Grenz found that neither of these approaches to scriptural authority and truthfulness could endure the withering philosophical and scientific criticism of late modernity, as well as the laissez-faire criticism of

---

icine, psychiatry, etc.

17. Note: This "co-opting" of philosophical positions is not necessarily a conscious activity of the 19th century Princetonians, Primitive and Landmark Baptists, etc. At Princeton, the focus of John Witherspoon's intellectual appropriation of commonsense realism, over time, migrates to the divinity faculty's constructs. Noll, 36ff.

18. Reid's "Common Sense Realism" has informed Evangelical theology for over 200 years. See Thomas Reid, *Essays on the Intellectual Powers,* (EIP 6.4, 464).6.4, 464. (Accessed at https://plato.stanford.edu/entries/reid/#ComSenFirPri, April 12, 2020).

the postmodern era. As the scientific and philosophical approach of the neo-evangelical Carl Henry reached its zenith, and then began to lose relevance, the question of the authority and veracity of Scripture began to resurface. Grenz's conclusion was that, if the authority and truthfulness of Scripture needed apologetic verification, then verification should come from the Triune God. Grenz, claimed, and rightly so, to be a "pietist with a PhD," understanding himself as a "Christian, a Baptist and an evangelical."[19] Coming out of this heritage, Grenz was committed to a theological grounding of the authority and veracity of Scripture that was not indebted to an Enlightenment epistemology, the priority of scientific method, or an evolutionist worldview. For Grenz, the Bible was a spiritual document whose authority and veracity is best understood through its origin in the Triune God.

With the advent of the postmodern critique, the modernist philosophical foundations of biblical authority are first questioned, then slowly rejected by many in the academy.[20] However, outside Grenz, there are no sustained attempts to ground the authority of Scripture within the doctrine of the Holy Spirit and the coherentist-pragmatist language games matrix that Grenz gives to his understanding of postmodern theological epistemology.[21] The contemporary Christian is faced with two very different approaches to the Bible. The modernist view of the Bible is that of a disparate collection of historical and moral writings forged into a book by the theo-political powers of the late Roman Empire.[22] The classical spiritual view of the Bible is of God-breathed, God-spirited, *inspired* Scriptures that describe the creative and salvific work of God, and serve as the formative *Word* for the Christian life. It is the latter position that was embraced by Grenz and many other contemporary Christians. It is the position that drives Christian biblical

---

19. Grenz's understanding of the inspiration and authority of Scripture comes out of this spiritual matrix. See Stanley J. Grenz, "Concerns of a Pietist with a Ph.D." accessed on May 20, 2020 at http://www.stanleyjgrenz.com/articles/pietist.html.

20. See Stanley J. Grenz and John R. Franke, *Beyond Foundationalism: Shaping Theology in a Postmodern Context* (Louisville: Westminster John Knox, 2001).

21. Grenz, *Renewing the Center*, 190-203.

22. See Bart Ehrman, *The Orthodox Corruption of Scripture: The Effect of Early Christological Controversies on the Text of the New Testament* (Oxford: Oxford University Press, 2011) and *Misquoting Jesus: The Story Behind Who Changed the Bible and Why?* (San Francisco: HarperOne, 2009).

scholars to mine the theological depths of Scripture.

The Church's position on the authority and veracity of Scripture dictates its mission, worship and doctrine. If one affirms the dynamic spiritual authority of the Bible, then its descriptions of Jesus, the cross and resurrection, salvation, personal and corporate empowerment by the Holy Spirit, and the mission of the church becomes the dynamic reality of the Christian. As Christians gather under this perspective, the congregation—now church—stands as a testimony to the love of God, and becomes a spiritual movement dedicated to the redemption and renewal of the world. If one affirms a modernist approach to Scripture, which views the Bible as a collection of historical and moral writings, then the gathering of believers serves to affirm the particular cultural thought of the congregation, with its affiliated causes. "Church" in this sense becomes a particular cultural obligation, as opposed to a dynamic, living, and moving expression of God.

Throughout Western culture, the concept of "church as obligation" has become as commonplace as the proliferation of biblical translations in the commercial market. Part of the legacy of the church in Western Protestant culture has been to identify with a particular denomination of Christianity because that is where family loyalties lie. An even more prominent mark of identification is that of doctrinal position. When new Christians are looking to become a part of a church, they look for a church that identifies doctrinally with their theological values. How has the "church as obligation," or "church as doctrinal position," become the norm for Western Christians, in contrast to the "church as the movement of God's love?" When we read Scripture as the Spirit-infused, Spirit-inspired and Spirit-illuminated Word of God, our vision of the church is much different. The church is not a static gathering of people once a week, but rather an 'In-spirited" movement, viral in nature, as its nature and *ethos* transform those who encounter it. Both the doctrine of Scripture and the doctrine of the church's mission should inform one another. To that end, we must understand the evolution of "church" from the various contexts in which it matured; for it is from these contexts that we are able to identify the church we have received, and rethink the church for our postmodern context and beyond. To the church and its mission we go next.

SCRIPTURES, SCHOLARSHIP, AND THE PEOPLE OF GOD

The 'Received' Church and the Recovery of Mission

The twenty-first century church in Western culture has a case of Dissociative Personality Disorder which has plagued it since its inception over two thousand years ago. Early in its life, the church argued and divided over several doctrinal questions, such as "Is Jesus God?", "If Jesus is God, is Jesus human?", "Is the Holy Spirit divine?", and "If so, how can the three different divine entities—Father, Son, Holy Spirit—constitute one God?" In 1054 the Catholic church split—the Latin West from the Orthodox East—over doctrinal questions about the procession of the Holy Spirit, as well as the power and control of Christendom.[23] This 'split' continued from century to century. In 1521, Martin Luther, a German monk and professor of theology in Wittenberg, began a "protest" movement that had unintended consequences: the break-up of the Roman Catholic church in northern Europe into a variety of "protest" churches, usually organized around national and theological affinities. This division resulted in the birth of the Lutheran Church in Germany, the Reformed Church in Switzerland and the Netherlands, the Anglican Church in England, the Presbyterian Church in Scotland, the Anabaptists (Mennonites) in portions of Germany, and the Baptists in England. Each sect had its own set of theological priorities, doctrinal particularities, and liturgical orders. The most prominent commitment they held in common was the priority of Scripture over church tradition as the rule of faith. Over time, the Protestant churches, as they are now known, continued to disagree over doctrine, and continued to split into Methodism, General and Regular Baptists, Assemblies of God, etc.[24] This continual disagreement over doctrinal issues continues to plague Protestant denominations to this day.

Interestingly, there is a growing movement of Christians throughout the world, who are reassessing their priorities as the "church." They are asking questions such as, "Should doctrine have the place of priority in our fellowship?", "Can Christianity be reduced to belief and the transformed

---

23. Called the "Great Schism." See Henry Chadwick, *East and West: The Making of a Rift in the Church from Apostolic Times Until the Council of Florence* (Oxford: Oxford University Press, 2003).

24. Cf. David Buschart, *Exploring Protestant Traditions: An Invitation to Theological Hospitality* (Downers Grove, IL: Intervarsity Press, 2006).

life, evidenced in following the way of Jesus?" "What place do baptism and the eucharist have in the rhythm and liturgy of the church?", "Should we own property that is exclusively for liturgical use?", "and "With such a high value placed on spiritual character development, and the witness of the gathered church, how are we to understand the nature and purpose of the church's mission?"

The Church of Empire

To get answers to these questions, it's important to return to the fourth century, when Diocletian, Galerius, Maximian and Constantius revoked the rights of Christians, and began the "Great Persecution" that lasted from 303 to 311. By 311, Galerius admitted that the persecution had failed, and, with Constantius's successor—his son, Constantine—issued the Edict of Toleration. In 324, Constantine became the sole emperor of the Roman empire.[25] Two items are notable. First, Constantine was a Christian in a very Roman sense of the term. Eusebius goes to great lengths to affirm the Emperor's faith, and select orations by Constantine affirm that, indeed, the emperor followed Christ. On the other hand, Constantine was a shrewd Roman politician. His battles with Maximian, and later with Licinius, as well as his battles with various barbarian armies, reveal Constantine as the quintessential Roman soldier. With relative peace now in the Empire, Constantine turned his attention to the various theological and liturgical quarrels in the church.[26] If, as Constantine believed, Christianity should be accorded the same privileges as other religions in the empire, is it possible that Christianity could become the unique religion of the empire? If so, should it not, in true Roman fashion, become uniform in beliefs and liturgies? Constantine was made aware of the various differences in belief and practice when he was a young Caesar. After the Donatist[27] controversy

---

25. See Eusebius, *The History of the Church*, ed. Andrew Louth (New York: Penguin, 1990) for a broad overview of this period of church history.

26. As the church was exposed to a wider ethnic and philosophical constituency (Greek, North African, Roman, Gallic, the Germanic people and Steppe tribes) the Christians in those groups began to articulate hybridized philosophical, theological and ethical versions of the faith.

27. Donatists asserted that Christians—lay and priest alike—who had handed over the sacred writings (Old Testament, copies of New Testament letters, etc.) to civil authorities were traitors and could not be readmitted to the church. Priests who had handed over sa-

erupted in 311, a church council was called by Constantine in 314 at Arles. At this council Donatism was condemned. Not satisfied, and still believing they were the pure church, the Donatists appealed again to Constantine, who, predictably, sided with the Catholic bishops.[28] Constantine spent the rest of his reign as emperor moderating doctrinal controversies in the church.

Arianism: The Great Theological Heresy

Arius, a deacon in the Alexandrian church, was at the root of the next major controversy. Arius had taught that Jesus was begotten, and thus could not be God: "If the Father begat the Son, he that was begotten had a beginning of existence: hence it is that there was when the Son was not. It follows then of necessity that he had his existence from the non-existence."[29] Arianism, as it came to be called, was not contained in Alexandria by Bishop Alexander, but began to spread around the empire. Eventually, Constantine was forced to call an ecumenical council at Nicaea in 325 to deal with Arius and Arianism. Rather than attend himself, Bishop Alexander sent Athanasius, an archdeacon in Alexandria. Eventually, Arius was judged to be a heretic, and Arianism a heresy. Out of the council a creed was formulated to protect the divinity of the Son. To do so, the Greek word *homoousios* was utilized to describe the essence of the Father and the Son as being "consubstantial" or "of one substance." It is said that Emperor Constantine presided at the council, and it was he who decided on the use of *homoousios*.[30] Athanasius, successor to Alexander as Bishop in Alexandria, was to become the apologist for Nicaean Christology. The balance of the fourth century and the beginning of the fifth century were to see a continuation of both the Donatist and Arian struggles. Additional controversies over the teachings of Bishop Apollinaris of Laodicea (Apollinarianism

---

cred writings could not administer sacraments.

28. "Catholic bishops," were those bishops who sided with Constantine on the Donatist schism. Like Constantine, these bishops believed that all confessing Christians, even those who had surrendered their "holy books" should be allowed to return to the church in full fellowship.

29. Mark A. Noll, *Turning Points: Decisive Moments in the History of Christianity* 3rd ed. (Grand Rapids: Baker Academic 2012), 45.

30. Norman H. Baynes, *Constantine and the Christian Church* (Oxford: British Academy, 1972).

argues that Jesus had a divine mind, but a human body), Bishop Nestor of Constantinople (Nestorianism argues for the full humanity of Christ), and the supposed teachings of the British monk, Pelagius (Pelagianism argues for human free will in the quest for salvation)[31] were to occupy several emperors well into the fifth century. The councils were often argumentative, and on several occasions, violent.[32]

The Consequences of Heresy and Homogenized Theology

The quest for Constantine's "uniform theology and practice" had several important outcomes for the Christian faith: a focus on doctrinal homogeneity; a questionable division between what is orthodox and what is heresy; a regulated priesthood; an authority and power structure that could be manipulated economically, and politically; and a reductionist understanding of both the function of the Holy Spirit and mission. I will call this the "Received Church." With these outcomes in mind, the church we experience today—the Received Church—is the inheritor of roughly seventeen centuries of controversy, division and violence, with an ever-increasing impotence where the *ethos* of the Gospel and mission are concerned.

Did Constantine intend this "sabotage" to the apostolic church we experience in the book of Acts, and the letters of Paul, Peter and John? Absolutely not. Constantine's mother was a practicing Christian, and Constantine understood the truth and power of the faith; however, Constantine was also a Roman soldier and shrewd politician. He believed that Christianity could unify the empire, but it would have to be acceptable to the citizens of the empire. To accomplish this, theological, liturgical and administrative disagreements had to be "fixed". The "disunity" of the Christian faith that Constantine experienced was the result of a collision between several different cultures: North African (Arabic, Berber, and West African), Semitic, Germanic and Greco Roman. Add to this the poor moral condition of humankind with its propensity towards power, and the accompanying subterfuge, intimidation, and violence. A Semitic faith collided with a Graeco-Roman philosophical and political machine that reinterpreted,

---

31. Ali Bonner, *The Myth of Pelagianism* (Oxford: British Academy, 2018).
32. See Michael Gaddis, *There Is No Crime for Those Who Have Christ: Religious Violence in the Christian Roman Empire* (Berkley, CA: University of California Press, 2005), 68-102.

repackaged, and then began to *consume* the faith, as they would almost any other religion in the empire.[33] Additionally, the church leadership of the time became complicit in this transition. What occurred was nothing less than a fundamental restructuring of the Christian faith: consuming it, as opposed to living it.[34] Christianity became a religion alongside the Orphic and Eleusinian Mysteries, the Cult of Isis, and the Pantheon of Graeco-Roman gods. This uneasy relationship between Christianity and paganism was resolved by Theodosius I in 381 when he declared Christianity as the exclusive religion of the empire, complete with enforcement policies for reluctant Roman citizens, in the Edict of Thessalonica.[35]

The fifth century was filled with the continuing drama of defining "orthodox" belief over "heretical" views. The Apollinarian, Nestorian and Pelagian controversies were at the forefront of the conflict between the different sees of the church. Church fathers such as Alexander, Athanasius, Cyril, Nestor, Eusebius of Caesarea, Hilary of Poitiers, Basil the Great, Gregory of Nazianzus, Gregory of Nyssa and Augustine of Hippo were some of the primary participants in this conflict in the fourth and fifth centuries. The nascent theology of the 'Received Church' was formed in the controversies surrounding orthodoxy and heresy in the Roman Empire. More than anything, the confrontation regarding church belief was not so much a theological one, although theology was derivative of the conflict; the confrontation was about power and politics. The great centers of Christian thought at the time, Alexandria and Antioch, were constantly at odds over theological issues, and were especially attentive to what side of the argument the Roman emperors favored. Until the great ecumenical council at Chalcedon in 451, the factions most commonly at odds were those who argued that Jesus and the Father were of the "same" substance,

---

33. In this sense, 'consuming' religion is equated with 'objectifying' religion. Religion becomes one object among many that shapes a person's worldview. This is opposed to becoming subject to divinity in a fashion that gives the divine a priority in shaping a person's life and worldview. Hence the idea that Christianity is a "relationship" rather than a religion.

34. Wes Howard-Brook, has proposed a viable theory of how the church became the "religion of empire," beginning in second century and continuing to the fall of Rome. See Wes Howard-Brook, *Empire Baptized: How the Church Embraced What Jesus Rejected in the 2nd-5th Centuries* (Maryknoll, NY: Orbis Books, 2016).

35. See *Codex Theodosianus* XVI.1.2 [Henry Bettenson, ed., *Documents of the Christian Church*, (London: Oxford University Press, 1943), 31.

or that Jesus and the Father were only of "like" substance.³⁶ In the midst of this ecclesial conflict, the western half of the Roman Empire was collapsing due to incursions of the Germanic and Hunnic people. As the pressure of these raids grew, the military and political power of the empire crumbled. R. P. C. Hanson maintains that neither Rome nor the Christian church saw this coming, until it arrived.³⁷ None believed that the Roman Empire could fall, and most believed that the empire would last several more centuries. Although the pagan historian Ammianus Marcellinus believed that the empire was "now in its old age," he never imagined that it was now in its "hour of death."³⁸

The Church in the "Dark Ages" and the Holy Roman Empire.

After the collapse of the western Roman Empire with the ascendancy of the Teutonic (Herulian) King Odoacer³⁹ in 476, the Catholic church survived through its administrative and political savvy.⁴⁰ Unlike the Roman Empire, the Catholic church had a structure by which its life did not depend upon the Empire. Although it benefitted greatly from its relationship to Rome in terms of wealth, prestige and political acumen, it did not depend on the Empire for education or ultimate survival. The church would not only survive the various barbarian incursions, it would learn to thrive

---

36. Those bishops who affirmed the "same" *(homoousion)*divine substance were the Nicaean Catholics. Those bishops that affirmed the "like" *(homoian)* substance were the those influenced by the teaching of Arius. For example, although Constantine affirmed *homoousion*, his son, Constantius affirmed *homoian*. For this interesting perspective, see Michael Kulikowski, "The Making of the Constantinian Empire," in *Imperial Tragedy: From Constantine's Empire to the Destruction of Roman Italy AD 3636-568* (London: Profile Books, 2019), 7-15.

37. R. P. C. Hanson, "Reaction of the Church to the Collapse of the Western Roman Empire in the Fifth Century," *Vigiliae Christianae* 26:4 (December 1972): 272-87.

38. Ibid., 274-75.

39. Odoacer's ethnicity is debated to this day by historians. He has been placed with the Goths, the Huns or most prominently with the Heruli; a Teutonic tribe from southern Scandinavia. E.g. Michael Grant, *From Rome to Byzantium: The Fifth Century AD*. (London and New York: Routledge, 1998); Guy Halsall, *Barbarian Migrations and the Roman West, 376-568* (Cambridge: Cambridge University Press, 2007); A. H. M. Jones, "The Fall of the Western Empire and the Barbarian Kingdoms," *The Later Roman Empire, 284-602: A Social, Economic, and Administrative Survey*, Vol. I. (Baltimore, MD: Johns Hopkins University Press, 1964).

40. Hanson, 279.

politically and economically. Hanson states:

> One reason for the employment of bishops in secular activities was that the barbarian rulers when they gained possession of territories formerly belonging to the Roman Empire found themselves very short of trained and experienced administrators. They found it advisable to make little alteration in the existing system of taxation. They naturally turned for help to the bishops of the Church who were well educated and trained in administration and not inexperienced in financial affairs…By the second half of the fifth century, therefore, clergy were increasingly the only educated…and the barbarian ruler had no option but to employ them in his civil and diplomatic service.[41]

Thus, by making itself indispensable to the Goths and others who invaded the empire, the Catholic church not only survived, but thrived. As the Catholic church, the papacy, the local bishops and other clergy proved their worth to their new overlords, the church strengthened its position in the growing feudal culture of the Middle Ages.

With the crowning of the Frankish King Charles Martel as the Holy Roman Emperor in 800 by Pope Leo III, a new era of the church's existence began. Charles the Great(aka, "Charlemagne") was already a baptized Christian, and had established positive relationships with the Frankish bishops and clergy. The impetus to bring Charlemagne to Rome for his coronation as Emperor was not coincidental or accidental. Pope Leo had reasons to acknowledge him as Emperor; on the other hand, King Charles (it is said) would not have accepted the crown had he been told in advance.[42] Einhard, a loyal servant and chronicler of Martel, wrote:

> When he made his last journey thither, he also had other ends in view. The Romans had inflicted many injuries upon the Pontiff Leo, tearing out his eyes and cutting out his tongue, so that he had been compelled to call upon the King for help [Nov 24, 800]. Charles accordingly went to Rome, to set in order the affairs of the Church, which were in great con-

---

41. Hanson, 280-81.
42. Einhard, *The Life of Charlemagne*, trans. Samuel Epes Turner (New York: Harper & Brothers, 1880), sec. 28. Accessed on May 20, 2020 at https://sourcebooks.fordham.edu/basis/einhard.asp

fusion, and passed the whole winter there. It was then that he received the titles of Emperor and Augustus [Dec 25, 800], to which he at first had such an aversion that he declared that he would not have set foot in the Church the day that they were conferred, although it was a great feast day, if he could have foreseen the design of the Pope.[43]

In practice, Pope Leo III was simply following the precedent that Pope Stephen had set by crowning Pippin III, Charlemagne's father, King of the Franks in 754. However, Pope Leo III's crowning of Charlemagne as *Holy Roman Emperor* brought to the Catholic church the privilege and power of regal confirmation in a renewed Roman Empire—the Holy Roman Empire.[44] Pope Leo and the church needed the protection of King Charles, and this act sealed an already powerful relationship.[45] Yet this act opened a door of power that could be easily abused, and ultimately brought about the Protestant Reformation. The church was now not only in partnership again with the state, but had more authority to utilize coercive power to meet its objectives.[46]

It is interesting that during this period of time, the older idea of evangelism as preaching the gospel, where the Holy Spirit brought repentant men and women to the church voluntarily, had become anachronistic.[47] In the mid-eighth century, one will find Charlemagne issuing edicts regarding the conversion of Saxons in Capitulatio de Partibus Saxoniae, a series of legal missives which called for the forcible conversion of the Saxon people to Christianity on pain of death.[48] In 775 the Carolingian Chronicles recorded that Charlemagne "resolved to wage war on the perfidious and

---

43. Ibid.
44. See Horace Mann, The Lives of the Popes in the Early Middle Ages, vol. 2 The Popes During the Carolingian Empire: Leo III to Formosus (St. Louis, MO: Herder, 1906), 11ff.
45. See Horace Mann's account of the attack on Pope Leo by his rivals at the procession of Greater Litanies in 799. Horace Mann, "Pope St. Leo III," *Catholic Encyclopedia*, volume 9 (New York: Robert Appleton Co., 1913). Retrieved May 27, 2020 from New Advent: http://www.newadvent.org/cathen/09157b.htm
46. See McKitterick's study on the union of Charlemagne and the objectives of the Catholic church in Rosamond McKitterick, "Correctio: Knowledge and Power," in *Charlemagne and European Identity*, (Cambridge: Cambridge University Press, 2008), 292-372.
47. Hanson, 282.
48. See "Revised Annals of the Kingdom of the Franks," in P. D. King, *Charlemagne: Translated Sources* (Kendal: P. D. King, 1987), 110-111.

treaty-breaking people of the Saxons and to persevere with this until they had either been overcome and subjected to the Christian religion or totally exterminated."[49] The relation of church to empire not only became stronger, but gave the church more access to military power. An example of the exercise of this power is the Albigensian Crusade or Cathar Wars beginning in 1208. The Cathar religion, a form of Gnostic dualism, was prominent in the Languedoc area of southern France. Over the twelfth century this religion grew in numbers and influence, to the point that Catholic churches were being abandoned. This led Pope Innocent III to call for a war against the Cathars in this region, promising all of the participants in this crusade the remission of sins and heavenly reward. Over forty years, thousands of the Languedoc people were killed, whether or not they were practitioners of the Cathar religion.[50] This abuse continued as the church became wealthier and more powerful than at any other time in its existence. However, this abuse of power ultimately led to the Protestant schism in 1521.

The Church of the Nation-State

For at least a century prior to Martin Luther's posting of his 95 Theses to the Wittenberg Castle church door, small enclaves of protesting churches began to take root in central and northern Europe. John Wycliffe and the Lollards in England (1381) as well as Jan Hus's Moravian Church in Czechoslovakia (1399) are prime examples of clergy and lay people who had become disenchanted with the abuses of the Catholic church. In 1521, Martin Luther, a professor and monk at Wittenberg in Saxony-Anhalt, protested Pope Leo X's policy of granting indulgences to those who contributed to the papal coffers for the rebuilding of St. Peter's Basilica. Johann Tetzel, Pope Leo's 'Grand Commissioner for Indulgences' in Germany, preached a message that encouraged listeners to purchase their loved ones' release from Purgatory and entrance into Heaven. Luther bristled at this heretical message. Pope Leo's refusal to acknowledge the legitimacy of Luther's complaint eventually led to the Protestant Reformation. The Catholic churches among the various principalities in northern Europe splintered,

---

49. Bernard Scholz and Barbara Rogers, trans. *Carolingian Chronicles: Royal Frankish Annals and Nithard's Histories* (Ann Arbor, MI: University of Michigan Press, 1970), 51.

50. See Jennifer K. Deane, *A History of Medieval Heresy and Inquisition* (New York: Rowman & Littlefield, 2011), 25-56.

not simply in protest of the pope's policies, but because the prince-electors in this region wanted to be free of the coercive power of the papacy.

But the protest that began with Luther shattered quickly into several splinter groups, each being more radical in their reform than Luther himself. Indeed, with the Holy Roman Empire moving into its twilight years, individual nation states began to claim their own church. In the territory of what would later become Germany, the Lutheran Church became the church of state. In Switzerland and the Netherlands, the Reformed Church of John Calvin took root. In Scotland, the reformation movement took on a new persona as the Presbyterian church. In England, King Henry VIII took over the Catholic church and pronounced himself as head of the new "Church of England." In the process of taking over the church, King Henry executed Sir Thomas More, who had refused to acknowledge Henry as the head of the Anglican church. Henry's successor, his daughter Mary, attempted to put England back in the arms of the Catholic church. In this attempt, she had a number of Protestant clergymen burned at the stake for their failure to recant their error.[51] The violence of non-conformity only grew. Correct doctrine, ecclesial loyalty, and liturgical uniformity[52] have become the marks of the church since the Constantinian adaptation of the church to empire. Between the reign of Theodosius I (380) through Pope Leo X (1521), the church had become wealthy and adapted itself to the use of secular-style governance and military power. This would begin to change in the sixteenth century as the authority of the church waned with the ascendance of Enlightenment philosophical thought and disillusionment with church theology and politics.

---

51. Anglican bishops Hugh Latimer, Nicholas Ridley, and Thomas Cranmer were the Oxford Martyrs of 1555. John Calvin's execution of Spanish theologian Michel Servetus by burning at the stake serves as another example of what happens when the church attempts to settle doctrinal difference by drawing from the state's coercive power. See Roland H. Bainton, *Hunted Heretic: The Life and Death of Michael Servetus, 1511-1553* (Boston, MA: Beacon Press, 1960).

52. In 1549, King Edward VI introduced the Book of Common Prayer, reflecting the theology of the English Reformation, was introduced. The enforcing of the English language in worship services was fought by traditionalist Catholics in Cornwall and Devon, where revolt broke out. The revolt was put down at a cost of over 3,000 lives. See Nicholas Pocock, ed. *Troubles Connected with The Prayer Book of 1549* (Oxford: Camden Society, 1884)

The Church in the Modern World: Democracy

Scholars will argue that the Age of Enlightenment began as early as the work of Leonardo da Vinci, the publication of Michel de Montaigne's *Essays,* or the philosophical work of René Descartes. These great thinkers lived and wrote from the late fifteenth century through the early seventeenth century, and their work not only grounded and inspired the later work of thinkers such as Immanuel Kant, John Locke, David Hume and Georg Hegel, but also the political revolutionaries such as Thomas Paine, Voltaire, and Samuel Taylor Coleridge. It is here, in the sixteenth, seventeenth and eighteenth centuries, that the church's relationship to empire and state was changed. The authority of the church was first questioned, then marginalized, and finally ignored.

In the seventeenth and eighteenth centuries, certain radical Protestant sects, who found their presence in Europe was without promise, were given the opportunity to leave England, the Netherlands, and German states for a better place in the New World. Puritans, Baptists, Mennonites, Quakers, Shakers, Methodists, and the Amish came to America for a new start, out from under the control of their respective countries of origin. America, and to some degree Canada, were very much shaped by these religious sects and their quest for freedom of religion. In America particularly, the two most powerful forces affecting the formation of the United States were the Enlightenment philosophies of Locke, Hume and Shaftesbury, and the quest for religious freedom and its practice.[53]

Early American framers of the U.S. Constitution and Bill of Rights sought to enshrine religious freedom, and the separation of church and state in these founding documents. In the 244 years since the United States was established, this commitment to religious freedom and the separation of church and state has been challenged continuously. As Western culture has become more diverse, its religious populations have become more diverse. This diversity has been very difficult for some Christian denominations to accept. Christians have always struggled with theological differences, and

---

53. Tom Schacthman, *Gentlemen Scientists and Revolutionaries: The Founding Fathers in the Age of Enlightenment* (New York: St. Martin's Press, 2014), and Frank Lambert, *The Founding Fathers and the Place of Religion in America* (Princeton, NJ: Princeton University Press, 2003).

today the interdenominational struggles have turned into interreligious struggles. As the culture has become morally permissive and religiously shallow, Christian denominations have become divided and combative along cultural and political lines. Additionally, the United States' commitments to a Lockean political philosophy of law and government, and its staunch devotion to the democratic process, have created an atmosphere of constant, often rancorous argument. In recent American politics, the conservative political faction has very intentionally courted the conservative religious faction. Once again, the Church's desire for political recognition and power has linked it to empire—except that it is not the Roman, Holy Roman, or British empires, it is the American Empire.

The Death of Christendom: The Rise of the Church

As in the fall of the Roman Empire, the waning of the American Empire has gone unnoticed by some, and misjudged by others. The postmodern criticism of the modern philosophical assumptions, upon which much of contemporary Western and American culture was grounded, has 'unmoored' the Church and its understanding of the faith. According to the most reliable polls conducted in America today, the church in the United States is in a steady decline, and an irreversible transition.[54] Over the last thirty years, there has been a concerted effort politically and liturgically to reverse the decline.

In order to 'save the current model of the 'Received Church', different denominations and individual congregations have turned to various forms of a consumer model. Consumer model A focuses on culturally hip, theologically light, and fashionably time-consuming worship music, a trendy, casual, but biblical sermon, and a myriad of opportunities and methods to contribute financially. There are few actual discipleship classes, but plenty of 'home' groups. The focus is to get contributing individuals and families into the building where they will encounter a culturally relevant worship setting. Consumer Model B focuses on a particular theological position, usually a form of Fundamentalism, Biblicism, Pentecostalism, Calvinism

---

54. See Mark Chaves, *American Religion: Contemporary Trends* 2nd ed. (Princeton, NJ: Princeton University Press, 2017), 117-122; and Joseph Baker, *American Secularism* (New York: NYU Press, 2015), 66, 201-217.

or Liberalism. The congregation has a regular, specific liturgy, inclusive of hymns, responsive readings, creedal recitations, an offering plate and a sermon in the style dictated. The congregation usually continues to offer a form of discipleship, usually Sunday School. The drawback to the consumer model is that it continues to echo the Nicaean-Constantinian form of the church. In other words, church is still about what you believe, and where you attend. Are you a Nicaean—Baptist, Episcopalian? Are you a Donatist—Independent Baptist, Bible Church? Are you a Montanist—Pentecostal, Charismatic? Are you an Arian—Congregationalist, some Methodists, Presbyterians? Are you a Marcionite—some Baptists? Are you a Nestorian—spread throughout the denominations? Are you a Pelagian—spread throughout the denominations? It is not difficult to find Protestants split over Jesus' divine status, the nature and gifts of the Holy Spirit, or the nature of the Bible. Young men and women, often called the "I" generation, or "millennials," are very clearly rejecting this form of church. Many of these young adults consider themselves to be "spiritual, but not religious." Their frustration has given some of them no recourse but to claim agnosticism, and others, atheism.

The very idea of 'Christendom', as conceived during the fourth century, and reconceived over time in a multitude of variations, has been rejected by this generation. This is a generation that wants meaning, spirituality and truth. It is a generation that does not settle for easy answers and cultural copies. For this generation, if faith is not 'real', if it does not make a difference, and if it does not embody the "love of God" they have heard so much about, they will not waste their time or energy on it. The "Boomer" generation and "Generation X" would like to save Christendom—i.e., the 'Received Church'—simply because this is the only form of the church they have known. However, this will not be a profitable course. Christendom is dying, and will end with their generation.

Conclusion: The Church is a Movement

The church will not die. The church is the keeper, and instrument of the gospel, the habitation of the Holy Spirit, the executor of Christ's mission, priest to the world, and fountain of the love of God. Even as I write, God is raising up the form of the church that is necessary for this time and place. The church—the *ekklesia,* the ones who are called out—has its roots in the assembly of Greek citizens who were called out to do the business of the city-state of the day.[55] In the case of the church, the application would seem to be obvious: those who are in Christ are called out and equipped by the Holy Spirit to accomplish the mission of Christ according to the will of the Father.

Recent missiological work has sought to recast the work of the church as primarily mission. Authors such as David Fitch, Darrell Guder, J. R. Woodward, Christopher Wright, Michael Goheen, Craig Van Gelder, Craig Ott, Paul Williams, Stuart Murray, Alan Hirsch, Alan Roxburgh, and many others, have been addressing the pressing issue of the church and its mission for the past thirty years. J. R. Woodward and Dan White Jr. have even touched on the conception of the church as a movement.[56] Using the theological concept of incarnation, in which the Christian, and the church as a whole, embodies the life of Christ in the power of the Spirit, the church *becomes* mission. Mission ceases to be external to the life of the church, and becomes internal, natural and crucial to its existence. Reconceiving the "ecclesial architecture" of the postmodern, post-Christendom church is critical to its life as the movement of God's love. Woodward and White forcefully make the argument that the church of Christendom has been hobbled by a confused self-understanding: "The church is not a building, a weekly gathering or a program, but a people that God has called out of the world and sent back into the world to redeem and renew the world."[57] Woodward and White have outlined in very practical terms how the church can reconceive itself in a time of transition. Utilizing the work of contemporary theological and biblical scholars such as Miroslav Volf, Stanley Grenz, N. T. Wright, and Walter Brueggemann, Woodward and White construct an ontology of the church that is essentially *mission.*

The Johannine idea that "God is Love" and that the essence of the human life in God is "to love God" and to "love neighbor" describes an ontology of act, in which being is subsidiary to, and defined by, *agape.* As Stanley Grenz described it, we are created in the image of a "social God,"

---

55. See R. K. Sinclair, *Democracy and Participation in Athens* (Cambridge: Cambridge University Press, 1988).
56. J. R. Woodward and Dan White, Jr., *The Church as Movement: Starting and Sustaining Missional-Incarnational Communities* (Downers Grove, IL: InterVarsity Press, 2016).
57. Woodward and White, 114.

and thus the Christian "self" is not the isolated individual of modernity, but rather a self determined by its relations to God, other human beings and the balance of creation.[58] In his 2006 Pierre Marquette lectures, Larry Hurtado raised the question of why people in the first three centuries became Christians, considering the hardship and persecution they endured. He postulated the concepts of a "loving God" and the promise of "eternal life" as the appealing factors in Christian conversion.[59] What was essentially implied, but unstated in Hurtado's text, is the *experience* of the loving God and the tangible hope of eternal life, both aspects of the believer's experience of Christ through the dynamic presence of the Holy Spirit. In light of these thoughts, the church *is* a movement of the *imago Dei*, constituted by the love of God, through the indwelling of the Spirit in the life of the community of believers. The other-focused nature of the love of God means that the church exists for the sake of redemption and renewal in the world. The narrative of Scripture from Genesis to Revelation stands in witness to this fact. The church worships God in spirit and truth, obedient to the mission of loving neighbor as much as it loves God. Buildings, liturgies and theology serve the missional life of the church, rather than the opposite. The Scriptures stand as a testimony to the charter of God's people: the church is mission. One could assume then that if our theology of Scripture does not serve our theology of mission, then our theology of Scripture must change, and vice versa. The two doctrines dynamically inform each other. The church that understands itself as the love of God *in action* is the church that will be relevant in the twenty-first century.

Professor Soderlund was not the voluminous writer like some of his Regent College colleagues. His body of writings were focused on the Bible, or served as tributes in honor of his colleagues. In what I can only assume was an intentional choice, Sven made his major investments in life as a scholar-teacher, and a churchman, living the Kingdom of God so that others might benefit. His passion for understanding and applying Scripture to the Christian life and the mission of the church was undeniable. Because of his passion for the dynamic nature of Scripture and the dynamic being

---

58. Stanley J. Grenz, *The Social God and the Relational Self: A Trinitarian Theology of the Imago Dei* (Louisville: Westminster John Knox, 2007).

59. Larry W. Hurtado, *Why on Earth Did Anyone Become a Christian in the First Three Centuries?* (Milwaukee, WI: Marquette University Press, 2006), 121-129.

of the church on mission, Sven was one of the best examples of theology "Under the Green Roof." Sven Soderlund is one of my favorite illustrations of what it means to be a Christian witness, in a postmodern, post-Christendom world: a man who loves Christ, hears the Spirit speak in the Scriptures, and lives the life of mission with the church.

10

From Library to Pulpit

The Role of Research and Scholarship in Expository Preaching

David J. Montgomery

Sven Soderlund's Regent College colleague Gordon Fee often said that he desired to be neither a scholar on ice nor a fool on fire, but a scholar on fire; and Sven himself, in his own way, has embodied this calling. Regent College in the 1990s was flush with the best in evangelical biblical scholarship and it was Sven's Greek exegesis classes and his seminar class on Text and Canon that I remember most clearly and which cemented my confidence in the text that I, as a preacher, have been called to communicate.

Most of the preaching I heard in my early years could have been described in one of two ways, not unlike Fee's axiom. It was either passionate communication with little biblical foundation underneath the enthusiasm and rhetoric, or else a detailed exposition of the text which was little more than a verbal montage of commentaries, with an application that seldom went beyond "be more prayerful" or "be more trusting"; what Bryan Chapell coined as "the deadly Be's."[1]

It seemed that the expositional preaching which prevailed in my tradition was a little like attending a webinar on the internal workings of a

---

1. Bryan Chapell, *Christ-Centered Preaching* (Grand Rapids: Baker, 2005), 289ff.

computer: it is fine for a technician with specialized interests, but will do nothing to help me get my email working again or get the most out of my iCloud storage—the things I really need in order to get me through each day. The preacher, in this analogy, gives us a tour of lexicons and commentaries and leaves us either feeling confused and inadequate, or in awe of their erudition. One is a failure of the calling to "set forth the truth plainly" (2 Cor. 4:2); the other is a failure of character (see 1Cor. 2:4; 9:16; Jas. 3:1).

For contemporary evangelicalism as a whole, however, the failings may be different: communication at the expense of content, a default towards anti-intellectualism, and an age-old dichotomy between scholarship and spirituality. The onset of the digital age has exacerbated this, in terms of preachers losing confidence in the power of the word preached, but it is not new. The advent of television in the mid-twentieth century brought its own challenges and there have been many voices since, clamoring to proclaim that the era of the traditional sermon is past.

The arguments may be philosophical (Richard Eslinger, claiming that "the old rational homiletics is obsolete")[2] or cultural (Lamin Sanneh arguing that the tradition of exegesis on which most Western preaching is based "has run its course…(and is) little more than cultural filibuster")[3] or methodological (Lowry's preference for "Sermon as Art" where he encourages "wandering thoughtfulness" because "the sermon is not a doctrinal lecture"). According to Lowry, the sermon is "an *event-in-time*, a narrative art form more akin to a play or novel in shape than to a book. Hence we are not engineering scientists, we are narrative artists by professional function".[4]

However, none of these voices have dealt a fatal blow either to systematic expository preaching, nor to historical grammatical exegesis, both of which continue to have a lively and fruitful influence on contemporary preaching. Hamilton, for example, writes:

---

2. Quoted in Donald L. Hamilton, *Homiletical Handbook* (Nashville, TN: Broadman Press, 1992), 30.

3. Quoted in Thomas G. Long, *The Witness of Preaching*, (Louisville: Westminster John Knox, 2016), 77.

4. Eugene L. Lowry, *The Homiletical Plot: The Sermon as Narrative Art Form* (Louisville: Westminster John Knox, 2001), xx.

> It is interesting to note that the same authors who condemn the concept of propositional truth do so almost exclusively through means of propositional argumentation.... Those involved in espousing a "new homiletic" seem to be contradictory in the way they communicate *their* ideas about preaching in comparison to the way they say sermonic ideas themselves must be communicated.[5]

Likewise, there are many examples of non-Western sermons, or creative narrative sermons, that lose nothing of their cultural or artistic authenticity while still being based on solid exegesis and robust hermeneutics.[6]

The dilemma many preachers face a short time into their post-seminary preaching ministry is how to use the theory and training they have received and the tools at their disposal in the very particularized locus of the congregation. The temptation to default towards pragmatism and to shelve the learning in exchange for immediacy and 'relevance' is always strong.

Greidanus observes that the danger is "that the purpose of the preacher will overrule the purpose of the text and in effect silence the text."[7] Eager for relevance, the minister will ignore the real meaning, and application will therefore dominate interpretation. There is a cartoon of a pastor in his study wondering whether or not to use an entertaining story in his sermon. He has an angel on one shoulder and a demon on the other. The demon is saying, "It's okay, it's only an obscure verse in the minor prophets," while the angel responds, "Your exegesis, pastor, your exegesis!" Where should the preacher begin? Sinclair Ferguson writes:

> It is tempting for those involved in theological education to say 'the first step is to reach for the Hebrew Bible or the Greek Testament'. At the other end of the spectrum, it seems likely that some preachers enter

---

5. Ibid., 28.

6. See especially the contributions on Hispanic, African, and Asian preaching, and first-person narratives in Haddon Robinson & Craig Larson (eds.), *The Art and Craft of Biblical Preaching* (Grand Rapids: Zondervan, 2005), chapters 51, 52, 53, 121; and in Raymond Bailey, ed., *Hermeneutics for Preaching: Approaches to Contemporary Interpretations of Scripture* (Nashville, TN: Broadman, 1992).

7. Sidney Greidanus, *The Modern Preacher and the Ancient Text: Interpreting and Preaching Biblical Literature* (Grand Rapids: Eerdmans, 1988), 107.

their pulpits Sunday by Sunday not only not having consulted their original texts, but perhaps not even knowing where in the muddle of their studies their original language tools are to be found![8]

So, in the years since Regent College, I have struggled somewhat with the relationship between scholarship and preaching. I am burdened to communicate the most precious message entrusted to human beings, but am concerned at the lack of substance in what passes for preaching in many evangelical pulpits. Coming from a Reformed church that has historically held to the ecclesiastical office of Doctor, I see few, if any, contemporary examples of this in the English-speaking world. It appears to be a tradition that is more honored in the breach than in the observance. David Wells remarks how, historically, even the role of 'pastor' in Reformed circles had an understood element of scholarship involved. 'Scholar-saints' led the church, pastors who were "as comfortable with books and learning as with the aches of the soul."[9] Or, as Strachan observes:

> Unlike our more recent history, when pastors were urged by some to busy themselves with the pragmatic matters of everyday ministry and some scholars focused less on the church and more on high-level academic questions, pastors and scholars throughout the larger span of church history have blended these roles. Pastors worked out of a burden to bless their people with rich biblical theology even as scholars labored to nourish, strengthen, and captivate the church through their scholarship.[10]

As a preacher, I have always needed scholars committed to the truth of Scripture who will be my companions on the journey from text to sermon and who will enlighten and inspire me, but often I am frustrated that so much scholarship seems pre-occupied with its own issues (largely irrelevant to, and ignored by, the Christian community) and too many scholars

---

8. Sinclair Ferguson, "Exegesis," in Samuel T. Logan Jr., ed., *The Preacher and Preaching: Reviving the Art in the Twentieth Century* (Phillipsburg, NJ: Presbyterian & Reformed, 1986), 199.
9. David Wells, *The Courage to Be Protestant* (Grand Rapids: Eerdmans, 2008), 40.
10. Owen Strachan and David Mathis, eds., *The Pastor as Scholar and the Scholar as Pastor: Reflections on Life and Ministry* (Wheaton, IL: Crossway, 2011), 13.

can live in their own echo chamber rather than seeking to discover how their calling and gifts can be used to serve the church.

So there is a plague in both houses, as it were: preachers who have sold out to communication at the expense of content, and scholars who have sold out to the expectations of academia at the expense of edifying the community of faith. Is there a way of piecing these two together? How could the in-depth biblical scholarship and the exegetical tools to which I had been exposed in my seminary training best be utilized not just for furthering the biblical literacy and theological understanding of my community, but for their (and my) spiritual growth in grace?

The contexts in which I have sought to do this have been varied: from a highly educated suburban congregation with an expectation of deep scriptural teaching (some of whom were even acquainted with the original languages), to a small town church with no such history but deep piety, to a more recent role with IFES, teaching and equipping students. Although the congregations and contexts were different, the challenge was the same: how to bring the word to life so that it would first move the heart and engage the mind, and then transform the life of both preacher and hearers (1 Tim 4:16).

Rather than seeking to re-state what can be found in some of the best homiletics manuals or the most accessible Biblical Studies textbooks, this chapter is more of a reflection on a personal journey—an account of how I, as a quite inadequate practitioner, have sought to bring these two worlds together. It is also a plea for preachers to continue to engage more with the world of scholarship and for scholars to think more intentionally about the needs of the church in general, and of preachers in particular.

Scholarship and Preaching: An Incompatible Marriage?

A look through some of the classic preaching texts will reveal how little is actually said on the importance of research (outside of commentaries) or even how best to use or assess the commentaries themselves.[11] Most will remind the preacher of the basics of exegesis and the use of the original

---

11. For example, Michael Duduit, ed., *Handbook of Contemporary Preaching* (Nashville, TN: Broadman, 1992) contains 51 chapters from different contributors but with virtually nothing on exegesis, languages or scholarship.

languages, if possible, but even here this is often underplayed and, in some cases, even discounted. This is particularly true when 'good communication' is highlighted as an essential goal of preaching. An example of this in popular preaching literature is *Stop Preaching and Start Communicating* by Tony Gentilucci,[12] but with a recommendation and foreword from the esteemed homiletician Haddon Robinson. In an effort to encourage preachers to be better communicators and to learn from television, the author is explicit in eschewing the original languages:

> When I was in seminary, I got into the habit of defining key Greek or Hebrew words from the passage I was preaching from. I heard others do the same, so I did it, but [after a conversation with a listener] I have never mentioned another Greek or Hebrew word during any of my messages since... Ultimately, that's not what most people are interested in. People are interested in finding answers to life's daily challenges.[13]

This overt discarding of the original languages is echoed in the writings of other significant popular evangelical writers. Gentilucci quotes both Rick Warren and Chuck Swindoll. Warren writes: "some pastors like to show off their knowledge by using Greek words and academic terms in preaching. Pastors need to realize that no one cares as much about Greek as they do." He agrees with Swindoll, whom he quotes as saying that an overuse of the original languages actually "discourages confidence in the English text."[14] If this is the case, then in looking at preaching and scholarship we are indeed looking at two completely different and parallel disciplines that are destined never to intersect.

While Gentilucci's experience can easily be put down to bad praxis and an inappropriate lack of contextualization, Warren's and Swindoll's criticisms are more serious. A good mentor could have encouraged Gentilucci to keep doing his rigorous preparation, confidently grounding his sermon in the biblical text, and then being equally rigorous in discerning how best to apply that text in the context of the prison congregation he was

---

12. Tony Gentilucci, *Stop Preaching and Start Communicating: Communication Principles Preachers Can Learn from Television* (Pickering, ON: Castle Quay Books, 2010).
13. Ibid., 115.
14. Ibid., 116.

serving. However, instead of changing his style and being more selective about what he communicated, Gentilucci seems to have misdiagnosed the problem as being rooted in the use of scholarship itself.

Yes, there is a problem if, in Warren's words, the scholarship is used to "show off," but there is a danger that, in undermining the use of Greek in the pulpit, pastors adopt a crass utilitarian approach to preaching and lose confidence in the use of the languages in the study. It is even more concerning if, following Swindoll's argument, they believe that linguistic and other research is not only unnecessary but actually harmful, leading to a loss in confidence in Scripture.

We must be careful not to patronize congregations. While they may not be interested in technical linguistic issues, they do want to know what the Bible actually says, and to have confidence in the preacher. When I visit my physician, I don't want to be blinded by multi-syllabic medical terms that mean nothing to me; I want to be told in layperson's terms what is wrong and what I need to do, *but* I need to trust that the physician understands the science and anatomy and has done her research work competently.

How then can scholarship inform and enable better preaching? And how can preachers use their research effectively and wisely in the pulpit? As Koessler asks, "How do you capitalize on the inexhaustible riches of Scripture in your preaching, without sounding like a Bible commentary?"[15] The following sections of this chapter will work towards a reconciliation between scholarship and preaching, and then offer a couple of worked examples.

Understanding the Differences *between* the Two Disciplines

The criticism of Gentilucci and others is probably best explained by their failing to take into account the essential differences in the goals, purpose and callings of the two roles. While a student or scholar who becomes "too preachy" in his writing will likely face justifiable criticism from faculty and peer reviewers, the preacher who is too abstract and academic in her delivery may not have the same corrective mechanisms readily at hand (save, perhaps, for rapidly emptying pews and declining congregations weary of

---

15. John Koessler, "Getting the gold from the text," in Robinson & Larson, *Art and Craft*, 221.

hearing lectures.) Boice maintains that the sermon is not a lecture: "it is an exposition of a text of Scripture in terms of contemporary culture with the specific goal of helping people to understand and obey the truth of God. But to do that well the preacher must be well studied."[16] Carson writes that even scholars should not pursue their calling in a vacuum. All their intellectual endeavour must be undergone "as part and parcel of worship." Nor should they lose sight of their responsibility to the church at large: "Scholarship inevitably cares about innovation, fresh discoveries, new insights. Such strengths are not to be dismissed. But if a scholar makes that sort of pursuit his or her primary passion, it will become easy to overlook or marginalize the gospel once for all delivered to the saints."[17]

The foundational nature of authorial intent to all interpretation was defended by no less a literary luminary than C. S. Lewis, who said, speaking of literature in general, "Find out what the author actually wrote and what the hard words meant and you will have done far more for me than a hundred new interpretations or assessments could ever do."[18]

However, the role of the preacher will always go further than that of the scholar. Long writes of "the extra step the preacher must make that the exegete need not."[19] While the scholar's task ends with the interpretation of the text, the preacher then has the further task of asking "so what?" In the words of Greidanus, "One may not simply draw a historical equation mark between God's revelation in the OT and God's message for today… God's revelation in the past is not necessarily his final word for people today."[20]

Understanding the Variety that Exists within the Two Disciplines

Just as preachers will approach a passage with different theological assumptions and presuppositions regarding, for example, the authority of the text and the role of the Spirit in preaching (to name just two), so too biblical scholars will approach their discipline with a diversity of pre-commitments.

---

16. James Montgomery Boice, "The Preacher and Scholarship," in Logan, *Preacher and Preaching*, 91.
17. Don Carson, "The Scholar as Pastor," in Strachan & Mathis, *Pastor as Scholar*, 75.
18. Quoted by Earl Palmer, "Five Bird-dogging Questions for Biblical Exposition," in Robinson & Larson, *Art and Craft*, 234.
19. Ibid, 77.
20. Ibid., 121.

Within the evangelical tradition, some of the reticence towards listening to the insights of biblical scholarship stems from a misunderstanding that engaging in, or consulting, scholarly research inevitably involves employing a hermeneutic of suspicion towards the text. While this may be true of certain branches of scholarship, it is of course a lazy stereotype and an unwarranted generalization.

Preachers who genuinely desire to hear God speak through the text, and to hear him speak to their congregations through it, will need to be aware of these presuppositions when undertaking their research. For example, if the preacher believes the text is authoritative for today and is trustworthy in what it affirms, he or she will want to have their interpretative antennae well tuned when consulting scholars whose approach to the text is radically different from theirs, otherwise the very purpose of their preaching will be undermined.

Sidney Greidanus helpfully points out how one branch of scholarship, the historical-critical, has proved particularly barren territory for the preacher. Highlighting some of the assumptions of the method (the similarity of texts, similarity of events and a closed universe) he points out that whatever the benefits to academia of such debate, if it finds its way into the pulpit it can only lead to a serious loss of conviction in the preacher and a loss of confidence in the text on the part of the congregation:

> The historicity of the events proclaimed in Scripture is under a cloud of suspicion today, and as long as that suspicion (or scepticism) remains, these narratives and other genres cannot be preached with the same point and conviction as they were by their biblical authors.[21]

While a measure of doubt is appropriate when approaching any historical document, it is pertinent to ask how radical the doubts need to be, and how long they should persist. Are we asking of the biblical text an unreasonable level of proof that we do not demand of other texts? Is there an unspoken assumption that extra-biblical sources are more reliable than biblical ones (despite the textual evidence to the contrary) and that therefore if two texts disagree the critic will automatically side with the

---

21. Ibid., 24.

non-biblical text? Greidanus thinks so: "Because of the historical-critical method's approach of doubt, the burden of proof has shifted so that now the biblical reports are required to *prove* their historicity."[22] He acknowledges the important role of the historical-critical method within academia but believes there has been a cost:

> Although this [historical-critical] method has booked many gains, the overall results in biblical studies have been the separation of the biblical narrative from its underlying history and … some biblical scholars have fled from history into the safety of a nonhistorical or suprahistorical realm.[23]

Where preachers have followed scholars in this 'flight to safety' it is not hard to see the detrimental effect this has had on both the power and authority of the word preached.

As preachers we need to return to the fundamental questions, not just of *what* was written, or by whom, but why they wrote it. Discerning authorial intent is an essential part of preaching any text, and this has been an early casualty of both modernist and postmodernist readings. Greidanus quotes literary critic Northrop Frye, who said of literary criticism in general, "[too many scholars] approach the text like a picnic where the author brings the words and the readers bring the meaning." For Greidanus, "rank subjectivism is the death of biblical interpretation."[24] G. B. Caird agrees:

> We have no access to the mind of Jeremiah or Paul except through their recorded words… We may disbelieve them, that is our right; but if we try, without evidence, to penetrate to a meaning more ultimate than the one the writers intended, that is our meaning, not theirs or God's.[25]

This is not to advocate a simplistic, naive or monochrome approach to the text. Discerning authorial intent does not preclude acknowledging that there may be many and diverse 'intents' behind the authors' words. While some purposes are stated (Proverbs 1:1-6; Luke 1:1-4; John 20:31;

---

22. Ibid., 30.
23. Ibid., 27.
24. Ibid., 106-7.
25. Quoted in Bailey, *Hermeneutics for Preaching*, 31.

Acts 1:1-3; Jude 1:3) many are not. They could be explicit in their diversity (see 1Cor. 7:1) or implied from other parts of the text (was Philippians, for example, occasioned mainly because of the dispute between Euodia and Syntyche, mentioned in 4:2)?

Nor does authorial intent deny the existence of the *sensus plenior*—the 'fuller reading'—which takes account of God's progressive revelation and how later Scripture interprets and applies earlier texts. The author's original intent "does not *exhaust* the meanings ... especially in more poetic and predictive writings. Ultimately God is the author of Scripture, and it is his intention alone that exhaustively determines its meaning."[26] Or, in the words of La Sor, "[the *sensus plenior*] is not a reading into the text of theological doctrines and theories, but a reading from the text of the fullness of meaning, required by God's complete revelation."[27] While some scholarship will be of little use to the preacher, there is a growing corpus, from a diversity of ecclesiastical and theological traditions, which treats the text, its human authors, and its Divine Author with respect and which has the potential to inform and enhance any preaching ministry. The following sections offer four principles that will nurture a respectful co-relation of the disciplines.

Don't skimp on the exegesis

In discussing the interplay between biblical studies and preaching there is, of course, an assumption being made that, above all, our preaching must be *biblical*. As Piper remarks, "The very existence of the Bible as a book signals that the pastor is called to read carefully and accurately and thoroughly and honestly. That is, he is called to be a scholar."[28]

Sinclair Ferguson asserts that "from one perspective all preaching that is truly Christian preaching is exegetical in nature... [Preaching] may be a creative discipline, but it does not create *ex nihilo*."[29] Therefore any sermon that skips or skimps on the exegetical process will struggle to remain grounded in the text and be subject to a myriad of pitfalls. This is the most obvious place where the scholar and the preacher interact.

---

26. Greidanus, *Modern Preacher*, 111 (Italics original).
27. Ibid., 111.
28. John Piper, "The Pastor as Scholar," in Strachan & Mathis, *Pastor as Scholar*, 66.
29. Ibid., 192.

Most preaching textbooks will give one or more chapters to the exegetical process[30] and the elements outlined vary little. J. J. Kim's summary will suffice as an example:

> The interpreter of the Scripture engages in a process of discovering all the elements related to the text: the author and recipients, occasion and purpose, language and culture, literary form and theological truths, and how it has been interpreted throughout the history of the church.[31]

However, there is no consensus regarding the amount of time to be spent on this part of the process or the place of the original languages in the pulpit or even in the preparation. J. A. Broadus, a leading homiletician at the turn of the twentieth century, cautioned against "losing in the pulpit what had been gained in the study", but even he was quick to point out the limitations of scholarship and the inadvisability of bringing too much of the study into the pulpit:

> An acquaintance with the original language will enable us to judge, with greater confidence and correctness, among the various interpretations, though it be not likely that we shall strike out anything new, without a profounder knowledge than is often attained. Such an acquaintance will also sometimes save us from the disheartening notion that scholarship would make it all plain.... [If the preacher uses] the original languages in his interpretation, there is the danger of being misled by superficial knowledge or hasty examination.[32]

Later he points out that exegesis for the pulpit is a very different thing from scholarly research:

---

30. Although see Ernest E. Hunt III, *Sermon Struggles: Four Methods of Sermon Preparation* (New York: Seabury Press, 1982). He acknowledges that within his particular denominational context preaching occupies a subordinate role and this is reflected in his book. He outlines four methods, of which only one is primarily textual, and the sources listed in sermonic examples rarely mention anything more than one favorite commentary series and a Bible reference book. The other three methods rarely integrate any scholarship at all.

31. Julius J. Kim, *Preaching the Whole Counsel of God: Design and Deliver Gospel-Centered Sermons* (Grand Rapids: Zondervan, 2015), 38-39.

32. John A. Broadus, *A Treatise on the Preparation and Delivery of Sermons* (New York: Hodder & Stoughton, 1898), 41.

> We have here ... to present results and not processes. We must omit various matters, which have perhaps greatly interested ourselves, because they would not interest the people, or do not pertain to the object of the present discourse... There must of course be no parade of acquaintance with the original languages, and there should be no morbid fear of being charged with such parade... To repeat lists of strange and high-sounding names in favor of this or that interpretation is always useless, and is in general a very pitiful display of cheap erudition.[33]

On the surface this appears good practical advice. No-one wants their weekly worship to be interrupted by a lecture on some grammatical point of little interest to them. But, as was the case in the majority of preaching textbooks that followed over the last 100 years, while the dangers of preaching exegesis, unapplied research, and even "cheap erudition" were highlighted, few offered advice on how scholarship *could* be usefully and practically employed by the preacher. Given contemporary cultural anti-intellectual tendencies, and the perennial temptation for busy pastors to rush preparation, one wonders whether, for twenty-first-century preachers, the wrong dangers are being highlighted and the balance needs to be redressed. Is the problem not so much an over-use of scholarship, but either a wrong and thoughtless use of it, leading to tedious unapplied sermons, or an avoidance of it, leading to homilies heavy on illustration and application but without foundation on the text?

Ferguson brings us back to the hub of the matter: "To an extent this intramural debate between scholars and practitioners often centres on the wrong issues.... This focus on linguistics *simpliciter* is a mistaken one." He maintains that the emphasis should be on understanding the text and that "such an understanding demands some kind of appreciation of the language" but how and to what extent will vary, and the primary purpose is always the same, namely, "coming to an understanding of the meaning of the text to the best of our ability.... Pure linguistics are of limited help for the composition of a sermon, but they are of fundamental help if it is our concern to interpret Scripture correctly."[34]

Furthermore, we should always remain aware of the limitations of

---

33. Ibid., 156.
34. Ibid., 199-200.

the exegetical method in itself. Long encourages all preachers to keep this part of the process in perspective. Overconfidence in objective exegetical methods, he believes, can end up "muting the voice of Scripture, turning biblical interpretation into an autopsy of a dead text rather than a hearing of the lively and active word of Scripture."[35] Similarly, Farris reminds us again of the important difference between exegesis *in ecclesia* and exegesis *in academia*. Exegesis done in sermon preparation will be "subtly but substantially different" from exegesis done for academia. "Such an exegesis will make the fullest possible use of the preacher's intellectual and academic resources, but in the end it will be primarily a spiritual exercise."[36]

Very often, though, the biggest obstacle to preachers engaging more with the scholarly community is not philosophical or theoretical, but practical: the enemy of time. Here Koessler offers practical advice on how to maintain good research practice amid the other demands of pastoral life:

> You have to do the hard work of exegesis before you think about any other issues of style or application.... You must not rush this phase.... Discipline yourself so your exegetical work doesn't take place the same week as your sermon preparation.[37]

Let Scripture speak to Scripture

It is important that we do not imagine that the only, or even the main way, in which scholarship can inform preaching is in the form of secondary sources—background reference works, commentaries, journal articles. A vital part of the exegetical process is allowing Scripture itself to interpret Scripture. First, this will involve being clear about what the text in question actually is, and lexicons, grammars, and the textual apparatus will help us here. Second, a good working knowledge of the text of all sixty-six books should be developed, particularly where there is clear evidence of intertextuality. The cross-references in, for example, the UBS Greek New Testament should not be forgotten.

This is particularly true when it comes to the New Testament's use of

---

35. Ibid., 76.
36. Stephen Farris, *Preaching that Matters: The Bible and Our Lives* (Louisville: Westminster John Knox, 1998), 39.
37. Ibid., 225.

the Old. Here, in the words of Beale and Carson, "one of the distinctive differences one sometimes finds between the way NT writers read the OT and the way that their non-Christian Jewish contemporaries read it is the salvation-historical grid that is often adopted by the former."[38]

Such a reading is central for those Christian preachers who want to ensure that their preaching is both Christological and redemptive and whose sermons therefore regularly have to bridge the contextual chasm between ancient Israel, first-century Palestine and today. Scripture itself can be the guide, and the preacher should not be fearful of making those connections, as the New Testament writers themselves did.

While not denying some of the hermeneutical complexities regarding how NT writers employed OT texts, "we sometimes need reminding that the NT authors would not have understood the OT in terms of any of the dominant historical-critical orthodoxies of the last century and a half."[39] Bearing in mind the limitations of some such methodologies that we have highlighted above, the preacher should be encouraged by this and have the confidence to make Scripture itself the starting line and finishing post, regardless of what other pitstops are made along the way.

Consult the scholars – later!

In terms of these pitstops, if some preachers, in a bad week, forgo research altogether, it is likely that many more of us, most weeks, will be tempted to short-circuit the process and jump straight to the commentaries. However, much will be lost when this happens: our acquaintance with the languages diminishes, we become less able to discern whether or not the commentator is being fair to the text; we may even struggle to read some of the better technical commentaries and therefore be restricted to using more popular volumes based on the English text. Most of all, we will not have the same familiarity with the text as we would have if we had spent time working slowly through it in the original. One advantage of beginning with the Greek or Hebrew text is that a relatively slow reading ability (alongside, for example, a Metzger lexical aid or an Armstrong, Bus-

---

38. G. K. Beale and D. A. Carson, eds., *Commentary on the New Testament Use of the Old Testament* (Grand Rapids: Baker Academic, 2007), xxvi.
39. Ibid., xxviii.

by and Carr Reader's Lexicon)[40] gives us more time *in* the text, in contrast to a speed-reading or superficial reading of an English translation.

Furthermore, as Long argues, a premature use of secondary sources will prevent the sermon from being uniquely ours. We bring in the scholars late in the process so as "not to stifle the creative interactions that can and should occur between the preacher and the text. Preachers need to get to know these texts ... before allowing the voices of 'authoritative scholars' to narrow the range of interpretative possibilities."[41]

The vast array of commentaries and scholarly articles could easily be intimidating for the preacher, but need not be. Experience will help you discern which journals and series are usually most helpful, and which are accessible in terms of your linguistic proficiency. Commentaries are still the obvious place to begin once the lexical work has been done. Darrell Johnson in *The Glory of Preaching* has arguably the most comprehensive and balanced chapter on sermon crafting,[42] and also cautions that this phase should remain a much later part of the process. He has four main steps to preparation: the devotional, the exegetical, the hermeneutical and the homiletical, with eighteen sub-sections in total. Sub-sections seven through fifteen will involve some research but commentary consultation comes only at sections fourteen and fifteen, with the earlier sections devoted to working with the original.[43] Johnson refers beautifully to this stage as "consulting the brothers and sisters", reminding us that scholars and preachers are first and foremost family.

Don't neglect the older material. While new discoveries and theories may render some older works less useful, especially in the area of archaeology and cultural background, this is not always the case. The Keil and Delitzsch Old Testament commentary series,[44] for example, is still unsur-

---

40. Bruce Metzger, *Lexical Aids for Students of New Testament Greek* (Princeton, NJ: self-published, 1991). T. A. Armstrong, D. L. Busby & C. F. Carr, *A Reader's Hebrew-English Lexicon of the Old Testament* (Grand Rapids: Zondervan, 1989).

41. Ibid., 77.

42. Darrell W. Johnson, *The Glory of Preaching: Participating in God's Transformation of the World*, (Downers Grove, IL: IVP Academic, 2009).

43. In fact subsection 11 is headed "Don't consult the commentaries at this stage." Similarly, in Long, checking the commentaries is step 10 of 11, but earlier sections are strongly exegetical and require the use of research tools.

44. C. F. Keil & F. Delitzsch, *Commentary on the Old Testament*, 10 vols. (Peabody, Mass.:

passed in many instances where lexical issues arise in the Hebrew (if one can bypass the interaction with long-dead, invariably German, scholars).

Don't forget the reference works. Many preachers will have a number of reference volumes on their shelves but forget to consult them. These may be lexical[45] or general.[46] The articles are short and will still give you more than many commentaries are likely to supply.

Look for helpful journal articles. For guidance on articles, use at least one commentary series with a good bibliography. The Word series is useful here.[47] If the commentator quotes a source in relation to a particular verse, and it is crucial to your homiletic argument, refer to the bibliography and take time to read the article in context, rather than just taking the commentator's word for it. Since many of these journals are now available online the significant previous obstacle of not having library access no longer applies.

Apply the text – redemptively

We must not forget that ultimately the goal of the preacher, having garnered the material and consulted the brothers and sisters on the page, is to speak life to the sisters and brothers in the pew. Thomas Long writes of how preachers are taught to take the social location of the text seriously, but this should include the social location of the congregation: "There is one aspect of social location that the preacher knows well but is mostly lacking in biblical scholarship, namely that the preacher is not interpreting texts in general but always on behalf of those who will hear the sermons." The preacher cannot and should not "filter out local circumstances from the interpretation of Scripture."[48]

For Long, biblical interpretation is dynamic, because "texts are living realities."[49] Furthermore, the biblical element of our preaching should not

---

Hendrickson, 1996). Now online at https://www.stepbible.org/version.jsp?version=KD.

45. For example, William A. Van Gemeren, ed., *The New International Dictionary of Old Testament Theology and Exegesis*, 5 vols. (Grand Rapids: Zondervan).

46. For example, David N. Freedman, ed., *The Anchor Yale Bible Dictionary* (6 vols) (New Haven, CT: Yale University Press, 2007), or the 8-volume IVP Dictionary Series. These can often sit on the shelf as reference books but be overlooked because we are narrowly focused on a particular passage.

47. Word Bible Commentary Series (Waco, TX: Word Publishing).

48. Ibid., 77.

49. Ibid., 79.

end with our exegesis. As Koessler notes, the whole sermon must continue to be biblical: "We talk about the grammar, the syntax, and maybe the cultural background. Then we move to application. But often when we get to application, we forget about the text."[50] Or, in the words of Dockery, too often the text read and the sermon preached are like "strangers passing in the night."[51]

What many preachers find counter-intuitive is that the text can be our friend in this regard. Rather than viewing the research as the 'necessary, but not very interesting' part of the sermon before we get to the 'bit that really matters,' the sheer wealth and diversity of scriptural texts means that good research and solid exegesis should provide us with plenty of applicatory material. The problem with starting with application is that we usually have a very myopic view of our felt needs and those of our congregations, so we find a limited number of well-known texts to fit our purpose, and sermons can too easily descend into moralism.

One of the best guides in helping the preacher to apply passages in a way that is redemptive, treating both the text and the context into which it is to be applied with integrity, is Bryan Chapell's *Christ-Centered Preaching*. Chapell recommends that the preacher learns to discern in the text what he calls the 'Fallen Condition Focus'. This approach involves using as lenses of interpretation the two key questions, What does this text reveal of God's nature that provides redemption? and What does this text reflect of human nature that requires redemption? He continues:

> This does not mean that the lenses make the person or name of Jesus magically appear from the bushes of every biblical account. Rather they enable us to see reflected aspects of divine character and human fallenness that provide or require the grace of God ultimately manifested in the person and work of Christ.... Preachers should not pretend that every text specifically mentions Jesus if one has the right decoder ring. Rather, they should demonstrate how every text reflects aspects or needs of his grace that are made plain in the fullness of time.[52]

---

50. Ibid., 223.
51. David S. Dockery in Bailey, *Hermeneutics for Preaching*, 49.
52. Ibid., 284. Chapell argues that every passage will have one or more of these four redemptive foci: it will tell us something that is predictive of the work of Christ, preparatory

So, as an example, when preaching on the Sermon on the Mount recently, which is so tempting to preach moralistically, and the verses regarding walking the extra mile and turning the other cheek (Matt. 5:38-42), instead of a quasi-humanistic approach I opted for a structure like this, where each of the points offers plenty of room for contemporary application:

1. We think "there's only so much you can take," but he took so much more for us (v. 39).
2. We think "there's only so much you can give," but he gave his all for us (v. 40).
3. We think "there's only so far you can go." but he went the distance for us (v. 41).
4. Therefore, his grace gives us the power to take, to give, and to go, for the sake of his kingdom.

Worked examples

I would like to use the second half of this chapter to illustrate how this could work itself out in specific sermons. In each case the passages preached contained textual variants and I referenced these in the sermon, either because they were fundamental to my message, or because, as Johnson warns us, the alert listener will inevitably have questions about them.[53] In one case it is a disputed word, in another it is a sentence, and in the third, an entire pericope.

Worked example 1: 1 Kings 19:1-18

My preferred preaching method has been consecutive and expository.[54] In preaching through 1 Kings I had already dealt with Elijah's emergence in chapter 17, his encounter in Zarephath, and his victory on Carmel. This is the immediate context for chapter 19 and his flight into the desert. The

---

for the work of Christ, reflective of the work of Christ and/or resultant of the work of Christ.
53. Ibid., 112.
54. For an excellent example on how merely 'preaching the lectionary' can undermine the canonical context of texts see Farris, *Preaching that Matters*, 48-49, and his defense of *lectio continua*. Ferguson also makes the point that congregations learn from the pulpit not just in terms of what is said, but how it is said. Consecutive exposition "teaches the congregation to read the Bible for themselves; they follow the method they are exposed to Sunday by Sunday". Ibid., 195.

problem comes in verse 3, where the Masoretic text reads (*wayyar'*) "and he saw," but most translations and ancient versions have repointed it to (*wayyira'*) "and he was afraid." In favor of the emendation there is the external evidence of the ancient versions, and internally, the context of Jezebel's threat and the subsequent phrase "he ran for his life / he ran to save his life;" plus, grammatically, the verb *r'h* ("see") usually takes an object.

In favor of the Masoretic reading, in addition to the external evidence of the MT there is the wider context which looks not just at the immediate threat but at chapters 18 and 19 as a whole and the reasons behind Elijah's flight and subsequent depression. While, as a general rule, the Hebrew variants to the MT are worthy of close consideration,[55] the need for a compelling reason to change the MT, the principle of *lectio difficilior potior*, and given that the verb *yr'* ("to be afraid") also usually takes an object, and even an intensifying adjective (which one might expect here, "he was greatly afraid", or "he feared her"), there seems no compelling reason to change the reading from "he saw" in the MT, the reading which best describes the emergence of the others. Furthermore, while commentators disagree, I was able to consult a more in-depth treatment in a journal article by Allen, whose arguments I found convincing.[56]

So how did this work itself out in the sermon? My text is in italics with structural markers and explanatory comments in parentheses.

Title: From Disillusionment to Re-commissioning

A. [Introduction: context]
In 1 Kings 18 we have had the literal mountain-top experience, the climax of Elijah's prophetic career on Mt Carmel: fire from heaven, the defeat of Baal. We would expect Elijah to be living on the adrenalin of that for quite a while, and yet in chapter 19 he is in the desert complaining to the same God whose power he had seen so vividly only a few days before.
B. [Outline of problem. Solving this issue is not essential to every sermon on 1 Kings 19, but given the title of the sermon it is important to my thesis that Elijah is not so much frightened as depressed. Secondly, the presence

---

55. See Ernst Würthwein, *The Text of the Old Testament* (Grand Rapids: Eerdmans, 1988), 113ff.
56. R. B. Allen, "Elijah the Broken Prophet," *JETS* 22 (1979):193-202.

of the alternative reading in the footnote makes it easier for the congregation to follow.]

Now, if you look at verse 3, most of our English translations tell us that "Elijah was afraid." But this presents a problem. Why was he suddenly so frightened? Why would a prophet that had already stood up and spoken truth to power so forcefully and successfully be afraid? Why, when he had already taken his life in his hands and known what it was to stand alone when everyone else was against him, would he now be fearful for his life? Why would a prophet who had seen Yahweh vindicated and the enemy forces routed, run away on the word of one paranoid woman? And why would he run to save his life, and then beg to die?

C. [Outline of solution: I try to deal with the textual issues in an economy of words, always bringing it back to the importance of the choice. The vast majority of my listeners use either the NIV or ESV where the footnote gives the alternative reading.]

I think the solution can be found if you look at the footnote in your Bible. In Hebrew the words for "he was afraid" and "he saw" look exactly the same. They are simply pronounced differently, and the oldest standard Hebrew text has "he saw." Other ancient versions and manuscripts do have "he was afraid," but it is possible to see how the change could have happened since, <u>on the surface,</u> it appears to suit the context better: Jezebel issues a threat, Elijah is frightened, Elijah runs for his life. But only on the surface. As I've said, it actually creates more problems in terms of what has gone before, and how the story develops. Elijah is not the sort of guy to get frightened easily.

D. [An outline of why this is important and its connection to the rest of the sermon]

So then, what does it mean that "Elijah saw"? Think of where he has been—all that had happened in chapter 18 on Carmel. It looked like the tide had turned, the nation was spiritually back on track, the people had bowed down and declared that "the Lord he is God!" Elijah had been used by God in a mighty way. Revival! The pinnacle of his prophetic career. And then what? Was Jezebel repentant? Was she deposed? Was she licking her wounds and keeping a low profile? Not at all! She was breathing out threats more fiercely than before.

So Elijah <u>saw</u>. He saw that the revival, such as it was, had not permeated the higher echelons of society; he saw that the powers-that-be were as corrupt as *ever; he saw that all he could do, seemingly, was to apply the brakes temporarily to a runaway culture; he saw that he wasn't after all going to be the one to bring a comprehensive change to the nation. As he would tell God later in the chapter, he was no better than his forefathers.*

And so he flees, broken and disillusioned, running not to save his life (because he wants to die), but to prevent Jezebel from having the satisfaction of taking it. "Running for life" is an intensified phrase; in The Message we read "he ran for dear life." This was an "I'm outta here" moment! In fact we go on to see that he wasn't so much running from Jezebel as running from God. That is the significance of what we read immediately afterwards: he leaves Israel (Beersheba was the southern border town); he leaves his ministry by dismissing his servant, and he also wants to leave life itself. He's resigning his parish, resigning his calling, and resigning from the most precious gift of all—the very life God had given him.

E. [Explanation of how this reading fits in thematically with the previous chapters, with an applied link to the Gospels and personal experience.]

In 1 Kings 19 we see not so much a frightened fugitive but a disillusioned servant. In chapter 17 he had been used to restore life, now his own life was in desperate need of restoration. In chapters 17 and 18 he had performed extraordinary miracles, but now he was so depressed he couldn't even feed himself. Sitting in utter exhaustion and despair, he says, "God, I've had enough!" Often the deserts can follow swiftly on the heels of the mountaintop: the broom tree after Carmel, the demoniac after the transfiguration. Elijah was clocking off, handing in his notice, walking away. And like many of us in that situation he is completely self-absorbed. We'll notice in a moment how often in this chapter he talks about himself, what he has done for God. But God wanted to lift his vision a little higher.

F. [The main part of the sermon would now follow, looking at how Elijah received renewed strength (self-care), renewed vision of God (spiritual renewal) and a new task (revived vocation) plus the concluding encouragement that he was in fact not alone (v. 18). The redemptive focus came through in an emphasis on God as the agent of all these renewals, the one who lifts our eyes from ourselves to Him, and the one who became abandoned—"the only one left"—so that we would never be.]

Worked example 2. Luke 9:43b-56

Luke 9:51 is often seen as a fulcrum for the whole Gospel.[57] However, separating it from what immediately precedes can result in the loss of some important connections. While the preacher could justifiably end one sermon at v. 50 and begin another with 51ff, it would be equally justifiable to take 43b-56 as a unit, contrasting the cosmic significance of what Jesus was saying in vv. 44-45 with the pettiness and vindictiveness of what follows. In fact it would still be possible to reference the importance of the turning point of v. 51 to illustrate that while, for Jesus, his life and work is now entering a new phase and that a new trajectory of events is beginning to unfold, yet for his disciples nothing has changed. Jesus still has the same slow-of-mind and small-of-faith band of disciples with him making the same mistakes today as they did yesterday.

In taking vv. 43b-56 as the sermonic text we see a clear progression in the pride and prejudice of James and John, and we see it in three separate but connected pericopes. There is the in-group fighting requiring personal humility (46-48); there is the territorialism of the disciples in terms of the wider community of Jesus-followers requiring a more generous understanding of who is a disciple (49-50); and this is followed by their nationalistic sectarianism towards the unbelieving and unwelcoming Samaritans (51-56).

In the translations that most of my congregation will have in front of them, verses 54-55 read simply:

> And when his disciples James and John saw it, they said, 'Lord, do you want us to tell fire to come down from heaven and consume them?' But Jesus turned and rebuked them. [ESV]

However, the Western text has a couple of interesting additions (in italics):

> And when his disciples James and John saw it, they said, 'Lord, do you want us to call fire down from heaven to destroy them, *as Elijah*

---

57. For example, David Gooding, *According to Luke: The Third Gospel's Ordered Historical Narrative* (Belfast: Myrtlefield House, 2013).

did?' But Jesus turned and rebuked them, *and he said 'You do not know what manner of spirit you are of, for the Son of Man came not to destroy people's lives but to save them.'* [ESV margin cf. NKJV]

There is a degree of internal evidence for its inclusion. For example, in each of the previous two stories we are told the content of Jesus's rebuke (vv. 48, 50) and his words in each case are not without significance. In v. 48 he gives an object lesson in humility and outlines what it means to be 'great' in Kingdom terms. In v. 50 he shatters their self-constructed boundaries regarding who is "in" and who is "out" and he broadens their horizons to include those who are not part of their clique. The shortened v. 55 therefore seems abnormally truncated. We are expecting more.

Furthermore, in terms of the content of what Jesus says, vv. 55b-56a in the longer reading fits perfectly with what has gone before (and adds weight to the argument that this incident belongs with vv. 43-50). Having redefined greatness, and expanded their horizons in terms of who was 'with them', Jesus now reminds them of the purpose of his own mission and ministry. His was prompted by a different 'Spirit' and was about bringing life, not death.

All very good, except the external evidence is overwhelmingly in favor of the shorter reading. So, once again *lectio difficilior potior* would point us to conclude that the longer reading is not Lucan but was a later addition, possibly even added for sermonic purposes. In fact, while some English translations will place the quote in brackets, others in a footnote, some, such as the NIV, regard the manuscript evidence for the longer reading as being so weak that they don't even reference the alternative reading at all. However, it is important to remember that addition does not mean invention and it is not unreasonable to assume that the longer reading is likely to have been taken from another source and is still authentically Jesus, even if it is not Lucan.

Many sermons could be preached on this passage, of course, without making reference to the existence or content of the alternative reading, but what if, as one is crafting a sermon on this pericope, the less-attested reading does say something important and coherent to the theme?

In one sermon I was preparing on this passage, I wanted to take the three episodes and address the congregation on the issues of inappropriate competitiveness among believers, self-righteous exclusivism towards other Christian groups, and bitter sectarianism or racism in society. I wanted to show how this was a trajectory where one could easily feed the other—where the seemingly insignificant and petty (competitiveness) could be the feeding ground for the violent and hate-filled (fire from heaven against our enemies).

As my default in any sermon is to look, not just for judgement, but for grace in the passage,[58] I needed my hearers to leave, not feeling scolded, but equipped to live and think differently by the power and the Spirit of Christ. Therefore, v. 55b could be an important reference-point in my application: "You know not what 'Spirit' you are of."[59] We take our stand on the side of humility and inclusion and reconciliation, not because these are ends in themselves, but because they are fundamental to who we are as those born of a different Spirit.

Furthermore, this episode in Luke 9 is particularly poignant when one reads it alongside the pneumatological episode in Acts 8. One of the wonderful ironies in the growth of the early church is that John, who wanted to destroy the Samaritans, was one of those chosen by God to witness the Holy Spirit descend on them (Acts 8:14-17). The spirit referenced by Jesus in the longer reading of verse 55 becomes a textual foreshadowing of the Spirit whom John and the Samaritans later received in Acts.

I was also struck by how coherent Jesus' rebuke was, both to the immediate context and to the wider context of his whole ministry. We know from Luke 6:9 and John 10:9-10 that he proclaimed his ministry as life-saving (*sōzō*), in direct opposition to life-destroying (*apollumi*).

So there were numerous ways in which the longer reading gave me helpful and important material for my main points. However, while the contested verses reinforced my points, they did not form the basis of it.

---

58. I am grateful to Dr. Ross Lockhart of St. Andrew's Hall, Vancouver, for this thought, which he attributes to Paul Scott Wilson.

59. For convincing arguments on how the majority of NT references to *pneuma* refer to the Holy Spirit, as opposed to the human spirit, see Gordon Fee, *God's Empowering Presence* (Peabody, MA: Hendrickson, 1994). While Fee's work is confined to the Pauline corpus, his arguments on the Greek not having an equivalent to the French *esprit de corps* to signify human commonality (745) are relevant here, particularly when one bears in mind Jesus' other references to the Spirit and the link to Acts 8.

My use of the longer reading stemmed from the fact that everything in the contentious verses was still consistent with the literary and theological context and was actually useful for making connections—both retrospective, in terms of Elijah, and prospective, in terms of Acts 8. It would be an unnecessary indulgence—and bad homiletical practice—to talk about the textual issues and then never again make any reference to the content of the omitted verses.

So, given that some of the most widely used translations did not even footnote this, I have a dilemma. Do I deal with the variants at all? How much should be said about the reasons behind the exclusion without confusing the listeners or taking away from the main thrust of the sermon? How would it look in a sermon manuscript? Below is one attempt to reference the textual issues in a way that will engage the curious listener who has questions about why a verse has been omitted, while making sure that the sermon continues to flow and that the themes that the omitted sentences introduce (Elijah, the Spirit, salvation and the purpose of Jesus's mission) continue to form a major part of the sermon. Here the issues arise in the third section of the sermon.

Title of sermon: Pride and Prejudice

A. [Introduction to third point: initial mention of variant as I bring in the Elijah theme]
Thirdly, at the larger communal level, we encounter a bitter sectarianism. The Samaritans refuse to receive this entourage, and the disciples get a little antsy with the potential celestial resources they think are at their disposal. "Do you want us to call fire down from heaven to destroy them?" they say, and then some manuscripts add (it may be in your footnote) "as Elijah did?" referring back to 2Kings 1. Whether or not that phrase was written by Luke, it certainly captures the thought in the back of the disciples' minds.
B. [Outline and resolution of problem: to keep this as brief as possible, I mention what may be in some footnotes and say a little about how the Gospel writers utilized other sources, but I go straight to a part-solution here and mention a possible reason for the insertion.]
You see, at this point in the story we have one of those occasions where the New Testament manuscripts differ slightly. Some of your Bibles may show this in the footnotes, where the words of Jesus' rebuke are inserted: "You do

not know what spirit you are of, for the Son of Man came not to destroy men's lives but to save them". It's likely that Luke simply wrote "he turned and rebuked them." But of course, there were many other witnesses to what Jesus said, and many other actions and teachings which were not recorded in our four Gospels—the final verse of the Fourth Gospel makes this clear (John 21:25). So it is certainly possible that, since we have Jesus' words recorded in the first and second stories, someone 'filled in the blanks' here, both in terms of what James and John said ("we want to be Elijah") and in terms of what Jesus said—and they did so from another authentic source of Jesus' words that was available at that time.

C. [Further resolution showing coherence of longer reading with the wider context and theme of the passage]

Be that as it may, we know that Jesus, for the third time, rebukes them. What do you think he said? Well, frankly, knowing Jesus, thinking of the context, weighing it up with other sources and stories of other Samaritan encounters, and Jesus' own statements elsewhere in the Gospels about his purpose and mission, I guess he probably said something like, "You do not know what Spirit you are of, for the Son of Man did not come to destroy men's lives but to save them!"

D. [Cultural application: wanting fire from heaven]

Inter-ethnic suspicion and violence are prevalent the world over, but sadly it is not absent from the church. Read some of the accounts of racial conflicts in North America, of the Rwandan genocide, of the Balkan conflict, and of course I come from one part of the world where this is so. I witnessed people fresh out of prayer meetings, where ostensibly they have been baring their souls before Almighty God, they hear of some shooting or bombing on the car radio and they descend to uttering fierce invectives against their neighbors, self-righteously calling down fire from heaven to burn them to hell!

E. [Theological application: Elijah, James, John and us]

What James and John failed to grasp was that there was an epoch-shattering difference between being an Elijah—a man of God, who, at infrequent times, may have stood in the place of God as a type of proto-Messiah, being the occasional, temporary channel of God's righteous judgement—and being a disciple—the ongoing permanent channel of God's Holy Spirit. Living in the last days, God has appointed us, the men and women of God, to preach the eschatological gospel of transforming grace and to leave the eschatological judgement to his own day and hour.[60]

F. [Christological turn: fire of judgment falling elsewhere. Here, I reprise some of the vocabulary of the longer reading: "Son of Man," "what Spirit."]

Little did James and John know (although bearing in mind that Jesus had just predicted it, they should have known) that their salvation lay not in calling down fire from heaven on the Samaritans, but in seeing that fire of judgment fall on the one they loved. "The Son of Man came not to destroy but to save." The only life he came to take was his own. This is the gospel.

G. [Concluding application and summary: a different fire falls on the Samaritans.]

Sadly, if my own experience is anything to go by, Christ's rebuke can still be so relevant to us, can't it? You do not know what Spirit you are of. So instead of a spirit of competition and petty-mindedness we have a spirit of complementarity and partnership, instead of a spirit of exclusivism we have a spirit of generosity, instead of a spirit of bitterness we have a spirit of grace.

These dangers and temptations may pursue us to the grave, but by his Spirit, not ours, they can be conquered. It's wonderful, isn't it, that when the Samaritans eventually received this Spirit of God one of the apostles chosen in Acts 8 to lay hands on them was John. John did get to see fire from heaven fall on the Samaritans—but not in the way he imagined.

Conclusion

Carson writes that it makes no sense to pretend you are something you are not. Some scholars will never display great pastoral or preaching gifts; some pastor-preachers will never function as gifted scholars.[61] But there is certainly a need for more engagement and interdependency between the two. Sven, of course, would point us to no less a person than the Apostle Paul. In 1995 he led a workshop on "Paul, pastor and theologian" and debunked the idea that there was a disjunction between these two aspects of Paul's character and writings. I am also reminded of his other Regent colleague, Bruce Waltke, who would tell students who enquired about

---

60. Some of my vocabulary will change according to my audience. This text was for a professional audience with a high number of third-level educated congregants. In other contexts I may say something like "the gospel of transforming grace for our day, and to leave the final judgement to his own day and hour."

61. Carson, "The Scholar as Pastor," in Strachan & Mathis, 74.

doctoral studies that if they did follow that path they should always be pastoral scholars, and if they did not they should still be scholarly pastors. The church needs both.

For the latter, the temptation will be to forget the broader horizon of the pastor-preacher's vocation and to see the preaching of deeper and more nourishing sermons as the primary goal. For that reason this chapter should more accurately have been entitled *From the Prayer-room to the Library to the Pulpit and Beyond,* because our work neither begins nor ends in research or delivery, but with God in prayer and meditation and then back to God again in the living sacrifices of his people, inspired and transformed by his Spirit.

11

Disability and Dependency

Toward a Theology of Weakness

Toni Kim

When Galileo argued that the earth revolves around the sun, biblical interpreters condemned him as heretical. Why? On the surface, it was because his teachings appeared to contradict verses like Psalm 104:5, which explicitly declares, "He set the earth on its foundations; it can never be moved." Galileo's ideas seemed patently false when held up to the written word of God. The problem was that biblical interpretation was being filtered through the common perception of the day that the earth was the center around which the sun revolved. The unexamined presupposition of geocentrism limited the viewpoint of the theologians and led them to conclude that any denial of geocentrism was tantamount to rejecting the authority of the Bible. Pope John Paul II declared Galileo "a sincere believer" and accurately summarized:

> [T]he geocentric representation of the world was commonly admitted in the culture of the time as fully agreeing with the teaching of the Bible, of which certain expressions, taken literally, seemed to affirm geocentrism. The problem posed by theologians of that age was, therefore, that of the compatibility between heliocentrism and Scripture. Thus the new science, with its methods and the freedom of research which they

implied, obliged theologians to examine their own criteria of scriptural interpretation. Most of them did not know how to do so.[1]

This inability to "examine their own criteria of scripture interpretation" pertains not just to medieval Catholic theologians but to all of us, because of the human tendency to assume that our understanding of the truth is equal to the truth itself.

The theologian Thomas Reynolds, who has a son with complex disabilities, posits that modern theologians and laypeople alike fall under the sway of what he calls the "cult of normalcy,"[2] which unconsciously limits how we interpret Scripture. Building on Stanley Hauerwas' "tyranny of normality,"[3] Reynolds exposes how every culture has its own definition of what it means to be normal and how these beliefs dictate the ways we view and treat others. In the modern western world, we have come to define normalcy as being self-sufficient, rational, productive, and with physical bodies over which we have control. We talk about wanting people to be "contributing members of society," or we lament how some are "a burden on the system." Christians are not immune to this negative valuation of disability, weakness, and those who exhibit either or both.

Disability shatters our normative lens that spotlights strength in the Bible and filters out weakness. With fresh eyes we can see how God through Jesus Christ embraces weakness, reverses exclusion, inverts weakness, and redeems weakness. Weakness is not simply a quality that some humans endure for a season; weakness is endemic to human existence and is actually

---

1. Pope John Paul II, "Address to the Plenary Session on 'The Emergence of Complexity in Mathematics, Physics, Chemistry and Biology'" Oct 31, 1992 to the Pontifical Academy of Sciences. http://www.pas.va/content/accademia/en/magisterium/johnpaulii/31october1992.html#5, accessed Oct 1, 2020.

2. Thomas E. Reynolds, *Vulnerable Communion: A Theology of Disability and Hospitality*, (Grand Rapids: Brazos, 2008). Stated positively, "Full personhood is neither diminished by disability nor confirmed by ability. Instead, it is a factor of the interdependent relationships we share with one another as creatures loved into being by God and created in the image of God" (Reynolds, 42–43).

3. Stanley Hauerwas, "Community and Diversity: The Tyranny of Normality," 37–43, in *Critical Reflections on Stanley Hauerwas' Theology of Disability: Disabling Society, Enabling Theology*, ed. John Swinton (Binghamton, NY: Haworth Pastoral Press, 2004). Originally published in *Suffering Presence: Theological Reflections on Medicine, the Mentally Handicapped, and the Church* (Notre Dame, IN: University of Notre Dame Press, 1986), 211–17.

one means by which we are conformed to the image of Christ.

The cult of normalcy looks down on people with disabilities as being aberrant, inferior and even somehow not fully human. This prejudice is rarely stated. It is typically implicit and is an unintended byproduct of the explicit values of independence, rationality, and control: "Regarding people with disabilities, the (generally unspoken) logic is that since attributes like reason, sensory abilities and strength are what make people in the likeness of God and thus worthy of protection, those deficient in such attributes are not as worthy as others."[4] Few Christians would admit to condescension toward people with disabilities, but most fear that having a disability themselves would lead to their own diminishment.

The marginalization and denigration of people with disabilities bleeds into multiple sectors, including science:

> In its modern form, biomedical science conceives of disability as the epitome of suffering, an exemplary tragedy located within the individual, sometimes regarded even as a form of living death.... I see the genetic revolution as premised on the idea that humanity should be delivered from disability. Disability and its correlate, suffering, shapes the development of genetics.[5]

Disability is assumed to be something negative that should be minimized or eliminated if possible. This type of attitude usually results from equating disability with a medical condition like an illness that should be cured or eradicated. There are certainly medical aspects to many disabilities, and the amelioration of pain is a good goal. However, not all disabilities involve suffering, and some disabilities bring attendant strengths that could be lost as a result of any so-called "healing." People on the autism spectrum may struggle with certain social interactions but can have a hyper-focus and attention to different details that lead to breakthroughs, like Temple Grandin, who credits autism for her ability to understand animals

---

4. John F. Kilner, *Dignity and Destiny: Humanity in the Image of God*, (Grand Rapids: Eerdmans, 2015), 101.

5. Christopher Newell, "On the Importance of Suffering: The Paradoxes of Disability" in *The Paradox of Disability: Responses to Jean Vanier and L'Arche Communities from Theology and the Sciences*, edited by Hans S. Reinders, {Grand Rapids: Eerdmans, 2010), 172.

and design humane ways to slaughter farm animals.[6]

A recent study of teenagers and adults with Down syndrome revealed that an overwhelming majority of them are happy with their lives, with 97 percent being happy with who they are, and 96 percent happy with how they look.[7] Children with Down syndrome are more likely to develop acute myeloid leukemia, but their survival rate is more than twice as high as those without Down syndrome.[8] Would genetic removal of the extra twenty-first chromosome in every cell heal developmental delay but result in an increase in self-hatred—or an increased mortality rate for leukemia? "Healing" a disability is a complicated concept.

Historically, biblical interpretation has been tainted by the cult of normalcy and the medicalization of disability.[9] Blindness, deafness, and lameness are often equated with sin and are thus considered to be evils that should be eliminated. Strength is praised and sought; weakness is condemned and shunned. Striving to be like God entails pursuing attributes which the normative culture considers positive: strength, power, self-sufficiency, and beauty. The cult of normalcy focuses on the biblical passages that promise blessing.

And yet, Jesus is clear that He came "not to be served, but to serve, and to give his life as a ransom for many" (Mark 10:45). To be like Christ is to be a servant, to be considered weak by others. Whereas we default to focus on being like Christ in his resurrected power, the Apostle Paul makes clear that power is ontologically coupled with "participation in his sufferings, becoming like him in his death" (Phil 3:10). There is no resurrection apart from crucifixion. We cannot skip death if we want resurrection. The

---

6. Temple Grandin, "From *Thinking in Pictures, and Other Reports from My Life in Autism*," in *The Norton Psychology Reader*, ed. Gary Marcus, (New York: W. W. Norton & Company, 2006), pp. 358–364, here 361–2.

7. Brian Skotko, Susan Levine and Richard Goldstein. "Self-perceptions from People with Down Syndrome," *American Journal of Medical Genetics* Part A 155:2360–2369. Published online 2011 Sep 9. doi: 10.1002/ajmg.a.34235.

8. J. Timothy Caldwell, Yubin Ge, and Jeffrey Taub, "Prognosis and management of acute myeloid leukemia in patients with Down syndrome," *Expert Review of Hematology*, 7/6 (Dec 2014): 831–840. Published online 2014 Sep 18, doi: 10.1586/17474086.2014.959923.

9. For a comprehensive historical survey of biblical interpretation with regard to disability, see Amos Yong, *Theology and Down Syndrome: Reimagining Disability in Late Modernity* (Waco, TX: Baylor University Press, 2007), 19–42.

gateway to glory is always suffering. Jesus explained to the disciples on Emmaus Road in Luke 24, "Did not the Christ have to suffer these things and then enter his glory?" As we seek to be like Jesus, we are confronted with the fact that he often chooses weakness, and so we need a theology of weakness.

Before proceeding, there need to be several caveats. As averred above, disability, weakness, and suffering are not synonymous. They are overlapping domains. The Bible has a varied vocabulary within the semantic domains of weakness and suffering, and so passages about weakness and suffering will be used to address matters of disability. These applications do not assume equivalence but rather relevance, often by analogy.

Finally, we have to be careful that we do not objectify people with disabilities, whether by treating them as objects of mercy or as saints to be idolized. They do not exist solely for the purpose of educating or training the rest of us. Each of us is an individual made in the image of God, however imperfectly, and we are more alike than different. We affirm our common humanity and our common weakness.

Disability, Dependency and Human Weakness

Those of us who see ourselves as normal want disability to be something that affects other people, not us. We want disability to be an abnormality to which we are immune. Unfortunately, the line between ability and disability is sometimes blurry and never static. Disability can be a matter of degrees rather than distinctions. There may be a wide intellectual gap between a learned professor and a nonverbal person with profound disabilities, but they share the same desire for love, the same craving for affirmation, the same need for salvation in Christ, and the shared fate of certain death. Despite our differences, people of all abilities and disabilities journey on the same path together and are always vulnerable to additional weaknesses. An accident or stroke can result in a physical, mental, emotional and/or social disability at any age; no one is inoculated. This means there is a great commonality among all people, as Jürgen Moltmann writes:

> In actual fact the distinction between the healthy and the handicapped [*sic*] does not exist. For every human life is limited, vulnerable, and weak. Helpless we are born and helpless we die. So in reality there is no

such thing as a handicapped life. It is only the ideal of health set up by the society of the capable which condemns a certain group of people to be called "handicapped."[10]

The reality is that all human beings are dependent and have experienced, are experiencing, and/or will experience some degree of disability in our lifetimes. This does not discount the fact that some people's experience of disability is more pronounced than others. It simply decries the dichotomization of humanity into arbitrary categories of "normal" *vis à vis* "disabled" and between those who offer help and those who need help. We are all in need of help, and we all have something to offer others.

This interdependency of humanity is not a product of the Fall but is actually one of the ways in which we bear the image of the triune God who is love. In the beginning God created humanity male and female, because "it is not good for the man to be alone" (Gen 2:18). Humans were created to be in interdependent relationship with one another and in dependency upon their Creator God. Sin has complicated those relationships but did not manufacture them. In the new creation, people will be at peace with one another and be joined in the united but diversified praise of God (cf. Rev 5:9-10).

Two scholars combined their academic expertise in theology and disability studies with their experience of raising their daughter with Rett Syndrome to produce a book. They write that disability does not divide humanity but instead confronts us with our common weakness:

> The Trinitarian paradigm emphasizes the vital, universal need for human relationship. It illuminates and grounds human interdependence... [D]isability heightens awareness of our corporeality and mortality, and debunks modern myths of individual autonomy, control, and human perfectibility.[11]

---

10. Jürgen Moltmann, "The Liberation and Acceptance of the Handicapped" in *The Power of the Powerless*, (San Francisco: Harper and Row, 1983), 137. Quoted in William C. Gaventa, "Learning from People with Disabilities: How to Ask the Right Questions," in *The Paradox of Disability: Responses to Jean Vanier and L'Arhce Communities from Theology and the Sciences*, edited by Hans S. Reinders, (Grand Rapids: Eerdmans, 2010), 103-112, here 105.

11. Myroslaw Tataryn and Maria Truchan-Tataryn, *Discovering Trinity in Disability: A Theology for Embracing Difference*, (Maryknoll, NY: Orbis, 2013), 22.

The Old Testament: God's people are weak

Throughout the Old Testament we see God's preferential treatment for the oppressed, including the poor, orphans, widows, and those with disabilities.[12] At various times and in various ways, God's people have taken seriously this call to minister to those who are weak. What God's people have so often failed to realize is how the cult of normalcy feeds the false assumption that we are normal, and the weak are limited to those to whom we minister. We see others as weak and in need of the mercy that we can impart from our strength. There is much in Scripture that talks about how God blesses us in order to bless others. Serving the needy is indeed scriptural, but it is not complete. The Old Testament is full of God's proclamation that his people are themselves weak and in need of mercy. In a culture that prizes normalcy and certain visions of strength and beauty, God wants his people not just to minister to the weak but also to understand that we ourselves are weak.

Human weakness is an intrinsic part of the legacy of God's chosen people. To make it clear that his people are not natural but supernatural, God works through barren women. Abraham's wife Sarah (Gen 16:2; cf. Rom 4:19), Isaac's wife Rebekah (Gen 25:21), and Jacob's wife Rachel (Gen 29:31) all needed divine intervention to bear their sons of promise. God was not bound by the ancient customs of primogeniture, where first-born sons are given primacy in treatment, title, and inheritance. The election of God's people bypasses many first-born sons. Abraham's first-born son Ishmael, "born according to the flesh," is passed over in favor of Isaac, "born as the result of a divine promise" (Gal 4:22). Isaac's oldest son Esau is passed over for his younger twin brother Jacob, the father of twelve sons. Jacob's fourth son Judah is promised the scepter (Gen 49:10). Generations later, David is the youngest of eight boys and has to be called in from tending sheep in order to be anointed king (1 Sam 16:11). God chooses his people according to his divine will.

God's election does not protect his people from hardship. Joseph endures the personal trials of being sold by his older brothers and being abused and neglected by others. God works through this to bring the Isra-

---

12. See e.g., Deut 10:18, Psalm 82:3, Jer 22:16, and Lev 19:14.

elites to Egypt, where they flourish – for a season. Professor Bruce Waltke notes that Israel's divine election as the seed of God's blessings includes Egypt's oppression of them: "God's elect must suffer. But this suffering is not punitive; it is part and parcel of God's plan for the redemption of the world."[13] God has promised a holy seed that will one day crush Satan's head, but not before one's heel is crushed (Gen 3:15).

Whom does God raise to deliver his people from slavery in Egypt? His servant Moses, who describes himself as "slow of speech and tongue"[14] (Exod 4:10). When Moses balks at God's assignment, the Lord makes it clear that he made Moses that way: "Who gave human beings their mouths? Who makes him mute or deaf? Who gives them sight or makes them blind? Is it not I, the LORD? Now go; I will help you speak" (Exod 4:11). God knows that "Aaron, your brother ... can speak well" (Exod 4:13) but purposefully chooses Moses as his instrument. Moses' speech impediment does not discount him from doing God's work.

The Lord repeatedly reminds his leaders and his people of their weakness. Before they enter the Promised Land, God gives this pep talk:

> Hear, Israel: You are now about to cross the Jordan to go in and dispossess nations greater and stronger than you, with large cities that have walls up to the sky. The people are strong and tall... Understand, then, that it is not because of your righteousness that the LORD your God is giving you this good land to possess, for you are a stiff-necked people (Deut 9:1–2, 6).

The Israelites should be under no illusion that it is their strength or righteousness that distinguishes them from other people. God commands them to remember that they were slaves in Egypt (Deut 5:15) until he delivered them. This memory of helplessness, weakness, and being foreigners is meant to lead to compassion and just practices for others, as well as complete dependence on him, not on their own strength.

---

13. Bruce Waltke with Charles Yu, *An Old Testament Theology: An Exegetical, Canonical and Thematic Approach*, (Grand Rapids: Zondervan, 2007), 356.

14. This Hebrew phrase refers to "impeded speech of some kind." Saul Olyan, *Disability in the Hebrew Bible*, (Cambridge: Cambridge University Press, 2008), 132, n.9.

The New Testament: Jesus Christ Became Weak

One shocking truth about the Christian faith is that God himself becomes weak. Paul's hymn in Philippians 2 describes the intentional descent into weakness of Christ Jesus:

> Who, being in very nature God, did not consider equality with God something to be used to his own advantage; rather, he made himself nothing by taking the very nature of a servant, being made in human likeness. And being found in appearance as a man, he humbled himself by becoming obedient to death—even death on a cross! (Phil 2:6–8).

The infinite, all-knowing God, who spoke creation into existence, entered the world as a completely helpless, speechless, dependent baby with an impure genealogy tainted by sin. The angels trumpeted Jesus' birth, but then the all-powerful God-made-flesh spent three decades in relative obscurity as a carpenter's son. The anonymity of his early life is a picture of true humility that embraces weakness. Once he initiated his public ministry, Jesus was on a constant path down to Jerusalem to his crucifixion. Jesus performed many acts of mighty power, but resisted being made into an earthly king (John 6:15). He repeatedly chose the path of weakness, rather than availing himself of power: "Do you think I cannot call on my Father, and he will at once put at my disposal more than twelve legions of angels?" (Matt 26:53).

Jesus insisted that he "must suffer many things and be rejected by the elders, the chief priests, and the teachers of the law, and that he must be killed and after three days rise again" (Mark 8:31). Jesus was mocked, beaten, tortured, and crucified. This way of deliberate weakness, suffering, and death is not just for Jesus, but is paradigmatic for his people: "Whoever wants to be my disciples must deny themselves and take up their cross and follow me" (Mark 8:34). The Apostle Peter agrees: "Christ suffered for you, leaving you an example, that you should follow in his steps" (1 Pet 2:21). Suffering is not to be avoided but actually followed as the path to glory.

In Philippians 3:10 Paul declares, "I want to know Christ—yes, to know the power of his resurrection and participation in his sufferings, becoming like him in his death." The Greek structure makes it clear that the power of

Christ's resurrection and the participation in his sufferings are two inseparable sides of the same coin of knowing Christ. The participation in his sufferings is further developed by a third phrase, "becoming like him in his death." We are specifically called to be conformed to Christ *in his death*—a suffering conformity. Christ's death is a picture of ultimate dependence on God. Death makes us rely not on ourselves but on God, who raises the dead (cf. 2 Cor 1:8–10). It is a profound mystery that Jesus had to rely upon the Father to save him from death: "During the days of Jesus' life on earth, he offered up prayers and petitions with fervent cries and tears to the one who could save him from death, and he was heard because of his reverent submission. Son though he was, he learned obedience from what he suffered" (Heb 5:7–8). Dependence on God—not self-sufficiency—is our goal.

Resurrection is preceded by death, just as glory is preceded by suffering. As New Testament scholar Luke Timothy Johnson summarizes: "Everywhere in these [NT] writings the image of Jesus involves the tension-filled paradox of death and resurrection, suffering and glory."[15] Romans 8:17 names us co-heirs with Christ "if indeed we share in his sufferings in order that we may also share in his glory." Suffering itself is not an inherent good or something we should seek to maximize. Suffering and weakness also do not necessarily make people into saints; sometimes they just make people bitter and angry. But something changes when we contemplate that "God, for whom and through whom everything exists, should make the pioneer of their salvation perfect through what he suffered" (Heb 2:10). We realize that "we do not have a high priest who is unable to empathize with our weaknesses, but we have one who has been tempted in every way, just as we are—yet he did not sin" (Heb 4:15). Knowing that Jesus willingly suffered enables us to "approach God's throne of grace with confidence, so that we may receive mercy and find grace in our time of need" (Heb 4:16). There is no shame in having need; instead, there is an open invitation to receive mercy and find grace. Christopher Newell, a priest and academic theologian with multiple physical disabilities that cause him a lot of pain,

---

15. Luke Timothy Johnson, *The Real Jesus: The Misguided Quest for the Historical Jesus and the Truth of the Traditional Gospels*, (San Francisco: Harper, 1997), 166. Quoted in Marva Dawn, *Powers, Weakness, and the Tabernacling of God*, (Grand Rapids: Eerdmans, 2001), 58.

has found great comfort through Christ's suffering:

> For me, suffering is crucial to the narration of what it is to be a Christian because, within the broken incarnate God, I find the particular attributes essential for upholding and embracing my life and making sense of my complex journey. In particular, the centrality of the suffering of Jesus – not just in persecution during his life, death, and resurrection but also in his experience of being other – means that I can relate in a very intimate way to a very human God.[16]

This suffering God calls us to suffer with him: "Jesus also suffered outside the city gate to make the people holy through his own blood. Let us, then, go to him outside the camp, bearing the disgrace he bore" (Heb 13:12–13). Therefore, rather than trying to avoid or eliminate suffering, we can embrace suffering, weakness, dependency, and even disability as a way to be like Jesus:

> Jesus is the exemplar of the fully human life because he embodies God's loving regard for, and gratuitous solidarity with, humanity precisely in its incapacity, vulnerability, and indeed its brokenness. Rather than shunning weakness, Jesus embraces it as a means of becoming available to others.[17]

Weakness is not ontologically a part of God, but it is inherently a part of becoming like him. This is a radical re-conception of weakness and suffering: rather than seeing it as something to be avoided or eliminated, we recognize that it leads us into the path of knowing God and being like God. The Bible subverts all worldly values: those who are rich are made poor, while the poor become rich; the last will be made first, and the first, last; whoever wants to be greatest must be least of all. Similarly, Scripture has a pattern of including those who are excluded.

Disability, Exclusion, and Inclusion

The Bible often seems to perpetuate the cult of normalcy by treating disabilities as something aberrant—a sign of God's judgment or a curse. The

---

16. Newell, "On the Importance of Suffering," 177–178.
17. Reynolds, *Vulnerable Communion*, 199–200.

Old Testament is replete with adulation of perfection and denigration of anything imperfect. Offerings given to the Lord must be "without defect[18] or blemish[19] to be acceptable" (Lev 22:21; cf. Num 19:2, Mal 1:14). Specifically, the Passover lambs had to be "year-old males without defects" (Exod 12:5), and none of their bones could be broken (Exod 12:46, Num 9:12).

In addition, those who approached the holy God to present those unblemished sacrifices also needed to be without defect:

> The LORD said to Moses, "Say to Aaron: 'For the generations to come none of your descendants who has a defect may come near to offer the food of his God. No man who has any defect may come near: no man who is blind or lame, disfigured or deformed; no man with a crippled foot or hand, or who is a hunchback or a dwarf, or who has any eye defect, or who has festering or running sores or damaged testicles. No descendant of Aaron the priest who has any defect is to come near to present the food offerings to the Lord. He has a defect; he must not come near to offer the food of his God. He may eat the most holy food of his God, as well as the holy food; yet because of his defect, he must not go near the curtain or approach the altar, and so desecrate my sanctuary. I am the Lord, who makes them holy' " (Lev 21:16–23).

This exacting standard of physical perfection will ultimately find its fulfillment through the spiritual perfection of Jesus, but we need first to acknowledge that passages like these can be disturbing and feel discriminatory toward people with disabilities. Theologian Amos Yong lists three helpful insights about interpreting this passage: 1) The context of laws concerning the priesthood in Leviticus 21–22 reveals a long list of reasons for exclusion, of which disability is only one; 2) eating holy food was still allowed, meaning "blemished priests were not completely barred from priestly functions;" and 3) the listed blemishes are all visually perceptible,

---

18. The Hebrew word תָּמִים "blameless, perfect" is translated almost forty times in the Pentateuch as "without defect" when describing offerings. When not applied to a sacrifice, the word describes the blamelessness or perfection of God's people (Deut 18:13, 2Sam 22:24), God's ways and works (Deut 32:4, 2 Sam 22:31), and even God Himself (Psa 18:25).

19. This word מוּם refers primarily to a physical defect but can also describe a moral blemish (Prov 9:7, Job 31:7).

which implies there is no equivalency between disabilities and disqualifying blemishes. Nevertheless, Yong acknowledges that these allowances do not overcome the basic normative presupposition that physical blemishes and disabilities are profaning and thus disqualifying.[20]

One interpretive key is found by understanding that these restrictions are not permanent. For example, Deuteronomy lists an assortment of people who are banned from entering the assembly of the Lord, starting with eunuchs: "No one who has been emasculated by crushing or cutting may enter the assembly of the Lord" (Deut 23:1). This prohibition is completely overturned by the prophet Isaiah:

> Let no foreigner who is bound to the Lord say, "The Lord will surely exclude me from his people." And let no eunuch complain, "I am only a dry tree." For this is what the Lord says: "To the eunuchs who keep my Sabbaths, who choose what pleases me and hold fast to my covenant, to them I will give within my temple and its walls a memorial and a name better than sons and daughters; I will give them an everlasting name that will endure forever" (Isa 56:3–5).

This radical reversal includes a "counternarrative of the eunuch's inclusion and even privilege,"[21] because the eunuch does not need to be "healed" in order to please God; he who cannot physically have children will be given a memorial and name "better than sons and daughters." In a parallel situation, Ammonites and Moabites are forbidden to enter the Lord's assembly (Deut 23:3) and yet are included in the house of prayer for all nations (Isa 56:6–7). Most notably, Ruth the Moabitess secures a place not only among God's people but actually in the royal lineage of the Savior. God's people are formed by faith, not by flesh.

---

20. Amos Yong, *The Bible, Disability, and the Church: A New Vision of the People of God*, (Grand Rapids: Eerdmans, 2011), 18–20. He argues that even damaged testicles have a visually discernible effect.

21. Olyan, *Disability in the Hebrew Bible*, 11. Olyan's book details references to disability throughout the Old Testament and comes to the unfortunate conclusion that the biblical texts consciously and unconsciously stigmatize and marginalize people with disabilities, with only rare exceptions like Isaiah 56:3–7 and circumcision as a positive defect. He reads these texts apart from their fulfillment and transformation through the perfect work of Jesus marked by weakness.

The move from exclusion to inclusion is effected through Jesus, who is both the Great High Priest and the Passover Lamb. As the eternal High Priest, he embodies the undefiled Levitical priesthood and extends the priesthood to all believers. God's people become "a royal priesthood" (1 Pet 2:9), and those with disabilities are explicitly invited: "the poor, the crippled, the lame, the blind" (Luke 14:13). This new kingdom also includes the previously proscribed eunuchs, as evidenced by Peter's baptism of the Ethiopian eunuch in Acts 8. Picking up on language from Leviticus, Jesus is "a lamb without blemish or defect" (1 Pet 1:19) whose single sacrifice completes all Old Testament requirements: "we have been made holy through the sacrifice of the body of Jesus Christ once for all" (Heb 10:10).

Importantly, Jesus fulfills these two functions *through* suffering and weakness, rather than in spite of them. Emphasizing Christ's perfection as priest and sacrifice can inadvertently lead to reinforcing the stigmatization of those with imperfect or broken bodies. To counterbalance the normative bias against defects and brokenness, Christ's suffering must be understood to be inclusive of his perfection: "Christ is considered the unblemished and undefiled, in the sense of the sinless Great High Priest, yet on the other hand, his crucifixion means that he fulfills his priestly functions with an impaired and disabled body."[22] Jesus "through the eternal Spirit offered himself unblemished to God" (Heb 9:14) by suffering a painful bodily death on a cross.

Leviticus did not permit someone with a defect to "go near the curtain or approach the altar" (Lev 21:23), but when Jesus died, the curtain of the temple was torn in two (Matt 27:51; cf. Mark 15:38, Luke 23:45), opening access to the Most Holy Place. The author of Hebrews identifies that curtain as Jesus' body: "... we have confidence to enter the Most Holy Place by the blood of Jesus, by a new and living way opened for us through the curtain, that is, his body" (Heb 10:19–20). Jesus' broken, disfigured body opened access to God. Thus weakness and "defects" are not obstacles to God's work but the actual mechanisms through which we are blessed.

Weakness Inverted

Embedded in all the above is the recognition that God inverts weakness

---

22. Yong, *The Bible*, 29.

and strength. This is prefigured in the priorities of God the Shepherd in Ezekiel: "I will bind up the injured and strengthen the weak, but the sleek and the strong I will destroy. I will shepherd the flock with justice" (Ezek 34:16). God's advantage goes to the weak. God's people default to strength and power, however.

When God chose to reveal himself, he did not come as the world expected, which is why the world he created did not recognize him (John 1:10). Instead of coming in power and glory, God came through weakness and vulnerability. Jesus as the Good Shepherd cares for the weak by laying his life down for them as the sacrificial lamb: "He was led like a lamb to the slaughter, and as a sheep before its shearers is silent, so he did not open his mouth" (Isa 53:7).

The Apostle Paul's preaching of "Christ crucified, a stumbling block to Jews and foolishness to Gentiles" (1 Cor 1:23) seemed an oxymoron: "*Messiah* meant power, splendor, triumph; *crucified* meant weakness, humiliation, defeat. Little wonder that both Jew and Greek were scandalized by the Christian message."[23] Paul goes on to re-define foolishness and wisdom, as well as weakness and strength:

> For the foolishness of God is wiser than human wisdom, and the weakness of God is stronger than human strength. Brothers and sisters, think of what you were when you were called. Not many of you were wise by human standards; not many were influential; not many were of noble birth. But God chose the foolish things of the world to shame the wise; God chose the weak things of the world to shame the strong. God chose the lowly things of this world and the despised things—and the things that are not—to nullify the things that are, so that no one may boast before him (1 Cor 1:25–29, emphasis added).

As he did with the ancient Israelites, God makes it clear that his people are not chosen because of human standards of excellence or normalcy. God chooses the foolish, the weak, the lowly, and the despised. This means that only those who will admit to weakness can access the wisdom and power of God:

---

23. Gordon D. Fee, *The First Epistle to the Corinthians*, NICNT (Grand Rapids: Eerdmans, 1987), 75.

Such "weakness" in God is scandalous to those who think of themselves as righteous and thus in no need of forgiveness; but to those who recognize themselves as in need of mercy this is the good news that sets us free to follow him. Thus this weakness is also the ultimate power, and therefore the final wisdom of God.[24]

Paradoxically, weakness becomes strength. Paul therefore learns to "boast all the more gladly about my weaknesses" (2 Cor 12:9) and to "delight in weakness ... for when I am weak, I am strong" (2 Cor 12:10). This inversion of human values is possible because of the radical truth that Jesus himself "was crucified in weakness, yet he lives by God's power. Likewise, we are weak in him, yet by God's power we will live with him in our dealing with you" (2 Cor 13:4). Theologian Marva Dawn says that weakness is God's *modus operandi*:

> Even as Christ accomplished atonement for us by suffering and death, so the Lord accomplishes witness to the world through our weakness. In fact, God has more need of our weakness than of our strength.... By our union with Christ in the power of the Spirit in our weaknesses, we display God's glory.[25]

Disability, Mutuality and the Church

Professor Sven Soderlund reminds us that Christianity is always to be lived out communally: "No one lives in Christ alone, by himself or herself. Life in Christ is inseparable from life in community.... Once you live in Christ, you live with a host of others who are also in Christ."[26] The theology of weakness therefore applies not simply to personal transformation but also to ecclesiology:

---

24. Fee, *First Epistle*, 78.
25. Dawn, *Powers*, 47.
26. Sven Soderlund, "Living in Christ", Regent Chapel lecture, Nov 17, 2015. Accessed via https://www.regentaudio.com/collections/sven-soderlund/products/living-in-christ, June 7, 2019. Professor Soderlund, to whom this article is dedicated, has faithfully created community for so many people. He embodies a divine hospitality that welcomes people to the table, whether a physical table in his home or at a conference, or a metaphorical table, by really listening to, dialoguing with, and remembering personal details about others. He fosters a real sense of belonging and bestows upon each person a real dignity.

> The Pauline texts about Jesus crucified in weakness and inviting us to be crucified with him, the Petrine texts about following in the footsteps of Jesus, whose suffering has left us an example, and the Revelation texts urging perseverance in affliction all raise crucial questions for churches in our time. We must remember that what is true of Jesus, Peter, and Paul is no doubt also true for churches.... The Scriptures repeatedly show that the way of God is through weakness.[27]

The church is called to embrace weakness, model it, and subvert it. Doing so requires fighting against the pride that divides. The Roman church consisted of both Jews and Gentiles, whose mysterious union in Christ is described in Romans 9–11. In Romans 12, Paul addresses the need for humility and interdependence:

> For by the grace given me I say to every one of you: Do not think of yourself more highly than you ought, but rather think of yourself with sober judgment, in accordance with the measure of faith God has given you. Just as each of us has one body with many members, and these members do not all have the same function, so in Christ we who are many form one body, and each member belongs to all the others. We have different gifts, according to the grace given us (Rom 12:3–5).

Paul told the Jews that they should not think themselves superior simply because they were natural descendants of Abraham. He also warned the Gentiles not to be arrogant or conceited. This is an example of the cult of normalcy in action. The Jews think they are normative: they are God's chosen people. However, the Gentiles think they are the superior ones, the ones grafted in by choice. Each thinks that their own experience defines what is normal and what is best. That is why Paul enjoins them to refrain from thinking of themselves more highly than they ought. Instead, they need to understand that they are all part of the body of Christ.

Just as the Jews and Gentiles had to learn that they needed each other to be one body, so we need to understand that the church of God is disabled without the presence of, and ministry alongside, people with disabilities. If we do not proactively welcome people with disabilities into our presence,

---

27. Dawn, *Powers*, 57.

we are missing important parts of our body. We need each other. People with disabilities are not mere objects of mercy; they also have the Spirit of God and are given spiritual gifts for the building up of the church: "to each one is given the manifestation of the Spirit for the common good" (1 Cor 12:7). Disability ministries is not about what able-bodied folks can do for the non-able-bodied, but how we can learn from each other, how we can bless each other, how we can receive from each other, and how together we can glorify God.

According to the Centers for Disease Control and Prevention (CDC), 61 million adults in America live with a disability, or about one in every four American adults.[28] That's 25 percent of the population. However, most churches today display a tragic exclusion of people with disabilities, whether by never welcoming them into their buildings or by segregating them into separate programs removed from the rest of the congregation. When disability ministries first started, they were often considered ministries of mercy. People with disabilities were seen as objects of mercy—the poor, helpless people who were in need of our assistance and rescue. In this way, disability ministries ended up unfortunately being de-humanizing, feeding the cult of normalcy that prized able bodies which are readily controlled. Rather than treating people with disabilities as people, as brothers and sisters in Christ, mercy ministries can sometimes reinforce the chasm between the able-bodied who have all the privileges and those who have disabilities and are mere recipients of care. This is why we need Paul's warning: we are not to think of ourselves more highly than we ought. We are all members of the same body of Christ, and we need each other: "Disability is part of the fragile character of human existence in general, wherein we can find genuine good in relationships of mutual vulnerability.... Our weaknesses open us to each other."[29]

People with disabilities can break the mold of normalcy and reveal that to be truly human involves interdependence, not self-sufficiency: "We build systems of support and service to help so-called dependent people develop more independence; but in the process of getting to know them as

---

28. Statistics are from 2018. See https://www.cdc.gov/ncbddd/disabilityandhealth/infographic-disability-impacts-all.html, accessed 7/30/2020.

29. Reynolds, *Vulnerable Communion*, 118.

individuals, we become more profoundly aware of how all of our lives are interdependent."[30]

This is especially true in the church. In both Romans 12 and 1 Corinthians 12, the Apostle Paul talks about the body of Christ being comprised of members who are different from one another. A body cannot function if everyone is conformed to one particular body part. Paul reasons, "If the whole body were an eye, where would the sense of hearing be? If the whole body were an ear, where would the sense of smell be?" In order for a body to function, it requires many different parts. In particular, "those parts of the body that seem to be weaker are indispensable" (1 Cor 12:22). Here again, weakness is inverted, and we are reminded that weakness pertains not just to others but to ourselves as well: "To look at other people's brokenness and limitations without seeing our own is a gesture of power; to acknowledge our own brokenness and limitation in the face of theirs is a gesture of community."[31] By honoring those who are weak and identifying with them, we live out our interdependency in a way that glorifies God.

Weakness and Suffering Redeemed

The interpretative lens of normativity tends to filter out weakness by focusing on its eradication. This is especially true with regard to eschatology. God's people rightly revel in the promise of the new order of things, when "there will be no more death or mourning or crying or pain" (Rev 21:4). This is very good news. However, the normative assumption is that because disability equals pain, it will therefore be eliminated in the eschaton. But not all disability is pain and suffering, and there are some aspects of having a disability that are actually strengths. The danger in assuming the eradication of disability in the new kingdom is the (often unconscious) concomitant denigration of those with disabilities in the present age.

Instead, Amos Yong reminds us that when the resurrected Jesus appeared to his disciples and especially to Thomas, his scars were visible in his hands and side (John 20:20–27). Therefore, Yong posits that "the resurrected body does not necessarily have to be free of the marks of our present

---

30. Gaventa, "Learning from People with Disabilities," 108.
31. Hans S. Reinders, "Human Vulnerability: A Conversation at L'Arche" in *The Paradox of Disability*, 6.

impairments; rather, the resurrection will transform not only our bodies but also the world's scale of values as a whole."[32] There will be no more death or mourning or crying or pain, but perhaps in some mysterious way so-called disabilities will be present without being debilitating. Is it possible that it is not individuals' bodies that are solely to blame for disability, but rather the world's value system? Although we cannot know definitively what it will look like when our body that "is sown in weakness ... is raised in power" (1 Cor 15:43), can it be that the even greater transformation will be not in our bodies but in our hearts? We know that "The Lord does not look at the things people look at. People look at the outward appearance, but the Lord looks at the heart" (1 Sam 16:7). Reynolds concurs: "Jesus transforms what it means to be human, reversing conventional standards of human worth."

In the Book of Revelation, the Apostle John is given a vision of the very throne room of heaven. John begins to weep, because there is a scroll which no one is able to open. Then one of the elders says to John, "Do not weep! See, the Lion of the tribe of Judah, the Root of David, has triumphed. He is able to open the scroll and its seven seals" (Rev 5:5). The story builds up the expectation of the unveiling of the great Lion of Judah, who is Christ with a gloriously resurrected body. But when John looks, Revelation 5:6 says, "Then I saw a Lamb, looking as if it had been slain." Not a mighty and triumphant lion, looking as if it had never been slain, but a lamb, looking as if it had been slain. Somehow the wounds and suffering of Jesus are still perceptible. This lamb is triumphant, because it is "standing in the center of the throne, encircled by the four living creatures and the elders" and has "seven horns and seven eyes, which are the seven spirits of God sent out into all the earth" (Rev 5:6), with the horns representing power and the eyes representing complete vision.[33] There is indeed power and glory, but not to the exclusion of some sign of suffering and brokenness.

The most common title for Jesus in Revelation is the Lamb, used 27 times. New Testament scholar Gregory Beale suggests:

---

32. Yong, *The Bible*, 122.

33. See Robert H. Mounce, *The Book of Revelation*, NICNT, (Grand Rapids: Eerdmans, 1977), 145.

Disability and Dependency

John is attempting to emphasize that it was in an ironic manner that Jesus began to fulfill the OT prophecies of the Messiah's kingdom. Wherever the OT predicts the Messiah's final victory and reign, John's readers are to realize that these goals can begin to be achieved only by the suffering of the cross.[34]

Jesus came to proclaim the good news of a kingdom that overturned the world's values. People were expecting a victorious and powerful lion but instead found that God revealed himself as a lamb whose triumph came through death. Or, as Beale puts it, "Christ as a Lion overcame by being slaughtered as a Lamb."[35] God defies our expectations and inverts our values.

In addition to Revelation 5:6, two other verses mention his slaughter, including the mighty chorus of worship, "Worthy is the Lamb, who was slain, to receive power and wealth and wisdom and strength and honor and glory and praise!" (Rev 5:12), and a reference to "the Lamb who was slain from the creation of the world" (Rev 13:8). Why mention three times that the Lamb was slain? Why not eradicate all traces of the shameful death of Jesus? Why not begin the new creation with a clean slate?

John's apocalyptic and eschatological vision is meant to show us how to live as God's people now. It teaches us that God's power is manifest in weakness that is embraced, inverted, and redeemed. God includes that which has been excluded. He upends the world's values. It is precisely through death that resurrection life comes. It is through suffering that glory comes. It is through weakness that true strength is manifest. Weakness and suffering are not to be swept under the rug. Instead, they are transformed! Death has been swallowed up in victory; it has lost its sting (1 Cor 15:54–55). Suffering has no more power. The God who redeemed the weakness and suffering of the perfectly innocent one and transformed them into glory is the God who is able to redeem all of our weaknesses and suffering—not by hiding it, but actually somehow transforming it, so that all glory redounds to God. The God who himself suffers ushers in a completely new reality: Jesus "shared in their humanity so that by his death he might break the power of him who holds the power of death—that is, the devil—and

---

34. G. K. Beale, *The Book of Revelation*, NIGTC (Grand Rapids: Eerdmans, 1999), 353.
35. Ibid., 352.

free those who all their lives were held in slavery by their fear of death" (Heb 2:14–15). We are freed by God's sacrifice and example of suffering transformed.

This eschatological hope enables us to embrace weakness, not just in "others" with disabilities, but primarily in ourselves. Because we know that the Lamb was slain to grant us access to the living God, we can spend our days in joyful dependence on him, and invite others to a beautiful mutual interdependency with each other and worship of the triune God. We look forward to that day when God alone defines reality, when "we shall be like him, for we shall see him as he is" (1 John 3:2). On that beautiful day, our faith shall at last be sight. As the Lord says in Jeremiah 31:33–34,

> "This is the covenant I will make with the people of Israel after that time," declares the LORD. "I will put my law in their minds and write it on their hearts. I will be their God, and they will be my people. No longer will they teach their neighbor, or say to one another, 'Know the LORD,' because they will all know me, from the least of them to the greatest," declares the LORD. "For I will forgive their wickedness and will remember their sins no more."

Conclusion

God establishes his kingdom with a completely new value system, which includes overthrowing the human cult of normalcy that privileges strength over weakness and defaults to avoiding suffering. God reveals himself as the God who suffers, the God who enters into weakness, and the God who is the perfect, eternal High Priest who willingly and joyfully lays his life down as the sacrificial Lamb to be slaughtered. In so doing, God redefines what it means to be human and what it means for humans to be like God.

Humanity can theoretically be divided between those who have disabilities and those who do not yet have disabilities, but the better way to define what it means to be human is our common dependency on God that leads to interdependency with all our fellow humans, no matter our ability or disability: "Dependency, not autonomy, is one of the ontological characteristics of our lives. That we are creatures, moreover, is but a reminder that we are created for and with one another."[36] We are made by God and called

---

36. Stanley Hauerwas, "Timeful Friends: Living with the Handicapped," in *Critical Re-*

to complete dependence on him and mutual dependence with each other.

These radical truths have broad implications for the church. The church cannot act faithfully as the people of God if we lack the presence and the ministry of people with disabilities. We cannot accurately portray who God is if we fall prey to the assumption that normalcy, rationality, and self-sufficiency define what it means to bear the image of God. "The church is not sustained by intellect or reason but by grace which is manifested in the various gestures of love and revelation which form the fabric of meaningful community."[37] The church is called to be like God through the self-giving sacrifice of love.

Fortunately, we do not have to accomplish any of this by our own strength. The triune God meets us in our weakness and becomes our strength. We are adopted as children of our heavenly Father. We become "heirs of God and co-heirs with Christ, if indeed we share in his sufferings in order that we may also share in his glory.... In the same way, the Spirit helps us in our weakness. We do not know what we ought to pray for, but the Spirit himself intercedes for us through wordless groans" (Rom 8:16-17, 26). To the prayers of the Spirit are added the sacrifice and intercession of the Son: "Christ Jesus who died—more than that, who was raised to life—is at the right hand of God and is also interceding for us" (Rom 8:34). Therefore, nothing can separate us from the love of God which is in Christ Jesus our Lord, to whom be praise in our lives and in his church forevermore.

---

flections on Stanley Hauerwas' Theology of Disability: Disabling Society, Enabling Theology, ed. by John Swinton, (Binghamton, NY: Haworth Pastoral, 2004), 16. Originally published in *Sanctify Them in the Truth: Holiness Exemplified*, (Nashville: Abingdon, 1999).

37. John Swinton, "Hauerwas on Disability," in *Critical Reflections on Stanley Hauerwas' Theology of Disability: Disabling Society, Enabling Theology*, ed. by John Swinton, (Binghamton, NY: Haworth Pastoral, 2004), 7.

12

Accounting for the "Good" in "Toronto the Good"

Bill Reimer

Swedish immigrants to Canada have been described as possessing a "low profile" but having in common a propensity to help less fortunate others.[1] Sven Soderlund entirely fits this profile. Sven Soderlund was born in 1941 in the Estonian capital city of Tallin, during a repressive Soviet occupation that had begun in 1939. His father, Alexander, and mother, Maria, were both Swedish Estonians, born in 1900, whose families went back generations in Estonia. The Soderlund line of the family went back to at least the early eighteenth century. Indeed, the Swedish community in Estonia went back to the thirteenth century when Swedish traders settled there.

Beloved Uncle Herman Soderlund, a Pentecostal pastor in Tartu, perished in pre-trial imprisonment somewhere in the Gulag apparatus of Siberia after being arrested by the Soviets in 1941.[2] In tandem with the German invasion of Russia in 1941, German troops occupied Estonia after

---

1. Elinor Barr, *Swedes in Canada: Invisible Immigrants* (Toronto: University of Toronto Press, 2015) pp. 3-13. Barr mentions that for many years Sven conducted the early Christmas morning Julotta service for Vancouver's Swedes at the Danish Lutheran Church. Barr p. 98.

2. Atko Remmel, "Believers, human rights and freedom of speech in Soviet Estonia" in the Estonian academic journal *Tuna* [Past], no 3/2013, pp. 65-81.

inflicting horrendous casualties upon the Russians. The Germans proved not to be liberators and tens of thousands of Estonians perished. Most of the country's 4,300 Jews fled to Russia or were murdered. Tallin was home to 2,300 of Estonia's Jews and this once vibrant community ceased to exist.

In 1943, Sven and his family were among 3,700 Estonian Swedes who were evacuated by the Swedish government with the permission of the German authorities. The Soderlund family settled near Stockholm, where they stayed until 1951 when Alexander received a call from a group of his former Estonian parishioners who had settled in Toronto. Thus, Sven and his family, minus an older sister who stayed behind to marry, set out by ship from Gothenburg and arrived in Halifax at Pier 21. Canada was an adventure! Their cross-country train arrived at Union Station in Toronto where they were met by their Estonian friends from Tallin.[3]

A young Sven at age ten was able to explore the city around him by streetcar and gained a sense of independence, even if there was the loneliness and insecurities that came with his family's constant moves and the continuous experience of being "the new kid on the block." While there was not a hostility shown to immigrants, one could sometimes sense the "DP" (Displaced Person) label whispered behind one's back. But Toronto at least had the advantage of being a "safe place" for a young person like Sven.

Because the services in his father's church were all in Estonian, a language that Sven did not understand, he travelled on his own to other churches on Sundays. For a period, he did not attend church, but Toronto, the "City of Churches," was a cafeteria of churches, including the Pentecostal flavor that was familiar to him. By 1953 his Sunday exploring took him to the Stone Church on Davenport Road. Later Sven found Danforth Gospel Temple on Pape Avenue, a church that became a formative place for him.

But Sven found that there was a disconnect between his Sunday church-going and his life at school, where he sought to fit in with his friends. In the summer of 1957, at the end of Grade 10, he landed a job at Woodland Beach, Georgian Bay, north of Toronto. He would have freedom from parental controls, the presence of friends, with even a slick dancing

---

3. The biographical details are based on an interview that I conducted with Sven Soderlund on August 19, 2020.

hall on the premises! But on that first long weekend in July, Sven clearly remembers being in his room, and sensing that he was at a "fork in the road." He got down on his knees and made a decision to turn to God and not to follow the "crowd." Life was changed!

Returning to high school at North Toronto Collegiate Institute (NTCI), Sven began living the Christian life. He found a new interest in studies and climbed to the top of the class list. Upon graduation he entered the University of Toronto and earned a B.A. in English Literature. Varsity Christian Fellowship along with Campus in the Woods were key influences in his university life. At Danforth Gospel Chapel Sven was mentored by Dr. Harry Faught, whom he remembers with a deep respect for his pulpit teaching and personal guidance.

Toronto was a haven for the Soderlund family as it had been to so many immigrants, albeit those of European stock. Its extensive grid of churches, along with associated voluntary agencies, served to propagate the Christian faith but also historically served as the safety net for the poor and disadvantaged. Tens of thousands of postwar immigrants carried with them memories of unspeakable pain and suffering but saw Toronto as a hopeful frontier.

Sven has positive memories of safely moving about his new city on his own as a young person. He attended the Canadian National Exhibition without his parents, sometimes with a cousin. As a delivery boy for a local drug store, he rode a bicycle that was never stolen, despite a rather flimsy lock that he can't remember even using. "Homeless" people were not in evidence on the sidewalks of Toronto, even in the more transient Parliament-Wellesley area of town. Drugs were unheard of at NTCI and alcohol was not a prominent part of high school life. Students did not get in "trouble with the law" although there were a couple of "hoods" with black leather jackets and there was a rumour of a knife fight taking place one night but this was the exception to the rule. Sven is unable to recall any friends with divorced parents. This anecdotal evidence is consistent with interviews that I have conducted with other individuals who lived in Toronto in slightly earlier or contemporaneous time periods.

The school population was "pretty white" with a sizeable number of Jewish students and no Asians, although he does remember a Chinese student in elementary school. This is in keeping with the often repressive and exclusionary immigration practiced by Western governments. However, in the postwar period these practices were increasingly liberalized and humanized, and in this one can follow a humanitarian impulse that reaches back to abolitionist movements from the previous two hundred years of British history.

How does one account for the relatively "good" place the Soderlund family found upon arrival in Toronto in 1951? The following essay will reach back into Toronto's early years and then sketch an argument that relies on tracking a moral impulse within Toronto's culture over the course of the last half of the nineteenth century. There are manifold complexities as to how cultures develop and social capital is amassed, but the attraction of Canada and Toronto for hundreds of thousands of migrants, crossing an ocean of water to "arrive," beckons an explanation that reaches back in time.[4]

A Genealogy of Reform in Late Victorian Toronto

On December 14, 1893 thousands of Toronto's citizens braved "the piercing wind and flying snow" to pay their last respects to their former mayor and city philanthropist, William H. Howland. The weather with its sense of desolation seemed all too appropriate to the *Globe* writer who no doubt shared the feelings of the many who had gathered for the sorrowful occasion.

> In many walks of life the dead man had been known as a benefactor, and from every corner of the city came tokens of the esteem in which he had been held, and of the deep and sincere grief which filled every bosom... Workingmen, clad in their best, could be seen in the early morning hurrying in the direction of Simcoe Street; old men and women could be seen tottering along all through the morning; sisters of mercy were going there, too, religious differences sunk in the presence of death; toddlers from the mission schools were on their way thither, to be lifted by kindly hands to look into the casket, and in their innocence gleefully to cry "I see him!"; business men and clerks were tarrying on their way

---

4. For the larger argument that Toronto was a relatively peaceful culture with low rates of interpersonal violence, substantially due to the presence of a British Evangelical Protestant impulse, see William Reimer, *Revisiting "Toronto the Good": Religion, Violence and Culture in a Late-Victorian City* (Winnipeg: Gerhard & Co., 2016).

down town; and poor people and Christian workers were on their way thither—all to the same goal, to bid a last farewell to a good man, a man for whose presence Toronto is much better... At the head of the procession marched 150 of the boys from Mimico Industrial School, an institution that owes its very existence to Mr. Howland's long-sustained efforts, and in whose welfare he took the keenest interest to the last. The boys tramped, four abreast through the deep snow ... and followed by 30 little fellows from the Mission Avenue Ragged School... All along the route to the Necropolis groups of citizens watched the slowly moving line of vehicles and spoke in softened, kindly, respect of the dead.[5]

While poor people were an important part of the funeral entourage, the *Globe* reporter gave equal billing to the prominent citizenry in attendance. First mentioned was a partial listing of "the very large attendance of clergy." Although with the eventual eclipse of religion in Canadian culture their names are not remembered today, and their placement in the article strikes one as even odd, at that time clergy were highly esteemed and even wildly popular.[6] Following the names of clergy in attendance were lists of public officials, men with military rank, business men, and elected officials.

Howland, son of Sir William P. Howland the former Lieutenant Governor and a father of Confederation, had been at most a moderately successful businessman in the insurance field. Although one-time head of the Toronto Board of Trade, the Dominion Board of Trade, and the Manufacturers' Association of Ontario, Howland had made his mark as an evangelical Anglican layman who was a leader in a variety of mainly religious voluntary associations ranging from the YMCA to the Prisoner's Aid Society. His evenings were said to have been spent giving "religious

---

5. "The People's Tribute," in *The Globe*, December 14, 1893, p. 2. One might ask whether the attendees from the Mimico Industrial School would have chosen to be there but still the outpouring of poor people seems to be out of genuine adulation. In this there is resemblance to the throng of poor that attended Lord Shaftesbury's funeral at Westminster Abbey in 1885. See Georgina Batiscombe, *Shaftesbury: The Great Reformer 1801-1885* (Boston: Houghton and Mifflin, 1975), 332-333.

6. See for example G. Mercer Adam, *Toronto, Old and New: A Memorial Volume* (Toronto: The Mail Printing Company, 1891), 66-88. A chapter listing denominations and their pastors comes after a chapter on city officials but before those on the law courts, education, medicine, real estate and business.

and temporal aid" to the poor in St. John's Ward.[7] It was during Howland's two-term mayoralty during the 1880s that the city came to be dubbed with the epithet "Toronto the Good."

Howland's Toronto mirrored the rapidly urbanizing, progressive Victorian city.[8] On the fringe of the archipelago of the Empire the character of its immigration marked the Toronto of 1893 as a British city with 96% of its inhabitants claiming origins in the British Isles. Furthermore, it was a Protestant city with 85% claiming Protestant affiliation and less than 1% listing no religious affiliation in the 1891 census. At a time when all of Britain was said to be tinged with the "dominance of evangelicalism"[9] and that evangelicalism had the power to sway all of the English-speaking world, Toronto, at least by the count of census takers, was arguably the capital city of this evangelical world. Not only did evangelicalism "sway" Late Victorian Toronto, its religious discourse shaped the social and political institutions of Toronto, as is evident in the life of Mayor Howland.

If industrialization was the engine of the Victorian city, then philanthropic voluntarism would be its heartbeat, serving to humanize life on a capitalist frontier. Frank Prochaska argues that Anglo-Saxon Protestantism provides a powerful expression of "public spirit" that filled the "moral space" between rulers and ruled. As Victorian cities expanded, charities and other communal forms acted as "schools of citizenship" for both political insiders and outsiders.[10] The myriad of Victorian social agencies is difficult to fathom or reconstruct not least because of the tendency for contemporary historians to conflate nineteenth-century Victorian charities with twentieth-century government social services.[11] In the Victorian city associational philanthropy "saturated people's lives."[12] The extent of it

---

7. Ronald Sawatsky, "William Holmes Howland," in *Dictionary of Canadian Biography*.

8. For a recent study of the Victorian city see Tristram Hunt, *Building Jerusalem: The Rise and Fall of the Victorian City* (New York: Metropolitan Books, 2005).

9. See David W. Bebbington, *The Dominance of Evangelicalism: The Age of Spurgeon and Moody* (Downers Grove, IL: Intervarsity Press) especially pp. 250-252. See also by the same author *Evangelicalism in Modern Britain: A History from the 1730s to the 1980s* (London: Routledge, 1989).

10. Frank Prochaska, *Christianity and Social Services in Modern Britain* (Oxford: Oxford University Press, 2006), 5.

11. Ibid., 17-23.

12. Ibid., 23.

is staggering: in the 1890s the charitable receipts for London alone were greater than the total budgets of several European countries.[13] Toronto was no "mean city" when it came to voluntary, charitable associations. By 1890, Toronto church and associational budgets exceeded $1 million, at a time when the budget for the Province of Ontario was less than, $4 million.[14] Writing in 1891, G. Mercer Adam listed a sampling of such associations, including the Home for Incurables, the House of Industry, the Infants Home and Infirmary, the Prisoners' Aid, the Haven for Discharged Female Prisoners, and the Newsboys' Lodging and Industrial Home.[15] Howland at one time or other served as a board member for many of the key Toronto charitable associations. While corporate boardrooms and government chambers were strictly male preserves, a high percentage of charitable association volunteers were female. These associations combined with church and Sunday Schools provided a wide public sphere of influence for entrepreneurial and activist men and women.

Slavery in Upper Canada and in Memory

Howland stood in a line of Toronto Protestant moral reformers that extends back to the early beginnings of the European settlement then known as York. John Graves Simcoe, Lieutenant Governor of Upper Canada from 1791-94, left his mark on Toronto's moral landscape when he abolished the slave trade in British North America well before its abolition in the Empire in 1807. While there is no direct link between Howland and Simcoe, other than the evangelical texture of their Anglican beliefs, Simcoe in some immeasurable sense reduced a "dynamic" of extreme violence that accompanies the practice of slavery and in this bequeathed a measure of humanity that later reformers were heir to.

Simcoe's abolitionist beliefs are understudied and obscure but seem to stem from a religious conversion that he underwent while convalescing in England following imprisonment during the American Revolutionary

---

13. Frank Prochaska, *The Voluntary Impulse: Philanthropy in Modern Britain* (London: Faber and Faber, 1988), 60.

14. For 1891, total expenditures by the Province of Ontario were $3.9 million. See Ontario Legislative Assembly, *Ontario Sessional Papers* xxiii—part v (Toronto: Queen's Printer, 1891), 301.

15. G. Mercer Adam, *Toronto, Old and New*, 114.

War. Elected to the House of Commons in 1790 he had a very brief parliamentary career that went almost unrecorded. However, he seems to have come within the circle of the evangelical abolitionist William Wilberforce as there is an apparent record of Simcoe speaking out in favour of a motion to abolish slavery.[16] Certainly Simcoe, if present, would have cast his vote against the trade in April 1791 when, in the words of Wilberforce, "the character, talents, and humanity of the House were left in a minority of 88 to 163."[17]

Appointed Lieutenant Governor of the new Canadian province of Upper Canada, Simcoe arrived in late 1791 reaching what is now Niagara-on-the-Lake in the summer of 1792. No doubt he had received reports of the April 1792 debates on slavery with their graphic details of the routine torture and execution of African slaves. Once again the abolitionist MPs were routed by an even wider margin of 87 to 234.[18] In addition, Secretary of State Henry Dundas, the cabinet official that Simcoe reported to, played a key role in the defeat to such a degree that in 1796 the West Indian traders and planters thanked him "for the effectual opposition he thereby gave to the Bill for the Abolition of the Slave Trade."[19]

While still in Montreal in May of 1792, Simcoe made clear his intentions regarding slavery and Upper Canada. In a letter to a Quaker in Pennsylvania concerning immigration possibilities to Upper Canada, he writes:

> The principles of the British Constitution do not admit of that slavery which Christianity condemns. From the moment that I assume the Government of Upper Canada, under no modification will I ever assent to a law that discriminates by dishonest policy between the natives of Africa, America, or Europe.[20]

---

16. See S. R. Mealing, "John Graves Simcoe" in *Canadian Dictionary of Biography*.
See also Mary Beacock Fryer and Christopher Dracott, *John Graves Simcoe, 1752-1806: A Biography* (Toronto: Dundurn Press, 1998), p. 112.

17. Roger Anstey, *The Atlantic Slave Trade and British Abolition* (Atlantic Highlands, New Jersey, 1975), p. 273.

18. See the report of the April 3, 1792 debate in *The Times*, Tues. April 3, 1792, Issue 2271, p. 1. The role of Dundas in the defeat of the bill is briefly described.

19. Ibid., p. 314.

20. E. A. Cruikshank, ed. *The Correspondence of Lieut. Governor John Graves Simcoe*, Vol. 1 (Toronto: Ontario Historical Society, 1923), p. 153.

Upper Canada was the only province to ever legislate against slavery. In March of 1793 Simcoe went on the offensive with his slave bill that eventually received passage in June. It was a compromise in that it banned the importation of slaves but allowed continued bondage until death for existing slaves.[21] Given that many in the Lower House owned slaves and that six of the sixteen members of the Upper Canada legislature were slaveholders, as were three of the seven Legislative Council, the passage of the abolition bill must have involved considerable finesse and "strong-arming" on the part of Simcoe and the Attorney General.

Certainly, Simcoe cut deeply against the grain in proposing abolition in 1793. In Britain abolition experienced vigorous opposition with the coming of the French Revolution and the Haitian Revolution beginning in 1791. Writing to Dundas in September Simcoe states without apology:

> The greatest resistance was to the Slave Bill, many plausible Arguments of the dearness of Labour and of the difficulty of obtaining Servants to cultivate Lands were brought forward. Some possessed of Negroes knowing that it was very questionable whether any subsisting Law did Authorize Slavery, and having purchased several taken in War by the Indians at very small prices wished to reject the Bill entirely, others were desirous to supply themselves by an importation for two years. The matter was finally settled by undertaking to secure the property already obtained upon condition that an immediate stop should be put to the importation and that slavery should gradually be abolished.[22]

Simcoe left Canada for good in 1796. Later that year he went on to San Domingue, where he governed and led British forces against a slave army. The war was a fiasco for the British, who withdrew in ignominy. The history of the experience of Simcoe and Britain in Haiti disappeared into silence.[23]

---

21. Allen P. Stouffer, *The Light of Nature and the Law of God: Antislavery in Ontario 1833-1877* (Montreal and Kingston: McGill Queen's University Press, 1992), pp.12-17.

22. E. A. Cruikshank, ed., *The Correspondence of Lieut. Governor John Graves Simcoe*, Vol. 2, p. 53.

23. For references to Simcoe in Haiti see Roger Norman Buckley ed., *The Haitian Journal of Lieutenant Howard, York Hussars, 1796-1798* (Knoxville: University of Tennessee Press, 1985), pp. 75-77, 82, 95, 96, 150. On the silence of Simcoe's military experience in Haiti

Accounting for the "Good" in "Toronto the Good"

In 1798 Upper Canada administrator and slaveholder, Peter Russell, introduced a new bill into the Lower House of Upper Canada allowing for slaves to once again be brought into the province because of the scarcity of labour. After considerable debate the bill was approved by a margin of 8-4 but in the end was simply "shelved." Slavery gradually petered out with slaves escaping by the hundreds via an "underground railway" of sorts to free territories in the U.S.[24]

On March 25, 2007 Jason Kenney, representing the Canadian Government, announced the commemoration of the 200th anniversary of the 1807 bill to abolish the slave trade in the British Empire. In the communiqué Upper Canada is labelled a "pioneer" in the abolition movement with John Graves Simcoe playing a "key role" in the passage of the 1793 slavery legislation.[25] What is not mentioned is Simcoe's role in leading the fight against the ancestors of the current Governor General, nor the presence, for a time, of an "underground railway" from Canada to parts of the U.S.

Despite the abolition of the trade, slavery continued for a time in York (Toronto), the capital that Simcoe had established on Lake Ontario. At the end of the eighteenth century an advertisement described in the following way appeared in a York newspaper:

> Nor, despite early legislation against slavery, was the holding and transfer of human chattels wholly unknown at this period. While we hear of slaves being manumitted, we also hear of their being sold or offered

---

see for example Simcoe's biographer Duncan Campbell Scott, who states at the end of his section on the American Revolution that Simcoe was "never again to employ his undoubted genius on the field in fighting the battles of his beloved king and country." In *John Graves Simcoe*, The Makers of Modern Canada (Toronto: Morang and Co., 1910), 37.

24. Slavery, for example, was forbidden in the Territory of Michigan beginning in 1787. Slaves were able to escape to freedom across the Detroit River. For large extracts of original source material on the abolition of slavery in Ontario see William Renwick Riddell, "The Slave in Upper Canada" in *Journal of the American Institute of Criminal Law and Criminology*, Vol. 14, No. 2, Aug., 1923, pp. 249-278. For the "silence" surrounding the Haitian Revolution see Michel-Rolph Trouillot, *Silencing the Past: Power and the Production of History* (Boston: Beacon Press, 1995). Trouillet would no doubt differ with aspects of this paper.

25. "Canada's New Government Commemorates 200th Anniversary of the 1807 Act for the Abolition of the Slave Trade", Ottawa, March 25, 2007. https://www.canada.ca/en/news/archive/2007/03/canada-new-government-commemorates-200th-anniversary-1807-act-abolition-slave-trade.html

for sale. In the *Gazette* of the time, Mr. Peter Russell, then administrator of the affairs of the Province [Upper Canada], advertises for sale "a black woman named Peggy, aged forty years, and a black boy, her son, named Jupiter, aged about fifteen years, both of them the property of the subscriber! The woman," so sets forth the advertisement, "is a tolerable cook and washerwoman, and perfectly understands making soap and candles." The price set upon Peggy is $150, and upon Jupiter Junior $200, "payable in three years, with interest from the day of sale, and to be secured by bond." His Excellency is good enough to say, however, that "one-fourth less will be taken for ready money!"[26]

Following Simcoe's brief tenure in Upper Canada, at a time when abolitionist groups were in full swing in Britain and the U.S., it appears that Canada's would-be abolitionists were content to sit on the sidelines. While there were certainly individual abolitionists such as the writer and evangelical, Susanna Moodie,[27] and efforts to ameliorate the conditions of African American refugees,[28] it was the arrival of key abolitionists from the British Isles in the 1840s that stoked the fires of abolitionism.

Brian Harrison argues that there are vertical linkages between Late Victorian voluntary and philanthropic reform groups and earlier antislavery movements. In Britain, once humane principles were articulated in abolition, this "reforming dynamic" moved on to encompass a variety of causes from climbing boys, to prostitutes, vivisection, temperance, to persecuted Bulgarians, and even murderers. Libertarian principles advanced through the causes of Catholic and Jewish emancipation to the enfranchisement of women. The dynamic of reform itself rapidly uncovered additional areas of perceived evil in a continuous process.[29]

---

26. As quoted in G. Mercer Adam, *Toronto, Old and New: Historical, Descriptive and Pictorial* (Toronto: The Mail Printing Co., 1891), 22. "His Excellency" meaning Peter Russell who administered Upper Canada from 1797 to 1799 following Simcoe's leave.

27. Carl P. A. Ballstadt, "Susanna (Moodie) Strickland", *Dictionary of Canadian Biography*. Research among the members of the Upper Canada Bible Society could yet yield abolitionist material. For the philanthropic activity of, for example, Jesse Ketchum, see Lillian F. Gates, "Jesse Ketchum", *Dictionary of Canadian Biography*.

28. Robin W. Winks, *The Blacks in Canada: A History* (Montreal and Kingston: McGill-Queen's University Press), 114-141.

29. Brian Harrison, "A Genealogy of Reform," in *Anti-Slavery, Religion and Reform: Essays in Memory of Roger Anstey*, ed. Christine Bolt and Seymour Drescher (Folkestone,

Foremost and most formative was the abolitionist movement of the late eighteenth and early nineteenth century. Out of this movement a continuity of personnel and technique bound causes together. Family connections were a distinctive characteristic of a wide variety of nineteenth-century reform movements. These family connections linked contemporaneous movements horizontally and maintained vertical connections over time.[30]

In John Graves Simcoe linkages with a growing evangelical abolition movement in Britain are seen. These abolitionist beliefs were imposed on Upper Canada in military style and left their mark on Toronto's moral landscape. It is difficult to predict how long slavery would have lingered in Upper Canada without this imposition, although certainly it would have ended in 1833.[31] The early disappearance of slavery gave Canada increasingly an appearance of a safe haven for escaped slaves and other African Americans.

Abolitionism in Ante-Bellum Toronto

The arrival of key abolitionist leaders from the British Isles circa 1840 galvanized an Anglo-Canadian abolitionist movement centred in Toronto. The majority of these leaders hailed from Scotland and had belonged to abolitionist movements dedicated to eradicating American slavery. Foremost in the group were Michael Willis, a Free Presbyterian minister who took up residence as principal of Knox College, and Peter Brown, editor of the *Banner*, a Presbyterian newspaper, and his son, George, who founded the national newspaper *The Globe* in 1844. Other key leaders included Isabella Henning, George Brown's sister, and Thomas Henning her husband, Irish Methodist minister William McClure, Free Presbyterian minister Robert Burns, and the Scottish Presbyterian Charles Stuart, a retired magistrate and soldier who had been an abolitionist for a number of years in the U.S.[32]

With the passing of a harsh, new federal Fugitive Slave Law in 1850, the flow of both runaway slaves and free African Americans crossing the border into Canada increased exponentially. *The Globe* claimed that within

---

Kent: Wm Dawson and Sons, 1980).

30. Ibid., 124-133.
31. Robin Winks (*The Blacks in Canada*, p. 48) makes mention of illegal sales of slaves in Canada as late as 1832.
32. Allen P. Stouffer, *The Light of Nature and the Law of God*, 128-141.

a month of the passing of the law, 3,000 refugees fled across the border into Canada.[33] Recognizing the crisis, Toronto's abolitionists gathered on February 26, 1851 at City Hall to form the Anti-Slavery Society of Canada (ASC). *The Globe* announced that the intention of the meeting was to:

> express the feeling of this community on the subject of American slavery... It is right that the Canadian people should give their testimony on this question, and their neighbours that they feel ashamed and indignant that their common civilization, common country, and (alas!) common Christianity should be outraged by the foulest system of iniquity to be found on the face of the earth.[34]

The meeting was reported to be the "largest and most enthusiastic Meeting we have ever seen in Toronto."[35] The officers of the new association were as follows:

President
Michael Willis
Secretary
Secretary, Rev. William McClure
Corresponding Secretaries
Thomas Henning, Capt. Charles Stuart
Treasurer
Andrew Hamilton
Committee
Samuel Alcorn   T. J. Short
W. R. Abbott   Oliver Mowat
Peter Brown   Rev. John Roaf
Rev. Dr. Burns   John McMurrich
Dr. Connor   A. T. McCord
George Brown   Angus Morrison
John Doel Jr.   John McNab
Rev. H. Essen   G. P. Ridout
James Foster   J. Laidlaw

---

33. Ibid., 110.
34. *Globe*, Tues. Feb. 25, 1851.
35. *Globe*, Thur. Feb. 27, 1851.

Accounting for the "Good" in "Toronto the Good"

Patrick Freeland Mr. Peal
Rev. A. Geikie Rev. J. Pyper
James Lesslie T. J. Tyner
John Shaw J. Woodhouse
Rev. A. Lillie Rev. James Richardson
Dr. Russell

Of the 34 men elected to office for the year 1851, 28 have separate entries in the *Dictionary of Canadian Biography*. Using these entries and supplementing them with lists of the annual report listings of officers of voluntary organizations, I have been able to match many of these men and/or their descendants with voluntary activities during the last two decades of the century (see Appendix).

Among the stated purposes of ASC was this statement:

> That slavery is the wanton and forcible bringing into bondage, and retaining indefinitely in that state, of rational beings, is an outrage on the laws of humanity, and of the Bible; and that the continued existence of the practice on the continent is a just cause of grief, and demands our best exertions, by all lawful and practical means, for its extinction.[36]

Further resolutions passed were that the Fugitive Slave Laws were "at open variance with the best interests of man, as endowed by our great Creator," and that the Society should work to "aid in the extinction of slavery all over the world" by means of "tracts, newspapers, lectures and correspondence."[37]

At an ASC meeting the next year, the St. Lawrence Hall, with a capacity of 1,000, was said to be "densely crowded." The report of the meeting in *The Globe* occupied fully seven columns of fine print at a time when the newspaper page count was only four. The annual report stated that the Lady's Association had assisted more than 100 Black refugee families.[38]

The Ladies' Association for the Relief of Destitute Coloured Refugees

---

36. *Constitution and Bye-Laws of the Anti-Slavery Society of Canada* (Toronto: "Globe" Office, 1951), 1-7.
37. Ibid., 4-5.
38. *Globe*, March 27, 1852.

(Toronto), a parallel society to the ASC, functioned as much more than an "auxiliary," raising its funds and navigating on its own. Indeed, it appears that the Ladies' Association was involved in considerably more activities than the ASC, aiding 450-500 fugitive slaves, for example, in 1857.[39] Thomas Henning in his report (his wife Isabella along with Mrs. Willis led the Association) stated that "the operation of the Society, since the last public meeting had been carried on chiefly through the agency of the Ladies' Association."[40] Here is evidence of voluntarist activities of women in the Victorian era that can often only be accessed through newspapers and annual reports.[41]

The ASC was largely ineffectual in the total scheme of abolition. It did support several chapters with active Black leaders in towns closer to the border where refugees tended to settle. Slave-born Samuel Ringgold Ward worked on behalf of the ASC for several years as a lecturer and fundraiser.[42] Often relations with Blacks were tinged with paternalism. Black newspaper editor, Mary Ann Shadd Cary bitingly asked:

> We have had many inquiries made of us recently, as to the movements of the Toronto Anti-Slavery Society, not one of which we could answer… We think, however, that there is a prospect of its being found about the "middle of June," anxious inquirers will then be able to see and hear to their satisfaction.[43]

---

39. *Globe*, Sat., May 2, 1857. See also Allen P. Stouffer, *The Light of Nature*, pp. 119-122, 125-127, 129, 133, 139, 141, 218.

40. *Globe*, Sat., May 2, 1857.

41. See also Karen Leroux, 1996. "Making a claim on the public sphere: Toronto women's anti-slavery activism, 1851-1854." Master's Thesis, University of British Columbia. The Ladies Association collected the signatures of 14,000 Toronto women for an abolition petition in 1853, an enormous accomplishment since the 1851 census listed just 30,000 men and women as city residents. No doubt the effort ventured outside the city limits but the petition was signed by a majority of women. The petition called for the emancipation of all American slaves. Leroux, pp. 50-54.

42. At an ASC meeting in 1852 it was reported that Ward had given 108 lectures during the year. *Globe*, Sat., Dec. 18, 1852, p. 2. See also Samuel Ringgold Ward, *Autobiography of a Fugitive Negro* (New York: Arno Press and the New York Times, 1968).

43. Here of course Cary is making reference to the annual meeting. C. Peter Ripley ed. *The Black Abolitionist Papers Vol. II Canada, 1830-1865* (Chapel Hill: University of North Carolina Press, 1986), 290. However, for an ad listing daily hours for the ASC office at 53 King St. see *Globe*, Sat., Jan. 27, 1855. Evidently the office was later closed down.

All told, perhaps 40,000 Black Refugees[44] came to Canada through the end of the Civil War with a reported 6,000 living in Toronto alone at a time when the city's population totalled only 45,000. These statistics may indicate some hyperbole in Cary's editorial comments. Winks writing on post-Civil War Toronto concludes that "the virus of anti-black prejudice spread less deeply there," that schools were integrated (unlike other parts of the province), and that sometimes African Canadian businessmen could experience "modest successes."[45]

Whatever the degree of its modest accomplishments, the ASC was the only significant abolitionist society in Toronto.[46] Its most important contribution is no doubt seen in the extent of the writings of key members. Here prime consideration should be given to the newspapers founded by Peter Brown (*The Banner*, 1843-48) and George Brown (*The Globe*, 1844-). Paul Rutherford argues that *The Globe* was Canada's first newspaper to "merit the term *popular*."[47] Brown's presses boasted the latest technology and made use of the telegraph wires for news stories and in the process became a regional newspaper.

The Browns were unwavering in writing a continual stream of blistering editorials and articles condemning slavery and arguing for the unity of the human race. At the end of one meeting of the ASC George Brown concluded a speech with a flourish:

> The question is often put, What have we in Canada to do with American slavery? We have everything to do with it. It is a question of humanity, and no man has a right to refuse his aid, whatever it may be, in ameliorating the woes of his fellow-men. It is a question of Christianity; and no Christian can have a pure conscience who hesitates to lift his voice

---

44. James W. St. G. Walker, "African Canadians," in Gerald Hallowell, ed., *Oxford Companion to Canadian History* (Toronto: Oxford University Press, 2004), 24-25.

45. Robin W. Winks, "Wilson Ruffin Abbott," *DCB*.

46. It should be pointed out that there were a number of Black Fugitive newspapers in Canada as well as networks of refugees that were involved in settlement work. See C. Peter Ripley ed. *The Black Abolitionist Papers Vol. II Canada, 1830-1865*.

47. Paul Rutherford, *A Victorian Authority: The Daily Press in Late Nineteenth-Century Canada* (Toronto: University of Toronto Press, 1982), 40.

against a system which, under the sanction of a Christian altar, sets at defiance every principle of Christianity.[48]

Calling for a ban on the use of American Sunday School Union materials because of its refusal to condemn slaveholding, Thomas Henning echoes similar language:

> No respect for ecclesiastical prestige should interfere with our denunciation of those "Who preach and kidnap men! Give thanks and rob God's own afflicted poor! Talk of Christ's glorious liberty, and then Bolt hard the captive's door!"[49]

At a time when new racial theories were in the vanguard, the evangelical abolitionist emphasis on the unity of humanity (monogenesis) did temper a hardening of racial categories and arguably contributed toward continuing humanitarian reform efforts in Toronto in the coming decades. The built-in resistance towards the new racial theorizing can be seen in the scientific work of University of Toronto President and an evangelical reformer, Daniel Wilson, who conducted research on the skulls of Native Canadians. Chastising "new" approaches of scientists who argued for a discontinuity between races, he argued that "the crania everywhere, and at all periods, have conformed or even approximated to one type."[50]

The significance of the Anti-Slavery Society for this study lies in the fact that through the ASC we have a window into the operation of an evangelical voluntary society in the early decades of Toronto's history. In the years circa 1840 a significant number of Scottish evangelical abolitionists

---

48. Alexander Mackenzie, *The Life and Speeches of George Brown*, 260.

49. Thomas Henning, *Slavery In the Churches, Religious Societies, Etc.* (Toronto: Globe Book and Job Office, 1856), 28.

50. Daniel Wilson, "On the Supposed Prevalence of One Cranial Type Throughout the American Aborigines," in *Edinburgh Philosophical Society Journal*, New Series, Jan., 1858, p. 31. CIHM 63246. For an analysis of Wilson's views on the subject see Bruce G. Trigger, "Prehistoric Man and Daniel Wilson's Later Canadian Ethnology" in Marinell Ash and Elizabeth Hulse, eds, *Thinking with Both Hands: Sir Daniel Wilson in the Old World and the New* (Toronto: University of Toronto Press, 1999). For the nineteenth-century evangelical resistance to polygenesis in the context of slavery see Colin Kidd, *The Forging of the Races: Race and Scripture in the Protestant Atlantic World, 1600-2000* (Cambridge: Cambridge University Press, 2006), 121-167.

had arrived in Toronto. This group represented a considerable number of years' experience in the "front lines" of the recently ended battle against slavery in Britain.[51] In many ways George Brown, through *The Globe*, became the most powerful voice that emerged out of this period. Through the end of the century *The Globe* espoused a Liberal political agenda and was a key print medium for promoting broad, non-sectarian evangelical social reform movements.

Vertical and horizontal linkages can be followed over the subsequent decades within evangelical Protestant reform movements in Toronto by using abolitionism as a "marker." The nexus of Protestant social reformers of the 1880s and 1890s appears to have many direct and indirect connections with abolitionism. As mentioned, George Brown, a father of Confederation and an evangelical Presbyterian, was probably Canada's foremost abolitionist among white elites. Daniel Wilson, President of the University of Toronto, was a fellow abolitionist with Brown in Toronto (although not serving on the ASC committee) and even prior in an abolitionist society in Edinburgh, where they were classmates. Likewise, Oliver Mowat, longtime Ontario premier and President of the Ontario Evangelical Alliance, was a young abolitionist in the Brown circle in Toronto. Toronto lawyer Samuel Blake and his brother Edward, leader of the federal Liberal Party, were both sons-in-law of the evangelical, abolitionist Bishop of Huron, Benjamin Cronyn. Samuel Blake served with Howland on the boards of multiple voluntary organizations and charities. Another key evangelical abolitionist in the 1850s, with Brown, was the Liberal politician and evangelical Presbyterian John McMurrich, father of William M. McMurrich, erstwhile mayor of Toronto and philanthropic associate of William Howland, Toronto's reforming mayor of the 1880s.[52]

Arguably the influence of this same group of individuals, or their as-

---

51. The members of this group were primarily from Glasgow in Scotland, which was a hotbed of abolitionism and other reform activities. See Duncan Rice, *The Scots Abolitionists, 1833-1861* (Baton Rouge: LSU Press, 1981). The Free Church had broken away from the Church of Scotland in 1843 over the issue of state control of clerical appointments. This Great Disruption no doubt sharpened further the radical edges of Free Church participants in abolition.

52. For these overlapping associations see Allen P. Stouffer, *The Light of Nature*, esp. pp. 110-114. This is a broad sketch of key linkages. For more detailed linkages see the Appendix.

sociates, can be followed within the Liberal Party at the federal, provincial, and municipal levels of government. Prior to Confederation Robert Baldwin and George Brown, both evangelical Protestants, led the Reformers to power in the 1850s. Edward Blake served as Prime Minister of Ontario before handing the reins to longtime Ontario premier Oliver Mowat, member of the ASC. Alexander McKenzie, a Baptist, held office as Prime Minister of Canada from 1873 to 1878 and after being defeated handed over leadership of the party to Edward Blake.[53] Toronto was decidedly Tory at the municipal level but nevertheless elected evangelical Liberal mayors numerous times during the last two decades of the nineteenth century.

"Peace, order, and good government" was a popular slogan in the political debates surrounding Confederation and after. The discourse on peace and order continued to infuse Canadian civic life. In the month after Howland's death *The Globe* published Chief Constable Grassett's annual report on crime in Toronto, a subject that was of special interest to a voraciously newspaper-reading public. In it he wrote that it was a "matter for sincere congratulations that murder, the darkest crime of all, has almost disappeared from the records."[54] No doubt if Howland had been alive to read the report, he would have nodded in approval. The social world of the Toronto of 1893 was vastly different from that of 1800 in ways that go far beyond simply the physical size of the city. By 1893 slavery was a long-forgotten institution, duelling had disappeared, the voting franchise had been extended to all males and increasingly to women, health and sanitation regimes were much in evidence, capital punishment had been increasingly restricted, and I argue, there were decreasing levels of interpersonal violence.[55] These changes were certainly tied to the broad processes that brought about the heightened industrialization, urbanization, and capitalization but also were tied to a religious discourse that had helped shape the Toronto of 1893.[56]

---

53. McKenzie was Brown's first biographer and compiler of select speeches and correspondence. See Alexander Mackenzie, *The Life and Speeches of Hon. George Brown* (Toronto: Globe Printing Co., 1882).
54. *The Globe*, January 29, 1894, p. 3. The lone "murder" for the year was due to the death of a woman who died after undergoing an abortion.
55. See William D. Reimer, *Revisiting "Toronto the Good"*.
56. Here I have no "measuring device" that can distinguish between changes brought

Accounting for the "Good" in "Toronto the Good"

The streetcars that ran on Toronto's streets were powered by electricity but they did not yet run on Sunday. The prominent edifices that lined downtown streets were still largely churches. I argue that the same religious discourse that shaped streetcar schedules and much of the outstanding city architecture also had a powerful effect on human behaviour and placed increasing constraints on male interpersonal violence in Late Victorian Toronto. These constraints extended on into the Toronto that Sven Soderlund came to know in the 1950s. The complexities of the issues involved must be acknowledged but the phenomenon of a relatively peaceful and religious Toronto remains.

---

about by the Enlightenment, industrialization, or religion. I would argue that key changes came about in Toronto, that include reduced rates of interpersonal violence, and that these changes came about as a result of a religio-Enlightenment complex. I make use of the theory of Norbert Elias in some key respects. For arguments that connect economic and religious change see Lenore Davidoff and Catherine Hall, *Family Fortunes: Men and Women of the English Middle Class, 1780-1850* (Chicago: University of Chicago Press, 1987). See also Boyd Hilton, *The Age of Atonement: The Influence of Evangelicalism on Social and Economic Thought, 1795-1865* (Oxford: Clarendon Press, 1988). For a sweeping account of a massive religious movement during the period see David Hempton, *Methodism: Empire of the Spirit* (New Haven: Yale University Press, 2005).

I have not tried to affix a rigid definition to "evangelical." In the context of Victorian Toronto, I would regard "evangelical" primarily as an outlook or spirit that is Protestant and assumes the central place of the Bible in life and practice, and emphasizes prayer and devotional practices in communal contexts. It was conversionist in varying degrees, optimistic, humanitarian, and it tinged all sectors of the Protestant church in nineteenth-century Toronto. Ontario evangelical leaders were almost all Liberal in political persuasion, anti-Clergy Reserves, opposed to sectarian education at both the elementary school level and often the university level, were increasingly opposed to capital punishment and were often proponents of temperance. Of course, when imbibed by a culture, deeply moralistic tendencies could be produced. For an example of a scholar who attempts to "nail down" the term "evangelical" see David Bebbington, *Evangelicals in Modern Britain: A History from the 1930s to the 1980s* (London: Routledge, 1989), 26-74.

Appendix: Biographical Sketches of the Executive and the Committee of the Anti-Slavery Association of Canada, 1851

Willis, Rev. Dr. Michael. President. b. 1798 in Renfrew, Scotland, d. 1879. Free Church, President of Knox College, Toronto. Vice-chairman of the Glasgow Emancipation Society, first and only president of ASC, Buxton Mission, Elgin Association. DCB

McClure, Rev. William. b. 1803 in Antrim, Ireland, d. 1871. Methodist minister. Involved in temperance work, Anti-Clergy Reserves Association, YMCA and the Young People's Mutual Improvement Association. DCB

Henning, Thomas. Corresponding Secretary. b. ? Graduate of the University of Toronto, educator at the Toronto Academy, secretary-treasurer of The Globe, married to Isabella, sister of George Brown.

Stuart, Capt. Charles. Corresponding Secretary. b. 1783 in Jamaica of Scottish parents. Soldier and magistrate. Presbyterian. Life-long friendship with Theodore Dwight Weld, American abolitionist, was an agent for the Anti-Slavery Society of the United Kingdom, worked with abolitionists James Scoble and Lewis Tappan and was involved in temperance and church work. Left Toronto in 1852. DCB

Hamilton, Andrew. Treasurer. Not identified.

Abbott, Wilson Ruffin. b. 1801 in Richmond, VA, d. 1876. Coloured Wesleyan Methodist. First Black Toronto Alderman, member of the central committee of the Reformers in Canada West and the Elgin Association. Helped purchase freedom for some slaves. Mrs. Abbott organizer of Queen Victoria Benevolent Society to aid indigent Black women. Son, Anderson Ruffin the first Canadian-born Black to receive a license to practice medicine, was a classmate with Samuel Ringgold Ward at Oberlin College. DCB

Alcorn, Samuel. Not identified.

Brown, George. b. Alloa, Scotland, d. 1880. Free Presbyterian. Owner and publisher of The Globe. Edinburgh Society for the Abolition of Negro Slavery with his father Peter and Daniel Wilson. Leader of the Reform party during the Great Coalition and a father of Confederation. Leader in the Reform party with W. P. Howland, whom he appointed Postmaster General and with Oliver Mowat, whom he persuaded to lead the provincial Liberal party. Close political ally of Alexander Mackenzie, the later leader of the Liberal party and Prime Minister of Canada. Close political ally of federal Liberal party Edward Blake, brother of Samuel Blake (both sons-in-law of abolitionist Bishop Cronyn), who in turn was a close colleague of W. H. Howland. Edinburgh Society for the Abolition of Negro Slavery. DCB

Brown, Peter. b. Edinburgh, Scotland, d. 1863. Free Presbyterian. Merchant and publisher. Edinburgh Society for the Abolition of Negro Slavery. DCB

Burns, Rev. Dr. b. 1789 West Lothian, Scotland, d. 1869. Free Presbyterian. Minister and educator at Knox College. French Canadian Missionary Society, Sabbath schools, tract and Bible societies, charity schools, infirmaries, temperance, Anti-Clergy Reserves Association, Highland famine relief, and the Elgin Association. DCB

Connor, George Skeffington. b. 1810 in Dublin, d. 1863. Anglican. Lawyer, politician, and judge. Immigrated to Canada with his brother-in-law W. H. Blake (father of Edward and Samuel), and with Bishop Cronyn (later father-in-law of Edward and Samuel Blake). Established a legal firm with W. H. Blake, whom he later replaced as Professor of Law at King's College. Chancellor of University of Toronto. QC. Appointed Solicitor General by George Brown.

Doel, John Jr. b. 1790 Wiltshire, England, d. 1871. Methodist Episcopal. Brewer, businessman, and politician. Radical Reformer and colleague of William Lyon Mackenzie. Arrested three times, rebels had met at his brewery. Trustee of the Toronto General Hospital. Is he "Jr." or is this a son? CDB

Esson, Henry. b. 1793 Banacraig, Scotland, d. Toronto. Free Presbyterian minister, educator, and author.

Foster, James. Not identified.

Freeland, Patrick. Not identified.

Geikie, Rev. Adam Archibald. Free Presbyterian minister. Could not locate an entry, only one mention. Son W. B. a professor at the University of Toronto Medical school. DCB

Laidlaw, J. Not identified.

Lesslie, James. b. 1802 Dundee, Scotland, d. 1885. Baptist. Merchant, publisher, and politician. Reformer, associate of William Lyon Mackenzie but rejected the use of force. Anti-Clergy Reserves, school trustee, Mechanic's Institute, alderman, House of Industry, Canadian Alliance (Reform movement), Bank of the People. DCB

Lillie, Rev. Adam. b. 1803 in Glasgow, Scotland, d. 1869. Congregational minister and educator. Anti-Clergy Reserves Association. DCB

McCord, Andrew Taylor. b. 1805 in Belfast, d. 1881. Baptist. Public servant and philanthropist. City treasurer and Reformer. Upper Canada Religious Tract and Book Society, Upper Canada Bible Society, Toronto City Mission, Toronto Temperance Reformation Society, Toronto Athenaeum, trustee of the Toronto General Burying Grounds, Irish Protestant Benevolent Society, House of Industry, Newsboy's Lodging and Industrial Home, Prisoners' Aid, and Home for Incurables. (Note W. H. Howland was on the board of directors of many of these organizations).

McMurrich, John. b. 1804 Paisley, Scotland, d. 1883. Free Presbyterian. Merchant, businessman, and politician. City Mission Society, Upper Canada Religious Tract and Book Society, Sabbath Observance Association, Toronto Home for Incurables, Anti-Clergy Reserves Association, Reformer and close political associate of Brown, Liberal MPP, Toronto Public School Board, Toronto Board of Trade charter member (W. P. Howland was president as later was W. H. Howland and both seemed to have overlapped with McMurrich), director of Western Assurance Company, and Royal Canadian Bank among other positions. Father of Toronto mayor William B. McMurrich, who was a close philanthropic colleague of W. H. Howland and leader of his mayoralty campaign. DCB

McNab, John. Not identified.

Morrison, Angus. b. Edinburgh, Scotland, d. 1882. Lawyer and politician. Worked as a clerk at the law office of W. H. Blake. Reform politician later turned Conservative. Three time mayor of Toronto. He negotiated the purchase of the exhibition grounds with W. H. Howland serving on the first board of directors of the Industrial Exhibition.[57] Restructured the Water Works Commission which was in turn reformed by Howland. DCB

Mowat, Sir Oliver. B. 1821 Kingston, Upper Canada (Scottish parents), d. 1903. Lawyer, judge, politician. Presbyterian. Clerk for John A. Macdonald. Upper Canada Bible Society, QC, alderman, Brown's chief lieutenant in the Legislative Assembly (1858-1864), and Upper Canadian Court of Chancery. At the urging of Edward Blake, George Brown, and Alexander Mackenzie he resigned his judgeship to become the Liberal Premier and

---

57. For Howland's involvement see Keith Walden, *Becoming Modern in Toronto: The Industrial Exhibition and the Shaping of a Victorian Culture* (Toronto: University of Toronto Press, 1997), p. 17.

Attorney General of Ontario with Blake (who had been Premier) and Mackenzie (who had been Attorney General) moving to federal politics as Liberals with Mackenzie eventually becoming Prime Minister. Mowat was Premier for 25 years and was concurrently President of the Evangelical Alliance, Upper Canada Bible Society. DCB

Pea, Mr. Not identified.

Pyper, Rev. J. Baptist minister. No other information. DCB

Richardson, Rev. James. b. 1791 in Kingston, Upper Canada, d. 1875. Methodist minister and bishop. Served in the War of 1812 losing an arm. Editor of the Christian Guardian. Upper Canada Bible Society, Temperance Reformation Society, and York Pioneer Society. DCB

Ridout, George Percival. b. Bristol, England, d. 1873. Anglican. Merchant and politician. Reformer and later sat as a moderate Conservative. President of the Toronto Board of Trade, president of the St. George's Society, alderman, board of trustees for Toronto schools, and worked for abolition of Sabbath labour. DCB

Roaf, Rev. John. b. 1801 in Margate, Kent, d. 1862. Congregational minister. Congregationalist Colonial Missionary Society of Upper Canada, Anti-State Church Association, sectarian free school advocate, Toronto Temperance Reformation Society, and commissioner of the Toronto Lunatic Society. DCB

Russell, Dr. Not identified.

Shaw, John. Not identified.

Short, T. J. Not identified.

Tyner, T. J. Not identified.

Woodhouse, J. Upper Canada Religious Tract Society. Only identification found.

Additional Linkages

Baldwin, Robert. b. 1804 in York (Toronto), d. 1858. Anglican. Politician, lawyer. Architect of responsible government in Canada, leader of Reform government in the Province of Canada. W. H. Blake was Solicitor General in his administration. Anti-clergy reserves, created the University of Toronto (formerly King's College). Long-time President of the Upper Canada Bible Society.

Blake, William Hume. b. 1809 Kiltegan, Ireland, d. 1870. Anglican. Lawyer, judge, politician. Immigrated to Canada with abolitionist Bishop Benjamin Cronyn, and brother-in-law George Skeffington Connor abolitionist member of ASC. Two sons Edward and Samuel married Cronyn daughters and a son of Cronyn married a daughter of Blake. Served with Baldwin as a Reform minister, Chancellor of Upper Canada, Chancellor of the University of Toronto.

Blake, Edward. b. 1833 in Upper Canada, d. 1912. Anglican. Lawyer and politician. Appointed QC possibly through the efforts of fellow Reformers George Brown and Oliver Mowat. Like his brother, married to a daughter of abolitionist Bishop Cronyn. Premier of Ontario. Recruited Alexander Mackenzie to his cabinet. Went to federal politics with Alexander Mackenzie, who became Prime Minister of Canada. After Mackenzie stepped down Blake became the leader of the federal Liberal party but was never elected Prime Minister. Wycliffe College, Home for the Aged, Prisoners' Aid Association. DCB

Blake, Samuel Hume Blake. b. 1835 in Toronto, d. 1914. Anglican. Lawyer and judge. Like his brother, married to a daughter of abolitionist Bishop Cronyn. Replaced Oliver Mowat in the Court of Chancery when Mowat became Premier. Served with W. H. Howland on the boards of many voluntary societies. Prisoners' Aid Society, YMCA, Evangelical Association, Wycliffe College, Bishop Ridley College, Havergal Ladies' College, Prison Gate Mission and Haven, Industrial School Association, international convention of Sunday schools, Evangelical Alliance, Protestant Churchmans' Union and Tract Society, Layman's Missionary Movement, Irish Protestant Benevolent Society, Toronto City Mission, Grace Church, Toronto Mission Union, Lord's Day Alliance, Toronto Humane Society, Society for the Prevention of Cruelty to Animals, Home for the Aged, Newsboys' Lodging, Willard Tract Depository, Bible League of Canada, YMCA, and the Dominion Alliance. Denounced the Boer War. Pallbearer at Howland's funeral and speaker at his memorial service. DCB

Howland, William Pierce. b. 1811 in Pauling, NY, d. 1907. Quaker. Businessman and politician. Reformer with George Brown. Lieutenant Governor of Ontario, Father of Confederation, constitutional Reform Association with Brown and Mowat. Nominated by Brown for Postmaster General. President of the Ontario Bank. DCB

Howland, William Holmes. b. 1844 Etobicoke, d. 1893. Anglican. Businessman and politician. President of Toronto Board of Trade, Dominion Board of Trade, Manufacturer's Association of Ontario. Wycliffe College, Willard Tract Depository, International Christian Worker's Association, Prisoners' Aid Association, Central Prison Mission School, Prison Gate Mission, Hillcrest Convalescent Hospital, YMCA, Mimico Boys' Industrial School, Grace Church, Toronto Mission Union, Children's Aid Society, Dominion Alliance, Newsboys' Lodging, Toronto Prohibition Alliance, Home for the Aged Poor, House of Industry, Home for Incurables, Boy's Home, Orphan's Home, Toronto Christian Institute, Toronto Coffee House Association, trustee Toronto General Hospital. Two-term mayor of Toronto. DCB

Cronyn, Bishop Benjamin. b. Kilkenny, Ireland, d. 1871. Anglican Bishop of Huron in London, Ontario. Travelled to Canada with William Blake and George Skeffington Connor, an ASC member. Cronyn worked with ASC to settle and educate Black Refugees in the London area. The Blake brothers married his two daughters and a son married a daughter of Blake. Founded Huron College out of which came the University of Western Ontario.

Gzowski, Sir Casimir. b. St. Petersburg, Russia, d. 1898. Anglican. Engineer and businessman. Wounded as a Polish insurgent and exiled to North America. Briefly overlapped with abolitionist Bishop Cronyn in London, Ontario and became an evangelical Anglican. Liberal, served Oliver Mowat as a commissioner and for a brief time filled in as Administrator of Ontario. Close associate in voluntary societies with Samuel Blake and William Howland. Wycliffe College, Toronto Coffee House Association, Newsboys' Lodging, Boys' Home, board of Shaftesbury Hall, Toronto Mission Union, YMCA. Son Casimir Jr. a pallbearer at the Howland funeral. Great great grandfather of Peter Gzowski. DCB

Henning, Isabella. Dates not identified. Daughter of Peter Brown. A leader in the Ladies' Association for the Relief of Destitute Coloured Refugees. Married to Thomas Henning of the ASC.

Alexander Mackenzie. b. 1822 in Logierait, Scotland, d. 1892. Baptist. Businessman, journalist, and politician. Close political ally of George Brown, Reformer. A member of the Ontario legislature with Edward Blake, in a key political move the two handed the provincial Liberal premiership to Oliver Mowat, with both moving to federal politics. Mackenzie and shortly after was Prime Minister of Canada. Blake later became the long-time leader of the Liberal party but was never elected Prime Minister. Compiled The Life and Speeches of George Brown. DCB

Wilson, Sir Daniel. b. 1816 in Edinburgh, d. 1892. Educator. Long-time President of the University of Toronto. Member with Peter and George Brown of Edinburgh Society for the Abolition of Negro Slavery. Polymath, coined the term "prehistoric." Grew up in abolitionist family and was insistent on the unity of humankind and rejected as ridiculous the notion that whites and blacks did not share common origins. Wycliffe College, Church of England Evangelical Association, YMCA, Newsboys' Lodging, Boys' Home, Upper Canada Bible Society.

Selected Bibliography

Soderlund, S. K. "The Oracles Against the Philistine and Edom in the Greek Text of Jeremiah: Chapter 29 as a Microcosm of the Problems Presented by the Septuagint Version of Jeremiah." (PhD diss., University of Glasgow, 1978).

———. "Christmas and the Shalom of God." *Crux* 16 (1980): 2-4.

———. "Focus on Philippians: A Review Article." *Crux* 20 (1984): 27-32.

———. *The Greek Text of Jeremiah: A Revised Hypothesis.* JSOTSup 47. Sheffield: JSOT Press, 1985.

———. "Burning Hearts and Open Minds: Exposition on the Emmaus Road." *Crux* 23 (1987): 2-4.

Soderlund, S. K., and N. T. Wright, eds. *Romans and the People of God: Essays in Honor of Gordon D. Fee on the Occasion of His 65th Birthday.* Grand Rapids: Eerdmans, 1999.

Soderlund, S. K., and J. I. Packer, eds. *The Way of Wisdom: Essays in Honor of Bruce K. Waltke.* Grand Rapids: Zondervan, 2000.

Soderlund, S. K. "Pastor Paul: From Eugene Peterson to Scot McKnight in Twenty Years." *Crux* 56 (2020): 31-36.

Appendix to Chapter 7

Table 1: NA28's 93 Variation Units

Entry #	Address	Type of Variation	NA28 Text Reading	Entry #	Address	Type of Variation	NA28 Text Reading
1	Phil 1:3	⌐ = Substitution	ευχαριστω του θεω μου	47	Phil 2:15b	⌐ = Substitution	αμωμα
2	Phil 1:4	T = Addition of και		48	Phil 2:19	⌐ = Substitution	κυριω
3	Phil 1:5	° = Omit	της	49	Phil 2:21	⌐ = Substitution	Ιησου Χριστου
4	Phil 1:6	⸔ 2 Transposition of words	χριστου ιησου	50	Phil 2:22	⌐ = Substitution	γινωσκετε
5	Phil 1:7	° = Omission	εν	51	Phil 2:24	T = Addition of προς υμας	
6	Phil 1:8	⌐ = Substitution/Addition/Omission	μου	52	Phil 2:26	⌐ ⸃ = Substitution	παντας υμας
7	Phil 1:9	⌐ = Substitution	περισσευη	54	Phil 2:30a	⌐ = Substitution	χριστου
8	Phil 1:11a	⌐ ⸃ = Substitution	καρπον δικαιοσυνης τον	55	Phil 2:30b	⌐ = Substitution	παραβολευσαμενος
9	Phil 1:11b	⌐ = Substitution	και επαινον θεου	56	Phil 3:1	T = Addition of το	
10	Phil 1:14	⌐ = Substitution	τον λογον	57	Phil 3:3	⌐ = Substitution	θεου
11	Phil 1:16-17	⸔ 2 (Transposition of the two verses)	οι μεν εξ αγαπης	58	Phil 3:6a	⌐ = Substitution	ζηλος
12	Phil 1:17a	° = Omission	τον	59	Phil 3:6b	T = Addition of θεου	
13	Phil 1:17b	⌐ = Substitution	εγειρειν	60	Phil 3:7a	° = Omission	[ΑΛΛ']
14	Phil 1:18	⌐ = Substitution	πλην οτι	61	Phil 3:7b	⸔ 2 = Transposition of words	ην μοι
15	Phil 1:19	⌐ = Substitution	γαρ	62	Phil 3:8a	° = Omission	και
16	Phil 1:20	⌐ = Substitution	αποκαραδοκιαν	63	Phil 3:8b	T = Addition of του	
17	Phil 1:22a	⌐ = Substitution	ει δε	64	Phil 3:8c	T = Addition of ειναι	
18	Phil 1:22b	⌐ = Substitution	αιρησομαι	65	Phil 3:10	⌐ ⸃ = Substitution	[την] κοινωνιαν [των]
19	Phil 1:23a	° = Omission	εις	66	Phil 3:11	⌐ ⸃ = Substitution	την εκ
20	Phil 1:23b	⌐ ⸃ = Substitution	πολλω [γαρ] μαλλον	67	Phil 3:12a	T = Addition of η ηδη δεδικαιωμαι,	
21	Phil 1:24a	⌐ = Substitution	επιμενειν	68	Phil 3:12b	° = Omission	και
22	Phil 1:24b	° = Omission	εν	69	Phil 3:12c	° = Omission	Ιησου
23	Phil 1:25	⌐ = Substitution	παραμενω	70	Phil 3:13	⌐ = Substitution	ου
24	Phil 1:27	⌐ = Substitution	ακουω	71	Phil 3:14a	⌐ = Substitution	διωκω
25	Phil 1:28a	⌐ ⸃ = Substitution	εστιν αυτοις	72	Phil 3:14b	⌐ = Substitution	εις
26	Phil 1:28b	⌐ = Substitution	υμων	73	Phil 3:14c	⌐ ⸃ = Substitution	του θεου εν χριστω Ιησου
27	Phil 1:29	⌐ = Substitution	υμιν	74	Phil 3:15	⌐ = Substitution	φρονωμεν
28	Phil 1:30	⬚ ⸃ = Omission	εν εμοι	75	Phil 3:16a	⌐ = Substitution	εφθασαμεν
29	Phil 2:1a	⌐ = Substitution	τι	76	Phil 3:16b	⌐ ⸃ = Substitution	τω αυτω στοιχειν
30	Phil 2:1b	⌐ = Substitution	τις	77	Phil 3:18	T = Addition of βλεπετε	
31	Phil 2:2	⌐ = Substitution	εν	78	Phil 3:21a	T = Addition of εις, το γενεσθαι αυτο	
32	Phil 2:3a	⌐ ⸃ = Substitution	μηδε κατα	79	Phil 3:21b	⌐ = Substitution	αυτω

Entry #	Address	Type of Variation	NA28 Text Reading
33	Phil 2:3b	⌐ = Substitution	ηγουμενοι
34	Phil 2:3c	⌐ = Addition of τους	
35	Phil 2:4a	⌐ = Substitution	εκαστος
36	Phil 2:4b	⌐ = Substitution	σκοπουντες
37	Phil 2:4c	° = Omission	[και]
38	Phil 2:4d	⌐ = Substitution	εκαστοι
39	Phil 2:5	⌐ = Substitution	φρονειτε
40	Phil 2:7	⌐ = Substitution	ανθρωπων
41	Phil 2:9	° = Omission	το
42	Phil 2:11a	⌐ = Substitution	εξομολογησηται
43	Phil 2:11b	⌐ ⌐ = Substitution	κυριος Ιησους Χριστος
44	Phil 2:12	° = Omission	ως
45	Phil 2:13	⌐ = Addition of ο	
46	Phil 2:15a	⌐ = Substitution	γενησθε

Entry #	Address	Type of Variation	NA28 Text Reading
80	Phil 4:1	⌐ = Substitution	αγαπητοι
81	Phil 4:3	⌐ ⌐ = Substitution	λοιπων συνεργων μου
82	Phil 4:7a	⌐ = Substitution	θεου
83	Phil 4:7b	⌐ = Substitution	νοηματα
84	Phil 4:7c	⌐ = Substitution	Χριστω
85	Phil 4:8	⌐ = Addition of επιστημης	
86	Phil 4:10	⌐ = Substitution	το
87	Phil 4:13	⌐ = Addition of Χριστω	
88	Phil 4:15	° = Omission	δε
89	Phil 4:16	⌐ ⌐ = Substitution	εις την χρειαν μοι
90	Phil 4:18	⌐ ⌐ = Substitution	δεξαμενος
91	Phil 4:19	⌐ = Substitution	πληρωσει
92	Phil 4:23a	⌐ ⌐ = Substitution	του πνευματος υμων
93	Phil 4:23b	⌐ = Addition of αμην	

Appendix to Chapter 7

Table 2: Manuscripts Ranked in Order of Agreement Rate with NA28

Rankings by Agreements with NA28	1	2	3	4	5	6	7	8	9	10	11/12/13			14	15	16	17/18/19			20/21/22			23	24	25/26		27	28
	016	01	1739	08	02	33	1881	04	1175	81	P16	025	365	104	P61	2464	075	P46	020	018	0278	1505	630	06	044	012	010	0282
Total Txt (2) + Txt/Maj (1/2)	18 = 86%	77 = 83%	76 = 83%	74 = 80%	73 = 78%	71 = 77%	70 = 76%	29 = 74%	68 = 73%	65 = 71%	7 = 70%	65 = 70%	65 = 70%	63 = 68%	6 = 67%	59 = 66%	61 = 65%	53 = 65%	58 = 65%	59 = 63%	36 = 63%	59 = 63%	58 = 62%	56 = 60%	55 = 59%	54 = 59%	56 = 58%	1 = 25%
Txt/Maj Rdgs (1/2)	13	51	54	46	49	47	53	18	49	47	5	54	53	52	6	46	51	34	57	57	26	55	58	40	49	38	40	1
Txt (non-Maj) Rdgs (2)	5	26	22	26	24	24	17	11	19	18	2	11	12	11	0	13	9	19	1	2	10	4	0	16	6	16	16	1

Table 3: Comparison of Manuscripts by Agreement Rate with THGNT

Rankings by Agreements with THGNT	1	2	3	4	5	6	7	8	9	10	11/12/13			14	15	16/17		18/19		20/21/22			23	24	25/26		27	28
	016	01	1739	02	04	33	03	1881	1175	81	P16	025	365	104	P61	075	2464	P46	020	018	0278	1505	630	044	06	010	012	0282
Total Txt (2) + Txt/Maj (1/2)	18 = 86%	79 = 85%	76 = 83%	75 = 82%	31 = 80%	73 = 79%	72 = 77%	68 = 75%	68 = 73%	65 = 71%	7 = 70%	65 = 70%	65 = 70%	63 = 68%	6 = 67%	60 = 65%	53 = 65%	58 = 64%	58 = 64%	59 = 63%	36 = 63%	59 = 63%	58 = 62%	57 = 61%	54 = 58%	54 = 58%	52 = 57%	1 = 25%
Txt/Maj Rdgs (1/2)	13	52	54	52	19	49	47	52	49	47	5	54	52	52	6	51	34	46	57	57	26	55	58	50	39	39	38	1
Txt (non-Maj) Rdgs (2)	5	27	22	26	12	24	25	16	19	18	2	11	13	11	0	9	19	12	1	2	10	4	0	7	15	15	14	0

Table 4: Comparison of Percentages of TuT2 and TuT1/2 Rdgs

Ms.	Total Entries	Total Agreements with NA28	TuT2 Readings	TuT1/2 Readings
01	93	77 of 93 = 83%	26 of 79 agreements = 33%	51 of 79 agreements = 65%
33	92	71 of 92 = 77%	24 of 71 agreements = 34%	47 of 71 agreements = 66%
104	93	63 of 93 = 68%	11 of 63 agreements = 18%	52 of 63 agreements = 83%
044	93	55 of 93 = 59%	6 of 55 agreements = 11%	49 of 55 agreements = 89%
630	93	58 of 93 = 62%	0 TuT2 Rdgs = 0%	58 of 58 agreements = 100%

Table 5: Comparison of Percentages of Special Readings

Ms.	Total Entries	TuT3⁺ Readings
012	92	30 of 92 = 33%
P46	81	27 of 81 = 33%
02	93	15 of 93 = 16%
04	39	7 of 39 = 18%
018	93	7 of 93 = 8%

APPENDIX TO CHAPTER 7

Table 6: 1739 and 1881 in Comparison

<u>1739</u> (93 Readings)　　　　　　　　　　　<u>1881</u> (92 Readings)

1739's 93 readings, with its 76 (82%) NA28 Agreements (TuT2 + TuT1/2) in **bold**:　　1881's 92 readings, with its 71 (77%) NA28 Agreements in **bold**:[1]

1 2 3 4 5 6 7 8 9 **10 11 12 13 14** 15 **16 17 18 19 20 21** 22 23 24 25 **26 27 28**　　1 2 3 4 5 6 7 8 9 **10 11 12 13** 14 15 **16 17 18 19 20 21** 22 23 **24 25 26 27 28 29**
29 **30 31 32 33 34 35** 36 37 **38** 39 **40 41** 42 **43 44 45 46 47 48 49 50** 51 **52**　　30 **31 32 33 34 35** 36 37 **38 39 40 41** 42 **43 44 45 46 47 48 49 50 51 52 53 54**
53 54 55 **56 57 58 59 60** 61 62 **63** 64 **65** 66 **67 68 69 70 71** 72 **73 74 75** 76　　55 **56 57 58 59 60** 61 62 **63** 64 **65** 66 **67 68 69 70 71 72 73 74 75** 76 **77 78 79**
77 78 79 80 **81 82 83 84 85 86 87 88 89 90 91 92 93**　　　　　　80 **81 82 83 84 85 86 87 88 89 90 91 92 93**

1739 and 1881 Combined Agreements
84 agreements in 92 commonly preserved Entries
(Agreement Rate of 91%)

23 non-Maj Rdgs (TuT2 + TuT3⁺) of 84 agreements (27%) in **bold**

1 2 **4** 5 7 9 **10 11 12 13 15** 16 17 18 19 **20** 21 **23** 24 **25 26** 27 28
29 **30** 31 **32** 33 34 35 **36** 37 **38 39** 40 42 43 44 **45 46** 47 **48 49** 50
51 52 53 **54** 55 56 57 58 59 60 61 **62** 63 64 65 66 67 68 69 70 71
72 73 74 75 77 78 79 81 82 83 84 85 86 88 89 **90 91 92 93**

---

[1] 1881's reading for Entry 80 (in gray) is idiosyncratic, if not non-sensical, rendering its witness nil for this variation unit.

313

Table 7: Alliance Groups B-Prime's Total Combined Agreements

Three Allies (01 02 and 33)	Four allies (01 02 33 04)
66 agreements in 92 commonly preserved Entries = 72%	25 agreements in 38 commonly preserved Entries = 66%
26 of 67 agreements are non-Maj (TuT2 + TuT3+) Rdgs (39%; in **bold**).	13 of 25 agreements are non-Maj (TuT2 + TuT3+) Rdgs (52%; in **bold**).

1 2 3 4 7 **8 9 10 11** 12 **13 14** 15 16 17 18 19 21 **22 23 25 26** 28 30 **31 32 33 34 36 37 38 39** 40 **41** 43 **45 47** 48 **49** 52 53 **54** 56 57 59 **60 61** 63 **66 67 70** 71 **72** 73 75 **76** 77 79 83 84 85 86 87 88 **90 92** 93

18 19 21 **22 23** 25 28 30 **31 32** 33 34 36 37 **38 39** 40 **41** 43 **45 47 49** 52 56 57

Table 8: B's Agreements with NA28

Alliance Group 01-02-33 Agreements with NA28	Alliance Group 01-02-04-33 Agreements with NA28
58 agreements with NA28 in 92 Entries commonly preserved by 01 02 and 33 = 63%	23 agreements with NA28 in 38 Entries commonly preserved by 01 02 04 and 33 = 61%
19 of 58 agreements are non-Maj Txt (TuT2) Rdgs (33%; in **bold**)	10 of 23 agreements are non-Maj Txt (TuT2) Rdgs (44%; in **bold**)

1 2 3 **7 8 9 11** 12 **13 14** 15 16 17 18 19 21 **23 25** 26 28 30 **32** 33 34 **36** 37 **38 39** 40 **41** 43 **45 47** 48 **49** 53 56 57 59 61 63 **66** 67 71 **72** 73 75 **76** 77 79 83 84 85 86 87 88 90 **92**

18 19 21 **23 25** 28 30 **32** 33 34 **36** 37 **38 39** 40 **41** 43 **45 47 49** 52 56 57

Appendix to Chapter 7

Table 9: X-XII' Total Agreements
Four allies (104 365 1175 and 81)
64 agreements in 92 commonly preserved entries (70%)
17 of 64 agreements are non-Maj (TuT2 + Tut3⁺) Rdgs (27%; in **bold**).

1 2 4 5 9 **10** 12 **14** 16 17 18 19 **20 22** 24 **26** 27 29 **32** 34 **36** 37 **38** 40 42 43 44 46 47 50 51 **52 53** 58 59 61 62 63 64 65 **66** 67 68 69 **70** 71 73 74 75 **76** 77 80 81 82 83 84 85 86 87 88 90 **91 92 93**

Table 10: RP's Total Agreements
Three Allies (018 630 and 020) Total Agreements
75 agreements in 89 commonly preserved entries = 84%
none of the 75 agreements are non-Maj (TuT2 + TuT3+) Rdgs).

1 2 3 5 6 7 9 14 15 16 17 18 19 20 21 22 23 24 25 26 27 28 31 32 34 35 38 39 40 41 42 44 46 47 50 51 52 53 54 55 56 57 58 59 60 61 62 63 64 65 66 67 68 69 70 71 72 73 75 76 77 78 80 81 82 83 84 85 86 87 88 90 91 92 93

315

Table 11: P46 Support Network: Readings Adopted by NA28

Support Network Key
- B': unanimous agreement of 01-02-33 (and 04 when preserved)
- b': majority agreement of B' or in rare cases, two members of four (Entries 35 51 55)
- X-XII': unanimous agreement of 104-365-1175-81
- x-xii': majority agreement of 104-365-1175-81
- RP': unanimous agreement of 018-020-630

	B'/b' Alliance Group	X-XII' Alliance Group	RP' Alliance Group	1739-1881	D-Txt/ d-txt:	CCW/ ccw:	Maj	Entries
P46	03	B'	X-XII'	RP'	1739-1881	D-Txt	CCW	Maj	56 71 75
P46	03	B'	X-XII'	RP'	1739-1881	d-txt	CCW	Maj	59 83 86
P46	03	B'	X-XII'	RP'	1739-1881		CCW	Maj	19 37 85
P46	03	B'	X-XII'		1739-1881		CCW	pm	81
P46	03	B'	X-XII'	RP'	1739-1881	D-Txt	CCW		49 78 92
P46	03	B'	X-XII'		1739-1881	d-txt	CCW	Maj	43
P46	03	B'	x-xii'		1739-1881	D-Txt	CCW		11, 23
P46	03	B'	X-XII'		1739-1881	D-Txt	CCW		36
P46	03	B'	x-xii'	RP'	1739-1881	D-Txt	CCW	Maj	56
P46	03	B'	x-xii'		1739-1881	d-txt	CCW		38
P46	03	B'	X-XII'		1739-1881		CCW		66
P46	03	B'	x-xii'		1739-1881	D-Txt	CCW	Maj	45
P46	03	B'	x-xii'		1739-1881		CCW		72
P46	03	B'	x-xii'	rp'	1739	D-Txt	CCW		8
P46	03	B'	x-xii'		1739				76
P46	03	B'			1881		ccw		3
P46	03	B'			1739		ccw	Maj	41
P46	03	B'				D-Txt	CCW		30
P46	03	B'				D-Txt	CCW	Maj	58

Appendix to Chapter 7

		B'/b' Alliance Group	X-XII' Alliance Group	RP' Alliance Group	1739-1881	D-Txt/ d-txt:	CCW/ ccw:	Maj	Entries
P46	03								
P46	03	B'							47
P46	03	b'	X-XII'		1739-1881	d-txt	CCW	Maj	29
P46	03	b'	X-XII'	RP'	1739-1881	D-Txt	CCW	Maj	74 82
P46	03	b'	X-XII'			D-Txt	ccw		55
P46	03	b'	X-XII'	RP'	1739-1881		CCW	Maj	5 68
P46	03	b'					CCW	Maj	48
P46	03	b'		RP'			ccw	Maj	91
P46	03	01							65
P46	03	33	X-XII'	RP'	1739-1881	D-Txt	CCW	Maj	51
P46	03		x-xii'	RP'	1739-1881	D-Txt	CCW	Maj	31
P46	03			RP'	1739-1881	d-txt	CCW	Maj	70
P46	03				1739-1881	d-txt	ccw		54
P46	03					d-txt	ccw	Maj	4
P46	03						ccw	pm	42
P46		B'	X-XII'	RP'	1739-1881	D-Txt	CCW	Maj	61
P46		B'	X-XII'	RP'	1739-1881	d-txt	CCW	Maj	16
P46		B'	X-XII'		1739	d-txt	CCW		14
P46		B'	X-XII'	RP'		d-txt	CCW	Maj	93
P46		B'	x-xii'	RP'	1739-1881	d-txt	CCW	Maj	7
P46		B'	x-xii'	RP'	1739-1881	D-Txt	CCW	Maj	21
P46		b'	X-XII'	RP'	1739-1881	D-Txt	CCW	Maj	44
P46		b'	X-XII'	RP'	1739-1881	D-Txt	CCW	Maj	69
P46		b'	104-365	RP'	1739-1881		CCW	Maj	35
P46					1739-1881	d-txt	ccw	Maj	10
P46		02	b'	rp'				Maj	89

Table 12: P46 Support Network: Readings Rejected by NA28

	B/b' Alliance Group	X-XII' Alliance Group	RP' Alliance Group	1739-1881	D-Txt/d-txt:	CCW/ccw:	Maj	Entries
P46	03	01			d-txt	CCW		24
P46	03		1175			CCW		15
P46	03			1739-1881	D-Txt	CCW		22
P46	03					2464		18
P46	03				d-txt	CCW		63
P46		B'			D-Txt			60
P46		02	x-xii'		D-Txt			46
P46		02		1739-1881		CCW		89
P46		01	1175	1739-1881	D-Txt	CCW		62
P46					D-Txt			39
P46					d-txt			67
P46					d-txt	1505		88
P46						0278		17
P46						81		20
P46							Maj	28
P46				365-1175	d-txt	CCW		33
P46				(singular or sub-singular) 6 9 32 40 52 57 73 77 84 90				

Editors and Contributors

Robert P. Gordon, Emeritus Regius Professor of Hebrew, University of Cambridge (UK)
Mariam Kamell Kovalishyn, Assistant Professor in New Testament Studies, Regent College (Canada)
Toni Kim, Former Minister, Park Street Church (USA) and Member of the Board of Governors, Regent College (Canada)
Joseph H. S. Lee, Adjunct Professor, Biblical Studies, William Jessup University (USA)
James M. Leonard, Former Adjunct Professor, LSU, Norte Dame Seminary, Loyola University, John Brown University (USA)
David Montgomery, Associate for Bible Teaching and Pioneering, IFES Europe (N. Ireland)
Ken M. Penner, Associate Professor, Religious Studies, St. Francis Xavier University (Canada)
Iain W. Provan, Marshall Sheppard Professor of Biblical Studies, Regent College (Canada)
Bill Reimer, General Manager, Regent College Bookstore (Canada)
Stuart T. Rochester, Senior Lecturer in the Unit for Reformed Theology, North-West University (South Africa); Tutor at Greenwich School of Theology (UK); Lecturer in New Testament, Asia Pacific Theological Seminary (Philippines)
Jay T. Smith, President and Bridger Professor of Theology & Ethics, Yellowstone Theological Institute (USA)
Marcus K. M. Tso, Senior Pastor, Newbern Alliance Church and Research Associate of the Dead Sea Scrolls Institute, Trinity Western University (Canada)
Bruce K. Waltke, Professor Emeritus in Old Testament Studies, Regent College (Canada)

www.ingramcontent.com/pod-product-compliance
Lightning Source LLC
Chambersburg PA
CBHW031723230426
43669CB00007B/218